The Blackwell Guide to
Recorded Contemporary Music

THE BLACKWELL GUIDES

The Blackwell Guide to
Recorded
Contemporary Music

Brian Morton

BLACKWELL
Publishers

DBN: 1421537

First published in UK 1996

Ref.
ML
111.5
.M67
1996

Blackwell Publishers Ltd
108 Cowley Road
Oxford OX4 1JF
UK

Blackwell Publishers Inc
238 Main Street,
Cambridge, Massachusetts 02142
USA

British Library Cataloguing in Publication Data

A CIP catalogue record for this book is available from the
British Library.

Library of Congress Cataloging-in-Publication Data
Morton, Brian, 1954–
    The Blackwell guide to recorded contemporary music / edited by
Brian Morton.
    cm. – (The Blackwell guides)
    Includes bibliographical references and index.
    ISBN 0-631-18881-9. – 0-631-20138-6 (pbk.)
    1. Sound recordings–Collectors and collecting.   2. Music–20th
century–History and criticism.   3. Music–20th century–
Discography.   I. Title.   II. Series.
ML111.5.M67   1996
016.78′026′6–dc20   95-11403
                                                                          CIP
                                                                          MN

Typeset in Palatino and Optima on 10/12 pt
by Acorn Bookwork, Salisbury, Wilts
Printed in Great Britain by T.J. Press, Padstow, Cornwall

Contents

Introduction

The Recording Angel that I am concerned with is not CBS ... but the One with the Big Book.

Igor Stravinsky: 1972

Even after his place in the Big Book was secure, Stravinsky had good reason to be grateful to CBS, who helped turn him into the first, and still arguably the greatest, of the twentieth century's composer–superstars. When in the early 1930s, American concert-goers voted Jean Sibelius their favourite composer *of all time*, they were still voting primarily as concert-goers rather than record collectors. No composer before Stravinsky had been so significantly reshaped by the recording industry and none fell so squarely athwart its inbuilt paradoxes of novelty and familiarity.

Stravinsky understood that while 'a disc or magnetic tape of a piece of new music can be several thousand times as powerful (influential) as a live performance', it did so at the price of a certain commodification of music. He was forced to recognize that sales of between thirty and fifty thousand for a recording of the early and now classic *Firebird* were required to underwrite more challenging later scores like *The Flood*. Inevitably, there was both a price and a pay-off. Like motor cars, recordings were subject to planned obsolescence, none more so than recordings of new music, which are – and should be – immediately superseded by interpretative improvement and finessing of a sort that is rarely necessary in longer-established repertoire. However, 'even a new (out of date) recording of new music seems worth while when one thinks of all those young musicians in Reno, Spokane, Talahassee, New York and other provincial cities who may hear a thousand performances of the 'New World' Symphony but who would never otherwise than on records hear such landmarks of contemporary music as [Arnold Schoenberg's] *Die Jakobsleiter* or [Pierre Boulez's] *Pli selon pli'*.

There is a discernible shrug in this, a hint of *'faute de mieux'*, but whether he entirely approved or not, Stravinsky had identified a major change in the dissemination of new music. In keeping with a wider cultural shift towards private consumption, replicable recording music assumed a far greater relative importance than the concert hall. To a large extent the underlying reasons were technological. In 1948 Columbia Records introduced the $33\frac{1}{3}$ microgroove 'long-playing' record, which allowed up to twenty-seven minutes of music per side. Stereophonic sound and multi-track recording emerged in the late 1950s, further improving recording fidelity, and progress has continued (though not without controversy and the occasional evolutionary cul-de-sac like cartridge eight-track and quadraphony) with the introduction of good quality tape cassettes, compact and laser discs. It is ironic but also fitting that Evan Eisenberg's stimulating 1989 book on record collectors should have been called *The Recording Angel*. These days, the Angel no longer attends concerts, but sits at home with the Ultimate Hi-Fi.

Like almost everyone else who came of age in the early 1970s, and who grew up away from the main concert centres (surprisingly enough, Xenakis and Ligeti were little known in Dunoon), my musical interests were formed almost entirely by records. With rock music, concert-going always seemed a second-order activity, a ritual obeisance rather than a strictly musical experience, and that was the way musicians seemed to regard touring, too. The technology has improved dramatically since then – no more wasted evenings listening to men in jeans intoning 'one-two, one-two', fewer squalls of feedback – but to a large extent the technology has taken over entirely, obliterating the once-cherished distinction between 'studio' and 'live' rock. With jazz, there was an even greater reliance on records. The casualty figures tended to be higher than in rock and a perversely satisfying number of the major figures were dead, the very point (equally perversely) that was always used to confirm the supposed irrelevance of classical music. From a British (and acutely from a Scottish) point of view, accessibility was a further problem, and occasional north of the border dates or southward trips to see jazz greats in London or in Europe acquired a special, but again largely ritual, significance.

In 1972 contemporary 'composition' was still in its conceptual phase. Performances were often extremely ephemeral affairs, puzzling, moving or infuriating as the case might be, but entirely lacking in external reference points. Even early twentieth-century classics were rarely included on concert programmes, or if at all only as unapologetically throw-away preambles (much as Haydn symphonies were once misused) to the real substance of an evening concert. The same people who would hiss and glare angrily at a muffled cough during a Mozart item would think nothing of waving and mouthing questions, or even of noisily reorganizing the seating, during a modern piece. In four years at the University of Edinburgh I managed to hear professional live performances of Schoenberg's *Verklärte Nacht* (twice) and Berg's *Lyrische Suite*, but nothing whatever by the unclubbable Anton Webern, and little if anything by contemporary composers.

There were, fortunately, adventurous student and amateur groups performing new repertoire and twentieth-century classics; there was a substantial amount of new music on BBC Radio 3 and within reliable shortwave reach on German and French radio; and there was a surprisingly substantial amount of new music on record. Deutsche Grammophon's 'avant-garde' imprint was a constant source of new and challenging repertoire, and the economic climate was still sufficiently buoyant to permit mainstream labels to run their own loss-leading side catalogues of frontier music: Decca's Headline imprint, Vox Turnabout, Nonesuch, and, perhaps most important of all, the composer-led CRI in the States. Lest it be forgotten, there was also a huge amount of new music coming out of the (then) Iron Curtain countries, poorly pressed but cheap and often superbly recorded sets from Hungaroton, from the Czech Supraphon and, unstoppably, from the state-backed Soviet Melodiya.

After a slump in the later 1970s and early 1980s, there has again been a substantial increase in the amount of new music on record and in the number of labels who take an active interest in new composition. Coverage is still inevitably patchy, but it is by no means unusual for contemporary works to have been recorded before they have received more than a tiny handful of concert performances. The Finlandia label (which, along with the Swedish BIS, accounts for an excellent current representation of Scandinavian music) has even issued live recordings of premiere performances.

The industry's enthusiasm for new music has not been entirely disinterested or altruistic. As rock has lapsed into repetition and nostalgia, and jazz has faced up to the imminent (surely?) exhaustion of blues and bebop harmony, younger listeners have begun to experiment with new music. A potentially lucrative 'cross-over' is reflected in such initiatives as the Munich-based ECM's carefully styled and highly successful 'New Series', and the Swiss hat ART's inclusion of Morton Feldman, John Cage, Giacinto Scelsi and lesser-known figures such as Galina Usvolskaya and Maria de Alvear alongside avant-garde jazz musicians. A number of other labels have explored similar territory, notably New World and Music & Arts, and CD technology and simplified distribution have encouraged the establishment of small specialist and composer-led labels, many of them modelled on Mimi Phillips's influential Lovely Music. Existing labels have greatly increased the profile of contemporary composition, 'signing up' marketable young composers and reissuing a back catalogue of twentieth-century classics.

Perhaps the most important defining precondition of the phenomenon we know as 'post-modernism' is the sense that all styles and all periods of art, literature and music are simultaneously available and equally valid. To an extent, classical music has always been dominated by the back catalogue. What is distinctive about the present period is that, as in rock music, the visual arts, poetry and the novel, there is no dominant style. Instead, one encounters an astonishingly broad spectrum of stylistic variables, sustained by a liberal consensus in favour of choice (which is, after all, the original meaning of eclecticism). There has been a widespread 'return to tonality', but it is still more than possible to write serial music; the creative tension between them emerges time and again in the essays that follow. Though minimalism has been perhaps the closest approximation to a dominant style, it won and maintained its constituency outside the academy long before it became a – or perhaps *the* – establishment style.

The 1980s have seen an end to the progressivist obsessions of the avant garde. Indeterminate scores are now rare. With a handful of exceptions and some shifts of emphasis, classical instrumentation is firmly back in the saddle, and the main classical genres are still viable, but perhaps only at the expense of a certain collapsing of musical history. There is now a strong appetite for the deutero-medievalism of composers such as Arvo Pärt, Ladislav Kupkovič and Henryk Górecki. Such a development may be no more than a reaction away from the perceived harshness of the serialism, but it puts a different, almost prophetic complexion on the cod baroque of Professor Peter Schickele, aka P. D. Q. Bach, who for three decades has sent up the pretensions of academic musicology and the 'authentic performance' movement.

However, even if perceptions about the 'total availability' of recorded music are accepted without question, it is clear that contemporary composition still represents only a tiny, unrepresentative, and largely submerged proportion of the total mass. Nine-tenths of the musical iceberg wobbles ludicrously in the air – what possible need can there be for *all* that Haydn, all those Mahler cycles? – while the less than 10 per cent that is new composition is pushed down below the level of consciousness by the sheer mass of the historical legacy. The Freudian analogy only breaks down because in music the past is now so insistently present and audible, because it is, arguably at least, *not repressed enough*. New music may be briefly fashionable, but it is rarely in a position to be perceived clearly and on its own terms. Perspectives are deceptive at the waterline. The critical enterprise endlessly runs aground, not on uncharted hazards but on all too familiar obstacles.

I am not a musicologist. This book is intended as a record of, and an aid to, the enjoyment of contemporary composition. It is addressed, at least implicitly, to those who may have come to contemporary music by a similar route rather than through a detailed study of the classics. I was brought up to believe that the only art that really matters is the art of one's own time (this was at a period when it was ideologically unsound to trust anyone over thirty). Later (around thirty, oddly enough), and under cover of a sudden revisionist darkness, I repitched my tent in the opposite camp. Now the antagonism of avant-garde and classical, progressive and canonical styles and forms seems more than ever a shadow-fight.

I have selected seventy-four recordings of pieces written in the half-century from 1940 to 1990. The pieces are chosen for a variety of reasons, not always consistent, not always quantifiable. Some are of uncontroversial historical significance on their own terms. Many are unabashedly 'conservative'. Some are used to suggest patterns of stylistic change or generic survival. Some are included, in a fashion which is not meant to be blandly tokenistic, to introduce the music of certain territories or countries. Some are merely (merely!) interesting or moving or very beautiful.

It is much easier – because it is ultimately less revealing – to tamper with geographical quotas than with chronology. I *have* tried to include as wide a range of nationalities as possible among the composers represented, but with the constant proviso that nationality and 'national style' are not concepts that particularly trouble me. So, there are works by a Korean and a Brazilian, a Scot and a South African; but a Korean who lives and works in Germany, a Brazilian who made his name in France, a Scot who transplanted to the United States, and a South African who continued his studies in Aberdeen, and then made his home in Ireland.

As will be readily seen from the dates of composition, the pieces I have chosen refuse to conform to an even chronological spread. Indeed, they seem fated to adopt little constellations round particular years, the components unrelated except by accidents of date.

My intention in every case has been to provide a context for listening, rather than a detailed guide to the work in question. Liner- or sleeve-notes, or specialist commentary in journals and books will usually be a far better guide to the internal workings of a piece for those who wish to understand them in greater detail. I have tried to present personal choices in such a way as to offer the reader points of entry to contemporary music at a number of levels, and to assist with the building of a representative but also widely ranging record collection. Inevitably, each essay is to some extent biographical, and provides some insight into the development of the composer in question. Almost all of them attempt something further: to locate that development within a rather wider frame of reference. This may be stylistic or generic; again, though, it is frequently national, suggesting ways into the music of a particular territory; and it may very simply concentrate on a particular instrument or ensemble.

I make no claim to definitive 'interpretation'. To a large extent, my responses document my own discovery of the repertoire and of a critical debate associated with it. Even given a broad consensus on who the most important contemporary composers are, any selection of works is bound to be controversial: 'Why the Second Symphony, and not the Fourth, or even the Eleventh String Quartet?' Such arguments are inevitable, and therefore pointless. I have tried to make a case for each inclusion on its own merits; the essays stand or fall on the conviction of the argument, not on the selection itself. If seventy-five seems an odd total, that is in order to pre-empt any suggestion that I am nominating a premier league of contemporary works.

After each essay I have given suggestions for further reading, but also some indication of where a listener whose attention has been caught by a particular work might go next. The obvious direction is further into the output of that particular composer; here my suggestions are reasonably uncontroversial and have mostly been signalled already in the essay. However, what I have called 'map references' may be more contentious. Again, there may be clues to these in the essay, references to putative 'influences' or a commonality of style or purpose. In some cases, they merely group together other works from the same territory or for similar instrumentation. Most are accessible on record and wherever possible brief discographical citations have been given. The orienteering aspect, how the listener might find a route from one work to another that may seem rather distant, is very much a matter of personal preferences and individual discoveries.

Stravinsky's point about the instant obsolescence of new music recordings still holds true. One of the problems anyone interested in contemporary composition regularly faces is the difficulty of judging how successful or even how correct a performance of new or unfamiliar material actually is. I have quoted Milton Babbitt's comments on the premiere of his *Relata I*; one has to assume that this too is merely the tip of a problematic iceberg.) Whereas any concert performance or new recordings of Beethoven's Ninth Symphony or Haydn's 'Emperor' Quartet will automatically be set against a general consensus (or in some cases an ongoing controversy) about which are the most accurate or authentic or emotionally satisfying interpretations, there is rarely any basis for similar accord or disagreement about new music recordings. The earlier pieces discussed, particularly those such as Messiaen's

Quatuor pour la fin du temps, Bartók's Concerto for Orchestra, Copland's *Appalachian Spring*, which are identified as 'modern classics', certainly exist in a great many recorded versions. Controversial scores like Shostakovich's Eighth Symphony are susceptible to quite startling variations in interpretation. In these cases, I have indicated – and attempted to defend – a strong personal preference. Readers who wish to take the issue further would be well directed to the cumulative wisdom of what is now the *Penguin Guide to Compact Discs and Cassettes* (currently in its umpteenth revision and second major revolution in format) but should be aware that Messrs March, Greenfield and Layton have generally preferred to concentrate on classical repertoire, where there are competing recorded versions, than on new music. The majority of works covered in the volume exist only in a single recorded version and have not, perhaps for that reason, been noted in the *Penguin Guide*.

Generally, I have devoted little space to recording quality or standards of performance. Where there is no point of comparison, it seems a little redundant to make too much of such considerations. I have, however, indicated where I think there are striking excellences or unavoidable shortcomings. Otherwise, I have preferred to treat each selection as a given. Those few which have not yet made the transition to CD will inevitably be harder to find and may require the services of a gramophone library or a specialist second-hand dealer.

At the end of the volume, there are two brief appendices. Though generally I have tried to avoid excessive technicality, there is a small class of terms which are specific to the music of the modern period. Many of these are invoked so frequently that they cannot be allowed to pass without some indication of how I, at least, understand them. The first appendix provides a brief glossary of such terms and their cognates, most of which were already in currency before 1940, and many of which - 'atonality', 'serialism' – have suffered from continual misuse, or at least imprecise usage. For more detailed discussion of such terms, readers should consult the latest (1980) edition of Grove's *Dictionary of Music and Musicians*. In keeping with 'map references', I have also included in the glossary notes on some of the major locations associated with new music, like the summer schools at Tanglewood and Darmstadt, and Pierre Boulez's innovative research centre at IRCAM.

Most of the composer entries offer some suggestions for further reading, either essays on the particular work in question or more general writing on the composer's work as a whole. In a final appendix, I have provided a brief, reasoned bibliography of works which will be of assistance to anyone interested in the music of the period. A significant number of these citations are to collections of interviews, on the assumption that an artist's testimony plays a particu-

larly resonant if not uniquely privileged part in reaching an understanding of his/her work.

As to how newcomers might most comfortably and effectively
approach new music, I can only again put forward my own experience.
My familiarity with much of the classical repertoire comes from hours
spent with the 1970 and later editions of *The Norton Scores: An Anthology for Listening*, where highlighting allows the listener to follow-the-
bouncing-ball of the most audible and functionally important lines. In
all conscience, I can not recommend this method, which subordinates
musical enjoyment to map-reading of a strictly armchair sort.

Instead, I think it is much preferable to follow Freud's advice to
trainee psychoanalysts, and strive for an 'evenly suspended attention
... in the face of all that one hears'.

> In this way ... we avoid the danger which is inseparable from the
> exercise of deliberate attention. For as soon as anyone deliberately
> concentrates his attention to a certain degree he begins to select
> from the material before him; one point will be fixed in his mind
> with particular clearness and some other will be correspondingly
> disregarded ... In making the selection, if he follows his expecta-
> tions, he is in danger of never finding anything but what he already
> knows; and if he follows his inclinations, he will certainly falsify
> what he may perceive.

That was written in 1912, the year of Schoenberg's extraordinary *Pierrot
lunaire*, Alban Berg's *Altenberg Lieder*, the bulk of Anton Webern's op.
10 *Fünf Orcheststück*, and of Igor Stravinsky's *The Rite of Spring*, the
year of Charles Ives's *Lincoln, the Great Commoner*, and of Claude
Debussy's *Syrinx*. These composers provide, if you like, the pretexts or
compass-bearings for what follows. It is not essential to know these
composers in order to know what follows (only Stravinsky appears in
the main text) but it is helpful to come to the music of the post-war
years with some understanding of what comes before. At the beginning
of the volume, I have provided a list of ten recordings which may well
be worth absorbing or listening to afresh before opening up to the
sounds that come after. If moonstruck enchantment, rustic song,
common speech and dance can be your guides, so much the better.

Brian Morton
London and Whitburn, 1993

Acknowledgements

Every book accumulates debts of gratitude. This one is significantly overdrawn. I would like to thank my patient editors at Blackwell, Alyn Shipton and Halina Boniszewska, for their unstinted faith in the project and their considerable patience; my copy editor Ingrid Grimes, for her scrupulous attention to detail; Richard Cook, for being the unwitting sounding-board for many of the ideas and impressions I have tried to convey; and, above all, Pam and Fiona, for putting up with loud, unceasing music, shouts of frustration and/or momentary break-through, and many, many unsocial hours in The Bunker.

This book is dedicated to two men who only met once, discovered absolutely nothing in common, and had the grace and good sense to recognize that that was the best possible basis for conversation. To my father Robert Morton, who died in 1990, beaten on penalties after extra time; and to Colin Smith (1945–88), the self-styled 'Kropotkin of Kirkin-tilloch', with whom I shared a musical and political education in Edin-burgh in the 1970s. They both played by ear.

BM

A Note on Numbers

On the vexed question of American as opposed to European or British versions, I have tried to give a version which indicates the identifying core number, without bothering unduly about territory-specific prefixes and suffixes. In the case of smaller labels, this will not be an issue anyway. In the case of corporate releases, which may have been re-numbered or which may exist in different versions, catalogues and dealers will generally be able to clarify any uncertainties. Most of the recordings listed will be available on compact disc; those that are not will indicate LP or in some few cases, cassette. I have therefore dispensed with suffixes, usually #–2, which indicate CD.

Compass Bearings

This is not intended to be a 'Top Ten' from before 1940. Even if such a thing were possible, it would be undesirable. Instead, I have tried to indicate ten recordings of pieces (listed here in order of composition) which seem to me to establish the basic language of modern music. In most cases, there are alternative recordings, and in some a plethora of rival candidates. However, these are the ones I have gone back to most often and which seem to me most consistently satisfying.

Charles Ives, *Central Park in the Dark* **(1898–1907)**
[with: Symphony: *Holidays* (1904–13); *The Unanswered Question* (1908)]
Chicago SO, Michael Tilson Thomas
CBS MK 42831

Claude Debussy, *Chansons de Bilitis* **(1909)**
[with: *Syrinx* (1912); Sonata for flute, viola and harp (1916), a.o.]
Catherine Deneuve, Ensemble Wien-Berlin
Deutsche Grammophon 429738

Maurice Ravel, *Gaspard de la nuit* **(1908)**
[with: *Menuet antique* (1898); *Jeux d'eau* (1901)]
Claude Helffer (piano)
Musique d'Abord HMA 190922

Richard Strauss, *Elektra* **(1908)**
Birgit Nilsson, a.o., Vienna PO, Georg Solti
London 417345

Anton von Webern, Five Movements for Orchestra op. 5 (1909)
[with: Passacaglia op. 1 (1908); Six Pieces op. 6 (1913); Symphony op. 21 (1928)]
Berlin PO, Herbert von Karajan
Deutsche Grammophon 423254

Arnold Schoenberg, *Pierrot lunaire* **op. 21 (1912)**
[with: *Das Buch der hängenden Gärten op. 15* (1907)]
Jan DeGaetani, Contemporary Chamber Ensemble
Elektra Nonesuch 79237

Igor Stravinsky, *Le sacre du printemps* **(1913)**
[with: *Petrouchka* (1911, rev. 1947)]
Cleveland Orchestra, Pierre Boulez
CBS MK 42395

Carl Nielsen, Symphony no. 4: *The Inextinguishable*
(1914–1916)
[with: Symphony no. 6 (1924–5)
Gothenburgh SO, Neeme Järvi
Bis CD 600

Edgard Varèse, *Intégrales* **(1924–1925)**
[with: *Amériques* (1918–22); *Arcana* (1927); *Ionisation* (1929–31); *Density 21.5* (1936)]
Ensemble InterContemporain, Pierre Boulez
Sony Classical SK 45844

Leoš Janáček, String Quartet no. 2: *Intimate Pages* **(1928)**
[with: String Quartet no. 1: *The Kreutzer Sonata* (1923)]
Smetana Quartet
Supraphon CO 1130

1940s

The decade was inevitably dominated by war. Increased mobility during the hostilities and after confirmed that music was a world phenomenon: henceforward, Balinese scales, Indian or African rhythms would make their way into Western concert music. The war also marked the consolidation of the United States as the *de facto* and presumptive heir of the European tradition in music. Whatever additional ideological or stylistic tinge it had, the music of the early 1940s was strongly coloured by nationalist sentiment or sheer expediency and was thus inclined to be more conservative than the music of the 'experimental' 1920s or the *engagés* 1930s. However, as with every other period in cultural history, any trend appears to embrace its own opposite, and the 1940s were also a seed-ground for the radical attitudes of succeeding decades. Technological development was greatly accelerated and the post-war sense of estrangement and dissociation from the recent past encouraged new ways of thinking about culture in general and, it seemed, music in particular …

1940   Béla Bartók emigrates to the USA.

1941   In December, following the attack on Pearl Harbor, the United States joins the war.

1942   Richard Strauss's last opera, *Capriccio*, an allegory about the creation and aesthetics of opera, is given its premiere in wartime Munich.

1943   Webern's last opus number, the Cantata no. 2, is completed, while its predecessor, the orchestral *Variations* receives its first performance.

1944   Paul Hindemith's *Symphonic Metamorphoses on a Theme of Carl Maria von Weber* underlines the post-war neo-classical temperament. Two years later, Hindemith takes American citizenship.

1945   Anton Webern, in whose tough dialect so much of the music of the period articulates itself, is shot in error and killed by an American soldier following the liberation of Austria. John Cage studies Zen under Daisetz T. Suzuki at Columbia University.

1946   Wolfgang Steinecke establishes the Kranichstein summer course in a new music at Darmstadt, West Germany. The once influential American journal *Modern Music* folds after two decades of publication.

1947   The first, and most successful, of the post-war international festivals is established at Edinburgh.

1948   First Congress of the Union of Soviet Composers, under the chairmanship of Andrei Zhdanov launches a campaign against 'Formalism'. Shostakovich becomes its most prominent victim. Pierre Schaefer experiments with *musique concrète*, completing his *Symphonie pour un homme seul* the following year.

1949   René Leibowitz publishes *Introduction à la musique de douze sons*. Meanwhile, Olivier Messiaen's composition *Mode de valeurs et d'intensités* points a route beyond serialism.

OLIVIER MESSIAEN (1908–1992)

Quatuor pour la fin du temps (1940)

FIRST PERFORMED: Stalag VIIIa, Görlitz, Silesia, 15 January 1941
SELECTED RECORDING: Deutsche Grammophon 423 247 2
   Luben Yordanoff (violin), Albert Tetard (cello), Claude Desurmont (clarinet), Daniel Barenboim (piano)
RECORDED: April 1978
DURATION: 45′ 48″

> I saw a mighty angel come down from heaven, clothed with a cloud; and a rainbow was upon his head, and his face was as if it were the sun, and his feet were pillars of fire. He set his right foot upon the seas, and his left foot on the earth, and standing upon the sea and upon the earth, lifted up his hand to heaven, and swore by Him that liveth for ever and ever, saying: THERE SHALL BE TIME NO LONGER.

In the dark days of 1940, minds turned with understandable readiness to images of Apocalypse, the end-of-everything. Hitler was rampant in Europe, the Allied nations were in recoil, the Soviet Union a seething Asiatic mass, the United States still effectively isolationist. The dominant mood was bleak, but somehow also pregnant with significance, and no single work of the time better expresses that complex mood (even though its author preferred to play down its contemporary resonance) than Olivier Messiaen's *Quatuor pour la fin du temps*.

At the outbreak of war Messiaen had been called up for military service, but was spared combat duty on account of defective eyesight and was posted to a medical unit as an auxiliary. When the Nazi invasion overran French resistance in May 1940, Messiaen was at Verdun, a fateful location in modern French history where a sizeable proportion of his father's generation had been lost in the First World War. As the French Army collapsed, Messiaen and three companions (who happened to be musicians) made their way south-east towards Nancy, but were overtaken and captured.

Messiaen spent the next two years at a prison camp in what is present-day Poland. Conditions were extraordinarily harsh – the composer has spoken about eating nothing for weeks on end except a thin, unsustaining broth – but the camp nonetheless saw the creation and first performance of one of the most significant works of modern times. Remarkably, perhaps, prisoners had access to musical instruments; there was a three-stringed cello, a damaged clarinet, and an upright piano with several defective keys. Messiaen was somehow able to extract stave paper form his captors and began to write a short sketch for his three comrades. It was tried out in the washrooms at Görlitz, and survives, with the addition of a piano part, as the brief fourth movement of the *Quatuor*. Some commentators have found this 'Intermède', which functions as a scherzo, unpleasingly vulgar, a false note amid music of otherwise visionary intensity (the same commentators have also carped at what can seem like blowsy sentimentality in the fifth and final movements) and it is important to keep this section firmly in focus, for it represents a valid and revealing point of entry to the work and the difficulties of performance it represents.

No contemporary performance will ever match the extraordinary circumstances of its premiere. The *Quatuor* was first performed in the Stalag at Görlitz in January 1941 by violinist Jean Le Boulaire, clarinettist Henri Akoka, and cellist Etienne Pasquier, with Messiaen himself taking the piano part. No fewer than 5000 fellow-inmates (an astonishing audience for a contemporary work; how often has it been matched since?) listened to Messiaen's profound music with rapt attention. One wonders what they made of it, but the very fact that so many men, from all walks and stations in life, even men starved of everyday comforts and entertainments, were prepared to listen to such a work with patient appreciation underlines an important point about the *Quatuor*. It is quite clearly an advanced work, but it has little of the alienating wallop of the serialist avant garde; unlike much of Messiaen's other work, and in particular the organ pieces, it is unmistakably a concert piece and not a contribution to the liturgy; it is irrepressibly rhythmic, albeit in a highly developed and personal manner; and though its themes and underlying programme are profound, even mystical, in substance and impact it is both immediate and accessible. That remarkable performance at Görlitz appears in hindsight as a point of focus, marking a mid-point in twentieth-century French music between Debussy and Boulez, uniting East and West, ancient and modern, high and low styles. As such, it encapsulates the central paradox about Messiaen, the qualities that humanize him; those who know him best, such as his former pupil the young British composer George Benjamin, agree that far from being a shy, difficult mystic, he was a man of great common sense and practicality, tolerance and charm, and reassuring fleshly concerns.

The *Quatuor* is, in one sense, relatively untypical of Messiaen's work. Apart from the organ works, he produced very little chamber music. The piece is not in any orthodox classical form, but in eight movements which, as Robert Sherlaw Johnson has shown, exist in precise, almost crystalline, interrelationships, all of them in some way over-determined by the appended passage from the tenth chapter of the Revelation of St John. The form may be influenced by Alban Berg's *Lyrische Suite* for string quartet (1927, some parts orchestrated 1928), but it also develops Messiaen's own practice in the *Quatuor's* immediate predecessor, *Les corps glorieux*, for organ. The *Quatuor's* unusual instrumentation was due in part to the availability of musicians but its main impetus comes from within. It is a beautifully balanced work, with an overarching structure echoed by the 'Fouillis d'arcs-en-ciel' – the 'cluster of rainbows' – of the penultimate movement. Though it makes the fullest possible use of its instrumental resources, only four of the movements are scored for quartet, the remainder for trio, duo or solo instruments; and it is the piano's (that is, Messiaen's own) absence in the central intermezzo that gives it its ironic force.

The *Quatuor's* mysterious quality comes in part from the unfamiliar rhythms Messiaen draws from Indian music, but also from the way its harmonic language fails to resolve into the conventional Western opposition of major and minor, but hovers ambiguously between the two; even so, the main tonal centre of the crucial middle three and last movements is E major, a key long associated (as in the work of Skryabin) with spiritual transfiguration. The dislocation of rhythmic and harmonic reference points (a method Messiaen had learned in part from his teacher Paul Dukas, composer of *L'apprenti sorcier*) contributes substantially to the work's deliberately ambiguous theme. The 'end of time' relates not just to historical time, but musical time as well.

Much critical effort has been expended in trying to separate Messiaen's spiritual intention from the circumstances in which the work was written. Perhaps too much; for it is clear that the two interact strongly. Living at the brink of starvation, Messiaen found himself in a strange, trance-like state in which he perceived sound as colour; it is a condition known as synaesthesia, one that was particularly important to the Surrealists, who are Messiaen's main artistic forebears. At Görlitz, he was particularly moved by a sighting of the aurora borealis in the cold northern sky, which seemed a confirmation of his spiritual vision.

In a note on the *Quatuor*, Messiaen states that he was 'drawn not to the cataclysms and monsters of the Apocalypse, but rather to its silences of adoration, its marvellous visions of peace'. The opening movement, entitled 'Liturgie de cristal', is anything but peaceful or contemplative. Messiaen builds up a rhythmic structure of unequal and overlapping values which is subject to constant and shifting repetition. The piano repeats what Messiaen calls a 'rhythmic pedal', derived from the *tala* of Indian music. This is based on seventeen rhythmic values, an indication of Messiaen's semi-mystical, but very practical, liking for prime numbers (seven has a powerful symbolic significance and the eighth, pendant movement of the *Quatuor* is intended to represent the transcendence of eternity and Resurrection); this is accentuated by a progression of twenty-nine chords and by the five-note motif articulated on the cello. Combined with the ambiguities of his harmony, this creates what Messiaen called 'stained-glass window' effects, a shifting chromatic language that constantly changes in value, and represents one of the ways in which he conveys musically the idea of eternity. The second is his use of extremely slow tempos in the fifth and eighth movements. The third, of course, is repetition. The repetitive structure is so complex that it would take considerably longer than the duration of the whole piece for the separate lines to move back into phase and return to the original configuration; this is a technique that became established practice with the American 'minimalists', and Messiaen discusses it with some reference to the 'Liturgie de cristal' in his 1947 book *Technique de mon langage musical*.

Messiaen's dynamic markings and instructions to performers are always highly personal and specific. Early in the first movement, the two string players are instructed to play 'comme un oiseau', a relatively early example (though it had made a first appearance in 1935, in the fourth meditation of the organ piece *La Nativité du Seigneur*) of his use of birdsong as a compositional device. Messiaen made thousands of transcriptions of birdsong throughout his career. They served him much like the Surrealists' *objets trouvés*, but with a superadded element of spirituality and transcendence. In the 'Liturgie de cristal', as in the third movement, the sound of birds evokes the spirit ecstatically bridging the enormous gulfs of eternity.

In the second movement, headed 'Vocalise, pour l'Ange qui annonce la fin du temps', Messiaen introduces the mighty angel of the Apocalypse with a beautiful arching song for violin and cello, set against the prismatic 'water drops' of the piano line. The third movement, entitled 'Albîme des oiseaux', is scored for clarinet alone and, as suggested above, opposes the enormous depths of the 'abyss' with the joyous call of the birds. After the central intermezzo, the character of the music deepens considerably. The fifth movement, like the last, is headed

'Louange [praise] à l'éternité et l'immortalité de Jésus', and is a gorgeous duet for cello and piano. Both of these movements are characterized in the dynamic marking as 'ecstatic', but clearly the other half of the marking to the fifth – 'Infinitely slow' – is logically impossible and has to be understood metaphorically and spiritually.

Getting these tempos right is absolutely critical. The 1978 Deutsche Grammophon recording was made in the presence of the composer, and has to be considered authentic in such regard. Some critics have found the music of the two 'Louanges' vapid and slightly syrupy, and Paul Griffiths quite rightly associates some of its essential elements with sentimental repertoire pieces like the 'Méditation' from *Thaïs*; but Messiaen himself insisted that the music of these movements should have a 'noble simplicity, unadorned, austere', and this is what distinguishes the recording by Barenboim and his colleagues from most of the others, which tend to gabble the slower tempos. Like much of Messiaen's work, and notably the brawling, sensual *Turangalîla-symphonie* of 1946 to 1948, even the most vigorous of the music is easily bruised by careless handling, and the more delicate parts are highly susceptible to banality; a recording by the American group Tashi is notably suspect in its treatment of the slower passages.

In between the two slow sections are contrasting movements for quartet. The sixth is called 'Danse de la fureur, pour les sept trompettes', and headed 'Décidé, vigoureux, granitique, un peu vif'. Messiaen varied the metaphor by likening this 'music of stone', with its romantic F sharp tonality, to steel and ice, and it is clear that the four instruments are also intended to evoke brass, first in the form of trumpets, later of huge gongs. The seventh movement recalls the annunciatory Angel of the second and varies and combines its thematic and dynamic characteristics into a whirling ecstasy of 'swords of fire, ... blue and orange lava flows, ... sudden stars'. This is the movement that brings the *Quatuor* to the portals of eternity, the absolute identity of sound and colour in what Messiaen identifies as a dream of 'classified chords and melodies, known colours and forms' that prefigures the stillness and utter peace of the closing 'Louange à l'immortalité de Jésus'. Time is brought to an end.

Discographical Information

Other recordings: Gruenberg, Pleeth, de Peyer, Beroff (EMI ASD 2470 LP); Meyer, Poppen, Fischer-Dieskau, Loriod (EMI Classics CDC 54935); Chamber Music North West [with: Bartók, *Contrasts*] (Delos D/CD 3043); Gavrilov, Deinzer, Palm, Kontarsky [with: *Turangalîla-symphonie*] (EMI CDS7 47463 8); Beths Pierson, Bylsma, De Leeuw (Philips 422 834 2); New York Philomusica Chamber Ensemble (Vox STGBY 670); Kavafian, Sherry, Stoltzman, Serkin (collectively Tashi) (RCA GD 87835); Brunner, Trio Fontenay (Teldec 9031 73239-2);

Ensemble Walter Boeykens (Harmonia Mundi HMC 901348); Le Dizes, Damiens, Aimard, Strauch (Adda CD 581029); Shifrin, Bae, Lash, Doppman (Delos CD 3043)

Other Messiaen: *Les corps glorieux* (1939, Unicorn-Kanchana DKPCD 9004); *Vingt regards sur l'enfant-Jésus* (1945; Unicorn-Kanchana DKP 9122/3); *Harawi* (1946; Bis CD 86); *Turangalîla-symphonie* (1946–8; Deutsche Grammophon 431781–2); *Et exspecto resurrectionem mortuorum* (1964; Summit DCD 122); *Livre du Saint-Sacrement* (1984; Unicorn-Kanchana DKPCD 9067/8).

Map references: Jules Massenet, 'Méditation', from *Thaïs* (1894; OSF 49012); Alexander Skryabin, *The Poem of Ecstasy*, op. 54 (1908; Chandos CHAN 8898); Paul Dukas, *L'apprenti sorcier* (1897; Chesky CD 61); Pierre Boulez, *Rituel: in memoriam Bruno Maderna* (1974–5; see p. 219); George Benjamin, *Antara* (1987; see p. 335); William Kraft, *Quartet for the Love of Time* (1987; CRI CD 639).

Further reading: R. Sherlaw Johnson, Chapter 8, *Messiaen*, London, 1975, 1989; P. Griffiths, 'Technique for the End of Time', Chapter 6, *Olivier Messiaen and the Music of Time*, London, 1985; P. Hill (ed.), *The Messiaen Companion*, London, 1994.

DMITRY SHOSTAKOVICH (1906–1975)

Symphony no. 8 in C minor (1943)

FIRST PERFORMANCE: Moscow, 4 November 1943
SELECTED RECORDING: Philips 422442 2
  Leningrad Philharmonic Orchestra, conducted by Yevgeny Mravinsky
RECORDED: March 1982
DURATION: 62'

Controversy stalked Dmitry Dmitryevich Shostakovich all his life and continues to haunt him beyond the grave. The ultimate truth of his work, and particularly of the fifteen symphonies, is probably now unrecoverable. Were they the work of a loyal Communist, who occasionally lapsed but reliably purged his contempt? Or was he a dissident, who from time to time bowed to the inevitable pressures of the system? Or was he an ironic jester, who played the duplicitous double game of the *yurodivi*, the Holy Fool who mocks the mighty with impunity? The problem with Shostakovich, or rather with his work, is that it has become a vast hall of mirrors in which it is virtually impossible to distinguish between genuine intention and distorted reflection, contemporary reality and *arrière pensée*, simple musical argument and carefully coded dissidence, subtle enough to fool Stalin's watchers. It has even become difficult to judge where Shostakovich, weakened by illness or by exhaustion, is writing incompetently and where he *might* be writing deliberately badly for satiric effect. There are, it sometimes seems, no terms of reference large enough to grasp the work objectively and entire.

Listening to Shostakovich at any length is an object lesson for anyone interested in the social construction of music. It is notoriously true – and something of a running joke in free jazz circles – that naming a piece 'Ode to Mandela' or 'Free the Penge Seven' guarantees it a totally different reception than calling the same piece 'Hebridean Sunset' or 'Evensong'. To some extent that is perfectly proper. Naming a piece is an ideological – if not always a directly political – act. Shostakovich's programme titles for the symphonies – 'May First' (no. 3) and 'The Year 1917' (no. 12) – must at some level be taken at face value. It is all too well known that Shostakovich worked and wrote under the shadow of a vast, over-determining political orthodoxy that sought to penetrate every aspect of social and cultural life. It is, or should be, equally obvious that no political system has ever attained such absolute control; the totalitarianism imagined by George Orwell in *Nineteen Eighty-Four* was, in the end, unworkably absurd because it was premised entirely on coercion. The truth of an artist's life and work must lie somewhere in between. The life and the work are not necessarily congruent in the way we might wish.

With Shostakovich's career, the logic of the Red Queen (the right colour at least) has prevailed. Writing about the notorious Fifth Symphony (1937), supposedly Shostakovich's line-toeing recantation of his bourgeois and formalist vices, Christopher Norris has warned against 'ideological reaction' in discussing the works. Anything can mean exactly what we choose it to mean ... *if* we accept the premise that everything in the symphonies is to be read as a direct expression of political views and feelings. That is the problem with the Fifth and even with the Seventh (which five years later became the apotheosis of politically correct wartime nationalism). But what does a particularly mechanistic and vulgar march actually satirize? What does a resounding C major resolution actually express? The Nazi invaders? The Cheka thugs? Socialist realism *in excelsis*? Or a sly use of convention to guy the conventional, like the sarcastic devoutness of the agnostic? Finessing such interpretations and second-guessing ideological responses has become a particularly redundant game.

I am certainly not arguing that the symphonies should be read as 'pure' or absolute works; apart from anything else that would set them counter to the essentially didactic and content-laden nature of Russian art. Nor am I claiming to offer a 'correct' interpretation; correctness was the province of Messrs Khrennikov and Zhdanov and those others who, in the name of Stalin, did litmus tests on art and literature to determine acceptable levels of ideological pH. But I do want to suggest that problems of interpretation in the case of Shostakovich are not always *where,* let alone *what,* they seem to be. In the case of the Eighth Symphony, I have to declare myself a counter-revisionist. Far from a world-weary botch, as it has been characterized, it seems to me one of the composer's very greatest works. I shall try to show why.

For the purposes of this book, the story effectively begins in the Siberian gateway town of Kuibishev where, on 5 March 1942, Shostakovich's Seventh Symphony was performed for the first time by the Bol'shoy Theatre Orchestra under the baton of Samuel Samosud. Its real premiere, though, came a few weeks later, on 29 March, in a worldwide broadcast from Moscow. The work instantly acquired enormous international significance as a symbolic expression of Russian resistance and stoicism; not even a Luftwaffe air raid during the performance managed to interrupt it. Shostakovich had completed the score just after Christmas and had inscribed it 'To the City of Leningrad'. On 9 August there was an emotional performance in Leningrad itself, with a scratch orchestra; the local battery commander had been instructed to silence as many of the German howitzers as he could on the evening, a detail that makes the occasional ping of digital watches and winter coughs at concerts seem absurdly trivial interruptions.

By the end of 1942, Shostakovich was the most famous living composer and the 'Leningrad Symphony' had been performed around the world, the score smuggled out of Russia on microfilm. Whatever doubts there may have been about Shostakovich's ideological reliability evaporated. The 'Leningrad' was read as a triumphant assertion of democratic and socialist values over the cynical tread of Fascism (the famous march in the first movement). No other interpretation seemed plausible. In his controversial *Testimony* (a ghosted autobiography edited – some would say confected – by one Solomon Volkov) Shostakovich appears to contradict himself, saying that the Seventh Symphony *had* to be written, and as an effort to 'create the image of our country in war'. Elsewhere, he made it clear that the work had been on his mind for some time, perhaps even before the Hitler–Stalin pact. Clearly, this is not a contradiction that need trouble anyone, since the first conception might well have the germ of a purely musical idea suddenly given force and urgency by the war. However, elsewhere Shostakovich was at pains to make clear that his symphonies from the suppressed Fourth (written 1936, premiered *1961!*) onwards 'and including the Seventh and Eighth' are about 'the terrible pre-war years', an extended requiem for all those who fell victim to totalitarianism.

The Seventh Symphony fell from favour after the war, everywhere but in Russia. Its martial air and triumphalist character were no longer musically pleasing. The Eighth almost inevitably suffered from being The One After the Big One, and it disappeared from the Western concert repertoire immediately after the war, and never received more than a lukewarm reception in the Soviet Union. However, during the cultural and political thaw of the 1960s, the Eighth assumed a new significance in the West which it has borne until relatively recently. Ian MacDonald, one of the harder-tackling music critics in Britain, set about the Eighth in his revisionist book *The New Shostakovich* (1990). MacDonald found it suspicious that of all the symphonies Shostakovich 'revised' in *Testimony* (in the terms quoted above) only the Eighth had been set above question 'as if the very idea of re-evaluating it is somehow in bad taste'.

Why should this have been? MacDonald suggests that before the publication of *Testimony* and the problematic revelation of a sceptical, dissident Shostakovich, 'Western liberals were able to assuage any guilt they harboured about admiring the work of an orthodox totalitarian by concentrating their praise upon the musical manifestations of what they saw as his copious grief for the victims of Nazism'. It had been 'chic' among leftist liberals to attribute the defeat of the Third Reich to the heroic sacrifice of the Russian people; clearly, if the Eighth were not about the war at all, then goalposts would have to be moved.

On one point at least, I agree with MacDonald. If the Eighth is controversial, it is so first and foremost on musical grounds. However, I cannot agree with his dismissal of the work. It seems to me that MacDonald fatally conflates inadequate *performance* with inadequate conception and a failure of imaginative control. He is clearly an able reader of scores, but surely to suggest that in the Eighth Shostakovich 'simply [*simply*!?] lost grip on his material under the weight of its emotional burden ... blew a fuse [in pushing through a work so demanding so soon after illness]' and produced an 'earthbound' work which lacks the '*vital electricity* which distinguishes Shostakovich's music from that of most [!] other composers', is to indulge a version of what Chris Norris called 'ideological [or in this case psychological] reaction'. It may be that in straining after controversy, MacDonald himself blew a fuse.

I can think of no major orchestral work, of any period, for which performance values vary so dramatically and over which conductors have taken more sizeable liberties with the composer's rhythmic and expressive markings. (Unlike the majority of selections in this book, I would strongly recommend listening to three or four versions; comparisons are more than academic.) Even without 'repeats', which can stretch or compact classical symphonies by several minutes, the Eighth is wildly variable in duration, and one has to assume that interpretative motivation has something to do with it. The composer's son Maxim Shostakovich turns it into a dark, personal odyssey and stretches it out to seventy minutes. Bychkov seems to want to reduce it to a sequence of bleakly nihilistic symphonic fragments and slows the first and last movements unbearably. Those conductors, pre-eminently Mravinsky and Haitink, who seem to have intuited the work's tightly organized (*pace* MacDonald) symphonic argument, bring it in around the hour mark. Admirable as Haitink's reading is, it is probably too architectural and impersonal. Mravinsky is able to balance dramatic and structural values in what seems to me an ideal reading, lent additional tension by the concert atmosphere of the recording.

Yevgeny Mravinsky (1903–88) was the dedicatee and first interpreter of the Eighth. He had visited Shostakovich at the Composers' Colony in Ivanovo during the writing of the piece and expressed his admiration for the first four movements; perversely, MacDonald attributes what he considers the relative vitality of the *Allegretto* finale to Mravinsky's encouragement. Shostakovich wrote the score, one of his longest, in just ten weeks, an achievement that suggests concentration of effort rather than a man on the brink of breakdown. Mravinsky wasted no time and on 4 November 1943 the Eighth Symphony was premiered in Moscow.

So what of the work itself? The Eighth exists as a complex of antagonistic interpretations, so it is difficult to describe neutrally. Certain details are incontestable. The work as a whole is dominated by a huge *Adagio* opening movement, which is twice the length of the finale and four times as long as movements two and three. However, the architectural balance of the piece is secured by playing the last three movements without a break, a device Shostakovich returned to in the Ninth Symphony (1945) and in the string quartets. The *Adagio* opens in the home key of C minor, a tonality that might recall the 'fate' motto of Beethoven's Symphony no. 3 or Schubert's so-called 'Tragic' Symphony no. 4. The lower strings establish a strong dotted phrase that gives the symphony a deceptively vehement beginning (and to my mind suggests that it begins *in media re*, as if the symphonies from no. 5 onwards are really part of an epic cycle). This gives way to a softer theme which is immediately reminiscent of the opening movement of the Fifth Symphony. Shostakovich instructed that the strings bow above the fingerboard, or *sul tasto*, a device that bleaches the sound of colour and reduces the intensity considerably. Bychkov's strings are positively anaemic and, with the tempo stalling disastrously, even show signs of heart failure. Inevitably, the music sounds artificially resuscitated as the theme gains weight and spirals upward. There is a throat-clearing interlude for the lower woodwinds before the second subject gets under way. Violins play robustly over a steady string pulse with violas and cor anglais emphasizing a sanguine and apparently optimistic mood.

With a return to the nervous opening figure, the flutes suggest that all is not as it seems. A militaristic drum beat establishes a note of urgency, though the basic pulse remains constant. There is an abrupt, powerful climax that completes the dynamic gamut from a near inaudible *pppp* at the start of the violin melody to a stunning *ffff* as the central conflict breaks. Suddenly up a gear, the woodwinds bleat ominously, while at some distance from the main action, the horns and cellos sound distant warnings of disaster. A heavy-footed march follows and it is hard not to picture the trumpets and glockenspiels of Nazi bands at Nuremberg. MacDonald considers the apocalyptic clashes and minatory blasts of brass that follow to be merely bruising. In keeping with his general reorientation, he suggests that all the vices ascribed to the Seventh – 'redundant longevity and repetition' – simply be re-targeted on its successor and that the Eighth's opening *Adagio* be dismissed as 'a bloated and unfocused mess'. Such a view might just be understandable from a critic reliant on Bychkov or Shostakovich *fils*, but not, surely, from anyone who has heard Mravinsky's magisterial and completely adult reading (which MacDonald himself recommends as 'classic' in his appendix).

He is equally severe on the plaintive cor anglais solo that follows the apocalypse. MacDonald considers it 'interminable', but it seems to me that it says no more than it needs to (which is little and tragic enough) before history in the shape of the supposedly over-extended second subject reasserts itself with a chastened character; all but Mravinsky and Rodzinski fail to observe the need for a subtle change of dramatic timbre at this point and so, instead of ending with a sense of heightened philosophical sophistication, most versions of the massive first movement merely end ambiguously.

The second movement is a scherzo with a surprisingly dour aspect. It recalls Shostakovich's more obviously satirical writing, but seems to have moved a step beyond merely guying Fascist goose steps to launch a more general attack on extremism of thought and the failure of intellectual generosity. The composer makes considerable use of widely spaced woodwind pitches over a basic D♭ tonality that is determinedly unsymphonic and banal in character. MacDonald again considers the movement 'ungainly' and 'tired', and seems resentful that the argument of the whole piece is steering steadily away from identifiable targets.

It is almost certain that the sound effects and battering ostinatos of the E minor third movement are intended to suggest military conflict. There are shell-bursts, machine gun fire, panicky musters and urgent high-pitched trumpet calls, but again the onomatopoeic and dramatic character of the music always seems prepared to be drawn up into something larger. In place of juxtaposition, Shostakovich allows the dissonant conclusion to dissolve into the succeeding *Largo*, which represents the heart of the closing meta-movement. It is cast as a passacaglia, a set of polyphonic variations over a ground bass, and the music transforms itself stage by stage from bleak defeatism (every phrase abruptly shut off or wearily attenuated) to a level of philosophical confidence that is too guarded and carefully mediated to characterize as optimism. Predictably enough, MacDonald considers the 'dirge-like' (again, not Mravinsky's) passacaglia to be a potent musical image of 'terminal exhaustion'. But here, too, it is as if Shostakovich is demonstrating the redundancy of the wand-waving triumphal affirmations that character-ized not just Soviet music (and not excluding his own) but symphonic music in general. Coincidentally (or not) Sergey Prokofiev (1891–1953) was to set his own farewell Symphony no. 7 (1951–2), dedicated to Soviet youth in the tough years of reconstruction, in the nearby but even more ambiguous C♯ minor key.

The transition to the *Allegretto* finale has always made me think of H. G. Wells in 1945, writing *The Mind at the End of Its Tether* immedi-ately after, *The Happy Turning: A Dream of Life*. The last section opens with a parping bassoon melody which sets in motion a sequence of rather languid philosophical discussions drawing in violins, a flute, cellos and oboes. There are quotations from earlier movements and from other Shostakovich works, most obviously the Stalin Prize-winning Piano Quintet of 1940 with its 'betrayal' motif, but there is no need to interpret such references too narrowly. It has become customary to hear the conclusion as devoid of animation, exhausted and ener-vated, but it sounds to me like the gesture of a composer who has already completed his argument and just spends a moment listening to it circulating, not quite reliably, round its orchestral 'audience'. I can see no warrant for MacDonald's finding that the final movement is ener-getic only in relation to its predecessors and then declaring that the energy is all deployed for the expression of ... nothing.

MacDonald finds that the Eighth 'swings a sandbag against the liste-ner's skull', but it is in many respects the least histrionic of the wartime group of symphonies. It is certainly in a different vein from the Seventh. Shostakovich's evacuation to Kuibishev afforded him a new perspective on the country that may have filtered through into the music, but whatever the reason, he conceived the Eighth in a much narrower, less staged way. There is far less inscape, far less newsreel, far less sound-tracking and special pleading. The Eighth is simply more *modern* than the Seventh or the Fifth, and when MacDonald says that 'what is wrong with [the opening movements] is that they are one-dimensional in the way that the works of composers like Penderecki or Schnittke are one-dimensional', the only word to quibble with is 'wrong'. The Eighth has an internal coherence and consistency of argument that does tend to unravel if it is forced to do service as underpinning for an emotional or political programme. It tells far more about war and intolerance and suffering, and about recovery and reintegration if it is simply experi-enced, and not interrogated.

Discographical Information

Other recordings: New York PO, Rodzinski (AS Disc AS 538); Scottish NO, Järvi (Chandos CHAN 8757/ABTD 1396); London SO, M. Shostakovich (Collins Classics 1271); London SO, Previn (HMV ASD 2917); Royal Concertgebouw Orchestra, Haitink (London 411616); Chicago SO, Solti (London 425675); USSR Television and Radio Large SO, Fedoseyev (London 425675); USSR Ministry of Culture SO, Rozhdestvensky (Olympia OCD 143); Berlin PO, Bychkov (Philips 432 090), St Louis SO, Slatkin (RCA 60145).

Other Shostakovich: Symphony no. 1 (1924–5; RCA Gold Seal 09026 60323); *Lady Macbeth of the Mtsensk District* (1934; EMI CDS7 49955); String Trio no. 2 (1944; CBS MK 44664); Violin Concerto (1947–8; Intaglio INCD 7241); Twenty-four Preludes and Fugues (1950–1; ECM New Series 1469/1470); *The Gadfly* (1955; Pro Arte CDD 551); String Quartet no. 8 (1960; Bis CD 26); String Quartet no. 10 (1968; Angel CDC 49269).

Map references: Sergey Prokofiev, Symphony no. 7 (1951–2; Chandos CHAN 8442); Rodion Shchedrin, Piano Concerto no. 1 (1954; Russian Disc RUS 11129); Sofiya Gubaydulina, *Concordanza* (1971; Mobile Fidelity MFCD 869); Alfred Schnittke, Symphony no. 1 (1974; Melodiya SUCD 10–00062).

Further reading: S. Volkov ('editor'), *Testimony: The Memoirs of Dmitry Shostakovich*, New York [NB], 1979; C. Norris (ed.), *Shostakovich: The Man and His Music*, London, 1982 [an essentially left-wing collection of essays]; I. MacDonald, *The New Shostakovich*, London, 1991.

BÉLA BARTÓK (1881–1945)

Concerto for Orchestra (1943, revised 1945)

FIRST PERFORMED: Boston, 1 December 1944
SELECTED RECORDING: Telarc Digital CD 80174
Los Angeles Philharmonic Orchestra, conducted by André Previn
    [with: Leoš Janáček, *Sinfonietta*, 1926]
RECORDED: 3 May 1988
DURATION: 38' 08"

In October 1940 Béla Bartók left his native Hungary for the last time. Ever afterwards, he behaved like a man brutally cut off from his own past. With the completion of the grotesque and ironic String Quartet no. 6 exactly a year before, and of its artistic twin, the brooding and fore-bidding Divertimento for string orchestra, Bartók seemed to have ended his creative journey. His mother had just died, and the brutal triumph of National Socialism cast into doubt the survival of a Slavonic culture he had done so much to energize. On a brief concert trip to the United States in April 1940, plans had been laid to secure a research appointment at Columbia University for Bartók, primarily to document Balkan folksong, but in the darkening context of that summer and autumn it must have seemed an increasingly bleak task, better suited to an obituarist than a committed musicologist. By then, Bartók's only close tie to his homeland was his son Péter, who remained in Hungary for a further two years.

These were bleak times for the composer. Much has been made of his precarious financial position in America. It is clear, though, that he was never as badly off in the United States as he frequently complained, and the recurrent obsession with money seems to have been little more than an exile's understandable projection of other anxieties. In other, equally significant regards, Bartók appeared even more depleted. He found performance exhausting, and the urge to compose seemed to have deserted him. More seriously, he had begun to suffer a series of high fevers which, after some hesitation, were attributed to leukaemia or polycythemia. The diagnosis was not at first disclosed to Bartók, which seems to have been sound judgement, for an artist who identified creativity with physical health and 'high-spiritedness' would have been utterly confounded by the rebellion in his blood, and it became clear later, once he began to write again, that regular creative activity was more beneficial to his health than anything his doctors could offer.

The Concerto for Orchestra is all the more remarkable for having emerged from a period of such sterility and depression. Few modern works have ever seemed so unsentimentally affirmative, balancing tragedy with a carefree playfulness, and there was little reason to anticipate the magnitude of Bartók's eventual achievement. As early as the spring of 1939, after the completion and premier of the Violin Concerto, there had been a suggestion that Bartók write a 'symphonic ballet'; two years later, at the nadir of his physical and spiritual fortunes, his publisher Ralph Hawkes was nudging him with the idea of an overture based on folk themes or possibly a series of concertante pieces, latter-day 'Brandenburgs'. It is not known how much material from any of these sources found its way into the Concerto for Orchestra, but it is clear that the work had a long, painful, and largely unconscious gestation.

Nothing brings a creative work to term more effectively than a firm commission. In the summer of 1943 Serge Koussevitzky, conductor and music director of the Boston Symphony Orchestra, responded to a suggestion by the violinist Joseph Szigeti (who had premiered the full version of Bartók's clarinet trio *Contrasts* with Benny Goodman and the composer for a Columbia recording in April 1940) and offered Bartók $1,000 from the Koussevitzky Foundation for an orchestral piece. It is not clear what was expected, and as with Ralph Hawkes, it seems that the assumption was that Bartók would produce only a relatively brief and undemanding overture, but it was immediately obvious that the commission sparked off something much more grandiose.

The Concerto for Orchestra became the largest concert score that Bartók was to write. At nearly forty minutes, it is longer than anything else in his output except the opera *Bluebeard's Castle* and the early orchestral Suite no. 1. In form the piece resembles a concerto grosso, with its opposition of a 'virtuosic' or 'soloistic' (Bartók's terms) *concertino* set against the replenishing *ripieno* of the whole orchestra and there were elements of this baroque practice in the Divertimento. However, it is clear that the Concerto for Orchestra is also Bartók's closest approximation to a symphony, in the stressed and personal form that survived into the twentieth century by the efforts of Nielsen, Sibelius and Shostakovich. It contains some of his most direct and clear-sighted scoring, drawing together musical elements from virtually every period in his career into a vast, asymmetrical arch.

The opening *Andante non troppo* has a quietly mysterious quality, fraught with potential. It is constructed largely of fourths, the interval that dominates the two end pillars of the Concerto for Orchestra, and establishes an opposition between a brash, assertive foreground dominated by flutes and trumpets and a quieter, more speculative and logical, secondary theme, which is taken up by the oboe. The introductory movement has an elegant contrapuntal inventiveness, a baroque anticipation of the whirling, folkish *perpetuum mobile* of the balancing final movement. That playful quality is explicitly taken up in the *allegretto scherzando* movement. This is headed 'Giuoco delle coppie' – 'play of pairs' – and may contain the most explicit reminder of the work's putative origins in the symphonic ballet discussed with Hawkes in 1939. The main part of the movement, interrupted (as the nearly symmetrical fourth movement is to be interrupted) by a brief chorale for brass and side drum, consists of thematically unrelated sections in which five pairs of winds each 'dance' to a different interval: bassoons in sixths, oboes in thirds, clarinets in clumsy sevenths, flutes in contrastingly well-balanced fifths, and trumpets in seconds reiterating the closeness of the opening pair. After the brief chorale, a recapitulation distributes the same pairings throughout the orchestra, thus intensifying the richness of texture and developmental significance.

The middle movement is an example of Bartók's characteristic 'night music'. In terms of the work's underlying programme, it represents an elegiac farewell to the communal 'dance', the unity of Bartók's native culture. The tone darkens into a funeral lament that may well refer to the death of the composer's mother, ending with a plangent piccolo figure that equally may stand for the isolation and failing voice of the exile. In the succeeding movement, a much-debated 'Intermezzo interrotto', the programmatic element is even more prominent. Bartók himself characterized the opening music for oboe and flute as the artist's declaration of love for his native land. This gives way to a romantic, cantabile string melody (with the violas prominent) which draws on a popular operetta theme. The opening material returns in a conventional ABA structure, but is rudely interrupted by a coarse, militaristic theme that shows (in the words of Bartók's own programme note) the artist 'seized by rough, booted men who even break his instrument'. The transparent reference to the Nazi invasion is underlined by Bartók's use of material from Dmitry Shostakovich's wartime Symphony no. 7, inscribed 'To the City of Leningrad', which had received its American premiere under Toscanini in July 1942, but which Bartók had apparently heard in a radio broadcast. It is to be wondered what Koussevitzky, a passionate propagandist for Shostakovich's music, felt about this apparently disrespectful quotation, with its farting brass effects, and some commentators have suggested that the 'interruption' was actually borrowed from operetta – perhaps Lehár's *Die lustige Witwe* – and that Bartók and Shostakovich were merely putting the same material to parallel but rather different use. Whatever the circumstantial truth, it is perfectly obvious what Bartók intends to convey. The invader may be violent but he is also transitory, and the older music reasserts itself as the movement draws to a dreamy close.

Like the opening movement, the finale begins with a fanfare that signals a new dawn and a new sense of community beyond the narrower folkishness of earlier movements. The music swirls up into two grandly inexhaustible developments – the first a *perpetuum mobile*, the second a more formal fugue – divided by a more sombre middle subject. György Kroó suggests that the massive closing fugue contains echoes of Beethoven's music of liberation in *Fidelio*, and once the connection has been made, it seems unmissable. Bartók's climax is a triumphant reassertion of humanity. There are faint bluesy overtones that are reminiscent of Dvořák, and equally difficult to characterize in national–cultural terms (Slavic? American? a new synthesis of Old World and New?), but that seem to deliver the ambiguous promise of the opening movement. If the Concerto for Orchestra was begun in despair, it ends with mature and chastened optimism. Only sickness prevented Bartók from giving final shape to the extraordinary outpouring of work that followed it.

Discographical Information

Other recordings: Cleveland Orchestra, Dohnányi [with: Lutosławski, Concerto for Orchestra] (London 425694); Czech PO Ančerl: (Sound CD 3439); New York PO, Bernstein [with: Music for Strings, Percussion and Celesta] (CBS MK 44707); Chicago SO, Solti [with: Mussorgsky, *Pictures at an Exhibition*] (Decca 417 7542); London SO, Frühbeck de Burgos [with: Kodály, Concerto for Orchestra] (Collins Classics 10912); Royal Concertgebouw Orchestra, Dorati [with: Janáček, *Sinfonietta*] (Philips 411 132 2); Berlin PO, Karajan [with: Music for Strings, Percussion and Celesta] (Deutsche Grammophon DG 415 322 2); New York PO, [with: Music for Strings, Percussion and Celesta] (CBS MK 37259); Montreal SO, Dutoit [with: Music for Strings, Percussion and Celesta] (Decca 421 443 2); there are many others, but note should be made of a CBS recording (MK 44526), performed by G. Sándor, of the composer's intriguing piano reduction of the full score.

Other Bartók: Suite no. 1, op 3 (1905, 1920; Hungaroton HCD 31045); *Bluebeard's Castle*, op. 11 (1911 [rev. 1912, 1918, 1921]; Mercury Living Presence 434325–2); *Contrasts* (1938; CBS MK 42227); Violin Concerto (1937–8; Angel CDH 69804); Divertimento 1939; Philips 432126–2); String Quartet no. 6 (1939; Collins Classics 11882); Sonata for solo violin (1944; ADDA 581131); Piano Concerto no. 3 (1945; EMI CDC 54770).

Map references: Jean Sibelius, Symphony no. 4 in A minor, op. 63 (1911; Chandos CHAN 6555); Zoltán Kodály, Concerto for Orchestra (1941; Collins Classics 10912 [see above, 'Other recordings']); Dmitry Shostakovich, Symphony no. 7 (1942; RCA Gold Seal 60293–2).

Further reading: [by Bartók] 'Hungarian Peasant Music', in *Musical Quarterly* xix/3 (Jul. 1933; writings on folk music published in English by New York Bartók Archive Studies in Musicology, ed. B. Suchoff, 1967 *et seq*.; [on Bartók and the Concerto], H. Stevens, *The Life and Music of Béla Bartók*, New York, 1953, rev. edns. 1964, 1993; G. Kroó, *A Guide to Bartók*, Budapest, 1971; L. Somfai and V. Lampert, 'Béla Bartók', in *Modern Masters* (*New Grove* Composer Biography Series, New York, 1984; M. Gillies (ed.), *The Bartók Companion*, London, 1993.

AARON COPLAND (1900–1990)

Appalachian Spring (suite) (1943–1944, 1945)

FIRST PERFORMED: New York City, 4 October 1945; original ballet version, New York City, 30 October 1944
SELECTED RECORDING: Deutsche Grammophon 427 335 2
    Orpheus Chamber Orchestra, unconducted ensemble
    Susan Palma (flute), David Singer (clarinet), Frank Morelli (bassoon), Wu Han (piano)
    [with: *Short Symphony* (no. 2) (1932–3); *Quiet City* (1939); *Three Latin American Sketches*: Estribillo, Paisaje mexicana, Danza de Jalisco (1959–71)]
RECORDED: March 1988
DURATION: 25′ 26″

If there is such a thing as a popular modern classic, *Appalachian Spring* must be among the most widely recognized. Even allowing that its best-known theme – widely known as 'Lord of the Dance' – was not actually written by Copland, the whole piece gives off an air of having been around for much longer than its fifty years, almost of having sprung spontaneously from the frontier soil. Ironically so, for this most 'natural', 'fresh' and 'spontaneous' of pieces is in fact a highly wrought musical confection, an artful manipulation of an 'expressive idea'. The title (which was choreographer Martha Graham's, rather than Copland's) comes from the poet Hart Crane, hardly a bard of innocence.

Appalachian Spring has been recorded countless times. The list below can only be partial and is inevitably of mixed quality. Though Copland's score is robust enough to survive some notably dreary performances, it is immediately striking how much more vivid the piece can sound when a conductor keeps in mind Copland's own conviction that 'orchestral know-how consists in keeping instruments out of each other's way'. I have picked a version – unconducted, as it happens – that returns to the uncluttered simplicity of the original, scored for just thirteen players (flute, clarinet, bassoon, piano and nine strings) because the band-pit at the Library of Congress, where the ballet was first staged, was too small to accommodate a larger orchestra. In 1945 Copland made a full orchestral arrangement of the piece, and this concert suite has become the most familiar version of the work; there is a 1959 recording with the Boston Symphony Orchestra conducted by the composer (see below), but the sound is very remote. In his entry on Copland in *The New Grove Dictionary of American Music*, William W. Austin suggests that far from congesting the clean lines of the original piece, Copland's orchestration adds subtle timbral values and harmonic richness. More bravura conductors like Leonard Bernstein (again see below) drive a horse and cart through any such subtleties. There is still much to recommend the chamber version, also recorded by Clark with the Pacific Symphony Orchestra and Davies with the St Paul Chamber Orchestra. The original ballet score for thirteen instruments can be heard on a recent recording by the Atlantic Sinfonietta (below), but the scoring is augmented on my selection with some extra strings, as Copland had permitted; the Deutsche Grammophon recording is notably clear and bright.

The famous melody in the seventh movement of *Appalachian Spring* is actually a Shaker hymn called 'The Gift to be Simple', which the hymnologist Edward D. Andrews called 'Simple Gifts' and also given as "Tis a Gift to be Simple'. Forty years later, Copland was quoted as saying 'Music that is born complex is not inherently better or worse than music that is born simple'. The echoes of Jean-Jacques Rousseau suggest that 'simplicity' was more than a technical device, an expressionism of the neo-classicism he learned under Nadia Boulanger in Paris, but also a spiritual and even political stance. If music was born free, then the twentieth century seemed to have clapped it in ever more elaborate and tangled harmonic chains. For Copland, too, there was a sinister hint of the lockstep in the dominance of Germanic forms; a

Brooklyn Jew who learned his music under Leonard Wolfsohn, Victor Wittgenstein, Clarence Adler and Rubin Goldmark, he had to watch much of his teachers' generation being herded off to the camps. Anyone who has doubted the political sincerity and bottom of the wartime *Lincoln Portrait* (1942) for speaker and orchestra, or the ubiquitous *Fanfare for the Common Man* (also 1942) need only listen to the orchestral *Statements* marked 'Militant', 'Cryptic', 'Dogmatic', 'Subjective', 'Jingo' and 'Prophetic', which he began a decade before and which were only heard in their entirety a few months before the Lincoln piece, in the immediate aftershock of Pearl Harbor.

Copland's musical style was forged as a response to, not a retreat from, history. He was perfectly capable of complexity and it is ironic, if predictable, that he should now be identified almost entirely with his 'simple' works, and with those – like *El Salón México* (1993–6), *Danzón cubano* (1942, orchestrated from two-piano version 1944), and *The Tender Land* (1952–4, suite from the opera 1956) – which made heavy use of folk or ethnic materials. While it is hard to dissent from the view of his biographer Vivian Perlis that Copland's major achievement as a composer was telescoped between those works, they were by no means his only significant achievements and they came at a very specific moment in American history, when the broad cultural and political consensus of the Popular Front offered a temporary truce between proletarian populism and the avant garde.

Appalachian Spring was Copland's fifth attempt at a ballet and, with the exception of the more rarely recorded *Dance Panels* (1959), it was to be his last. He made an abortive start in the early 1920s with *Grohg* (1922–5), of which only parts survived in the *Cortège macabre* (1923) and the *Dance Symphony* (1925). He enjoyed greater success in 1934 with the Chicago premiere of *Hear Ye! Hear Ye!*, now one of his less well known scores. It is important not to forget that until *Billy the Kid* (1938) and *Rodeo* (1942) the model for ballet in the United States, as in Europe, had been Russian. The impact of the Diaghilev company and of Vaslav Nijinsky had been definitive. To Martha Graham goes the credit for the virtual invention of a native American dance idiom, and Graham's characteristic introspection and reliance on patterns of tension and release, contraction and relaxation represent a physical objectification of Copland's music. Her ground-breaking *Primitive Mysteries* (1931) was choreographed to a score by Louis Horst, as was the later, more Copland-like *Frontier* (1935), in both of which the music is plainly (and not just with hindsight) subordinate to the rather abstract dance movement.

In *Appalachian Spring*, music and movement are more like equal partners and to some extent they work in parallel. There is a clearer narrative thread in the choreography, and Copland's music has a symphonic structure and robustness which had sustained the Suite in an independent concert and recorded life. There are one or two differences, apart from scoring, between the danced version and the later concert piece. The dance variations on the Shaker hymn are in a slightly different order and there is a long, sombre central section in the ballet version which is omitted. The ballet has been described as Copland's 'Rite of Spring', a reference to the Stravinskian neo-classicism he would have absorbed from Boulanger. The concert version slightly mitigates the darkness of the ballet and the orchestration (*pace* Austin) does occasionally blur the contours of Copland's musical landscape, but even so nothing further from Stravinsky's violent *Rite of Spring* (1911–13) could be imagined.

The scene is set in the Pennsylvania hills (Graham was born at Allegheny) in the early nineteenth century and centres on a springtime celebration round a newly built farmhouse. The central characters are a Revivalist Preacher and a Pioneer Woman, who represent the *yang/yin* oppositions of the American frontier life; a young Husbandman and his Bride (who in some reference books is unaccountably conflated with the older frontierswoman) and a group of four women who follow the Preacher. The opening movement – these are not individually cued in this CD version – is very slow and serves to introduce the dancers. Rising woodwind figures suggestive of sun-up and optimistic wakening are braked by deep, rather sombre chords from the piano, the two elements establishing a rhythmic and thematic subtext that will run through the young couple's relations with the Apollonian preacher and the 'experience' of the frontierswoman. The deliberately stilled 'white' tone of the clarinet, almost oboe-like in its simplicity and purity, establishes a frame that will be repeated in the 'quiet and strong' coda.

A bright *allegro* dance involves all the characters with counter-rhythms from piano and strings, bell-like effects and what sounds like a lark's morning song from the flute. There is a brief and slightly hesitant dance from the lone Husbandman and a prayerful theme for the four Followers which will reappear later in the blessing sequence. The Bride and her Intended 'enact [in Copland's words] the emotions, joyful and apprehensive, their new domestic partnership invites'. Characteristically, Copland sustains a considerable degree of dissonance and harmonic ambiguity within a generally tonal structure. In his work he frequently leans on the ambiguity of enharmonic notes – notes which are written differently and functionally separate but which are aurally identical – and on chromatic modulations which are one of Copland's most important borrowings from jazz. Though he used a carefully modified version of twelve-note technique in his Piano Quartet (1950) and elsewhere, Copland generally avoided such a systematic approach. His music is characterized by wide intervals, subtly propulsive syncopations and a degree of tension between melody and accompaniment which is ideally suited to dramatic dance contexts. It is particularly obvious in the *pas de deux*.

The Revivalist leads a fast dance which anticipates some of the material omitted from the later variations section and which is partly intended to warn the young couple of worldly perils. It combines a vigorous square-dance figure with more solemn hymnic underpinnings, and there are, perhaps, hints of a more secular beguilement in his attempt to recruit the Bride to his flock. The Pioneer Woman intervenes with a dance evoking 'the rocky confidence of experience', executed in a subtle rhythm which is not precisely quantifiable but relies (as with passages in the later *Dance Panels*) on sub-counts within the basic metre; without any overt jazz material, there is nonetheless a subliminal 'jazz feel' that allies the frontierswoman to Bessie Smith and other blues singers.

In response the Bride dances alone, joined briefly by her mate, at the end of which the Preacher blesses their union with a recurrence of the prayer motif. Typically, Copland leaves a tinge of ambiguity which will not be removed until the final section, as if the Revivalist has not quite relinquished his hold on the couple (or, more explicitly, on the Bride). There then follows the famous set of variations on 'The Gift to be Simple'. Unusually for Copland, the theme is played straight, with very little metrical distortion; when he returned to the hymn in the first set of *Old American Songs* (1950), arranged for Peter Pears and first performed at Aldeburgh, he subjected it to considerable chordal shifts. In *Appalachian Spring*, it becomes the basis for a relatively orthodox set of variations. The order is rather different in the concert version and, as mentioned above, a further attempt by the preacher to warn the young couple of 'the strange and terrible aspects of human fate' (violence and sexuality, one has to infer from the context) is omitted. It might be interesting to compare how Copland handles the Apollonian/Dionysiac oppositions of *Appalachian Spring* with Hans Werner Henze's equally symphonic treatment of a similar theme in *The Bassarids* (q.v.), another work which stands somewhere in the orbit of Stravinskian neo-classicism.

The Bride breaks away to pray, interrupting the preacher's last restatement of the dance-hymn. The Followers slowly join her and then are led off by the Pioneer Woman, beginning the symmetrical reversal of the opening sequence. The Preacher makes a last futile attempt to separate the Husbandman and his Bride but then quits the scene himself, leaving 'the couple ... quiet and strong in their new house'. The clarinet, which had sounded the Shaker theme with a full-voiced confidence over rippling cross-currents from the piano and strings, again returns to the slightly bleached tonality of the opening.

Appalachian Spring differs strongly from *Billy the Kid* in that its use of borrowed themes is not simply a matter of set-dressing and atmospherics. Nor is the hymn varied in a parodistic way, as were 'The Star-Spangled Banner' and the Wedding March in *Hear Ye!* It has a central functional significance in the music. Its intervals are implicit throughout, which is why it can be 'heard' in the opening group dance and the Bride's solo well before it has put in an explicit appearance. Copland also used borrowing later in his career – the Clarinet Concerto (1950) for Benny Goodman (a response to Stravinsky's 1945 *Ebony Concerto* for Woody Herman) was based on a Latin American theme – but never with such sophistication.

In later years, Copland was more of a tutelary presence than an active participator in American music. His is one of the great silences, punctuated by the odd occasional piece, like the CBS signature tune (1967), the inevitable *Threnody I: in memoriam Stravinsky* (1971; no. 2, for Bea Cunningham, followed in 1973, also for flute and string trio), and an often mangled version of the variations from *Appalachian Spring* for school orchestra (1967). If it was his gift to be simple, and that was his own determined conviction after the still-modernist *Symphonic Ode* (1927–9), it was probably inevitable that his interpreters, his critics and his public should have misread some of the scores as simplistic. Copland's synchronisation of harmonic detail and rhythm, particularly at slow tempos as in the dreamlike Piano Sonata (1939–41) and *Appalachian Spring*, is almost uncanny. He grew up in a thoroughly unmusical environment – 'It wasn't an absolute desert, but I don't think anybody ever connected serious music with the street [corner of Washington Avenue and Dean] on which I was born' – and came out of it with an innate gift that defies analysis and constantly transcends its origins.

Discographical Information

Other recordings: Minnesota Orchestra, Marriner [with: *Rodeo, El salón México*] (Angel 4DS 38048); London SO, Copland [with: *Fanfare for the Common Man, Rodeo*] (CBS MK 42430); New York PO, Bernstein [with: *Billy the Kid, Rodeo, Fanfare for the Common Man*] (CBS MK 42265; Los Angeles PO, Bernstein [with: Barber, Adagio for Strings; Bernstein, overture to *Candide*] (Deutsche Grammophon 413324 2/431048 2); Atlantic Sinfonietta, Schenck [with: Barber, *Cave of the Heart*] (Koch 3–7019 2); Los Angeles PO, Mehta [with: *Fanfare for the Common Man*; Gershwin, *Rhapsody in Blue*] (London 414468 4); Detroit SO, Dorati [with: Stravinsky, *Apollo*] (London 414457 2); Utah SO, Abravanel [with: Gershwin, *An American in Paris, Rhapsody in Blue*, overture to *Porgy and Bess* (MCA Classics MCAD 2–9800); London SO, Dorati [with: *Billy the Kid, Danzón cubano, El salón México*] (Mercury Living Presence 434 301 2); St Luke's Chamber Ensemble, Davies [with: Nonet, Two Pieces] (MusicMasters 7055 2); St Paul CO, Davies [with: *Short Symphony*; Ives, Symphony no. 3] (ProArte CDD–140); Philadelphia

Orchestra, Ormandy [with: *Billy the Kid*] (RCA AGK1 5202); Boston SO, Copland [with: *Billy the Kid*, overture to *The Tender Land*]. (RCA Gold Seal 6802 2); Pacific SO, Clark [original chamber version] (Reference RR 22CD); City of London Sinfonia, Hickox [with: *Quiet City*; Barber, Adagio for Strings; Gershwin, *Rhapsody in Blue*] (Virgin Classics VC 7 90766 2); many others.

Other Copland: *Symphonic Ode* (1927–9; Sony Classical SM2K 47232); Piano Sonata (1939–41; Cedille CDR 900000 005); *Lincoln Portrait* (1942; CBS MK 42431); *Threnody I: in memoriam Stravinsky* (1971; Northeastern Classical Arts NR 227); and items listed on recordings above.

Map references: Charles Ives, *Three Places in New England* (1903–14; Mercury Living Presence 432755–2); Roy Harris, Symphony no. 4: *Folksong Symphony* (1940; Vanguard Classics OVC 4076); Samuel Barber, *Capricorn Concerto* (1944; as for Ives, above); David Del Tredici. *Tattoo* (1986; Deutsche Grammophon 429231.

Futher reading: A. Copland, *What to Listen for in Music*, New York, 1939, and (with V. Perlis), *Copland* (2 vols), 1984, 1987; C. Gagne and T. Caras, interview in *Soundpieces: Interviews with American Composers*, Metuchen, New Jersey, 1982.

HEITOR VILLA-LOBOS (1887–1959)

Bachiana brasileiras no. 9 (1944–1945)

FIRST PERFORMED: Rio de Janeiro, 1945
SELECTED RECORDING: Lorelt LNT 102
   BBC Singers, conducted by Odaline de la Martinez
   [with: Lontano: *Sexteto místico* (1917, flute, oboe, saxophone, celesta, harp, guitar); *Two chôros bis* (1928, violin, cello); *Quatuor* (1921, flute, alto saxophone, celesta, harp, female voices); *Chôros* No. 7 (1924)]
RECORDED: 1992
DURATION: 9' 30"

If there is any validity in the Sheldonian classification of human types – worked out by William Sheldon in *The Varieties of Human Physique* (1940) – then Heitor Villa-Lobos was a classic example of endomorphy. Endomorphs are characteristically soft and heavy, somewhat attenuated in purely intellectual qualities, and dominated by the digestive tract. Villa-Lobos's appetite for music was gargantuan. He absorbed it greedily and undiscriminatingly (a passion that stemmed, perhaps significantly, from music-dominated dinner parties in his father's home and from the playing of *chôroes* or strolling groups who played the cafés of Rio de Janeiro. The most famous picture from his maturity has him grinning wolfishly with oversized teeth clamped round a luscious, loose-rolled cigar. He had all the brazen arrogance of the autodidact, arriving in France with the Wildean pronouncement that he had come not to learn but to show off his own achievements. His self-belief sometimes approached a conviction that he had invented music itself and he frequently said that whenever he felt himself susceptible to an artistic influence he quickly shook it off.

Characteristics like expansiveness, unstructured richness of resource, personal flamboyance have earned him a reputation – Sheldonian classifications at least have the merit of not being racially inspired – as the 'archetypal' Brazilian composer. He is unquestionably the most important, but his wider impact on Euro-American modernism has been slow to be recognized. (The Cuban-born Odaline de la Martinez, now based in Britain and director of the ensemble Lontano, was awarded the Villa-Lobos Medal by the Brazilian government in 1988 for her promotion of his work.) It is not strictly true to claim, as supporters and detractors do for precisely opposite reasons, that he left more than 2000 scores at his death. The actual number was pumped up by a lifelong habit of arranging many of his pieces (like the one above) for alternative instrumentations, thus multiplying the number of works in his already well-filled catalogue. The accurate figure is somewhere between 600 and 700 separate works; we will see that large numbers tend to recur throughout Villa-Lobos's career.

As a young man, he was intended for a medical career but rebelled and became a *chorão* or itinerant musician on the streets of Rio, making a slender living playing his cello in restaurant and theatre bands. (Though he also played clarinet and guitar, cello occupied a very special place in his affections. It *leaps* out of the ensembles in his string quartets and was the basis of the first of the *Bachianas brasileiras* in 1932, scored for eight, or alternatively a whole orchestra of, cellos.) When things got difficult, he raised money by selling part of his late father's library and set off to study and document the folk musics of northern Brazil; it is this experience more than anything else that distinguishes Villa-Lobos from the essentially aristocratic character of pre-war Brazilian modernism. In a neat turnaround of the metaphor, he claimed to have kept himself out of the digestive tract of some seriously endomorphic cannibals by improvising songs, but he cannot be trusted not to have made this up.

He was too footloose for a formal training and could not afterwards settle to his studies at the Istituto Nacional de Música. He was, however, producing copious amounts of music, writing with his guts rather than formal intellect. In 1915 a concert was given in Rio devoted exclusively to work that he described as by turns descriptive, mystical and free, 'representing the liberty of thought'. It was these qualities that attracted the young Olivier Messiaen, who told Claude Samuel in 1967 of his reaction to Villa-Lobos's sensational Paris début at the Salle Gaveau in 1924. The young Brazilian had come to the attention of Darius Milhaud, who visited Rio in 1917 as secretary to the French

Ambassador Paul Claudel. Villa-Lobos had just premiered the daring symphonic suite *Uirapuru*, which had caused a furore with its clanging dissonances and incorporation of folk instruments. Milhaud was almost as enchanted as the Indians in the forest legend Villa-Lobos had taken as his subject matter and became an enthusiastic supporter of his work. He also 'made contact' with another visitor to Rio, the pianist Arthur Rubinstein; Villa-Lobos and some friends simply gatecrashed the pia-nist's bedroom to serenade him like *chôroes* with some recent composi-tions. In February 1922, Rubinstein premiered the first *Prole do Bebê* (completed in 1918) during the Semana de Arte Moderna in Rio; the seventh movement, 'Polichinello', became a concert lollipop.

The piece Villa-Lobos finished for the pianist a few years later was anything but. Nicolas Slonimsky describes *Rudepoema* (1921–6) as 'trans-cendentally difficult', and it certainly quashes any naive notion of Villa-Lobos as a jovial and essentially simple-minded nationalist. It also over-turns a more seriously held view: that he began as a conservative and grew more radical as the years went by. It is true that some of the later scores are more obviously avant-garde in conception; the orchestral *New York Skyline* (1939) was devised by a process of 'millimetrization', placing silhouette photographs of the city over graph paper and tracing a melody from the outlines. However, in purely musical terms many of the earlier works were much more challenging and unorthodox. Among the pieces performed at the Salle Gaveau recital on 3 May 1924 were the *Quatuor* (1921, see above) for flute, alto saxophone, celeste, harp and offstage female voices, and the astonishing *Noneto* (1923) for flute, oboe, clarinet, alto saxophone, bassoon, celesta, piano, mixed chorus and an array of exotic percussion instruments including friction drums, rattles and the *reco-reco*, a notched gourd scraped with a stick. Opinion in Paris was as mixed as it had been after Rubinstein's Brazilian recital, but Villa-Lobos's name was made.

During his stay, he finished the series of *Chôros* (1–14, 1920–8; plus *Two chôros bis*, see above), for which he adapted the name of those guitar- and *violão*-dominated street groups. He intended the term to be understood generically, as 'a new form of musical composition, in which a synthesis of the different forms of the music of the Indian and popular music appear, having as the principal elements characteristic rhythmic and melodic types of expression which appear now and then, accidentally, always transformed by the personality of the composer. The harmonic processes are also a complete stylization of the original by the composer'. Or, as the Red Queen might have said: it means whatever I choose it to mean. It is ironic that the next phase of his career was to be as an educator.

By far the best known of the *Chôros* is no. 5 (1926), subtitled *Alma bra-sileira* or 'the Brazilian soul', and it is the one which seems most to preserve the root sense of 'weeping'. It is also one of only a pair – with no. 1 (1920, guitar) – for solo instruments. The others feature smaller or orchestral ensembles, sometimes with concertante elements. Villa-Lobos had written five early symphonies – including the *a guerre a vitória a paz* trilogy, nos 3, 4 and 5 (1919, 1920, 1921) – but has not been highly regarded as a symphonist. His next important cycle was the nine *Bachianas brasileiras* (1930–45). Apart from no. 6 (1938) for flute and bassoon and a first version of no. 4 (for piano 1930, orchestrated 1940), all were for orchestra or for large cello ensembles; the first, virtually a declaration of love for his own instrument, and the fifth, for soprano and cellos, remain the best known, but the sequence as a whole is probably his major achievement as a composer.

Villa-Lobos described his intentions thus: 'The *bachianas brasileiras* [lower case again suggests that he believed the pieces constituted a new genre] ... are inspired by the musical environment of Bach, considered by the composer as the rich, profound, and universal folkloric source of all popular musical materials of all nations, the intermediary of all peoples.' The intention was to do for the folk music of Latin America what Bach had done for the songs and dances of late seventeenth-century Europe. This strongly implies a pedagogical element and the *Bachianas brasileiras* are noticeably simpler and more tonal in conception than the earlier *Chôros*. There are no folk melodies and no traditional instruments; the basic structural device is the baroque fugue, which Villa-Lobos treats in a manner parallel to the round of solos and elaborations in Brazilian traditional music.

The series was begun after Villa-Lobos's return to Brazil on what was supposed to be a short visit. Dismayed at the poor penetration of the arts into the 'social organization', the one-time educational misfit presented a quite radical plan to reorganize the school system. It seemed at first as though his ideas had been politely filed, but just before his projected return to France, almost literally so, he was summoned to the presidential palace to explain his theories. He was invited to restructure the school curriculum in São Paulo and President Vargas, an amateur of the arts, appointed him national director of music education.

Villa-Lobos threw himself into the work heart and soul. In a country whose cultural apotheosis seemed to be association football, the stadium rather than the concert hall presented the best chance of revivifying national music. During the early 1930s, he dedicated himself to coaching and writing for huge 'orpheonic' choirs of children who were taught melodies by means of a rapid sol-fa system. Conducting and memorization were by a manual sign language – or cheironomy – similar to the 'Guidonian hand' devised by Guido d'Arezzo (*c.* 995–1050) as a mnemonic for choristers. Performance also included what the composer called 'orpheonic effects', hand-clapping, stamping and hissing or whistling, reactions that had been all too common at his early concerts; as early as the *Quatuor* (1921, above), he had experimented with similar devices, such as vibrating the lips with a forefinger while vocalizing, to produce rapid triplets. On Independence Day 1939, Villa-Lobos conducted a concert of 30,000 schoolchildren; in subsequent years, the numbers rose to a staggering 40,000, with over a thousand band instruments in support.

Working in such numbers encouraged him to use voices orchestrally. The better-known version of *Bachianas brasileiras* no. 9 is for strings, a version made because it was felt that the original choral arrangement, recorded here, was too difficult to perform. The BBC Singers give a precise, but by no means soulless, reading of a taxing score. The piece is in two movements, a brief 'Prélude' and a longer 'Fugue'. There is no text, just vocalized syllables and vowels, but with a complexity of texture that often suggests linguistic content. The opening section is oblique and mysterious, marked by the displaced accents which are typical of Brazilian music. There is, however, no explicit folkloric content, just an overall impression of the mystical and lyrical qualities of Indian music. The pace is deceptively slow, marked by asymmetrical accents and non-functional accents, while the six-part polytonal harmony is rather complex and evanescent, shifting constantly until the very last bar. Even here the resolution is highly ambiguous.

The Fugue is introduced in $\frac{11}{8}$ time, picking up the uncertain focus of the preceding section and sweeping it into a grand Bach-like development. Basses, tenors, altos and sopranos enter at surprising altitudes, and there is a further use of the delayed downbeat that was a feature of some of the earlier (and more authentically folkloric) piano pieces. As an integration of Bach's universalizing technique with the essentially modal music of the Brazilian hinterland, it is perhaps the most triumphantly successful work of the sequence. After the war, the composer returned to the international stage and became a major personality on the European and American scenes, conducting and recording. Between 1954 and his death, he documented a substantial body of his own work for Pathé-Marconi (see below) and taped a brief talk in slightly idiosyncratic French answering the question *'Qu'est-ce qu'un Chôros?'* and from which the definition above is quoted. The recording is fine for its period, but the version of *Bachianas brasileiras* no. 9 given, as on the Bátiz recording for HMV, is the one for strings. To appreciate the work fully, I think it is preferable to start with Odaline de la Martinez's radiant and idiomatic account of the choral version. The EMI box set of the Pathé-Marconi recordings is pricey but essential documentation for specialists. As an introduction to the composer's work, the Lorelt CD is hard to beat.

Discographical Information

Other recordings: French National Radio and Television Chorus and Orchestra, de los Angeles, Villa Lobos (EMI CZS7 67229); Hendricks, Osorio, Royal PO, Bátiz (HMV CDS7 47901); Orchestre de Paris, Capolongo (HMV CDC7 47357).

Other Villa-Lobos: [excluding *Bachianas brasileiras* and *Chôros*, many of which are included on the recordings above] *Uirapuru* (1917; Gega GD 102); *Prole do bebê* no. 1 (includes 'Polichinello', 1918, Audiofon CD 72023); *New York Skyline* (1939; Etcetera KTC 1123); *Erosão/The Origin of the Amazon River* (1951; Marco Polo 8.223357).

Map references: Camargo Guarnieri, *Dansa brasileira* (1931, piano; orchestrated a decade later; Sony Classical SNK 47544); Marlos Nobre, *Convergencias* (1968; Delos DE 1017).

Further reading: V. Mariz, *Heitor Villa-Lobos: compositor brasileiro* 5th edn, Rio de Janeiro, 1977; G. Béhague, *Music in Latin America: An Introduction*, Englewood Cliffs, NJ, 1979; D. P. Appleby, in *The Music of Brazil*, Austin, Texas, 1983.

BENJAMIN BRITTEN (1913–1976)

Peter Grimes (1945)

FIRST PERFORMED: London, 7 June 1945
SELECTED RECORDING: Decca 414 577
> Peter Pears (Grimes), Claire Watson (Ellen Orford), James Pease (Balstrode), Jean Watson (Auntie), Raymond Nilsson (Bob Boles), Owen Brannigan (Swallow), Geraint Evans (Ned Keene), Chorus and Orchestra of the Royal Opera House, Covent Garden, conducted by the composer
RECORDED: 1947
DURATION: 205'

Peter Grimes saved – or rather, reinvented – English opera. Its premiere is one of the key moments in British musical life since the war. Like any saviour or liberator, it has come to seem many things to many different people, interpretations which hinge on the interpretation of Grimes himself, but there is no mistaking its fundamental theme: the relationship between the individual and society. Whatever impression the social, political and cultural collectivism of the 1930s made on Britten, it was clear that his concern was always for the individual, the artist, the visionary, the man apart, rather than the mass.

Grimes's predecessor had been an unhappy collaboration with W. H. Auden, the virtually unlistenable-to *Paul Bunyan*. There the element of (literal) giantism meant that there was no convincing interplay between the protagonist and the other characters. In *Grimes*, Britten set out quite straightforwardly a conviction that was to become an incantation in the popular sociology of the 1950s and 1960s: that deviance and crime were the products of a sick and intolerant society, 'the more vicious the society, the more vicious the individual'.

Grimes's 'viciousness' goes to the heart of Britten's creative problems in writing the opera. The idea had come to him during his wartime exile in America, when he found a second-hand copy of George Crabbe's poem 'The Borough', which concerned a fishing town on the East coast of England. Crabbe had lived in Aldeburgh, where Britten was to make his post-war home and establish his festival. The location appealed to Britten as much as the theme, but he immediately baulked against Crabbe's portrayal of Grimes as an amoral brute, not least because the role was to be realized by Britten's lover Peter Pears. It was here that interpretative and practical considerations coincided. Normally, operatic villains were played by baritones or basses. Though Pears's voice had an unusual quality, which was sometimes characterized as light baritone, he was technically a tenor, and thus apparently unsuited to such a dark role.

In response, Montagu Slater's libretto offered a version of Grimes which suggested that he was, in another cant expression of the time, not bad but misunderstood, a man not untouched by goodness, and with a hint of visionary qualities in his turbulent personality; above all, a man at odds with his environment. (The suggestion that he is a repressed or closet homosexual may be obvious in the circumstances, and may even add a dimension to the role, but it is too reductive an interpretation.) The casting of Pears was improbable in one obvious respect. It is difficult to imagine him hewing away at fishing lines off the Suffolk Banks; later Grimeses – Jon Vickers and, in particular, Anthony Rolfe Johnson – were more convincingly physical. However, what Pears brought to the role was a wonderfully rich ambiguity, and this comes across very strongly in Decca's richly proportioned recording, one of the first major stereo projects undertaken.

The Prologue begins with an inquest meeting in the Moot Hall, investigating the death at sea of Grimes's young apprentice. It is chaired by Swallow, who is introduced by a nervy woodwind theme and then administers the oath to the fishermen, which Grimes repeats back an octave higher but with a slowed down delivery which already almost suggests fey detachment. Grimes describes the boy's harrowing death. Though there is a strong undercurrent of hostility, an echo of the hostile tides that led to the child's death, Grimes is comforted by the schoolmistress Ellen Orford. When the bustle of the courtroom dies down, she and Grimes are left alone. They sing in significantly contrasting keys – E major to Grimes's F minor – but conclude in friendship with a harmonic compromise that is to be one of the opera's motifs.

Peter Grimes is known even to people who have never heard it entire by the magnificent orchestral 'Sea interludes' which intersperse it. There are six of them, in a wide range of moods. The first is calm and untroubled, preparing the way for the quiet harmony of village life that opens Act I proper. Society is seen to be functioning normally, a pattern of interdependence that thrives on small consolations and a tinge of hypocrisy. The central figures are the apothecary Ned Keene and the sea captain Balstrode, who watches both sea and human behaviour with a different focus to any other character. Keene dispenses succour to the laudanum-drinking Mrs Sedley and in turn awaits comfort from one of the landlady Auntie's two 'Nieces'. The Vicar observes with toothless disapproval. Only Keene and Balstrode will help Grimes, now working alone, bring his boat ashore, but the apothecary tells him that a new apprentice has been found, an orphan boy and thus in breach of Swallow's inquest requirement that Grimes only hire an adult crewman.

Britten had intended to write a traditional 'number' opera, but hitherto there has been little extended lyrical writing. The carter's refusal to help bring the new apprentice to Grimes looks like being the first such passage, but it is interrupted, and it is Ellen, again coming to Grimes's assistance, who sings the first major aria. Much has been written about the difference between Claire Watson on this recording, and Joan Cross, for whom the role was written. Watson is supposed to lack character, but she exudes a warmth and humanity that sits at the heart of the opera, and it is important to recognize her importance, and Balstrode's, to the music.

The remainder of the act is played out against a symbolically rising storm, first noticed by Balstrode (of course), who sees the storm cone raised. There is a wonderful collective fugue, involving nearly all the principals and the chorus, before the scene moves to the pub, where the boy is to be brought and Keene is to give Mrs Sedley her pacifying tincture of opium. Balstrode gently suggests to Grimes, who prefers to stay outdoors in the storm, that perhaps this is not the place for him. Grimes replies with touching simplicity that 'I am native, rooted here', and not inclined to wander. The spectre of the dead boy comes back to him unbidden, in a passage marked by awkward, dislocated ninths, suggesting again that the man is far from unmoved by the tragedy.

Inside the pub, all is jollity, though Mrs Sedley's anxious presence creates a ripple of unease. There is also an ironic quality to the chorus which begins after a fight between Boles and Balstrode: 'We live and let live ...'. Grimes's entrance shortly afterwards is a clear signal that this is not the case, yet he seems curiously detached from the rabble in the Boar and sings his great meditative aria about the stars and human destiny,

'Now the Great Bear and Pleiades', with its tragic and poignant conclusion: 'Who, who, who, who can turn skies back and begin again'. The drinking round that follows, 'Old Joe has gone fishing', is deliberately bathetic, but also curiously aggressive, prefiguring the mob violence that is to come. Grimes's apprentice arrives, already half-drowned by the storm; Auntie wants to give him something warming, but Grimes insists on taking him off home, to the ironic jeers of the company.

The interlude that prepares the way for Act II is a light and buoyant theme first heard in the violas. Ellen and the boy come onstage while a church service is going on in the background, the collective worship of the community providing a wry counterpoint to her nervous catechizing of the abused child, who has an ugly bruise on his neck. When Grimes appears she reminds him it is the Sabbath and recalls their belief that his only salvation lies in solitary toil. He strikes her, and as the congregation sings the final Amen, he pronounces his own damnation: 'So be it, and God have mercy upon me.'

It is this theme which the trio of Bob Boles, Ned Keene and Auntie then pick up in the number that follows: 'Grimes is at his exercise.' The mood is darkening and Ellen's and Balstrode's efforts to calm the indignant crowd, who have heard the quarrel outside the church, is to no avail. A *posse comitatus* is called together and the mob heads off to Grimes's hut, to find out what is going on there; Ellen's protests have risen to an almost hysterical pitch, punctuated by Balstrode's firmness and calm. At this moment, one of the most remarkable sequences in the entire opera begins, a sign of its great psychological depth. Signalled by the sound of two flutes, the two Nieces, Auntie and Ellen sing a hauntingly beautiful 'trio' (the Nieces sing almost entirely in unison), in which they meditate on the fate of women in a world of violence and aggressive desire.

The opera revolves round this moment and the magnificent Passacaglia that follows, the most important of the interludes. At its heart is a plaintive viola melody which represents the boy in his ambiguous care. The whole of the next scene is an extended recitative and aria from Grimes, his most substantial singing in the piece. He wistfully describes his dreams of peace and contentment, but again he adverts to the horrifying scene in the fishing boat with the dying apprentice. As the aria ends, safely harboured almost as if in death, the noise of the village mob can be heard in the distance. Grimes reacts defiantly, but anxiously tells the boy to go down the cliff path, admonishing him to be careful. As he turns back to check the progress of the mob, there is a scream, the only sound the boy has made, as he falls to his death. Silence follows, interrupted by nothing but a glacial echo from the celesta. The visitors, led by the vicar, Swallow, Keene and Balstrode, arrive and find nothing amiss, beyond the fact that the hut door is open and the cliff edge so close at hand. Perhaps the persecution is at an end, as Swallow solomonically hopes.

The final act opens on a delicate moonlit scene tinged by flute and harp. The town dance is in progress and there is much movement between the Moot Hall and the Boar. Only Mrs Sedley, herself always hysterically out of key with the rest of the community, still wants to pursue and prosecute Grimes. As she hides in the shadows she hears Ellen and Balstrode discuss the discovery of the new apprentice's jersey, which the captain has found washed up sodden on the beach. Ellen's heartbroken aria, 'Embroidery in childhood was a luxury of idleness', is the longest in the opera, longer even than Grimes's in the previous act. It is also one of Britten's most beautiful creations and Claire Watson gives it a convincing edge of melancholy and despair.

Mrs Sedley goes to warn the townsfolk that Grimes's boat is in. Though the party is slow to break up, Swallow eventually takes the matter seriously enough to re-start the search. The crowd this time are not merely angry but positively murderous, calling out for vengeance against 'him who despises us'. Brutal cries of 'Peter Grimes!' bring the scene to an end. The final interlude is very brief and strange, dominated by a quietly mysterious horn chord that prefigures the repeated fog warnings of the closing scene. Wind-blown fragments of Grimes's earlier music reappear and are whipped away again. Into this strange atmosphere Grimes stumbles, now clearly beside himself with guilt and fear. As the chorus sings threateningly offstage and the fog-horn tuba intones menacingly, he rambles incoherently about his dreams and aspirations. In the tension of the moment, Balstrode lapses into speech and tells Peter to take his boat out to sea and scuttle her. He helps him to drag the craft to the water's edge and then quietly leads Ellen away.

As morning breaks, village life is getting back to normal, the never-ending round signalled by a return of the prelude music from Act I. There is no sign of the drama of the previous act, except that Swallow, looking out to sea with his telescope, notes that a boat is sinking in the distance. The waters have closed over Grimes's head; the community has had its revenge.

Other productions have given the opera – and its central characters – new inflections and interpretations, and two more fine records are listed below. None, though, has ever achieved the wholeness and range of expression achieved by Britten's own. Its status is as certain as that of *Peter Grimes* itself.

Discographical Information

Other recordings: Vickers, Harper, Summers, Bainbridge, Dobson, Robinson, Allen, Chorus and Orchestra of the Royal Opera House, Covent Garden, Davis

(Philips 432 578); Rolfe Johnson, Lott, Allen, Chorus and Orchestra of the Royal Opera House, Covent Garden, Haitink (EMI CDC7 54832).

Other Britten: *Les Illuminations* (1939; London 417153); *Serenade* (1944; London Historic 425996); *Peter Grimes: Four Sea Interludes and Passacaglia* (1945; Collins Classics 10192); *The Rape of Lucretia* (1946; London 425666); *The Young Person's Guide to the Orchestra* (1946 [with: *Sea Interludes*] Angel CDN 63777); *Suite no. 1 for solo cello* (1964; London 421859); *String Quartet no. 3* (1975; Collins Classics 10252); *Canticles I–IV* (1947–75; Hyperion CDA 66498).

Map references: Michael Tippett, *The Midsummer Marriage* (1946–52; Nimbus NI 53217; Hans Werner Henze, *The English Cat* (1978–82; Wergo WER 6204); John Adams, *Nixon in China* (1987; Nonesuch 7559 79177).

Further reading: P. Brett (ed.), *Peter Grimes/Gloriana*, ENO Guide 24, 1983; C. Palmer (ed.), *The Britten Companion* (1984); H. Carpenter, *Benjamin Britten* (1991).

WERNER EGK (1901–1983)

La tentation de Saint Antoine (1945, orchestrated 1952)

FIRST PERFORMED: Baden-Baden, 18 May 1947
SELECTED RECORDING: Deutsche Grammophon 429 858 2
  Janet Baker (contralto), Koeckert String Quartet, strings of the Bavarian Radio Symphony Orchestra, conducted by Werner Egk
  [with: Frank Martin, *Six Monologues* from *Jedermann* (1943–9), and *Three Excerpts* from *Der Sturm* (1952–4); Dietrich Fischer-Dieskau (baritone), Berlin Philharmonic Orchestra, conducted by Frank Martin]
RECORDED: November 1965
DURATION: 21' 40"

Though he was one of the most successful operatic composers of his day (with an output and impact comparable to those of Ernst Krenek or Hans Werner Henze), Werner Egk's reputation went into rapid reverse during his later years. He is rarely performed nowadays and is known, if at all, for largely extra-musical reasons.

In the first place, Egk was not his given name, and considerable, if pointless, ingenuity has been used to explain the derivation of his alternative self-designation. Born Werner Mayer in the small village of Auchsesheim, near Augsburg, he moved to Munich as a student, training under Carl Orff (1895–1982) and the pianist Anna Hirzel-Langenhan. It has been suggested that his assumed name is an acrostic of 'ein grosser Komponist', but Egk himself countered with the story that it was derived from his wife's maiden name Elisabeth Karl; the middle g is, in any case, silent. Far more significant and troubling, though, is the question of what Egk actually stood for during the war years. In

1936 he was commissioned to write music for the Berlin Olympiad, the games controversially commemorated in Leni Riefenstahl's documentary film *The Triumph of the Will*. Two years later Egk was appointed conductor at the Berlin State Opera, and between 1941 and 1945 he acted as head of the German Composers' Union, apparently enjoying the tacit support of Goebbels' Ministry of Propaganda.

Like Richard Strauss, he had to undergo examination by an Allied de-Nazification tribunal, but like his great role model he was discovered to be free of ideological contagion and *La tentation de Saint Antoine* was premiered openly. Egk seemed unshakeably disposed to controversy, however. His Faust ballet *Abraxas* (1948) was heavily censored on grounds of immorality; dismayed that he should have work suppressed in a 'liberated' country when he had been able to write freely in a 'totalitarian' state, he moved away from the residually theocratic atmosphere of Bavaria to the more cosmopolitan air of Berlin, where he headed the Hochschule for three years before returning south, partially reconciled, to spend the last three decades of his life in and around Munich.

In his work, Egk drew freely on Wagner, Richard Strauss and (as is evident in *La tentation*) on French neo-classicism, but the most direct and personal influence on his career was Orff, whose *Carmina burana* (1937) remains among the most popular 'modern' works in the repertoire. Orff was a pioneering educator, integrating musical performance on simple home-made instruments into the school curriculum, emphasizing melody, rhythm and harmonic straightforwardness, but strangely falling foul of the Nazis, who discovered something subversive or 'degenerate' in his use of folk materials.

In contrast to Orff, Egk always manages to sound sardonic. He had begun writing incidental music for puppet theatres while in Munich, and had gone on to compose operas to his own librettos, notably a fine radio work on *Columbus* (1933), which might have been worth reviving for the quincentennial celebrations, and a brave reworking of *Peer Gynt* (1938), which must have attracted widespread comparison with Edvard Grieg's original adaptation. The folksiness of this and *Der Zaubergeibe* (1935), which itself attracted comparison with a yet more famous model, was constantly ironized by Egk's growing tendency to stretch conventional tonality to a point where the rococo prettiness of his sung melodies began to disintegrate.

This is what lies behind the patent oddity of *La tentation de Saint Antoine*. The title page of the score indicates that the work is 'based on eighteenth-century airs and verses', and each of the dozen short sections specifies the source tune; all of these are French, as is Egk's text. The result is that the temptations which assail the saint are presented much as if they were plot devices in an early farce, marked by rapid entrances and exits, disguises and verbal bawdy far removed from the surreal, almost Boschian eroticism normally associated with the story of St Anthony. The opening scene is set in tones of high camp, reminiscent of an old joke about Hell: 'Oh, my dear, the *people*! And the *noise*!' The contralto voice (one wonders if Egk might have used a countertenor had he been writing many years later) only heightens this effect. Stanza 3 – to the tune 'Des folies d'Espagne' – introduces the troop of devils, 'from Cochin China and from Spain', some blonde, some red-haired, some grey, some carrying shadow puppets, and singing 'Ture, lure, lure. / Et flon, flon, flon'.

The atmosphere is hardly one of severe spiritual menace, but draws on a tradition of rather juvenile prankishness in the *Faust-Buch* (also reflected in Christopher Marlowe's *Tragical History of Dr Faustus*). The devils dress up St Anthony's pig as a monk, and there are more nonsense syllables, 'La faridondaine, la faridondon'. A she-devil reclines on a sofa, enticing the saint with her *décolletage*, almost as if she were costumed as Belinda in *The Rape of the Lock*. The Devil himself is discovered snoring on a throne (or perhaps a privy), wearing a fire-grate for a crown and carrying a poker by way of sceptre. Startled by his servants, he wakens abruptly and calls: 'Waiter!' Meanwhile, St Anthony, fearful of committing a sin, runs and hides under his counterpane where he finds 'Une con-, con-, con-, / Une cu-, cu-, cu-, / Une con-, une cu-, une concubine'. This combines parody of the elaborate 'stuttering' decorations of an opera singer with an obscene pun on 'con' and 'cul', the French equivalents of cunt and ass.

The contrast between matter and manner reaches its climax at this mid-point, but Egk continues to make bitingly ironic use of his French airs. The revised version with string orchestra increases the sense of distance between the vocal line and a shifting, indefinably threatening background in which the middle strings, violas and cellos in the main, mutter disaffectedly. Fed up at last with the noise and mess, as one might be with a party over which one has lost control and during which 'un derrière infernal, / Avoit fait caca' in a mixing-bowl, Anthony lays about him with holy water, putting the infernal gate-crashers to flight. The Devil is left wishing that he had taken female form as 'Toinette' and tempted the saint that way.

Egk's work is often dismissed as lightweight and insubstantial, but *La tentation* reveals an expert musical brain at work, no less subtle for being cast in such a playful form. Alongside the Swiss Frank Martin's *Everyman* and *Tempest* songs, Egk can sound a little capricious, and it is a pity that Deutsche Grammophon have broken up the original LP pairing of *La tentation* with Egk's own ballet after Hans Andersen, *Der chinesische Nachtigall* (1953), which gave a more balanced view of his sound-world. Janet Baker's voice is surprisingly well adapted to the score, though some of her diction is a little suspect, and she gives a more convincingly dramatic performance than Janet Walker on the Wergo version, who seems too intent on dotting the *i*s and crossing the *t*s of each and every joke. Perhaps Egk will have to wait until his centenary year for a second rehabilitation; in the meantime, this is a good place to start.

Discographical Information

Other recordings: this performance formerly released on Deutsche Grammophon SLPM 139142; Janet Walker, ensemble (Wergo WER 60179).

Other Egk: *Peer Gynt* (1938; Orfeo 005822); *Divertissement for Eleven Winds* (1948: Wergo WER 60179); *Die chinesische Nachtigall* (1953; Deutsche Grammophon DG SLPM 139142, as above).

Map references: Richard Strauss, *Salome* (1905; Decca 414 414); Ernst Krenek, *Jonny spielt auf* (1927; London 436631); Carl Orff, *Carmina burana* (1937; Angel CDC 54054); Hans Werner Henze, *The English Cat* (1978–82; Wergo WER 6204). Peter Dickinson, Organ Concerto (1971; EMI CDC7 47584–2).

VAGN HOLMBOE (born 20 December 1909)

Symphony no. 6 (1947)

FIRST PERFORMED: Copenhagen, 8 January 1948
SELECTED RECORDING: BIS CD 573
   Aarhus Symphony Orchestra, leader and soloist Hans Stengaard, conducted by Owain Arwel Hughes
   [with: Symphony no. 7 (1950)]
RECORDED: June 1992
DURATION: 31′ 23″

'Cosmos does not develop out of chaos without a prior vision of cosmos.' Virtually all of Vagn Holmboe's mature work – and it now constitutes an impressive musical universe – is in some degree an illustration of the Argument from Design. It represents not just his artistic philosophy, but a deep-seated metaphysical and even religious viewpoint. In its attempt to repair and rebuild bridges between the aesthetic, the ethical and the spiritual, it closely shadows the philosophic endeavour of the Danish philosopher Søren Kierkegaard. Holmboe's conviction that there is a natural order, to music as well as to the wider creation, is what sets his work beyond the reach of critics who would condemn or dismiss it as conservative and banally formulaic. Unlike another compatriot, the irrepressibly trendy Niels Viggo Bentzon (born

1919), who seems prey to a compulsion to make black marks on stave paper, Holmboe has managed to sustain a hugely prolific output in mainly classical forms without self-conscious experimentation but with no sign of flagging invention. Denmark's most important symphonist since Carl Nielsen (1865–1931) has throughout his career demonstrated the vitality of classical forms. In addition to twelve numbered symphonies written between 1935 and 1988 (as with other forms there are earlier scores which have been excluded from his work-list), there are many concerted works, with solo parts for such rarely featured instruments as recorder and tuba, more than twenty string quartets, and eighty-plus vocal and choral pieces.

Among his orchestral scores is a group of pieces – *Epitaph* (1956), *Monolith* (1960), *Epilogue* (1961–2), and *Tempo Variable* (1971–2) – which he called 'symphonic metamorphoses'. The principle of metamorphosis is the key to Holmboe's work. Though its roots (an appropriate enough metaphor) lie deep in the nineteenth century, with Berlioz and Wagner, and though he shares it with Bentzon and with the Hamburg-born Norwegian Hallvard Johnsen (born 1916), it is Holmboe who has been most closely associated with the metamorphic approach. Broadly, it involves the continuous transformation of basic harmonic or thematic material throughout the span of a musical movement or an entire work. The primary 'germ cells' can be likened to seeds or tubers in which all possible surface transformations are densely coded and to which the 'outer' aspects of a work, its instrumental branches, leaves and blossoms, bear an increasingly distant but genetically consistent relationship.

The analogy with organic processes is a rather obvious one. It is, though, in keeping not just with Holmboe's own philosophical standpoint but also with a widespread interest throughout Europe and America during the 1940s in the ideas of the Scottish zoologist and classical scholar Sir D'Arcy Thompson. Rather belatedly rediscovered, mainly by painters and sculptors, Thompson's most important book *On Growth and Form* (1917) had almost as great an impact on the arts as on the natural sciences. It offered a scientific but also somewhat mystical underpinning to efforts to reconcile the diversity of nature with the unity of the Creation, and it lent a certain legitimacy to archetypal and sometimes even atavistic forms in both the visual arts and music.

Throughout his career, Holmboe has stood apart from the avant garde, and since the end of the war has seen his once burgeoning reputation as a symphonist steadily eclipsed by the new music coming out of Darmstadt, Paris and Milan. On the surface, there seems much in common between the metamorphic approach and the transformational logic of the twelve-note approach. There are parallels, but to a composer of Holmboe's temperament, Schoenberg would have seemed a representative, if not necessarily a defender, of the quasi-Darwinism of the modern movement, in which forms are evolved in a fragmented, mechanical and self-conscious fashion rather than organically. If Schoenberg's music was symptomatic of a fatal un-rootedness, Holmboe had discovered the antidote in his researches into Romanian folk forms in the early 1930s (he married the Romanian pianist Meta Graf in 1934) and his discovery at the same time of Bartók's own musicological studies. His music is full of modal colours drawn from folk music, but there is little sign in it of the incorporation of both authentically and synthetically 'traditional' forms one associates with Sibelius. Holmboe's early development was consistent with, if not demonstrably influenced by the neo-classicism of Paul Hindemith (1895–1963) and early Stravinsky, and though the notion of a 'Nielsen influence' sounds both simplistically obvious and excessively parochial, it is nonetheless still the most convincing.

Holmboe shares with Nielsen not just an affection for classical counterpoint, which is another essential structural principle in his work, but a strong awareness of instrumental colour. Holmboe's orchestral scores are marked by detailed part-writing and vivid, often unexpected sonorities. The chamber concertos of the early 1940s, the period immediately before the crucial Fifth and Sixth Symphonies, are explorations of instrumental sound pure and simple, rather than of dramatic structure, and their impact can clearly be heard in Holmboe's dramatic use of solo parts in the symphonies. Nielsen had been particularly adept in this regard, even including an out-of-tempo snare drum solo in his Fifth Symphony (1921–2). The connection goes further and deeper. Behind Nielsen's colourful sonority and bright counterpoint was a spiritual dimension that was not merely personal and autobiographical. The titles of the Third (1910–11) and Fourth (1915–16) Symphonies – *Sinfonia espansiva* and 'Det uudslukkelige' – have proved resistant to straightforward translation; concepts such as 'Expansive' and 'The Inextinguishable', as well as the earlier 'Four Temperaments' subtitle to the Second (1901–2), have tended to be understood psychologically rather than philosophically, and it is perhaps only by reading Nielsen retrospectively in the light of Holmboe's less concentrated enterprise that their more purely musical and philosophical intentions become clearer.

Holmboe's work is not without its more straightforward references. The Fourth Symphony (1941–5), subtitled *Sinfonia sacra*, was revised in memory of the composer's brother, who died in a concentration camp during the Nazi Occupation. It is a passionate and very moving piece, with a prominent choral part based on the composer's own text, and it bears an obvious debt to Stravinsky's *Symphony of Psalms* (1930), which was premiered during Holmboe's period of study in Berlin. The Fifth Symphony (1944) was premiered in Copenhagen in the last days of the war in Europe; like its predecessor, it contained martial elements that were a clear reference to the war, and though it was too quietly stoical and reserved to gain anything like the heroic prominence of Shostakovich's 'Leningrad' Symphony, it established Holmboe's reputation. The Fifth is still redolent of mainstream neo-classicism, but it was Holmboe's first full attempt at the 'metamorphic' structure which was to reach its apotheosis in the dense single-movement form of the Seventh in 1950.

The Sixth is, stylistically as well as chronologically, an intermediate piece, and it remains one of Holmboe's most successful scores. Rather longer than the other symphonies of the time, it has a striking two-part organization which maximizes dramatic interest in the second, faster movement. The opening section is a patient exposition of growth and change. The movement begins *sotto voce* with a series of fourths which are perhaps intended to recall the opening of another wartime classic, Bartók's Concerto for Orchestra (q.v.). However, instead of being a foil for contrasting dramatic material, these soft string intervals and their languid rhythmic setting become the basis of the whole movement, merging with new material in the *Allegro* central section. Here the music quickens (in both senses) with the introduction of woodwind figures in $\frac{2}{4}$ time executing bright arabesques round a central pivot. The relationship between the two elements is not so much a dialogue as a form of symbiosis, each drawing on characteristics from the other. The movement builds into an impressive, brass-dominated climax, with a dramatic exchange of dynamic natures. There is a short violin solo before the music gradually settles back into the undisturbed calm and symmetry of the opening, which on its reappearance confirms a resemblance to Benjamin Britten's 1941 *Sinfonia da requiem*, a work Holmboe much admired.

If the Sixth Symphony has a programme, it might be the growth, interdependence and shared destiny of natural forms. As such, the opening movement serves as a prologue to the more overtly dramatic second half, in which Holmboe constructs a variety of musical life-forms out of a single rather mysterious scale, sounded affirmatively by brass and percussion at the start and then developed in three main blocks, the middle one a dark fugue. The opening motif and its associated scale are reintroduced just before the climax, but now they pave the way for a return of the first movement's underlying fourths. This raises the music quite suddenly, but with no sense of contrivance, to a new level of coherence in which simple mathematical transformations relocate the basic motifs in their harmonic environment.

The Swedish BIS label launched their Holmboe symphony cycle in 1992, filling a long-standing gap that had left him, increasingly unfashionable in the 1960s and 1970s, only poorly and intermittently represented on record. Owain Arwel Hughes favours a bigger, less obviously lyrical sound than his predecessor (and still honorary conductor) Norman Del Mar, but the Aarhus Symphony Orchestra sound completely idiomatic and there is no attempt to overdramatize the more obviously programmatic elements of this and the other three symphonies so far (March 1993) covered. Though less intensely focused than Nielsen and less overtly dramatic than his other countryman Rued Langgaard (1893–1952), Holmboe is a significant transitional figure in modern Danish music, pointing the way forward for important younger figures such as Per Nørgård (born 1932) and Hans Abrahamsen (born 1952), whose use of the simplest musical materials and basic oppositions can be seen as an extension of Holmboe's work. But he is important not just as an influence. On its own terms, his work represents one of the most dedicated applications in recent times of an individual musical philosophy untouched by schools or systems.

Discographical Information

Other Holmboe: *Benedic Domino* (1952); Concerto for cello and orchestra (1974), *Triade* (1975; all on Bis CD 78); Concerto for brass (1983; Bis CD 265).

Map references: Carl Nielsen, Symphony no. 5: *Sinfonia semplice* (1924–5; RCA Red Seal 60427); Ib Norholm, Concerto for violin and orchestra (1974–5; Kontrapunkt 32099), and Symphony no. 5: *The Elements* (1980; Kontrapunkt 320065).

Further reading: K. A. Rasmussen, *Noteworthy Danes*, Copenhagen, 1980.

JOHN CAGE (1912–1992)

Sonatas and Interludes for prepared piano (1946–1948)

FIRST PERFORMED: (in part) New York City, 14 April 1946; (complete) New York City, 12 and 13 January 1949
SELECTED RECORDING: Harmonia Mundi HM 730 LP
Maro Ajemian (prepared piano)
RECORDED: 1969
DURATION: 40'

John Cage lived and worked in a world of noise. Anyone who ever met or studied under him has remarked his blissful concentration on and apparent enjoyment of what seemed to others like cacophonies. It was the essence of Cage's aesthetic that music had to be released, not created. As a philosophy it was a delicate mixture of Zen Buddhism and old-fashioned American pragmatism.

In 1934 he began to study under Arnold Schoenberg, who had emigrated to the United States in October of the previous year. Schoenberg had worked briefly in Boston before crossing the country to live (improbably) in Hollywood. In 1935 he was made professor of music at the University of Southern California, but moved the following year to the University of California, Los Angeles, where Cage, a native Angelean, was able to continue what had seemed a promising early association.

Brief, and frustrating as it almost certainly became for both, the period under Schoenberg made a considerable impact on Cage's career. It was clear to both men that Cage had no strong feeling for harmony. Schoenberg predictably regarded this as an insuperable obstacle; Cage, equally predictably, did not. But when he asked the elder composer about serialist technique, he was told: 'That is none of your business', an example of Schoenberg's not-quite-idiomatic English expressing something other than he strictly intended. Cage had already experimented with serialist structures, using non-repeating pitch sets of twenty-five consecutive notes instead of the usual twelve, but these were not quite idiomatic either. He increasingly recognized that he inhabited a world not of *notes*, but of democratically undifferentiated sounds. This was entirely alien to Schoenberg, who told Cage he was beating his head against a brick wall. Cage vowed to continue, and quite literally began banging on things. Not in anger, which was the emotion most alien to his temperament, but with a conviction, encouraged by the film-maker Oscar Fischinger, for whom he had worked, that the spirit of objects could be released simply by setting them in vibration.

In 1939 Cage was working as accompanist for Bonnie Bird's dance classes at the Cornish School in Seattle. That year he founded a percussion group there and wrote what is perhaps his first major piece, *First Construction (in Metal)* (1939); six percussionists are required to play cow- and sleigh-bells, anvils, gongs (some of whose pitches were distorted by submerging them in water) and thundersheets, as well as industrial 'readymades' like suspension coils and brake drums. (Cage's artistic descendant John Bergamo has extended the transport metaphor as far as making drums out of engine nacelles from jumbo jets.) There were later *Constructions* (1940, 1941) for four percussion, but in between Cage had been introduced to the possibilities of electronics and sound manipulation and was experimenting with turntables, frequency recordings, tapes, oscillators and buzzers, setting off a sequence of *Imaginary Landscapes* (1939–52) for electronics and percussion.

In 1940, on a Tuesday (Cage is very specific), he was approached by the black dancer Syvilla Fort, who asked him to prepare some music; the piece was to be performed that Friday. There was no space in the small theatre for a percussion consort, no wings or band-pit, and Cage was obliged to work with the piano. He began by trying to devise an African-sounding note-row, but gave up and quickly concluded, with characteristic self-confidence, that 'what was wrong was the piano, not my efforts, because I was conscientious'.

This aspect of Cage – the conscientiousness, rather than the arrogant aplomb – is one that has often been overlooked. He is one of the great *technicians* of American music. His father, John Milton Cage Snr, had been an inventor and was responsible for a submarine detection system, as well as other more neutral and life-enhancing innovations, none of which made him any money. Cage had worked as the old man's research assistant and was genetically adept at technical improvisation using standardized everyday objects; Schoenberg even described Cage Jnr as 'an inventor of genius'. In his (deadline-haunted) effort to rethink the piano's sound, to make it more like a percussion instrument, he suddenly remembered having assisted Henry Cowell (1897–1965) on a piece called *The Banshee* (1925), one of the composer's Celtic–Irish fantasies. Cage had been sent to Cowell by the pianist Richard Bühlig, and in an interview with Richard Dufallo he recalls working the piano pedals while Cowell manipulated the strings with his fingers, both muting and plucking them.

Cage decided this was the key to his present difficulty. As he described to Richard Dufallo, 'I put a pie plate on the strings and it bounced; then I put a nail between the strings and it slipped. Then I found a wood screw and it stayed in position, and *I was able to repeat a sound.*' This last point was the crucial one, and is important to bear in mind when listening to the *Sonatas and Interludes*. Later composers and improvisers have been perfectly content with 'preparations' that varied during performance; the British pianist Keith Tippett, for example, uses small balsa blocks which are light enough to bounce off the piano strings each time they are struck. Cage, though, wanted to be able to fix certain timbres and sustain them for the duration of a performance. In addition to screws, Cage specifies coins and erasers, and there is a photograph, *c.* 1940, showing plastic spoons wedged between strings. I remember watching Yuji Takahashi (see below) setting up his piano for a performance of the *Sonata and Interludes* in the early 1980s and being surprised at how scrupulously he followed a written set of instructions; afterwards, it was said that Cage, who rarely commented or showed obvious interest in the conduct of a performance, had been satisfied with the way the piano had been prepared. The timbres are very exact and constant, and the pitching extremely complex; it is more or less impossible to identify many of the chords in the *Sonatas and Interludes*. The most obvious parallel, in terms of sound, is a gamelan orchestra, and there are moments in the *Sonatas and Interludes* where the irregular rhythmic patterns and pentatonic scales are strongly reminiscent of Balinese music.

This anticipates the story a little. Cage met his deadline successfully. *Bacchanale* (1940) was the first work for 'prepared piano'. (*The New Grove Dictionary of American Music* conflates the 1934 piano piece *Music for Xenia* [Andreyevna Kashevarov, his wife from 1935 to 1945] with the related *A Valentine Out of Season* (1944) for prepared piano which came at the unseasonal end of their marriage.) When he moved to New York, a city much less given – indeed, positively resistant in those years – to lateral thinking and experimentation, he no longer had access to like-minded performers, and spent more and more time alone at the piano. Between 1940 and 1946, there was a flurry of works for prepared piano: *And the Earth Shall Bear Again, In the Name of the Holocaust, Primitive* (a Cowell-like exercise, *sans* keyboard), *Amores, Tossed as it is Untroubled, Totem Ancestor, A Book of Music, The Perilous Night, Root of an Unfocus, Spontaneous Earth, The Unavailable Memory of, A Valentine out of Season, Daughters of the Lonesome Isle, Mysterious Adventure, Three Dances,* and *Music for Marcel Duchamp.* There was also the beautiful oddity of Cage's setting of Joyce in *The Wonderful Widow of Eighteen Springs* (1942) which calls for soprano and 'closed piano' and requires the accompanist to drum and slap on the lid and sound-box.

Labouring the list helps make one important point. By the time Cage came to write the *Sonatas and Interludes*, the prepared piano was no longer – if it ever had been – a gimmick; it had, in a sense, lost its inverted commas. There is an obvious contrast in the rather neutral, generic title and the programmatic, expressive, even impassioned titles of the preceding pieces. In 1945, the year of his separation from Xenia, Cage began to study Zen Buddhism, under the tutelage of Daisetz T. Suzuki at Columbia University. Thereafter his music was increasingly concerned with asking questions, less and less with expressing pre-determined solutions. In the later 1940s, Cage had begun to lose interest in music as an *expressive* medium at all, preferring to think of it and of all art as an 'experimental station' by no means discontinuous from any other living act whose end was in doubt.

It is perhaps odd that his first major existential work should bear such an old-fashioned title, but it is clear that with the *Sonatas and Interludes* he wanted to strip the music of any associative clutter. They are, in fact, oddly conventional and sound remarkably like a hybrid of keyboard works in the homophonic 'free style' of Domenico Scarlatti (1685–1757) and the mysterious Rose + Croix meditations of Erik Satie (1866–1925), particularly in Takahashi's notably brittle reading. One gets the same effect in Cage's nearly contemporary first String Quartet (1949–50), and in the Concerto for prepared piano and chamber orchestra (1951), an impression of very ancient music filtered through an entirely alien consciousness. Another early piece for piano (or harp), *In a Landscape*, written around the same time as the last of the *Sonatas and Interludes*, actually seems to imply a governing tonality, though of a rather extended, almost modal kind. The sixteen *Sonatas* are mostly in a simple binary form, like Bach's keyboard inventions; each comes in two sections with a modulation to the dominant (the fifth step in the octave) in the first part, and back to the tonic (the first or eighth) in the second. Needless to say, the prepared piano destroys any chance to read the tonality exactly, but as with *In a Landscape*, it is always implicit. Dramatic tension comes from the gap between what one somehow expects to hear and the sounds the piano is actually producing. Cage later stated that the greatest lesson he learned from Schoenberg was that the basis of all technical understanding was not rigour of application but the nature of *the questions asked*, and he claimed that Schoenberg 'would have liked the idea that in order to use chance operations you have to know all of the things that might happen when you ask a question that is answered by them'.

It would be wrong to present the *Sonatas and Interludes* as entirely emotionless. They are intended to suggest the emotions in a 'permanent', universalized configuration, almost like the Platonic Forms, and it is the function of their binary form to restore each of the emotions to a point of stasis or tranquillity. It was part of Cage's adaptation to Zen ways of thought that he came to reject the traditional artist's role of shaping and reshaping the world, and to accept a kind of creativity in which the artist adapted him/herself to the world. In this he was doubtless encouraged by his association with the dancer and choreographer Merce Cunningham (who became his lifetime partner, confirming dance's cornerstone place in his personal aesthetic) and by the radical pianism of David Tudor whom he met in the late 1940s. In 1951 Cage made his famous sojourn in the anechoic chamber at Harvard, and discovered that even 'pure' silence was interrupted by the thud of the bloodstream and the hiss of the central nervous system. A year later, his most famous work, 4′ 33″, which instructs 'tacet' – be silent – for any instrument or combination of instruments, established a caricature of modernism second only to Jackson Pollock's drips and splashes. It is very difficult after forty years to hear – or not hear – 4′ 33″ cold and without theoretical constructs; it must have been profoundly disturbing at the time. (I 'heard' Colin Smith, to whose memory this book is dedicated, 'play' the piece in 1976 and sat beside a woman who clearly had no notion of what was going on; her embarrassment and discomfiture could almost have been bottled.) Polemically, 4′ 33″ was once almost as important to the perception of contemporary music as the alien sound of *Sonatas and Interludes*, but time has diluted its impact, even as an occasional head-clearing exercise.

In later years, Cage extended very greatly the range of questions that could be asked of music and the other arts. Influenced by the I Ching, he experimented with chance operations, as in *Music of Changes* (1951). He suggested musical palimpsests, superimposing compositions over mostly electronic pieces like *Fontana Mix* (1958) or *Cartridge Music* (1960). He derived scores from the distribution of points on star-maps, as in *Etudes australes* (1974–5). Cage was also an important American *writer* (he was Charles Eliot Norton Professor of Poetry at Harvard in 1988 and 1989) and belonged to the lineage that connects Gertrude Stein with 'offshore Americans' like William Carlos Williams and Gilbert Sorrentino. *Silence* (1961) is a classic. He devised verbal pieces, like the Zen tales in *Indeterminacy* (1958), and mesostics derived from the initial letters of iconic names, James Joyce's or Merce Cunningham's. He lectured on mushrooms (including a prize-winning run on the Italian television quiz show *Lascia o raddopia*) and macrobiotics, wore deedle-bompers at a doctoral robing, espoused a kind of quietistic anarchism half-way between Prince Kropotkin and Marcel Duchamp (who taught him to play chess), and became – with Cunningham, and in a typically understated, non-activist way – a model for same-sex relationships.

There *are* recordings of 4'33" (I have one on Cramps CRSLP 6101), but they are somehow beside the point. Cage was for many years deeply ambivalent about the preservation of his music in mechanically reproducible forms, but towards the end of his life began to supervise a comprehensive documentation on the Mode label, which has become an important source. The *Sonatas and Interludes* have been recorded many times, complete and in part. Despite a strong conviction that Takahashi's very astringent and inexpressive CD version is the ideal performance, I have opted for an earlier LP recording by Maro Ajemian, who gave the premieres in 1946 and 1949. Like Takahashi, she has a dry, unfussy touch, combined with a briskness of attack that reduces the level of expressiveness almost to nothing. To a large extent, it is these pieces and not the more notorious 'silent' or 'chance' works which represent the *degré zéro* of modern music, the point at which it ceases to be a consumable artefact and turns into a participatory logic in which we are all, whether we wish it or not, complicit. It was Cage's greatness that he made music a social phenomenon again.

Discographical Information

Other recordings: Takahashi (Denon C37 7673); Members of American Festival of Microtonal Music Ensemble (Newport Classic NPD 85526); Pierce (Wergo WER 60156); Roggenkamp (Wergo WER 6074–2); also CRI 199; Decca Headline 9; Dial 19/20; Etcetera KTC 2001; Fylkingen FYLPX 101–2; Hungaroton HCD 12569; New World 203 (parts only); Tomato 2–1001.

Other Cage: *A Valentine out of Season* (1944; Etcetera KTC 3002); *Music of Changes* (1951; Wergo WER 60099), *4' 33"* (1952; Koch International Classics 3–7238–2); Concerto for piano and chamber orchestra (1951; Elektra Nonesuch N5 71202); *Indeterminacy* (1959; Smithsonian Folkways SF 40804/5); *Cartridge Music* (1960; Mode 24); *Atlas eclipticalis* (1961; hat ART CD 6111); Thirty Pieces for string quartet (1983; Mode 17).

Map references: Christian Wolff, *For Prepared Piano* (1951; hat ART 6101 [*The New York School*]); Earle Brown, Music for Cello and Piano (1954; as for Wolff); Morton Feldman, *For John Cage* (1982; Musical Observations CP2 101); try also sitting in an empty room with your eyes closed, just to see how much silence you don't hear.

Further reading: J. Cage, *Silence*, Middletown, Connecticut, 1961, and *I–VI* [Charles Eliot Norton lectures], Cambridge, Massachusetts, 1990; C. Tomkins, in *The Bride and the Bachelors*, New York, 1965 (repr. by Penguin as *Ahead of the Game*]; S. Sontag, 'The Esthetics of Silence', in *Styles of Radical Will*, New York, 1969; M. Nyman, *Experimental Music: Cage and Beyond*, London, 1974; D. Revill, *The Roaring Silence* [biography], London, 1992.

1950s

This was once routinely thought to be the decade of narrow conservatism in both politics and culture, a period of straitened caution, largely anaesthetized by post-war prosperity. It was, of course, a far more adventurous decade than 'the sixties', when the habit of thinking that decades really did represent definable cultural movements took a firm and lasting grip. Even if one accepts the general principle that nearly any 'innovation' can be traced back in time in an almost infinite regress, the 1950s are a significant moment. A great deal was happening technologically. The development of tape recorders, of the long playing record and 'stereo' sound, and also of the electronic computer, was to have varying but lasting effects on music, while the habit of thinking radically about music and its performance was so deeply engrained that almost nothing could be taken for granted...

1950 The magnetic tape recorder is perfected.
1951 The first electronic music studio is founded under the auspices of West German Radio in Cologne and under the directorship of Herbert Eimert. Arnold Schoenberg dies.
1952 John Cage unveils his silent piece, 4′ 33″.
1953 Pierre Schaeffer writes the electronic opera *Orphée 53*.
1954 Pierre Boulez's Concert Marigny/Domaine Musical series begins in Paris. Charles Ives dies.
1955 Karlheinz Stockhausen and Herbert Eimert establish *Die Reihe* – 'The Row' – an important listening post for the avant garde. In 1958 they edit a major retrospective consideration of Anton Webern.
1956 Russian and other Eastern bloc troops put down the risings in Hungary. Jackson Pollock, pioneer of 'action' painting and Abstract Expressionism, dies in a motor accident.
1957 Stereophonic recording is developed, becoming commercially available within the next two years. Also, the first computer composition, Lejaren Hiller's and Leonard Isaacson's *Illiac Suite*, is realized. Columbia releases Robert Craft's com-

pleted recordings of Webern's work.

1958   One of the centrepieces of the world exposition at Brussels is the Philips Pavilion, designed by Le Corbusier and his assistant Iannis Xenakis, and soundtracked by Edgard Varèse's

Poème électronique.

1959   First volume of Robert Craft's *Conversations with Stravinsky* published. Miles Davis records *Kind of Blue*, said by some to be the most important jazz recording since Louis Armstrong's Hot Fives.

ELIZABETH MACONCHY (1907–1995)

String Quartet no. 6 (1950)

FIRST PERFORMED: London, 1951
SELECTED RECORDING: Unicorn-Kanchana DKPCD 9081
  Bingham String Quartet: Stephen Bingham, Mark Messenger (violins), Brenda Stewart (viola), Miriam Lowbury (cello)
  [with: String Quartet no. 5 (1948); String Quartet no. 7 (1955); String Quartet no. 8 (1967)]
RECORDED: March 1989
DURATION: 19' 31"

At the age of sixteen Elizabeth Maconchy was turned down for the Mendelssohn Scholarship at the Royal College of Music in London. It was the view of the RCM director Hugh Allen that it would be wasteful to offer a prestigious award to a girl who would undoubtedly soon settle down to 'appropriate' female pursuits like child-rearing. Seven years later she did indeed marry and produced two daughters, one of whom herself turned to music, the fine English composer Nicola LeFanu (born 1947). However, Maconchy defied Allen's prediction and continued producing music of enormous distinction, often in the face of considerable personal difficulty.

It may seem odd to emphasize Nicola LeFanu's Englishness, but I do so to underline the enormous differences between the mother's and the daughter's backgrounds. Whereas Nicola LeFanu grew up in an actively musical family and attended contemporary music concerts with her mother from an early age, Elizabeth Maconchy, though born in Hertfordshire, was raised in rural Ireland during the latter years of the Ascendancy. Until her mid-teens and her arrival at the RCM, she had apparently attended just two concerts, one orchestral and one, significantly, by a string quartet. Since 1979, LeFanu has been married to the Australian composer David Lumsdaine (born 1931) and has even job-shared a readership at London University with him. Dame Elizabeth

– she was inducted DBE in 1987 – was married in 1930, to the medical historian William LeFanu, a descendant of the Irish novelist Sheridan LeFanu. Different attitudes prevailed before the Second World War and though undoubtedly supportive of his wife's music-making, LeFanu could not quite mitigate the critics' rather Dr Johnsonish condescension toward women composers. Composers of Nicola LeFanu's generation have been able to rely on a sympathetic infrastructure of performers and conductors, funding bodies and critics, all attuned to the notion of 'women's music', and in 1994 she was appointed to the prestigious professorship of music at the University of York. The only precedent available to the young Elizabeth Maconchy was the rather formidable and, yes, mannish figure of Dame Ethel Smyth (1858–1944), now being seriously reassessed but even during her lifetime somewhere between a musical establishment mascot and an outright joke; Henry Reed unmercifully spoofed her Germanic obsessions and megaphone conversational style.

There are also musical reasons for emphasizing Elizabeth Maconchy's un-Englishness. There is almost no sign in her work of the prevailing spirit of English pastoralism. Despite the longstanding friendship and support of Ralph Vaughan Williams (1872–1958), her main influences were European. In 1929 and 1930 she studied in Prague under the prominent Czech composer Karel Boleslav Jirák (1891–1972), who moved to the USA after the war. Janáček had just died, but it was his operas – more, at this stage, than the string quartets – that made the greatest impact on Maconchy. Her Concerto for piano and chamber orchestra (written in 1928, before going to Czechoslovakia) was premiered in Prague on her twenty-third birthday, and the fine orchestral suite *The Land* (1929) made a mark at the Proms that summer during the same week as her wedding to LeFanu. Her next substantial success was with the ballet music *Puck Fair* (1940). By this time, Maconchy had been diagnosed as consumptive and had returned to something like the rural isolation of her upbringing, an ironic turnaround for the most promising woman composer, and one of the most promising composers, of her generation. The war years were difficult for everyone, but Maconchy seems to have hit a fresh seam of inspiration at the end of the decade; 1950 alone saw concertos for oboe and bassoon, and for bassoon alone with strings, a palette she returned to the lovely *Variazioni concertante* (1964–5) and the Oboe Quartet (1972). It was, of course, also the year of the Sixth Quartet.

Setting Janáček alongside Bartók and late Beethoven, the other main influences on her quartet writing, it is tempting to assume that Maconchy's work in the medium is personal, 'existential' (in the proper sense) and expressionistic. To some extent that is, of course, the case. She has written fourteen string quartets to date and they reflect her changing attitudes and experiences. However they also embody in the clearest possible way her absolute insistence on structural values. The Hyperion series will eventually cover all fourteen and Maconchy has contributed illuminating liner notes, with a brief essay on quartet writing itself, charmingly dated by her analogies to sonnet-writing and driving a four-in-hand. In her essay she puts very deliberate emphasis on structural logic and careful musical navigation – no wild expressive gallops or unreined excursions – and suggests that the ideal virtues for the medium are 'corporate strength', 'economy and clarity', music that is 'precise and economical', 'logical, arresting and clear-cut'.

Protesting too much? Or merely overcompensating for generations of critical condescension during which it was casually assumed that women composers were not capable of rigorous organization and solid architecture? (Exactly a hundred years ago, George Bernard Shaw, not perhaps the man to look to for enlightened attitudes, registered a gasp of surprise when E. M. Smyth, composer of the powerful *Anthony and Cleopatra* overture, was revealed to be 'a lady'.) A few paragraphs later, though, Dame Elizabeth concedes that the abiding attraction of quartet-writing is 'the sense of excitement and exploration' they bring, one that she has maintained at a much subtler, less bellowing level than Dame Ethel. To some extent, the quartets do represent an autobiographical sequence, although there is no sense that she set out to write such a sequence, as Milhaud seems to have done, or Villa-Lobos, who declared that quartet-writing was 'a mania'.

None of the Maconchy quartets is as nakedly personal as Janáček's First, *The Kreutzer Sonata* (1923, the title came via Tolstoy's airlessly misogynistic story rather than from the Beethoven piece), or even the Second, *Intimate Pages* (1928). Nor is there much sign of Beethoven's own God-bothering intensity, but it is clear that Maconchy went to him direct for her basic idiom, refusing to rely on any intermediary. Maconchy's are classic string quartets rather than pieces for four string players, as had become the norm after Stravinsky and with increasing frequency once modernists like John Cage and Elliott Carter got their hands on the form. I have picked her Sixth because it comes halfway through the cycle and because it seems to me to combine a satisfying entireness with a deeply personal expression (the post-war years were not easy for Maconchy), but also because 1950 is the year of Cage's String Quartet in Four Parts (the title says it all) and the year in which Carter began writing his epochal String Quartet no. 1 (which I take a look at next). The comparison is striking.

Elizabeth Maconchy's String Quartet no. 6 derives most of its material from the five-note motif which sets the opening passacaglia in motion. Heard first in the cello, this figure consists of a broad upward sweep followed by two equal downward steps, solid-sounding thirds that give the figure an almost visible balance. Throughout the first movement, it can be detected in different instrumental and rhythmic configurations, or with its constituent intervals stretched and compressed, but always remaining instantly identifiable. The passacaglia is a dance built over a repeating bass pattern; as here, it is usually polyphonic and quite complex in structure, relying on a fairly strict pattern of variation. Interestingly, Benjamin Britten returned to the passacaglia, with its Venetian associations in his Third and last string quartet in 1975, having preferred the looser chordal homophony of the form's English variant, the 'Chacony' or chaconne in the massive closing movement of his Second (1945). Maconchy's passacaglia theme is almost as dominant, reappearing in her closing movement to give the piece a similar 'homecoming' symmetry.

The second part is a slightly dry little scherzo again built entirely on the melodic shape of the opening statement, which in this case is given to the first violin. If there is a major criticism of the Bingham Quartet's handling of Maconchy's 'middle quartets' it is a slight lack of flexibility in their handling of faster rhythmic modulations. As in the scherzos of the Fifth and Seventh (the latter boasts two, the first very fast), the coherence of the structure depends on a smooth integration of subtly contrasting patterns, and this the Binghams do not quite pull off. There is a virtuosic plucked middle section in which the violin theme is transformed and counterpointed; the extended use of pizzicato conjures up associations as far afield as Bartók and the Australian Peter Sculthorpe, and is certainly among the most un-English passages in Maconchy's output.

The viola takes its turn in the slow movement, essaying a quiet and rather melancholy tune; marked 'rubato', it sounds half-remembered, almost as if in reverie. The cello enters with a second 'more passive' theme, but one in which I can hear distant intimations of the returning passacaglia. This movement works by addition rather than subdivision or variation, and builds to a broad, affirmative climax that is as unambiguous as the culminating statement of the opening movement, with which it shares a sense of melodic continuity. The final movement starts as if in an entirely fresh direction but soon restores the definitive passacaglia theme which, having passed through all four instruments again, marks a powerful and utterly logical climax in its new, seemingly more positive transformation.

Such a description hovers close to reading into the quartet some half-buried psychological or emotional drama. One of the most impressive things about Maconchy's quartets is their ability to suggest moods and emotions without tying the music to a fixed programme. Even as she departed more and more confidently from tonality such moods never became abstract or remote. Maconchy is essentially a dramatic composer – her trilogy of operas *The Sofa*, *The Three Strangers* and *The Departure* (1956–61) are still too little known – with a brisk freedom from sentimentality. Piano pieces like *Mill Race* and *The Yaffle* (both 1962) stand comparison with similar essays by Bartók, and her 1985 treatment of Edith Sitwell's much-mangled lyric 'Still Falls the Rain' contains exemplary choral writing. Too little of her work has been made available on record. I remember fine versions of the Fifth and Ninth Quartets by the Allegri String Quartet on Argo (also loyal sponsors of Maconchy's near-contemporary Elisabeth Lutyens) and a creakier reading of the Tenth by the University of Alberta String Quartet on CBC. Beyond that, very little, until the inception of the Hyperion project.

Discographical Information

Other Maconchy: Symphony for double string orchestra (1953; Lyrita SRCS 116 LP); Quintet for clarinet and strings (1963; Hyperion CDA 66428); 'Take, o take those lips away' (1965; HMV HQS 1298).

Map references: Ruth Crawford Seeger, String Quartet (1931; Gramavision R21s 79440; Ralph Vaughan Williams, Partita for double string orchestra (1946–8; Angel Classics for Pleasure CDM 64114); Nicola LeFanu, *Deva* (1979; Chandos ABR 1017 LP).

Further reading: E. Maconchy, 'A Composer Speaks', in *Composer* winter issue (1971–2).

ELLIOTT CARTER (born 11 December 1908)

String Quartet no. 1 (1951)

FIRST PERFORMED: New York City, 26 February 1953
SELECTED RECORDING: Sony Classical S2K 47229
   Juilliard String Quartet: Robert Mann, Joel Smirnoff (violins), Samuel Rhodes (viola), Joel Krosnick (cello)
   [with: String Quartet no. 2 (1959); String Quartet no. 3 (1971); String Quartet no. 4 (1986); Duo (1974), Mann (violin), Christopher Oldfather (piano)]
RECORDED: December 1990
DURATION: 41' 45"

Elliott Carter has turned to the string quartet form at significant points in his career, moments when his stylistic development has been undergoing rapid acceleration or change. Almost always, a new quartet marks a point of transition between one of his characteristic syntheses of inherited procedures (David Mason Greene called him the 'eclectic's eclectic') and a new plateau in his own musical language. As a sequence – and there are two fine cycles currently available on record – the quartets are at once astonishingly varied and remarkably of a piece.

The First and Second (1959) are both intimately concerned with musical time. Looking back at them in 1970, Carter said 'I get the impression of their living in different time-worlds, the first in an expanded one, the second in a condensed and concentrated one', cautiously adding 'although this was hardly a conscious opposition at the times of their composition'. The difference between the two works, and the development it implies, is instructive in understanding how the First came to be. In the later quartet, Carter replaced the independent parallelism of the four instruments which had been such an innovative property of the earlier work with a more 'archetypal' approach in which each instrument was assigned its own expressive 'character' and idiolect, 'typecast' with 'its own repertory of musical speeds and intervals'. The terms are all Carter's, and he went further, suggesting that the later piece resembled an opera made up almost entirely of quartets, with one instrument dominating each scene as it invents its own material.

The dramatic separation of voices seemed to call for very strong stereophonic separation, which the 1970 Composers Quartet recording from Nonesuch offers with knobs on; useful for anyone interested in how the piece is put together, but rather distracting and artificial. The recording is very much of its time and there is no question of inappropriate interpretation; all three versions cited here were supervised by the composer, and so additionally represent a valuable insight into how *he* conceived and reconceived the piece. Later digital recordings offer a more subtle microphone placement and sound separation, ideally so in the Juillard Quartet's performance.

Technical and performance considerations were very much on Carter's mind in 1951 as he approached the First Quartet. He was already forty-three, a relatively slow developer. Despite the early patronage (much exaggerated in some critical accounts) of the great American outsider and radical Charles Ives (1874–1954), Carter had been steered towards neo-classicism and a more accessible style by the legendary Nadia Boulanger (1887–1979) with whom he studied in Paris. His music of the later 1930s and early 1940s reflected, as he has said, a 'natural desire to write something many people could presumably grasp and enjoy easily at a time of social emergency'. By the end of the war, though, he was dissatisfied and began to explore the distinctive characteristics of instruments themselves as his fundamental compositional resource. Though he pleads 'poor performing nerves', Carter has been almost uniquely responsive to the intrinsic character of instruments and to the capabilities of performers. In the important Piano Sonata (1945–6), he derived virtually all the musical material from the characteristic overtones of the instrument itself, all but eliminating the traditional assignment of theme and accompaniment to right and left hands respectively. In its successor, the Sonata for cello and piano (1948), he concentrated on the quite different playing characteristics of the two instruments, anticipating the way that in the First String Quartet the four players seem to move along parallel but quite independent lines.

Some have argued that this illustrates a leaning toward chance-based or even jazz-influenced improvisational freedom, but this is very far from Carter's intention. He has stated that he regarded jazz as liberating but not musically stimulating. The Cello Sonata did, however, find him using opposing rhythms, separate melodic lines and strongly differentiated articulation characteristics, sharing responsibility for the underlying pulse between the two instruments. This was part of Carter's search for what he called a 'focused freedom', a quality that would invest strictly notated music with some of the energies of jazz. It also emulated Haydn's gift in the great quartets for maintaining structural unity while avoiding the 'squared-off articulation' of classicism by assigning quite varied melodic and rhythmic characteristics to the instruments. Carter was very interested in the superimposition of choral voices in parts of Mozart and later composers like Modest Mussorgsky (1839–81), and all these considerations led him with every appearance of inevitability to a technique known (though not initially by Carter) as 'metric' – or 'metrical' – 'modulation'. This is a slightly misleading terminology, since it is not the metres that are varied but the speed of a particular line; 'tempo modulation', a variant favoured by Robert P. Morgan, Leonard Stein and Peter Zafares in their excellent but quite technical liner-note to the Juilliard Quartet recording, is a much more satisfactory version.

In order to write a work which stretched, rather than passively accommodated, the abilities of its performers and the susceptibilities of its putative audience, Carter removed himself from the everyday routines and compromises of New York City, where he had been teaching at Columbia University. He travelled to the Lower Sonoran Desert, near Tucson, Arizona. In the breadth and colour of its sound, the First Quartet partakes of the dramatically expanded horizons and outwardly undifferentiated, but actually highly expressive, landscape he found there. It marks too a sudden liberation of Carter's more avant-garde instincts. There are explicit musical references both to Charles Ives (the cellist quotes from the 1910 Violin Sonata no. 2 near the beginning) and to the radical Conlon Nancarrow, whose jazz- and blues-tinged first rhythmic Study for Player Piano (Nancarrow was born in 1912, but leaves his works undated) is quoted at the start of the final movement.

Carter himself has aligned these references with the allusive quality of modern literature, James Joyce in particular, and has frequently spoken about the First Quartet in terms of the cyclical, inwardly-directed and epiphanic quality of Modernist novels and other art forms. He is often quoted as saying about the piece that it was 'written largely for my own satisfaction and grew out of an effort to understand myself', a statement he actually borrowed from Joseph Wood Krutch's *The Modern Temper*, an influential work of criticism by a neighbour and friend in Arizona; and there is a strongly personal, almost *Bildungsroman* quality to the First Quartet that makes it one of Carter's most identifiably 'personal' pieces. One might say that the distance between the First and Second Quartets is that between Joyce's *Dubliners* and *Portrait of the Artist as a Young Man* on the one hand, and on the other *Ulysses* and *Finnegans Wake*; Carter has added a parallel between the early Thomas Mann and the mythical structure of the later novels.

However, the image that immediately triggered the First Quartet was the framing device of Jean Cocteau's visionary film *Le sang d'un poète* (1932), in which the action is compressed into the split second it takes a dynamited factory chimney to collapse. The image is intended to convey the difference between clock (or metronomic) time and the hugely expanded 'dream' time, with its Joycean 'stream of consciousness', illogical parallelism, notational oddities, and epiphanies, that Carter's new rhythmic conception is intended to set free. Just as Cocteau's movie is bracketed by an interrupted shot of the falling chimney, so Carter's piece achieves its sense of circularity by repeating an opening unaccompanied cello cadenza (representing objective time) in a closing statement by the first violin alone, also unaccompanied.

The contrast between real and subjective time is also conveyed by the structure of the piece. It is cast in four movements which flow continuously into one another (there are partial precedents for this in late Beethoven and elsewhere), but which are interrupted internally by two silences, midway through the *Allegro scorrevole* second movement, and after some 167 bars of the 'Variations' fourth movement. These abrupt interruptions divide the work into three roughly equal sections, which of course no longer coincide with the four named movements. By desynchronizing the conventional form in this way Carter mirrors the rhythmic and thematic complexity of the music with a kind of large-scale structural counterpoint, a process he was to develop three years later in the extraordinary, interactive *Variations* for orchestra (1954–5).

The two outside movements of the First Quartet are made up of a great many themes developed simultaneously, giving a sense of 'simultaneous streams of different things going on together'. The opening 'Fantasia' establishes four independent melodies (all derived from the tetrachord E–F–G♯–A♯) in a multiplicity of shifting permutations. Changes in tempo, which in this context serve almost the same function as changes of key, are not assigned to all instruments at once; though each of the four main ideas has an individual profile of intervals and absolute speed, it may change its rate of articulation even while the others remain constant. The polymetric relationships are very complex, sometimes calling for fifteen beats in one instrument to be synchronized against twenty-one in another (there is some preference for proportions of three to seven), creating what Stein and Zaferes describe as 'pulse streams'. (Much later in his career, notably in the Third and Fourth Quartets, the difficulty of co-ordinating separate rhythmic patterns became much more acute, even requiring the performers to follow a click-track on headphones during live performance.)

The effect here is somewhat like that of a river current, where the rate of flow is different according to depth and other factors; though of course in Carter's music there is no 'surface' line until the end of the music where the four main ideas come together simultaneously. A better analogy might well be some form of particle experiment in which sub-atomic entities of different classes can be speeded up or slowed, foregrounded or not, according to quite specific interventions, but without disturbing the overall stream of radiation.

The ending of the first movement is a passage of virtuosic counterpoint in which each of the main voices briefly claims precedence. It is immediately replaced by a scherzo in which the analogy with particle physics seems even more apposite. Marked 'scorrevole' (which means 'flowing' or, interestingly, 'sliding' as in slide rule) it might be described as pointillistic were not the individual points of sound subject to such dramatic excitation and movement. The music is extremely fragmented (Carter likened it to a mosaic) and placed against a harmonic background of almost eerie stillness. This is then interrupted twice, first by a huge, dramatic outburst which comes after twenty-three bars, then by the first of the piece's two internal breaks. The mosaic is then restored and continues until a further outburst signals the beginning of the *Adagio*.

The third movement introduces a device which was to become central to Carter's conception in the Second and Third Quartets, that of assigning individual expressive characteristics to the instruments, and, more radically still in the Third, of dividing the quartet into two independent duos who share no material whatever and are placed at opposite ends of the stage. In 1951 he pitched the higher instruments against the lower; twenty years later, he deployed the initially unlikely combinations of first violin with cello and second violin with viola, relying once more on stereo separation to underline the pairings. In the last respect, the Juilliard recording on Sony is once again technically superb, a significant advance even on their own prize-winning recording of the Second and Third Quartets for Columbia [M–32738]. For the First, this is not quite so critical, for the material is clearly differentiated; the violins (with their mutes in place) play a rarefied, almost meditative music over a gruffer and more earthy recitative from the viola and cello. The contrast represents, in Carter's view, 'the extreme point of divergence between simultaneous ideas'.

The final movement is a set of 'Variations' whose separate themes are repeated ever more rapidly, accruing thematic changes with each cycle of repetition and acceleration until they approach a 'speed vanishing point'. The exception is a slow, minor-third interval from the cello which runs through the entire movement (again interrupted by a pause) until it becomes a blurred tremolo at the end. The final variation is given to the first violin, which gradually transforms its material back into the cello cadenza at the start. Real time is unfrozen and the chimney completes its fall and disintegration.

Carter nursed few hopes for his First String Quartet, apparently quite sincerely regarding it as a technical and highly personal exercise that would not find favour with players or audiences. Within months of its premiere in New York, though, it was awarded First Prize in the prestigious Concours International de Quatuor à Cordes at Liège, and it has since been recognized as one of the most significant and influential works for string quartet written this century, a bridge between Alban Berg's stressed and personal *Lyrische Suite* (1925–6) and the more abstract sound-worlds of younger composers like Brian Ferneyhough and Wolfgang Rihm. Albeit from a very different aesthetic (and, one must say, historical) perspective, its use of shifting rhythmic textures and static harmonies anticipate some of the products of American minimalism: 'The effect I am interested in producing is one of perceived large-scale rhythmic tension, sometimes involving the anticipation of the impending final coincidence of all the disparate rhythmic layers' is a statement intent that would not have seemed alien to Steve Reich or John Adams in the early 1970s.

In its determination to break down the inherited, hierarchical coherences of string quartet writing, it draws as much from middle-period Haydn as it share with John Cage's String Quartet in Four Parts (1949–50), but what does link Carter and Cage and irascible Ives, otherwise so unalike in temperament, is their absolute Americanness. The First Quartet is an open, generous piece in which every sound manages to stand for itself, simply and literally, but also to touch on whole constellations of meaning beyond. In that sense, it is also, for all its complexities of language, a quintessentially democratic piece.

Discographical Information

Other recordings: Composers Quartet [with: String Quartet no. 2 and valuable sleeve-note by Carter] (Nonesuch H–71249); Arditti String Quartet [with: world premiere recording of String Quartet no. 4] (Etcetera KTC 1065); KTC 1066 includes String Quartets nos 2 and 3, and *Elegy*.

Other Carter: Variations (1954–5; New World NW 347–2); Double Concerto (1961; Elektra Nonesuch 79183–2); *Syringa* (1978; Bridge BCD 9014); Triple Duo (1982; Elektra Nonesuch 79110-4); Violin Concerto (1986; Virgin Classics VC7 91503/CDC 59271).

Map references: Alban Berg, *Lyrische Suite* (1925–6; Disques Montaigne WM 789001); Charles Ives, Violin Sonata no. 2 (1910 [with: nos. 1, 3, 4]; Bridge BCD 9024); Conlon Nancarrow, Studies for Player Piano nos. 42, 45 a/b/c, 48 a/b/c, 49 a/b/c (n.d.; Wergo WER 60165–50); Brian Ferneyhough, *Sonatas* for string quartet (1967; RCA Red Seal RL 70610); Wolfgang Rihm, String Quartet no. 4 (1979–81 [with: Alfred Schnittke, String Quartet no. 4]; EMI Classics CDC 54660).

Further reading: A. Edwards, *Flawed Words and Stubborn Sounds: A Conversation with Elliott Carter*, New York, 1971; 'Music and the Time Screen', in *The Writings of Elliott Carter: An American Composer Looks at Modern Music*, Bloomington and London, 1977.

MICHAEL TIPPETT (born 2 January 1905)

Four Ritual Dances from *The Midsummer Marriage* (1946– 1952)

FIRST PERFORMED: (as concert pieces): Basle, February 1953
SELECTED RECORDING: Philips 6527 112 LP
    Joan Carlyle (soprano), Alberto Remedios (tenor), Elizabeth Bainbridge (mezzo-soprano), Stafford Dean (bass), Chorus and Orchestra of the Royal Opera House, Covent Garden, conducted by Colin Davis [with: Benjamin Britten, *Four Sea Interludes* from *Peter Grimes* (1942–5)]
RECORDED: 1970
DURATION: 19' 15"

One of the striking things about Michael Tippett's work, and about his unusual willingness to discuss it in print, has been its reliance on what he himself calls 'images'. These are by and large archetypal forms conjured from the depths of a collective imagination (I think it has to be *a* collective imagination at this point) and then used as abstract polarities to give convincingly dynamic shape to the slight, occasionally even trivial materials out of which he has constructed his works. Ezra Pound's analogy of the magnet and the iron dust is immediately applicable, but it was from T. S. Eliot (the lesser craftsman of the two poets, by his own account) that Tippett drew many of his ideas, not least the universalized impersonality of great art.

Tippett is certainly not an expressionistic composer in any normal sense, and there is a certain chill around even his most extravagant scores. They are, however, intellectually passionate even when they remain inviolate in Eliot's rather prudish sense of resistance to abstract ideas. Unlike Eliot though, Tippett was, in his youth at least, a committed leftist who conceived of music in an explicitly social and broadly political way. He joined the Communist Party in 1935 and the Peace Pledge Union five years later, around the time he took over the directorship of Morley College in South London. Such a background may partly explain Tippett's dedication to substance and meaning over style and technical sophistication. Set alongside Benjamin Britten, as he is on this recording, or the younger Peter Maxwell Davies, it is evident that Tippett is not *il miglior fabbro*.

Tippett made his name with the jazz-tinged oratorio *A Child of Our Time* (1939–41). Though he has written four symphonies (1944–5, 1956–7, 1970–2, 1976–7), and impressive concerted works like the Concerto for Double String Orchestra (1938–9, perhaps his best-known and most recorded piece after *Child*), a Piano Concerto (1953–5), a Concerto for Orchestra (1962–3), and a brave try at the rarely attempted Triple Concerto (1978–9, violin, viola, cello, orchestra), together with a substantial body of chamber music, centrally the four string quartets (1934–5, 1941–2, 1945–6, 1977–8), it is as a composer of dramatic music that Tippett seems fated to have made the greatest contribution. His earliest documented work was a realization of the 1729 *Village Opera* by Charles Johnson, which Tippett staged with Oxted Players at his home in Surrey. Experience as organizer and conductor of workers' music groups in the 1930s (when the vogue for folksong opera was still in full force) gave him a lyrical directness which has served him well throughout his career. Ironically, *A Child of Our Time* is marred by sentimentality and a kind of emotional complacency (I find it almost literally unlistenable–to) that does not appear anywhere else in his output, though the trendiness of its jazz references was to be a nagging shortcoming of later operas like *The Knot Garden* (1966–9), with its yowling guitar part, and the recent *New Year* (1988), which unconvincingly imports street-music devices.

The model for much of Tippett's operatic writing was Eliot's still-underrated verse drama, in which, as in *The Waste Land*, mythic and universal archetypes coexisted with the shabby realities of present-day society. At one time, Tippett actually studied, albeit informally, under Eliot's guidance, a relationship that the composer's biographer Ian Kemp likens to that of master and apprentice. Despite obvious differences of intellectual temperament, they seemed to get on well, and

Tippett asked Eliot to write the libretto for *A Child of Our Time*. The poet's refusal (how different a work might it have been?) spurred Tippett to tackle the job himself, something he has done with growing confidence and sophistication ever since.

What interested him in Eliot's verse plays was not so much the narrative structure (which is schematic in any case) but the way in which sustained self-examination and the music of language could be made to reveal immense and universal truths about the human psyche. On the page, Tippett's librettos can be embarrassingly bland and sophomoric, and their claims to plumb the collective imagination are sometimes weakened by their utter Englishness. In context, though, Tippett's words are thoroughly embraced by his music, in accordance with a conviction that 'the music of a song destroys the verbal music of a poem utterly'. One of the problems with *A Child of Our Time* is that the verbal music remains all too intrusive. It would be tempting to suggest a connection between the rather bland cliché that opera represents an ideal if outmodedly one-sided 'marriage' between words and music, and the title of Tippett's first opera. In an important article in the *Times Literary Supplement*, published a day after his fourth opera *The Ice Break* (1973–6) was premiered, Tippett explained that he accepted Wagner's point that Shakespearian drama with its multiplicity of scenes was no longer appropriate to the social and cultural reality of the modern world. With the experience of two destructive world wars within his lifetime and society poised on the brink of the new social and aesthetic configuration he identified with the Age of Aquarius, Tippett was determined to find an operatic vehicle which was capaciously mythical and in which the *music* crucially – not the libretto – had the power to lift the ordinary and mundane onto a plane of transcendence.

Tippet worked long and hard on his first full-scale opera; Ian Kemp suggests that it occupied him in various forms for a decade. However, the basic material of *The Midsummer Marriage*, in keeping with Tippett's Jungian reliance on 'involuntary' or unwilled messages from the unconscious, was given to him in the form of an image: 'I *saw* a stage picture (as opposed to hearing a musical sound).' This was of a hilltop temple in which a 'warm and soft' young man was rejected by a 'cold and hard' young woman. The device of a lovers' quarrel in a midsummer landscape was one with obvious Shakespearian connotations, but Mark and Jenifer are also latter-day versions of Tamino and Pamina in Mozart's *Die Zauberflöte*, another hermetic opera much concerned with the progress of the self towards successful individuation by means of union with its opposites. Nevertheless, *The Midsummer Marriage* is not an 'opera of ideas' or of straightforward advocacy like the tragic operas of Alan Bush (born 1900), and it is much more obviously operatic than the 'musical theatre' of Peter Maxwell Davies or Harrison Birtwistle.

The *Ritual Dances* are (with one exception) embedded in the second act of *The Midsummer Marriage*. Though they have had a separate life as concert pieces and recordings, in order to understand how they function in the opera, it is necessary to give a sense of its curious schema and plot. The stage represents a hillside with a Greek temple at the top. To the right a flight of steps ends poised in the air; to the left another flight descends into the hillside itself. The imagery emerged directly from Tippett's original vision and constitutes one of the opera's central oppositions. A chorus of friends gather to celebrate the elopement of Mark and Jenifer, names with a strong mythical resonance for the adoptive West Countryman, Jenifer being a variant of Guinevere. The celebrants are halted by the sight of the temple and the magical music (celesta and flute, as in *Die Zauberflöte*) that issues from it. They hide and watch Strephon (who is to be Mark's 'shadow') emerge and dance with the Ancients. Mark interrupts, demanding a new dance for his wedding day, but is told not to intrude on the ancient ritual, until a male Ancient trips Strephon and the dancers depart with the promise that Mark *will* learn new steps before the day is out.

After a magnificent lyrical aria from Mark, Jenifer arrives, but without her bridal clothes. Explaining that she seeks truth, not love, she mounts the right-hand stairs (which represent the masculine principle of *animus*) and disappears. After hearing the voice of his fiancée's father King Fisher, Mark takes the left-hand flight down into Mother Earth. There is already a tonal code to the work in which A major seems to represent the principle of light and E♭ the shadow side of the Ancients. Virtually all the music works within some variant of that code and every vocal utterance has to be read or heard relative to its exact tonal coloration. Mark's aria explores the range with a mixture of superficial self-confidence and incriminating self-doubt. In order to achieve a meaningful union, Mark and Jenifer have to exchange some of their more entrenched characteristics.

King Fisher, whose name Tippett has likened to Duke Ellington's, but who is clearly also an inverted avatar of the mythological Fisher King, is identified by the same $\frac{3}{8}$ dance as the Ancients' and is the living symbol of authority. Not finding his daughter, he calls on his secretary Bella (the first of the 'rude mechanicals') to search for her. King Fisher cannot enlist the Ancients' help in finding the couple and is only able to buy the assistance of some of their male friends; the women remain obdurately loyal. Bella is sent to get her boyfriend Jack, a cheerful factotum with a limited unconscious life: his business card gives his trades and hourly rate, 'but it can't tell you what I dream'. Jack and Bella stand for the Papageno–Papagena pair in *Die Zauberflöte*, the simple souls who represent a comic foil to the two main characters.

Like Mark, Jack is warned off, but the men press forward until Jenifer, then Mark reappear, transformed into variants of Athene and Dionysus respectively. In two magnificent arias, accompanied by a girl trumpeter in Jenifer's case, a boy with cymbals behind Jack, they find themselves still at odds. As her father is pushed to the fringes of the scene, she holds up a mirror to Jack's animal nature, before dropping it and descending into the earth in an attempt to recover her spiritual balance. Jack departs by the opposite stairway. Their friends pronounce them 'the laughing children' (a variant on lines in Eliot's 'Burnt Norton'), which was at one point Tippett's first choice for the opera's title.

The second act begins after noon. The scene is the same as for Act I, but is now at a slightly different angle, a perspectival shift very typical of Tippett's work. Strephon begins to dance, but breaks off when he hears the chorus beginning their midsummer celebrations. As is traditional, Bella proposes to Jack, a beautiful duet that touches on Mozartian models. As they move off into the wood, Strephon strikes an attitude for the first of the three animal transformations and chases that make up the *Ritual Dances*. At their climax, with Strephon apparently about to be caught by the Hawk-dancer, there are screams of fright from Bella, who has been watching, and the magic is dispersed. There is a brief, comic–tender interlude in which Bella sings 'They say a woman's glory is her hair', before telling Jack that King Fisher has places for them both in a new plan to recover Mark and Jenifer. The act ends with an orchestral version of the magical music and with Dionysian cries offstage.

The final act begins at twilight. The temple is once again in the same configuration as Act I and the celebrants are finishing a meal. King Fisher calls up his clairvoyante Madame Sosostris, a figure familiar from *The Waste Land*. While Bella relays King Fisher's demands to the Ancients, the chorus bear onstage a shrouded figure, a false Sosostris played by Jack in his protean Trickster guise. In the confusion that follows, the real Sosostris appears, shrouded in veils. After an elaborate invocation, she sings of Jenifer's and Mark's mystical union, in which male and female elements are in perfect balance. King Fisher intervenes angrily, smashing to the ground the bowl from which Sosostris scries her wonderfully dramatic vision. He then attempts to suborn Jack again, offering him a gun and holster in order to unmask Sosostris. He refuses and goes off with Bella, and when King Fisher himself unveils Sosostris, it is to reveal a huge lotus bud. Inside, in the classic intertwined pose of Shiva and Shakti, are Mark and Jenifer. King Fisher aims the pistol at his daughter's lover, but at a glance from Mark–Siva, he falls dead to the ground and is borne away to a magnificent seventeenth-century antiphonal hymn. It becomes clear that he has been a priestly sacrifice. Strephon prepares the fourth and final *Ritual Dance*, this time celebrating fire; Mark and Jenifer join him in the lotus, which erupts into flame before the stage goes dark. As a misty dawn breaks, the couple can be heard again, asking in wonderment: 'Was it a vision? Was it a dream?' They reappear in human form and in wedding clothes and this time Jenifer accepts the ring from her husband.

Such an abrupt summary almost inevitably emphasizes those elements of *The Midsummer Marriage*, which are likely to seem pretentious and over-wrought, and occasionally bafflingly inconsistent. Fully staged, it has an internal coherence, derived largely from the music but also from Tippett's symbolic choreography. Why, then, separate the four *Ritual Dances*, which might seem to be the most carefully integrated element of the whole rather ramshackle structure? In the first place, they stand out precisely *because* they are so coherent and self-contained. They were written on a commission from the Swiss conductor Paul Sacher, and premiered by him almost two years before *The Midsummer Marriage* was first staged at Covent Garden. There is no doubt, however, that they were always intended to be an integral part of the opera. As Ian Kemp insists, 'they are in no way a *divertissement* or a concession to some operatic convention, [but are] inextricably connected with the nature and rationale of the work, a point confirmed by the fact that the ritual they enact is not completed until Act III, when the fourth dance takes place'. Though obvious, this latter point is often overlooked.

The dances are extremely stylized. Each is signalled by a group of solemnly ritualistic chords, somewhat akin to the Masonic chords in *Die Zauberflöte*. There then follows a 'transformation', in which Strephon and a girl dancer take on animal form, while the other dancers organize themselves as a stand of trees. In the concert suite Tippett wrote for Sacher, as Kemp and others have noted, these preparations seem a little orotund. In the stage version recorded here, trimmed for dramatic reasons at the time of Colin Davis's 1968 Covent Garden revival, they are tackled with great straightforwardness, there being no need for offstage changes of costume. The four dances represent a cycle of seasons and of the four mythological elements. The first represents 'The Earth in Autumn'. Strephon is transformed into a Hare, an animal with Trickster associations, and thus connected in Tippett's mythological schema to Jack, a country name for the hare, as well as to Mark. He is pursued by a girl-dancer in the shape of a Hound. The Hare's music, which is dominated by the magical sounds of horn, bell and flute, is skittish and deceptive, full of false trails and sudden changes of direction. By direction, his pursuer is conveyed by a solid ground bass, in darker earth tones from the harp, cello and double bass. The rhythm of pursuit accelerates, but the Hound is no match for the crafty Hare, who escapes to a bold and somewhat complacent theme.

This dissolves at the start of the second dance, which takes place in the chill of winter waters, suggested by rather colourless woodwinds, and by the shift of Strephon's theme from flute to clarinets. This time, he is transformed into a Fish, and his pursuer is an Otter; less dogged, perhaps, than the Hound, and with an unmistakable sense of fun, she chases him through an uncertain, swirling environment. As with the first pursuit, the dance music is divided into repeating segments, in each of which elements of the work's overall tonal progression can be heard. Essentially, the dances move from a resigned A minor through a rather hermetic E♭ minor (a tense and awkward key for the orchestra) to the mature individuation of D major and the 'springtime' key of A major, suggesting rebirth. There is a complementary and not always evident movement in the dance melodies from low E to C, which significantly recurs at the end, with the apotheosis of Mark and Jenifer.

In the cold stream, the Fish has miscalculated, and allows himself to be caught by a tree-root; the tree-dancers have lined the river bank. In pulling free, he tears his scales, and the triumphant dance of escape has an awkward syncopation which is startlingly like the movement of a tired and damaged fish at the end of its fight. In the archetypal drama, the Fish's wound will be passed on to the next avatar. In spring, Strephon is changed into a small Bird, while his pursuer is a Hawk. As he pecks grain in the cornfield sown by the other dancers, it becomes evident that he is hampered by a broken wing and unable to fly up to his mate: grounded bassoon and twittering oboe. Again Tippett gives the music a strongly representational cast, suggesting the Bird's awkward attempts to fly and the stealth and violent speed of the raptor who chases him (a sparrow-hawk or peregrine, I would guess, rather than a hovering kestrel). But it is clear that the Bird's time is almost up. Again the dance is made up of repeating sub-sections and these accelerate ominously. As we have seen, it is only Bella's scream that interrupts the dance and saves the Bird.

The final dance is located much later in the opera and is very much more abstract in character. After the dead march for King Fisher, the annunciatory chords are sounded again, but this time Strephon prepares a ritual fire, rustling friction from the strings and sudden sparks from a single trumpet. The chorus shouts ecstatically as the flames take hold, establishing the elemental significance of this final section, which is concerned with the sacrifice and sublimation of individual personality in the mystic marriage. The dance is a glorious, expressive canon. Fuelled by low shouts from the Ancients and Chorus and replenished by downward figures from the orchestra, Mark and Jenifer reach a climax – in every applicable sense – with shuddering cries of 'Rejoice! rejoice!', words which had not yet been devalued in British culture by political use but which sitting coldly on the page suggest nothing of the powerful tension-and-release, carnal passion and philosophical calm with which Tippett invests the final pages of the opera. The end, as in Eliot, is the beginning. The wedding vows are exchanged, and Mark and Jenifer walk off into the distance united.

Tippett has continued to write music into his ninth decade and must now be accounted the senior British composer since the death of Ralph Vaughan Williams. Though large, the discography is still patchy (there is no currently available version of *The Midsummer Marriage* as a whole). The *Ritual Dances* are perhaps now much better known than the opera as a whole. John Pritchard, who conducted the opera's premiere, gave a magnificent account of the concert suite on an Argo 2-LP set (see below) which paired the dances with *A Child of Our Time*. That is still worth seeking out, but Davis's reading is as powerful as one could wish, and overdue for CD transfer.

Discographical Information

Other recordings: Carlyle, Remedios, Bainbridge, Dean, Chorus and Orchestra of the Royal Opera House, Covent Garden, Davis (Philips 6527 112 LP); Morison, Bowden, Lewis, Standen, Royal Liverpool Philharmonic Choir and Orchestra, Pritchard (Argo ZDA 19/20 2LP); also Nimbus NI 5217; Pye CCL 30114/5; Philips 6580 093; EMI EL 27 0273 1; complete opera on Philips 6500 125/127.

Other Tippett: *A Child of Our Time* (1939–41; RPO Records 7012); String Quartet no. 3 (1945–6 [complete quartets]; Collins Classics 70062); *The Ice Break* (1973–6; Virgin Classics 59048); Symphony no. 4 (1976–7; London 433668); Triple Concerto (1978–9; Nimbus NI 5301); *The Blue Guitar* (1982–3; New Albion NA 032).

Map references: Ralph Vaughan Williams, Symphony no. 3: *A Pastoral Symphony* (1916–21; Classics for Pleasure CDEMX 2192); David Bedford, *Music for Albion Moonlight* (1965; Argo ZRG 638 LP); Richard Rodney Bennett, *All the King's Men* (1968; Abbey XMS 703 LP).

Further reading: M. Bowen, *Michael Tippett*, London, 1982; I. Kemp, *Tippett: The Composer and His Music*, Oxford, 1984.

BOHUSLAV MARTINŮ (1890–1959)

Gilgameš (1954–1955)

FIRST PERFORMED: Basle, 24 January 1958
SELECTED RECORDING: Marco Polo 8.223316

> Ivan Kusjner (Gilgamesh), Štefan Margita (Enkidu and The Hunter), Ludek Vele (The Spirit of Enkidu and Narrator), Eva Depoltovà (Woman), Milan Karpišek (Narrator [spoken]), Slovak Philharmonic Choir and Orchestra, conducted by Zdeněk Košler

RECORDED: 23 and 24 November 1989
DURATION: 55′ 24″

On the twentieth anniversary of his death, Bohuslav Martinů's remains were taken from Schonenberg in Switzerland, where he had spent the last two years of his life, and re-interred in a family plot at Polčka, in present-day Czechoslovakia. It was a slightly ironic homecoming, since the most profoundly Czech of modern composers had never been widely accepted in his native country, and had spent most of the second half of his life in exile. Until the centenary celebrations of 1990, his general reputation was a little depressed, presumably on the grounds that any composer who had produced so much music could hardly have lavished sufficient attention on individual works.

Martinů was certainly among the most prolific of modern composers, with an output that recalls Haydn (an influence on the 1949 *Sinfonia concertante*) and earlier eighteenth-century figures like Giovanni Sammartini and Boccherini, who could rely on a well-founded court and church patronage system. In his younger years, Martinů was forced to hack out a living writing for whatever medium – stage, concert hall, radio – offered a fee; he was a pioneering spirit in television opera, then a new and exciting form, with *Čimčlověkžije* (roughly *Reasons for Living*) and *Ženitba* (*Marriage*, both 1952). His work incorporated popular forms, such as the 'jazz' influences on *La revue de cuisine* (1927) and the patently misnamed *Jazz Suite* (1928), or the rumbustious crowd-effects of *Half-Time* (1924), a piece inspired by a football match. Only when the String Quintet (1927) – some historians indicate that it was the later String Sextet (1932) – won the Elizabeth Sprague Coolidge Prize were he and his wife able to step off the treadmill; for a time, Charlotte Quennehen had supported him by mending shirts.

Interestingly, Martinů saved his best work for last, though most of it has a chastened, almost tragic quality that stands in sharp contrast to the early work. The last of seven string quartets, known as *Concerto da camera* (1947), seemed the pinnacle of his ability to combine rhythmic folkish melodies with generous neo-classical counterpoint, learned in Paris in the mid-1920s. Like his compatriot Bartók, he had good reason to be grateful to America, which took him in on 31 March 1941 and in particular to Serge Koussevitzky, who commissioned the first of the symphonies (a form he could not have afforded to tackle thitherto). Between then and 1946 he wrote four more; the last, known as *Fantaisies symphoniques* (1951–3) and premiered in 1955, had been a commission from Charles Munch for the seventy-fifth anniversary of the Boston Symphony Orchestra, and was easily the best.

The war cut across Martinů's life, as it had Bartók's, disorientating him painfully, but also sparking some of his most intense music. The next significant accolade after the Elizabeth Sprague Coolidge award had been Martinů's inclusion by the Nazis in a list of 'degenerate' composers (a reliable confirmation at that time that an artist was working along the right lines). At the end of the war, the Communists had taken over in Czechoslovakia and it was impossible for him to return. Martinů had a serious fall in 1948 and the injuries undermined his health. Between 1953 and 1955 he lived in Nice, returning to the USA for a further year's teaching in Philadelphia before settling in Europe again, first in Rome, then finally in Switzerland. It was during this time in the south of France that he wrote *Gilgameš*.

It was an appropriate choice of text for a world that seemed to have been returned to the furies and demonic presences of ancient Babylon and which was only just picking itself up out of the rubble that was the destiny of all great kingdoms. Preserved on a dozen tablets from the library of the first century BC Assyrian King Ashurbanipal, and supplemented by more recent archaeological findings, *The Epic of Gilgamesh* is a tale of heroism with an impressively individualized and complex central character. Gilgamesh seems to have been an historical figure, one of the kings of Uruk in the third millennium BC, but having established the lineaments of his hero in the first section, Martinů concentrates on those later tablets that concern Gilgamesh's friendship with Enkidu, a warrior figure who in certain regards anticipates Adam, Samson, Esau, John the Baptist and Christ. It is a story of loyalty and loss, a society embattled by the gods, but able to sustain a certain human resilience even in the face of vast impersonal forces.

The *Gilgamesh* fragments were originally written in cuneiform Akkadian. In 1928 the first portions of an English translation became available, edited by Campbell Thompson, and it was this version that Martinů, never a comfortable English speaker, began to use, reverting to a Czech version for the final text. Thompson's work has been superseded by further archaeological discoveries (though there is no way of determining a canonical text of *Gilgamesh*) and by the work of later translators such as Stephanie Dalley, a Fellow in Assyriology at the Oriental Institute, Oxford. However, Martinů was less concerned with philological and archaeological precision and much more with the problems of investing the Gilgamesh and Enkidu story with the 'prayerful' and mysterious qualities demanded of the oratorio form.

Perhaps the most significant twentieth-century works in oratorio form had been written by the Franco-Swiss Arthur Honegger (1892–1955) who died not long after Martinů had completed *Gilgameš* and whose *Le roi David* (1921) and *Jeanne d'Arc au bûcher* (1934–5) were premiered in Basle exactly twenty years before Martinů's work was presented there. Though Honegger used identifiably Christian material, the two pieces saw him move away from orthodox Biblical texts and towards a more personal, psychologized perspective that also allowed him to take account of the redemptive hero(ine)'s interaction with the wider society of his/her times. This is essentially true of Martinů's treatment of Gilgamesh.

The musical setting is unmistakably solemn. Each of the three approximately equal length sections begins with dark, mysterious sounds and throughout the work Martinů uses spare instrumental textures to complement the voices. The work opens with the bass Narrator singing Gilgamesh's praises, soon to be joined by the chorus. There is no reference in Martinů's text to the hero's one-third divinity, nor does it follow the original text in likening him to a powerful bull or ox, but the music conveys a certain brutal power that renders the chorus's joyous acceptance – 'He is our shepherd, masterful, dominant!' – faintly ironic.

Embedded in the opening music, there are yearning, unresolved chords that suggest Gilgamesh's loneliness and underscore his people's sense that his appetites and energies are somehow beyond human scale. The goddess Aruru breaks off a piece of desert clay and shapes the warrior Enkidu, a shaggy figure with hair like a woman (the unaccompanied bass recitative is punctuated by a single ironic clarinet note at this point). Enkidu keeps to the wild places, feeding (and implicitly coupling) with the cattle and wild deer. As the tenor recounts in speech, this frightens a hunter, who turns to Gilgamesh (or 'his father' in Martinů's version) for advice. The bass suggests that Enkidu be tempted into the human world by the harlot Shamhat, and the chorus offers a lively account of the first encounter. The seduction itself is encouraged by the tenor in a beautiful rhapsodic melody over a rocking, almost sensual rhythm. The bass and chorus then confirm Enkidu's humanization, and, in a rapturous response to his caresses, the woman apostrophizes his Godlike form and leads him toward Erech (Uruk), whose beguilements are conveyed by wordless singing from the sopranos and altos. Personified by the tenor, Enkidu declares his challenge to Gilgamesh and the mighty contest that follows. Part 1 ends with the two heros reconciled in the accompaniment, firm friends.

Martinů opens the second part, 'The Death of Enkidu', with sombre tones from muted brass suggestive of a funeral march. The chorus sings mournfully of death, while the speaker reveals Enkidu's fatal sickness: he has been struck down for having rejected the advances of Ishtar, goddess of love, and having killed the bull she sends as his nemesis. The tenor rises out of a troubled accompaniment with an account of his death-dream, a disturbing vision which has him go down into the nether regions where he is seen by the Queen of the Underworld. From here to the end of the second section the music sustains a high level of emotion as Gilgamesh distractedly laments his friend's fading life while the chorus insistently reminds him that the power of life and death is not in man's hands but the gods'. The orchestra, in its fullest and most developed scoring so far, adds an elegiac note.

Part 3, 'Invocation', recounts Gilgamesh's attempts to contact his dead friend. In response to the soprano's question, he describes his loss. The speaker, accompanied by a wordless female chorus, recounts Gilgamesh's conviction that 'only the earth' has seized Enkidu, that he will return to the upper air. The soprano and the chorus join him in a long, impassioned prayer of intercession successfully to Enlil, to the Moon-God and to Eia, and at last Enkidu ascends. The music takes on an atmosphere of the profoundest mystery, as Enkidu (now represented by the bass) answers each of his friend's questions with an enigmatic 'I saw, I saw', and the music ends darkly and abruptly with the final mystery intact.

It is a powerfully dramatic moment, beautifully portrayed on the 1989 Marco Polo recording. Its predecessor on Supraphon was perfectly authentic in matters of phrasing and orchestration (and was attractively cheap), but it lacked the drama and the emotional wallop that the new recording has in abundance. Only in the wartime *Polníl mše* (*Field Mass* 1939) and in *Proroctví Izaiášovo* (*The Prophecy of Isaiah*, 1959) did Martinů harvest such a rich poetic yield as in *Gilgameš*, and he did not live to hear the later work performed. When *Gilgameš* was premiered, he was already showing symptoms of the cancer that was to kill him eighteen months later. It has taken even his admirers time to winnow out the chaff, but his work is now widely recognized and respected, and *Gilgameš* is rightly hailed as one of the uncontestably great vocal works of the period.

Discographical Information

Other recordings: Machotková, Zahradníček, Zitek, Prusa, Broušek, Czech Philharmonic Chorus, Prague SO, Behlohlavek (Supraphon 1121 808).

Other Martinů *Half-Time* (1924; Supraphon CO 1669); *Le revue de cuisine* (1927; Reference RR 29); *Field Mass* (1939; Chandos CHAN 9138); Symphony no. 1 (1941; Multisonic 31 0023); Symphony no. 6: *Fantaisies symphoniques* (1951–3; Bis CD 402); *The Prophecy of Isaiah* (1959, op. posth. Supraphon 11 0751).

Map references: Camille Saint-Saëns, *Le Déluge* (1876; Adda 581261); Arthur Honegger, *Le roi David* (1921; Supraphon 11 0132); and *Jeanne d'Arc au bûcher* (1934–5; Supraphon 11 057); Per Nørgård, *Gilgamesh* (1971–2; Marco Polo DCCD 9001).

Further reading: M. Šafránek, *Bohuslav Martinů; His Life and Works*, London, 1962; S. Dalley (trans. and ed.), *Myths from Mesopotamia*, Oxford, 1989.

IGOR STRAVINSKY (1882–1971)

Agon **(1953–1957)**

FIRST PERFORMED: Los Angeles, 17 June 1957
SELECTED RECORDING: Sony SM3K 46292
  Los Angeles Festival Symphony Orchestra, conducted by the com-
  poser
  [with: *Apollo*; *Le baiser de la fée*; *Jeux de cartes*; *Orpheus*; *Pulcinella*; *Scènes
  de ballet*; Tchaikovsky, arranged Stravinsky, *Bluebird pas de deux*]
RECORDED: 1957
DURATION: 23′ 44″

Unlike its predecessors, Stravinsky's last ballet has no mythological,
narrative or choreographic subject. It may sound as if it follows logically on from *Apollo* (*Apollon musagète*, 1927–8, 1947) and *Orpheus*
(1946–7), but it is quite independent of these, and the composer's only
intention was to illustrate a set of dances he had seen reproduced in a
French manual published in the 1600s. There are twelve of them in all,
and the number has a special significance, for *Agon* marks a highly significant point of change in Stravinsky's work.

He had been similarly inspired in his immediately previous dramatic
work *The Rake's Progress* (1948–51), written to a libretto by W. H. Auden
and Chester Kallman (see entry on Hans Werner Henze, p. 155). The
opera had been suggested by a set of prints after William Hogarth, and
has a breezy character quite appropriate to its eighteenth-century
subject matter and robustly moral stance. A matter of months after the
premiere, Stravinsky was still inclined to be dismissive of serialism;
expressing admiration for the 'discipline' and 'purity' of the serialists,
but suspicious of their thrall to the 'figure twelve'. For Stravinsky, there
was still 'quite enough to do with the seven notes of the scale'. This
sounds like a fairly confident reiteration of the neo-classical position,
but within three or four years, to the considerable surprise of everyone
who observed his progress, there were signs of a change of heart.

The Cantata on four anonymous English poems and the Septet, both
finished in 1952, contained some serial elements. These were developed
further in two more vocal pieces, an *In memoriam Dylan Thomas* (1954)
for tenor, string quartet and four trombones, and *Canticum sacrum ad
honorem Sancti Marci nominis* (1955) for tenor, baritone, chorus and
orchestra. What was most surprising was that Stravinsky should at this
point have gravitated to the most austere, least 'classical' of the serialist
trinity, Anton Webern. *Agon* is certainly marked by Webern's almost
anorexic self-sufficiency of material and instrumental textures; it is a
very stripped-down and austere score, conceived without reference to

staging or any other visual association. It calls for a very large orchestra, but uses it only in carefully judged subdivisions.

Agon has more faster passages than almost any of Stravinsky's postwar scores. Talking to his confidant and amanuensis Robert Craft, who conducted the Los Angeles premiere, the composer suggested that *Agon* contains 'three times as much music for the same clock length as some other pieces of mine', a development he linked to the 'operations of memory': 'We are located in time constantly in a polyphonic work, whether Josquin's *Duke Hercules Mass* or a serially composed non-tonal-system work.' The reference to Josquin des Prés (*c.* 1450–1521) offers an intriguing clue to the kind of music Stravinsky created in *Agon*, for simultaneously with his partial conversion to serial procedures he was also exploring the polyphonic part-writing of very early Renaissance music; a very similar synthesis can be traced in early, Stravinsky-influenced works by Peter Maxwell Davies.

The conversion was indeed partial. A composer of Stravinsky's intuitive brilliance was unlikely to submit to any ready-made system, and he was inclined to play down the more ideological implications of his change of style. Talking to Craft, he pointed to the difference between changes in scientific paradigms, where new discoveries tended to cancel out previously held truths, and artistic ideas, where innovation ideally joined a long continuum. Regarding his own *Elegy for J.F.K.* (1964), an astonishing piece scored for baritone, two clarinets and basset horn, he suggested that a 'serialist autopsy' was largely irrelevant because he had written the piece as a sequence of melodic fragments, with no hint of the predetermination that goes along with serial writing. He told Craft that 'the intervals of my series are attracted by tonality; I compose vertically and this is, in one sense at least, to compose tonally'. (There was a brief, but interesting argument about the validity of 'atonality' as a term. Schoenberg argued that it should be 'atonicality', since the absence of a tonic was what distinguished so-called atonal music; furthermore, 'atonality', construed logically, meant music with no tones. It is a minor point, but it reinforces Stravinsky's refusal to accept that he was 'no longer' composing 'tonally'.)

It was not until the *Mouvements* (1958–9) for piano and orchestra that Stravinsky wrote a concert work in which all parameters of the music, not just pitch, were determined by serial procedures. There is, though, a further element of serial organization in *Agon* in the disposition of the twelve separate dances, with three brief interposing sections and a coda. These begin with a 'Pas de quatre', which is completely non-serial, and dominated by a brilliant fanfare; in choreographic terms this piece is then doubled and tripled to introduce all twelve dancers, eight female, four male, and so complete the first section; the 'Pas de quatre' recurs at the very end of the piece. By using internal groupings of the orchestra in very distinct juxtapositions, Stravinsky gives the opening piece a marked late-medieval quality. After a short prelude, there follow a triple-time 'Saraband', a 'Gaillarde' (which was also known in England by the French name *cinq-pas*, after its fifth, skip step), and a 'Coda', which introduces a measure of serial organization at the exact centre of the piece. Tiny serial structures run through the 'Bransle simple' to the end of the eleventh dance, 'Four Trios', at which point the opening 'Pas de quatre' reaffirms itself. The row Stravinsky uses is E♭, D E F C B D♭, B♭, A♭, A G G♭. Disposed rhythmically, it gives the serial miniatures in the second half of *Agon* a symmetry and poise that is characteristic of the work as a whole. Stravinsky uses one or two slightly unconventional devices to marry the tonal (vertical) language with the rhythmic or horizontal. There are traces of jazz, reminiscent of his own earlier practice in *Histoire du soldat*, in the third section; referring to his use of it, Stravinsky said 'jazz is a mode, not a music', and made no effort to give it an authentic flavour. (He made a similar comment about 'Aléatorisme', contrasting it with 'Sérialisme' and silence, which had to do with the very body of the music, its order and duration.) In the opening section and the 'Gaillarde' he uses a mandolin (originally it was a guitar), sometimes paired with a harp; in the eighth dance, the 'Bransle gay', he uses castanets to count out a repetitive metrical pattern; in the interlude between groups two and three, the timpani repeat a D♭–B♭ figure which serves as the fulcrum of the whole suite.

As with *The Rake's Progress*, Stravinsky had been sparked off by visual images, in this case the illustrations to de Lauze's seventeenth-century *Apologie de la danse*. His scoring of the 'Bransle simple' was influenced by an engraving of two trumpeters in the manual. Elsewhere, the music has the same hard-edged simplicity of outline, favouring instrumental groups by virtue of timbre. After the 'Bransle double', Stravinsky returns to a more formal division of dances: a 'Pas de deux', four duos, four trios and, as a coda, a repeat of the opening 'Pas de quatre'. It is a simple way of asserting the coherence of the structure, but it is highly effective.

Discussing the work, Pieter C. van den Toorn (sounding breathless himself) suggests that 'it is *the whole of Agon* [his emphasis], the whole of its vast, pluralistic reach in historical reference, that is bold, unique, and – because the synthesis "works" – breathtakingly – well-nigh miraculous'. He says this because of the critics' tendency to regard the piece as a mishmash, knocked out at a time when Stravinsky was in transition 'from neo-classicism to serialism'. To some extent, Stravinsky and Craft colluded in that interpretation, in flat contradiction of the composer's previous refusal to accept 'progressivism' as a principle of art. The view stated in the *Conversations* (1959) is much closer to his usual position. (As with almost every page of Craft's copious transcriptions, it is difficult to hear Stravinsky – whose English was never good – actually *saying* such things; the composer sensibly insisted that Craft be listed as co-author rather than as mere amuensis, and we have to assume that at least some quotations are true to the spirit of Stravinsky's position if not an actual record of his words.) No one else who knew him at the time remembers him as being as tersely aphoristic as he appears in *Conversations*:

> Every age is a historical unity (...) I was born to causality and determinism, and I have survived to probability theory and chance ... But I was also born to a non-progressivist notion of the practice of my art, and on this point, though I have survived into a musical society that pursues the opposite idea, I have not been able to change.

(Some observers, obviously eager to preserve a neo-classical continuity have explained Stravinsky's 'turn' to serialism by reference to the death of Schoenberg – the last of the three founding fathers – in 1951, an event that, symbolically at least, moved serialism into the 'classical' past.)

This may have some incidental validity, but the premises are wrong. It is clearly as nonsensical to divide Stravinsky's career with a black line into the neo-classical and the serialist, as it is to suggest that *Agon* is a slipshod experiment. It is one of the most achieved and coherent of the late works, as van den Toorn suggests, and Stravinsky took great pains over it. The work had been commissioned – and was dedicated to – George Balanchine and Lincoln Kirstein, co-founders of the New York City Ballet. Stravinsky began writing, starting with the 'Pas de quatre' in 1953, but put the score aside, as he had done with *Le rossignol* (begun in 1908, finished in 1914, made into a ballet, *Le chant du rossignol*, in 1920 and further revised in 1962). He explained that 'such music cannot be composed in a hurry'.

By the time Stravinsky resumed the work in 1956, it was already clear that he intended something very different from the earlier ballets. 'I told [George Balanchine] he had done so well in adjusting dances to symphonies that I would like to write a special symphony with the dance in mind. It is to be a dancing symphony'. Far from being a peripheral, tentative work, *Agon* (a title the composer intended to be read quite neutrally as a 'dance match' or 'dance contest') joins that class of non-symphonic modern orchestral works – Bartók's Concerto for Orchestra most obviously – which nonetheless communicate the same grand structural unities and tensions as the classical symphony. It is time that *Agon* was treated more respectfully. Stravinsky's 'dancing symphony' is one of his greatest achievements and, relative to the composer's own lofty eminence in twentieth-century music, that places it very high indeed. Stravinsky was held in reverence by his fellow-musicians, and after he died in 1971 the man who had written so many touching memorials for friends and public figures (including T. S. Eliot and Aldous Huxley) himself became the object of an astonishing outpouring of emotion; threnodies for Stravinsky represent a virtual sub-genre. The only pity is that it and the emotion it expresses have misted up perceptions of the great man's own work.

Discographical Information

Other recordings: Melbourne SO, Iwaki (Virgin Classics VC 7 9101); Leningrad SO, Mravinsky (Olympia OCD 224); London Sinfonietta, Atherton (Argo ZRG 937); Boston SO, Leinsdorf (RCA Victor CSC 2879/RB 6673); South-West German Radio Orchestra Baden-Baden, Leinsdorf (Vega C30A/Wergo WER 50002); the 1964 Stravinsky recording has also been released on CBS BRG 72438, Columbia ML 5215, Philips ML 5215.

Other Stravinsky: [after 1939 only; see *The New Grove* or other sources for the Russian and neo-classical masterpieces] *Ebony Concerto* (1945; CBS MK 42227); Concerto in D (1946; Sony Classical SK 46667); *Orpheus* (1947; Chandos CHAN 9014); *The Rake's Progress* (1948–51; Sony M2K 46299); Double Canon (1959; Angel CDC 54347); *Tres sacrae cantiones de Gesualdo* (1960; Hyperion CDA 66410).

Map references: Nikolay Rimsky-Korsakov, *Dubinushka*; *chanson russe* (1905 [the year he began giving Stravinsky composition lessons]; Chandos CHAN 8783); Arnold Schoenberg, *Pierrot lunaire* (1911 [apparently the first work of the Second Viennese School Stravinsky encountered]; Elektra Nonesuch 79237); George Gershwin, Piano Concerto in F (1925; Angel CDC 54280); Anton Webern, Quartet (1930; Sony Classical SM3K 45845); Don Carlo Gesualdo's madrigals (*c.* 1585 [pub. Istituto Italiano per la Storia della Musica in 1942]; ECM New Series 1422/1423).

Further reading: E.. W. White, *Stravinsky: The Composer and His Works*, London, 1966, 2/1979; R. Craft, *Conversations with Igor Stravinsky* 1966, et al. (but see *caveat* in text); P. C. van den Toorn, *The Music of Igor Stravinsky* New Haven and London, 1983; many, many others.

TON de LEEUW (born 16 November 1926)

Mouvements rétrogrades (1957)

FIRST PERFORMED: Hilversum, 1957
SELECTED RECORDING: Olympia OCD 505 – *400 Years of Dutch Music*
    Het Residentie Orkest, The Hague, conducted by Ernest Bour
    [with: Matthijs Vermeulen, Symphony no. 4: *Les victoires* (1940–1);

Kees van Baaren, Septet (1952, violin, flute, oboe, clarinet, horn, bassoon, bass); Anthon van der Horst, Chorus II op. 67 ('La nuit') (1953–4, eight-part mixed chorus, orchestra); Otto Ketting, *Due canzoni per orchestra* (1957)]
RECORDED: 1980
DURATION: 11' 41"

With the Netherlands' industrial and commercial infrastructure almost wholly destroyed by concentrated Luftwaffe bombing and its civil society undermined by the depradations of the Nazi occupiers, Dutch culture found itself in a quite extraordinary position at the end of the Second World War, cut adrift even from its own recent past, a virtual *tabula rasa*. For Dutch musicians there was considerable symbolic significance in the destruction, during the German bombardment of Rotterdam in May 1940, of nearly all the scores of Willem Pijper (1894–1947), the most important pre-war composer in the Netherlands. Much of Pijper's work was later reconstructed by his pupil Karel Mengelberg; but when the war ended, it seemed necessary to younger composers (and to their government, which has been generous with commissions, travel grants and publishing awards) to begin afresh with a new musical language that had nothing to do with the past, or with prevailing Germanic models. There was no particularly vigorous nationalist or vernacular tradition in the Netherlands, no major repository of untapped folk music, and so younger Dutch composers inevitably began to look abroad.

Louis Andriessen (q.v.) has brought a satirical and politically committed edge to his work; born just as the war was beginning, he was drawn in his teens to American music, particularly that of Charles Ives, but also to jazz and popular forms, which were becoming the new international demotic. Ton de Leeuw, almost a generation older, and presumably able to remember the appalling destruction of the war years, looked even further afield, to non-Western musics. So did Theo Loevendie (q.v.), who had begun as a jazz clarinettist and led his own concert ensemble, but who fell under the spell of Turkish music on a visit there, starting to compose in earnest only relatively late. Few, interestingly, showed much interest in the dominant twelve-note style of the Darmstadt school, and Loevendie condemned Andriessen's former teacher Kees van Baaren (1906–70) for his 'conservative' decision to embrace serialism (as in the Septet, on the recording above). In fact, van Baaren had long been rather diffident about the serialist method; he had encountered the masters of the Second Viennese School on their home turf in the early 1920s, but on returning home had been warned off by Pijper, who considered serialism limiting. It is significant that van Baaren should only have turned to the method again in the immediate post-war period: symptomatic perhaps of an understandable appetite for ready-made systems.

De Leuw studied originally under Henk Badings (1907–89), a pupil of Pijper's and inheritor of the 'Pijper scale' of alternating tones and semitones (Rimsky-Korsakov had experimented with the same scale independently in Russia); among de Leeuw's first works was *Treuermuziek in memoriam Willem Pijper*, written in 1948. He was already showing an interest in non-European procedures when he went to Paris the following year to study with Olivier Messiaen and the Ukrainian-born Thomas de Hartmann (1885–1956), who had converted from Russian nationalism to embrace a rather mystical modernism. De Leeuw returned to the Netherlands in 1950 and studied for a further four years with Jaap de Kunst (1891–1960), curator of the Amsterdam Tropical Institute and the man widely credited with inventing the term 'ethnomusicology'.

After de Kunst's death, de Leeuw was to make study trips of his own to the Far East, visiting India and Persia, and later Japan and the Philippines; the first direct result of this experience was the orchestral dance *Nritta* (1961). However, his compositional philosophy was already developing in quite individual directions. *Job* (1956) was a prizewinning radio oratorio which exploited electronic tape; in 1958, he wrote the mostly serial String Quartet no. 1, but in the following year, he composed *Mouvements rétrogrades*, his most frequently performed and recorded work. It represents a significant point in his search for a music that dispenses with linear development in favour of a very static approach in which pitches are subject to quite different principles of organization than in Western music. Modal or scalar composition (which was also influential in jazz in the early 1950s) replaces the uniform hierarchy of the harmonic scale and its uneven steps and suspended resolutions with a system whereby any given note may be the root of a new scale or mode, without immediate reference to any other system. This is a limited interpretation of modality, which in Eastern musics, and most particularly in Indian composition, is extended to subsume every characteristic or parameter of the mode in question, giving it its individual identity and coloration. This is typical of Indian *raga* music, which utilizes individualized modes, with no harmonic progress or chord-changing whatever.

Scored for large orchestra, but imaginatively subdivided and often with the intimacy of chamber music, *Mouvements rétrogrades* consists of ten brief parts, each of which illuminates a different (often radically different) aspect of the same basic structure. These are divided into five main blocks with what de Leeuw describes as a 'musical mirror' at the centre. The opening section establishes the mysterious, non-progressive atmosphere of the piece, with dark sounds from cellos and basses following an opening articulation of a non-repetitive theme that is refracted through the succeeding sections. The second subdivision begins with soft bell tones on vibraphone and harp, with a solo violin playing a rhapsodic figure based on the first section, but sharing with a rising interval from the oboe. There are dark mutterings from the lower brass and an uneasy pizzicato throb from the cellos and basses again. The next section is a bright chase, embellished with piccolos and underlined by patterns on the snare drum. This gives way to the first big orchestral tutti, a brief quasi-march in double time which sounds like Shostakovich in his ironic mode. Skittish descending trills and triangle sounds lead into a restatement of the big orchestral figure on piano (another echo of Shostakovich, and particularly the Fifth Symphony), which suddenly seems transformed into one of the Eastern *tala* rhythms used by Messiaen in the *Turangalîla-symphonie*. This is taken up by the full orchestra, with brass dominant and timpani making their presence felt before the section comes to a strangely irresolute halt, just as the strings seemed ready to move off in another direction.

Dramatic drum rolls signal the next section, with brass breaking up the tempo of the fanfare-like opening. After a trumpet call and another response from the piano, the strings establish a mysterious atmosphere like that of the first section. This is the most developed section, with plaintive woodwinds establishing a new area of activity before re-emerging under the strings in a kind of dotted rhythm that recalls the *tala*-like figure of the previous part. There is a dramatic acceleration, signalled by percussion and strongly recalling Bartók, and the section ends with pounding brass and timpani, a reversal of the opening. The final part opens in the dominant dark mood, yielding to a probing, almost quizzical melody in the higher strings. There is a thunderous outbreak, echoing the end of the previous section, then a descent into a languid Bartókian 'night music', with a decidedly oriental feel. A sudden clarion call breaks briefly across the English horn's weaving, snake-charming line and the piece comes to a halt, with a sense of what de Leeuw calls a 'static equilibrium'.

In years to come, de Leeuw was to experiment with electronics in a much more structured way than he had with *Job*, and created one minor masterpiece in *Clair–obscur* (1981–2). At the same time, though, he also showed a growing interest in folkish scales with a clearly defined harmonic centre, moving away from the stasis of *Mouvements rétrogrades*. It remains, though, his most distinctive and completely original score, still much underrated but anticipating the work of such acknowledge geniuses of orchestration as Henri Dutilleux and Witold Lutosławski.

Discographical Information

Other recordings: [same performers, different issues] BFO/CVD 10; Radio Nederland RN 1965 109 531; Polygram 6814.781/786.

Other de Leeuw: *Nritta* (1961; RN Opus 65); *Spatial Music I* (1966; RN Opus 68); *Gending* (1975; Donemus CV 7602); *Car nos vignes sont en fleur* (1981; Donemus CV 8502); *Clair–Obscur* (1981–2; Donemus CVS 1986/6).

Map references: Willem Pijper, Concerto for piano and orchestra (1927; Olympia OCD 504); Charles Ives, Symphony no. 4 (1927, but only performed entire 1965; Sony Classical SK 44939); Thomas de Hartmann, *Concerto funèbre* (1939; RCA Red Seal 60370); Henk Badings, *Dialogues* (1967; Bis CD 160).

Further reading: T. de Leeuw, *Muziek van de twintigate eeuw* [Music of the twentieth century], Utrecht, 1964.

PETR EBEN (born 22 January 1929)

Nedělni hudba (1957–1959)

FIRST PERFORMED: Prague, 26 October 1959
SELECTED RECORDING: Supraphon 11 0564 2
   Kamila Klugarová (organ)
   [with: *Laudes* (1964) and *Hommage à Dietrich Buxtehude* (1987)]
RECORDED: September–December 1988
DURATION: 31' 10"

Arguably the two greatest organ composers of the twentieth-century died within a year of each other in 1991 and 1992. Both were Frenchmen, heirs to the great organ tradition of César Franck (1822–90), Charles-Marie Widor (1844–1937), Gabriel Pierné (1863–1937), Charles Tournemire (1870–1939), and slightly younger figures like Marcel Dupré (1886–1971) and Maurice Duruflé (1902–86). Olivier Messiaen studied with Dupré at the Paris Conservatoire and grew up listening to Widor at St-Sulpice and to Tournemire on the magnificent organ at Ste-Clotilde. Tournemire had inherited Franck's role as *maître de chapelle* there and his majestic organ symphonies and pancyclopaedic *L'orgue mystique* (1927–32) were a substantial influence on Messiaen, who nonetheless moved in a new and more exotic direction, exploiting the colossal tonal and coloristic range and multilinear capacity of the organ to reinforce his innovative conception of harmony and rhythm. By contrast, the blind Breton Jean Langlais (1907–91), Tournemire's successor at Ste-Clotilde, drew much of his basic material from Gregorian chant, but also from Celtic folklore. Langlais's abandonment of fixed tonality or regular barlines was often the result of his absorption in vernacular music, and he wrote surprisingly few straightforwardly fugal pieces, opting instead for a free, improvisational counterpoint that remains deeply refreshing.

There have been, of course, other contemporary composers for organ, though few as idiomatic as Messiaen or Langlais. In France, the hugely precocious Jehan Alain (1911–40) wrote well over one hundred works, mostly for organ, before his death in action. In the United States, Daniel Pinkham (born 1923) has been the most Messiaenic composer for organ, particularly in the fine *Toccatas for the Vault of Heaven* (1972) which also exploits electronics; an interest developed by the Dane Bengt Hambraeus (born 1928), who has exploited the huge clusters possible on the organ's multiple keyboard and pedals almost as if in imitation of the electronic music with which he was experimenting from the late 1950s, but with a vastly increased sonority. Hambraeus was also a distinguished interpreter of Messiaen's organ works, introducing them to Scandinavia. In Britain, the still vastly underrated Peter Dickinson (born 1934) has produced an impressive body of organ music in a work-list dominated by keyboard works, and including a superb Organ Concerto (1971).

No living composer, though, shows such an intimate and idiomatic grasp of organ as the Czech Petr Eben. He grew up in what he has described as the 'dreamy medieval town' of Cesky Krumlov, near the borders with Bavaria and Austria. Rapid conscription and mobilization at the start of the Second World War emptied the town of adult males and the ten-year-old Eben found himself in charge of the town organ. Imprisonment by the Nazis and subsequent Communist restrictions on cultural life lent his strong spiritual awareness a markedly humanistic coloration; he was influenced by the quasi-existentialism of the French philosopher and theologian Teilhard de Chardin, particularly the notion that the world is permanently in creation and that its perfectibility is advanced another step each time an act of creativity reduces the sum of disorder. This idea can be traced throughout Eben's work, much of which is programmatic or liturgical. The essential musical drama is the triumph of a freely rhythmic classical structure, usually played on full organ, over slight and metronomic themes which express temptation or repression, the beguilements of evil. This is true of the grand cycles *Faust* (1979–80), which was originally conceived as theatre music, and *Hiob* (1987), a hugely powerful reworking of the Book of Job that captured Eben's strong premonition (promptly fulfilled) that even the miseries of the Husák regime could not last for ever.

During the period of Communist rule, he regarded many of his pieces as coded messages of hope to his people. Perhaps his most important contribution to liturgical music was the *Missa cum populo* (1981–82), a post-Conciliar Mass for choir, brass, organ and congregation, premiered (appropriately) at Avignon the year after its completion. In 1990 the *Prague Te Deum* expressed Eben's joy at the 'velvet revolution' which had ousted the Communist Party and restored the continuum of Czech culture. Eben's classicism had steadily deepened during the 1970s as he moved away from his earlier synthesis of folkloristic themes (somewhat like Langlais's) with touches of Messiaen's almost surrealistic tone-colours. In *Greek Dictionary* (1974) for female chorus and harp, he produced his most explicit statement of the classical ideal, though its rote vocabulary lists perhaps also suggest how far modern culture has fallen away from that ideal. There is a hint of the same underlying sentiment in choral works such as *Desire of Ancient Things* (1984) and *Breath of Ancient Days* (1988), in the Ovid settings *Sempiternal Cosmetics* (1985), and in the earlier *Honour to Charles IV* (1978), in which the high cultural ideal is balanced by a heroic, almost military quality, conveying Eben's sense that civilized and spiritual values are not static or given, but require to be fought for.

That is very much the essence of *Nedělni hudba* or *Sunday Music*, a powerful symphonic work in the grand tradition. Along with *Windows* (1976) for trumpet and organ, a piece inspired by Marc Chagall's work in stained glass, it established Eben's reputation. The *Moto ostinato* third movement, with its grand battle theme, has become a popular organ showpiece, but the work as a whole is now among the most frequently performed and recorded in the contemporary repertoire. It is cast in four movements, and is broadly symphonic in outline, with a clearly discernible underlying programme. As in the *Symphonia gregoriana* (1954, organ, orchestra), the basic thematic material comes from plainchant. The opening 'Fantasias' draw on a *Kyrie* (or invocation) addressed to 'Orbis factor', 'Creator of the World'. Fantasia I develops the phrase into a linked series of rising trills, which grow out of a solemn but celebratory opening, constructing an elaborate cadenza that reaches its climax in a mighty restatement of the Kyrie on the full organ. Fantasia II has a simpler, but architecturally more ambitious structure, on which is suspended the sound of pealing bells. These are dispersed across the manuals and pedals as if to suggest a message (of hope? or warning?) being transmitted through the world. The opening *Kyrie* figure is again the basic material, but Eben breaks it into smaller units and widens the harmonic intervals considerably, giving this longer movement considerably more scope for development. Organ music devolves considerable responsibility to the performer, and is one of the very few classical genres which demands improvisation; Kamila Klugar-ová adds quite considerably to Fantasia II, extending it to over eight minutes, but without losing contact with the main development.

Eben has identified the famous third movement as a vision of primeval battle. Coming in place of the traditional symphonic scherzo, it has the same vivid energy and forward motion one might expect in such a place, except that Eben has constructed the movement over a relentless ostinato background which suggests a march even though the long–short–short metre, played on the trumpet stop of the organ is intended to suggest a call to battle. The *Moto ostinato* is a wildly exciting piece of music, with a tantalising promise of Apocalypse that never quite comes to pass, and it is an ideal place to start for anyone who has not hitherto experienced organ music as anything other than an emphysemic accompaniment to 'Rock of Ages'. The movement ends with an ambiguous stand-off, communicated by flurries of chords from all over the organ. The battle is not yet over.

The long, complex finale opens with the survivors regrouping under a new trumpet clarion, which develops into a hectic toccata, before disappearing in a fiercely dissonant haze, with long screaming runs up the keyboard. There is a sudden drop in volume, as if the conflict has broken off, and another plainchant theme becomes audible, symbolizing Christ's appearance on the eternal battlefield. This in turns develops canonically, bringing in more and more of the surrounding texture and perhaps symbolically beating the metallic weaponry of the battle scenes into ploughshares and pruninghooks. The final section begins with another virtual march, but a much less antagonistic one on this occasion, with joyous fanfares in the background and renewed hints of Christ's arrival. The closing recapitulation brings together the battle theme and the Christ theme in a heavy bass, harmonizing them until they are gradually overcome by a (literally) overwhelming welcome to the Mother of God, an apotheosis which symbolizes the final triumph of love.

Again, there is a degree of freedom (which will further depend on the instrument being played) as to how such passages should be realized. Organ scores are 'post-modern' to the extent that they only represent a partial specification of performances. Playing on the great organ in the Dvořák Hall of the House of Artists in Prague (Supraphon's headquarters), Klugarová does not give the final resolution quite the meltingly triumphalist impact that Haig Mardirosian does on the cathedral organ of St Thomas More, Arlington, Virginia, holding back just a little on the closing fanfares. Since her performance was supervised by the composer, it seems fair to assume that such an ending reflects his own interpretation of the drama. It certainly fits his broadly humanistic approach rather better than the more familiar ecstatic interpretation. The Supraphon recording also offers two later Eben works, which adds valuable context. The slightly later *Laudes* also draws on plainsong, but suggests very different interpretations of 'praise', which are quite consistent with the dramatic logic of *Sunday Music*. The opening *Largo* is solemn, almost processional, while the following *Lento* is mysterious and shifting, sounding in places almost like an electronically synthe-sized piece. In the third movement, marked *Fantastico*, the mood changes even more abruptly, introducing a jazz-based modal improvi-sation on the trumpet stops, while the fourth and last seem to reiterate some of the internal conflicts of *Sunday Music*, progressing *Gravemente* from doubt and irresolution to a carefully balanced triumph. The 1987 homage to the great Danish organ composer Dietrich Buxtehude (*c.* 1637–1707) is an additional bonus, though the Centaur pairing with the two Langlais works is also attractive.

Discographical Information

Other recordings: Mardirosian [with: Jean Langlais, *Suite breve* (1947), and *Three Characteristic Pieces* (1957)] (Centaur CRC 2042); many other recordings, includ-ing Audite 51004; Crystal S 182; CTS 801207; Christophorus Verlag LC 0612; Lyrinx 8204 031; Melodiya 33D 030347 48; Mixtur MXT 2 005 B; Pallas 120; Supraphon DN 5175; Teldec 6622038 01; Vista VPS 1062.

Other Eben: *Symphonia gregoriana* (1954; Motette CD 40151); *Suita balladica* (1955; Multisonic 310065–2); *Greek Dictionary* (1974; Thorofon CTH 2107); *Honour to Charles IV* (1978), *Faust* (1979–80; Etcetera KTC 1115); *Missa cum populo* (1981–2; Panton 81 1141–2911); *Hiob/Job* (1987; Multisonic 31 0095–2).

Map references: Charles-Marie Widor, Symphony no. 1 (date uncertain, rev. 1901; Novalis 150073–2); Olivier Messiaen, *Le banquet céleste* (1928; MD+G L3346), and *Les Corps glorieux* (1939; Unicorn-Kanchana DKPCD 9004); Maurice Duruflé, *Requiem* (1947; Jade JACD 033); Peter Dickinson, Organ Concerto (1971; EMI CDC7 47584–2).

Further reading: S. Lansdale, 'The Organ Music of Petr Eben', in *The American Organist*, 1979.

BERNARD HERRMANN (1911–1975)

North by Northwest (1959)

CINEMA RELEASE: 1959
SELECTED RECORDING: Unicorn-Kanchana DKP 9000 LP
  London Studio Symphony Orchestra, conducted by Laurie Johnson
RECORDED: 1979
DURATION: 35' 56"

American composers have generally had a happier time in Hollywood than American writers. Or so it appears. The corporate mind seemed to feel it had a right and the right qualifications to interfere in matters of scripting, less so in 'technical matters' like musical scoring. The studio system, with its compartmentalized approach and tendency to creation-by-committee, militated against very idiosyncratic or subjective musical ideas being applied to movie images, as was sometimes the case in Europe. But whereas in Europe – and particularly in the burgeoning Soviet film industry – 'serious' concert composers could expect to be approached by the studios, Hollywood exerted far less pull on composers than on dramatists, short story writers and novelists; Faulkner, Hemingway, Hammett, Nathanael West, and Mailer all obeyed the siren-call at one time or another. For its music, Hollywood preferred to mould specialists, leaving only worthily peripheral projects like documentary shorts and 'art films' to concert composers.

Between the 1930s and the late 1950s, a handful of figures managed to rise above the committee approach and stamped a distinct artistic personality on the *sound* of American movies. The best known of them were Max Steiner (1888–1971), Dmitri Tiomkin (1894–1979), Franz Waxman (1906–67), Miklós Rózsa (born 1907), Bernard Herrmann, and Leonard Rosenman (born 1924). Steiner's career began with *Cimarron* for Wesley Ruggles in 1931, took in *King Kong* (1933) and *Gone with the Wind* (1939) and extended as far as the popular theme for *A Summer Place* (1959). Tiomkin (1979) wrote atmospheric vocalises for *Lost Horizon* (1937), and jauntier scores for later Frank Capra films, before specializing in Western and adventure features like *High Noon* (1953) and *The Guns of Navarone* (1961). Waxman was valued for his ability to convey hyperthyroid emotion, as in *Sunset Boulevard* (1950) and *A Place in the Sun* (1951, incidentally a useful illustration of what Hollywood could do with a great novel, Theodore Dreiser's *An American Tragedy*). Rózsa began with *The Four Feathers* in 1939, won Academy Awards with his scores for *Spellbound* (1945) and *Ben-Hur* (1959), and was still writing effective 1940s pastiche, if nothing else, in the early 1980s, with his score for the Carl Reiner/Steve Martin comedy *Dead Men Don't Wear Plaid*. Rosenman helped establish the James Dean mystique with hard-edged and vaguely dissonant scores for *East of Eden* (1954) and *Rebel without a Cause* (1955); he later contributed substantially to the toe-curling properties of *A Man Called Horse* (1969), particularly to what might best be euphemized as the Pectoral Suspension Scene, not before or – mercifully – since a stock Hollywood device.

The names and the range of dates illustrate two significant points about Hollywood music. The studios tended to remain loyal to those composers who delivered, guaranteeing them long careers. By an historical accident, the majority of such composers were transplanted Europeans. Waxman – as Karl Wachsmann – had worked with Friedrich Holländer on *Der blaue Engel* in 1930 before fleeing the Nazis. Tiomkin's remarkable score for [*sic*] *Symphony for Six Million* (1932) used Jewish tunes and throbs uncomfortably with anticipations of an unwritten post-war 'Elegy for Six Million'. The *émigrés* brought with them a

conservative neo-romanticism and a symphonic style in the Tchaikovskian mould (Tiomkin's last project was the musical direction of
Ken Russell's 1971 biopic) that was to characterize American film
soundtracks throughout the 'classic' period. Atonality and/or currently
fashionable electronics were useful for suggesting youthful *anomie* as in
Rosenman's *East of Eden* score, extreme psychological states (like Ray
Milland's DTs in *The Lost Weekend*) or alien invasion (Herrmann's music
for *The Day the Earth Stood Still* and Louis and Bebe Barron's rather
cheapo all-electronic effects for *The Forbidden Planet* in 1956). Traces of
Americanism, of the folksy sort that Aaron Copland brought to *Our
Town* and *Of Mice and Men* in 1940, were equally rare and usually self-
conscious, like Tiomkin's interpolated ballads in *High Noon* ('Do not
forsake me, oh my darling') and elsewhere. The only American music
that made a substantial impact on the movies was jazz, often in
pastiche form, as in Elmer Bernstein's *The Man with the Golden Arm*
(1955), but often, too, refreshingly direct, as in Leith Stevens's superb
score for the ultimate biker movie *The Wild One* (1953) and Duke Ellington's for Otto Preminger's faintly misogynistic, and thus authentically
Hitchcockian, *Anatomy of a Murder*, made in the same year as *North by
Northwest*.

Another European transplant, Hitchcock is a central, catalytic figure
in the development of American film music. He also worked with
Tiomkin (*I Confess*, *Dial M for Murder* and *Strangers on a Train*) and with
Rózsa (*Spellbound*, which included a memorable use of electronics in the
Dalí-designed dream-sequence) but ironically his most distinctive
partner was the only American in the group above, apart from the
younger Rosenman. Herrmann wrote scores for five of Hitchcock's significant American films, *Vertigo* (1958), *North by Northwest*, *Psycho*
(1960), *Marnie* (1964), parting company only when the director bowed to
corporate pressure and rejected Herrmann's score for *Torn Curtain*
(1966); he also wrote scores for *The Trouble with Harry* (1955), *The Man
Who Knew Too Much* (1956) and *The Wrong Man* (1957). During their
association, they achieved a marriage of sound and images that has
scarcely been equalled in cinema. Though he occasionally experimented
with unusual instrumentation – *The Day the Earth Stood Still* included
amplified violin, electric bass and the electroacoustic Théremin – Herrman's gift was for full-scale orchestral writing. He was capable of virtuosic dramatic punctuation, onomatopoeic effects like the stabbing
string sound in the notorious shower scene of *Psycho* (on which he
managed to overrule the director, who had wanted the scene played in
silence), but he was rarely content to write literal reflections of the
action. Unlike the majority of film composers, he seldom used leitmotif
(a 'signature' device, associated with Wagnerian characterization), preferring to develop virtually all the musical material from one or two

contrasting melodic and rhythmic ideas which allowed him to convey the overall emotional or dramatic temper of the film in musical set-pieces. Herrman regarded it as axiomatic that he should be entirely *au fait* with the director's intentions before starting to write and then integrating a carefully wrought score with the narrative images.

This is not the place to attempt a scene-by-scene explanation of how the music 'works' in *North by Northwest*, but a measure of Herrmann's unselfish commitment to the film rather than to his own expressive ambitions can be gauged from the fact that its best-known sequence, when Cary Grant is attacked by a cropduster aircraft, is played out over a silence far more menacing than throbbing basses or off-key oboes and clarinets. Herrmann was convinced that film music was a significant and as yet underexploited artistic medium. Unlike the herd of 'Hollywood' composers (he never saw himself as the creature of the studios) he also wrote a substantial body of concert music, including an opera after *Wuthering Heights* (1943–51) and a remarkable cantata based on *Moby Dick* (1936–8).

Herrmann had been a musical prodigy. When he was only thirteen and a pupil at De Witt Clinton High School, he won $100 for *The Bells*, a setting of a Verlaine poem; he decided on the spot to become a composer. He trained at New York University under the weird but brilliant Australian Percy Grainger (1882–1961) and at the Juilliard School under Bernard Wagenaar (1894–1971). At the age of twenty, he founded the New Chamber Orchestra, wrote the fine ballet *Americana* (1932) and a number of pieces for the NCO, including *Marche militaire* (1932), which may be echoed in his score for the film of Norman Mailer's *The Naked and the Dead* (Raoul Walsh, 1958), *Aubade* (1933) and *Prelude to Anathema* (1933). In 1934 he joined CBS as a staff arranger and assistant conductor to the house orchestra. There he met Orson Welles and wrote music for the Mercury Theatre broadcasts. In 1941 Welles hired him to write the score for *Citizen Kane*, and the following years for *The Magnificent Ambersons*. The music for *Kane* is particularly brilliant and insightful, and contains a famous aria from an entirely imaginary opera based on Salammbo (not to be confused with the real opera of that name).

Brilliant as Herrmann's music for Welles undoubtedly was, it has a set-piece quality that is lacking in his later, more studied scores for Hitchcock. *Psycho* is still the best, largely because of the shower scene, but *North by Northwest* seems to me the most completely satisfying of the film pieces as an aural experience. It has the virtuosic elegance and dramatic modulation of the film itself and frequently suggests a dance score (a quality heightened by Grant's balletic and almost Chaplinesque mobility). The main title sequence provides the hectic rhythmic figure that runs through the entire film, culminating in the struggle on top of Mount Rushmore. This vigorous fandango, in double waltz time, is developed over Saul Bass's clever abstract representation of the Washington street-grid (and the maze of deception and misconception in which Cary Grant 'George Kaplan' finds himself); Bass's graphic is reminiscent of Piet Mondrian's canvas 'Broadway Boogie-Woogie', and Herrmann's $\frac{6}{8}$ rhythmic code has a similar structural function to Mondrian's mathematically exact proportions. It appears again and again through the film, driving on the action in what Herrmann described as its 'crazy dance'.

The opening was innovative for Herrmann's self-referential incorporation of the MGM lion's roar into the first bar of the music. Everything that follows is carefully signalled artifice. The meeting of Cary Grant and Eve Marie Saint, neither of whom are what they seem (he an innocent bystander, she a double agent, pretending to work for 'the enemy'), is represented by a tentative and harmonically ambiguous dialogue between clarinet and oboe which gradually opens into a languid Tchaikovskian swoon. The London Studio Symphony Orchestra play beautifully for Laurie Johnson, with the exactness of diction that Herrmann's music always demands. Though the idiom is thoroughly romantic, the music is never slushy or vague and contributes every bit as much to the dramatic tension as the schizoid string outbreaks in *Psycho*. The synchronization of music and action during the climactic dance on Mount Rushmore is breathtaking; watching the scene silently demonstrates how minimal Robert Burks's cinematography really is, just as watching Janet Leigh's final ablutions with the sound turned down robs the scene of anything but a mild prurient interest.

The vogue of 'symphonic' film scores was coming to an end with the close of the 1950s, but Herrmann lived just long enough to see it return in the mid-1970s, and paved the way for younger composers such as Elmer Bernstein (born 1922) and John Williams (born 1932). On the day he died, he had just completed recording the soundtrack for Martin Scorsese's hard-boiled *Taxi Driver*, a score that gives an almost 'balletic' coherence (the term was one Sam Peckinpah kept using of his own hyper-violent Westerns) to an otherwise numbing account of human degradation. Herrmann's own perfectionism allowed him to lift a corner of the curtain that obscured the obsessions of others; that was what he shared with Captain Ahab and Heathcliff and Kane, Norman Bates and even Travis Bickle. Few musicians in any style or genre have been able to make mood so frighteningly tangible.

Discographical Information

Other recording: original film soundtrack [overture only]; London PO, Herrmann (Decca 417 847 4).

Other Herrmann: *Moby Dick* (1936–8; Unicorn-Kanchana UKCD 2061); *Symphony* no. 1 (1941; Koch International Classics 3–7135); *Wuthering Heights* (1943–51; Unicorn-Kanchana UKCD 2050/51/52); *Souvenirs de Voyage* (1967; Bay Cities BCD 1014); also many film scores.

Map references: Virgil Thomson, *The River* (1937; ESS.A.Y CD 1005); Sergey Prokofiev, *Alexander Nevsky* (1938; Dorian DOR 90169); Dmitry Shostakovich, *The Gadfly* (1955; Pro Arte CD 551).

Further reading: B. Herrmann, 'Score for a Film', in R. Gottesman (ed.), *Focus on Citizen Cane*, Englewood Cliffs, NJ, 1971; E. Johnson, *Bernard Herrmann*: Hollywood's Music Dramatist, London, 1977.

BENGT HAMBRAEUS (born 29 January 1928)

Constellations II (1959)

FIRST PERFORMED: Copenhagen, 13 January 1960 (as radio broadcast)
SELECTED RECORDING: Philips 838 750 AY LP
    Hambraeus (organ)
    [with: *Interferences* (1961–2), Karl Erik Welin (organ)]
RECORDED: 1975
DURATION: 12' 04"

In 1952 a new edition of the seventeenth-century Danish composer Dietrich Buxtehude's organ works was published in Copenhagen by Josef Hedar. That summer Bengt Hambraeus was paying his second visit to the Ferienkurse für neue Musik at Darmstadt. These were the poles of his musical education: the organ repertoire of the baroque and the advanced sonic experimentalism of Boulez, Pousseur and Stockhausen. Mainly self-taught as a composer, Hambraeus had studied organ playing under Alf Linder and was largely responsible for introducing Messiaen to Scandinavian audiences. Messiaen's influence was already evident in the dramatic organ sonority of *Musik für Orgel* (1950), and was reinforced by Hambraeus's reading of the German cleric and organ scholar E. K. Rössler's complex theoretical *Klangfunktion und Registrierung* also published in 1952.

Hambraeus also claims credit as first Scandinavian composer to experiment with electronics. The two disciplines come together in the *Constellations* series (1958–83), dedicated to Rössler, which contains some of his most characteristic and idiomatic work. Hambraeu's first attempt at electronic music was in Cologne (the studio founded by Stockhausen) in 1955, where he realized *Doppelrohr*, named after Rössler's 'double reed' organ stop. Four years later, while at Berio's and

Maderna's Studio di Fonologia in Milan, he created the extraordinary *Visioner over en svensk folkvisa* ('Visions after a Swedish folksong') for Swedish Radio. He also did most of the work for *Constellations II*

The second piece in the series reflected his frustration with the technical limitations of existing organs, and his dream of 'a fantastic space organ, beyond all limitations' which would allow layers of sound to operate separately within a room (an idea he had encountered in his seventeenth-century researches) rather than compacted in the cabinet of a conventional pipe-organ. This new vision of 'Musik-im-Raum' (which does not mean quite the same thing as 'chambermusic') was dramatically simplified by his work at Cologne and Milan. Using loudspeakers and a two-track tape linked to a sound-board, Hambraeus devised an environment in which it was possible to let one set of sounds circulate freely (quadraphonically) while another is projected statically from a single point. I have no idea whether a quadraphonic version was ever released – the much-bruited 'quad revolution' now seems terribly old hat – but *Constellations II* sound extremely impressive in stereo, with distinct separations and smooth phasing from speaker to speaker.

The language is clearly very different from the neo-classical idiom of Petr Eben's music (see p. 79) and draws – *via* Messiaen – on the highly coloured language of Asian music. It also bears echoes of Edgard Varèse's experiments; did Hambraeus hear or read about Varèse's Brussels *Poème électronique* the previous year? Hambraeus has always regarded music as an 'adventure', not a purely intellectual discipline, and there is a vivid exploratory quality to his scores. The apotheosis of the new piece, if not entirely chance-determined, was at least unanticipated. Hambraeus has stated that natural sounds – wind, water, thunder, animal cries – have acted as a 'control signal' for almost all of his scores. So far as I know, he has never experimented with transcription in the field, but *Constellations II* evokes a sudden burst of morning birdsong; typically of such 'choruses', it sounds irrational but ordered, continuously varied in its development from simple coloristic ideas, and articulated without reference to a strict (or even implicit) pulse. For the composer, it expresses a 'rapturous constellation of untamed natural force, space (the cosmos, the universe, the heavens) and an all-encompassing playfulness'.

Constellations II was created by manipulating 'tone-points' taken directly from *Constellations I*; it is still possible to detect elements of the original piece, but only as a kind of after-image. The constituent sounds are nonetheless exceedingly bright. 'Constellations' is an interesting terminology, suggesting points of light (or sound) in visual (aural) proximity, but with no intrinsic relationship beyond that. As in astronomical observation, one seems to be dealing with events a long way removed from source. The logic of Hambraeus's work often defies strict analysis (where Messiaen's, for example, almost always yields to it), but the sequence of *Constellations* exhibits an evolutionary order. A third work (1961) used the tape from *II* under an entirely new organ score; a fourth and fifth (1978, 1982–3) added percussion and voices respectively. Written at the same time as *Constellations III*, *Interferences* (on the above recording) reinforces the important point that while Hambraeus has drawn considerable inspiration from electronics, he has not gone outside the organ's own resources to create either piece. The 'manipulation' of sound on *Constellations II* is simply that, and involves no electronic transformation; the descriptive subtitle 'for organ sounds' is quite literal. Among the defining sounds of *Interferences* are a weird fluctuation of pitch and what Hambraeus evocatively describes as 'swaying resonances'; these were created by switching on and off the instrument's motor during one of its many passages of sustained and otherwise static sound, a simple but extremely effective device which is presumably unique to the organ.

The piece was written for another Swedish composer and keyboard player Karl-Erik Welin, a disciple of Cage's friend and collaborator David Tudor and a leading light of the Scandinavian 'happening' movement. Welin was once carted to casualty after sawing up a piano (and parts of his own anatomy) onstage; he later restricted himself to gentler pursuits like brushing a teddy bear. His own organ works – the non-specific *Hommage à ...* and *Improvisations* (both 1969) – belong squarely to the sawing tendency and he has apparently not seen fit to return to writing for organ, preferring to restrict himself to performance, though a recent piece like *EssAEG* (1988) for two pianos and electronics, sounds as though it might have been conceived with organ in mind. Together with Hambraeus, Welin has made a significant impact on contemporary organ music, and composers such as Sylvano Bussotti, Mauricio Kagel, and György Ligeti have been influenced by or written for them.

Hambraeus emigrated to Canada in 1972, a move marked by a brief hiatus in his compositional output. He has, though, continued to write highly distinctive music. There have been fine orchestral scores, the Asian-sounding *Ricordanza* (1975–76) and the memorable *Litanies* (1988–9), dedicated to Jehan Alain (1911–40), a group of sacred vocal and choral works, and four operas spanning the unusual *Experiment X* (1968–9) and *L'Oui-Dire* (1984–6), but his most significant output remains for the organ. The extraordinary *Sheng* (1983) for oboe and organ, and the related *Après-Sheng* (1988) for organ alone, make virtuosic use of pedals and stops to create an entirely new sound for the instrument, delicately oriental and precise, chamber music rather than the throbbing symphonic approach of much organ music. If there has been an Ivesian quality to his recent orchestral scores, the chamber pieces show a marked debt to Webern. Hambraeus also writes very effectively for brass and has created original and very personal music for guitar and (a Scandinavian speciality) for free bass accordion; he makes frequent use of percussion. Unfortunately, he is not widely recorded and because he is not often featured on concert programmes in the United Kingdom or below the forty-seventh parallel in North America, he may be difficult to find.

Discographical Information

Other Hambraeus: *Doppelrohr* (1955; PS CD 41); *Mikrogram*; *Seven Aphorisms* (1961; Caprice CAP 1176); *Sheng* (1983; MAP R 8606).

Map references: Olivier Messiaen, *Livre d'orgue* (1951; Koch Schwann CD 315 024); György Ligeti, *Ricercar (Omaggio e Frescobaldi)* (1953; Adda 581240); Edgard Varèse, *Poème électronique* (1958; Neuma 450 74); Mauricio Kagel, *Rrrrr* (1980–1; Aulos PRE 66004).

Further reading: A. Hodgson, *Scandinavian Music: Finland and Sweden*, Cranbury, New Jersey and London, 1984; H.-G. Peterson, 'Bengt Hambraeus', in *Swedish Composers of the 20th Century* (English trans.), Stockholm, 1988.

GUNTHER SCHULLER (born 22 November 1925)

Abstraction (1959)

FIRST PERFORMED: New York City, 16 May 1960
SELECTED RECORDING: Atlantic 1365 LP – *Jazz Abstractions*
   Ornette Coleman (alto saxophone), Jim Hall (guitar), Scott LaFaro, Alvin Brehm (double basses), Sticks Evans (drums), Contemporary String Quartet – Charles Libove, Roland Vamos (violins), Harry Zaratzian (viola), Joseph Tekula (cello)
   [with: Schuller, *Variants on a Theme of John Lewis (Django)*, *Variants on a Theme of Thelonious Monk (Criss Cross)*, Eric Dolphy (alto saxophone, bass clarinet, flute), Ornette Coleman (alto saxophone on *Criss Cross*), Robert DiDomenica (flute), Jim Hall (guitar), Eddie Costa (vibes), Bill Evans (piano), George Duvivier, Scott LaFaro (double basses), Sticks Evans (drums), Contemporary String Quartet; Piece for Guitar and Strings, personnel as for *Abstraction*, but Ornette Coleman, Alvin Brehm and Sticks Evans do not appear, and add Alfred Brown (viola)]
RECORDED: 20 December 1960
DURATION: 4' 24"

Though less than five minutes in length, *Abstraction* is perhaps the purest and most representative work of the 'Third Stream'. It was

Gunther Schuller who gave the movement its name in the late 1950s, intending it to suggest a form which drew equally from formal modern composition (specifically the Second Viennese School of Schoenberg, Webern and Berg) and from vernacular traditions (mainly jazz and bebop, but including other, non-Western forms as well). 'Third Stream' was not merely an attempt to bring to jazz some of the formal rigour of serialist composition, nor to invigorate 'serious' music with unquantifiable characteristics like 'swing'. It was always Schuller's premise that the first and second streams would continue to develop unilaterally, uncolonized, but that there should also be a desegregated middle ground, with a common, esperantist currency.

Inevitably, the 'Third Stream' managed to please virtually no one, dismissed by hard core formalists for its improvisational slackness, too dry for many jazz fans. The very title *Abstraction,* and others like *Symphonic Tribute to Duke Ellington* (1955) and *Jumpin' in the Future* (*Atonal Jazz Study*) (1948), must have seemed like red rags to a notably bullish and separatist jazz audience. 'Third Stream' had largely derogatory connotations in the later 1960s and 1970s, when the main academic strand of formal composition was 'integral' or 'total' serialism (an approach that left no improvisational slack whatsoever) and when jazz was aggressively resistant to Europeanization in any form. Composers like Schuller, his colleagues at the New England Conservatory Ran Blake (born 1935) and Jimmy Giuffre (born 1921), John Carisi (1922–92) and others were marginalized, and only recently has Schuller's formidable output – over 150 original scores, mainly in orchestral and instrumental forms, but including songs, choral pieces and operas – begun to be reassessed in keeping with a new accessibility in formal music and a new tolerance toward structured composition in jazz.

Schuller's first musical career was as a horn player. He joined the brass section of the New York City Ballet orchestra in 1943 as a teenager and subsequently became principal with the Cincinnati Symphony and the Metropolitan Opera. His first major orchestral score was a Horn Concerto (1944); another followed in 1976. Later, there was a remarkable *Perpetuum mobile* for four muted horns with bassoon or tuba (1948), a set of pieces for five horns (1952), and the still more extravagant *Lines and Constants* for sixteen horns (1960). Schuller's more general gift for imaginative instrumentation developed rapidly, often drawing on quite extreme sonorities – Quartet for four double basses (1947), a rare Concerto for contrabassoon (1978) – and on instrumentation associated with vernacular ensembles, including the fine Concertino for jazz quartet and orchestra (1959), also released on Atlantic Records during the label's short but enthusiastic sponsorship of 'Third Stream' music.

Schuller brought an unmistakably American perspective to serial composition. He had studied essays like Arnold Schoenberg's 1941

'Composition with Twelve Tones', later reprinted in *Style and Idea* (New York, 1950), and developed the same strict but intellectually generous perspective reflected in composer Milton Babbitt's theoretical writings and scores of the 1950s, and in essays such as *The Hexachord and Its Relation to the Twelve-Tone Row* by another influential American composer and theorist George Rochberg (born 1918), published in the same year as *Abstraction*. Schuller's exploration of these ideas and procedures came at a time when advanced jazz musicians such as Ornette Coleman (born 1930) and Cecil Taylor (born 1933) were questioning the traditional approach to jazz as a set of harmonic improvisations on the chords of a popular tune. Coleman was experimenting with compositions which, unlike a conventional jazz 'standard', had no harmonic sequence and which used the 'rhythm section' as well as the traditional lead instruments like saxophone and trumpet to create a sort of free counterpoint of independent melodic lines; this was what Coleman later defined as 'harmolodics', a philosophy he has done more to propagate than to explain, but it also had much in common with Viennese twelve-note composition. Like Taylor's atonal jazz, Coleman's work in the 1950s was full of unexpected rhythmic displacements and jagged dissonances and seemed like a curious hybrid of Schoenberg with another of Schuller's longstanding idols, Charles Ives (1874–1954), whose radical modernism was accompanied by a lasting affection for popular forms. Jazz composers such as John Lewis (born 1920) of the Modern Jazz Quartet, and Tadd Dameron (1917–65), were exploring the possibilities of wholly scored pieces (like Dameron's 1952 *Fontainebleau*) and of structured integrations of jazz and formal music; Lewis, with whom Schuller had worked on the seminal 1949 *Birth of the Cool* sessions (somewhat misleadingly attributed to Miles Davis on their LP reissue), was the guiding spirit of the Atlantic 'Jazz Abstractions' project.

Schuller's treatment of Lewis's two-part 'Django' theme (with its remarkable pizzicato first variant and dramatic use of the gifted but tragic bass player Scott LaFaro) and of Thelonious Monk's 'Criss Cross' demonstrates how far jazz composition had progressed beyond the provision of adaptable tunes with a strong harmonic base for improvising. However puckish he and they seemed in performance, Monk (1917–82) wrote themes of great formal rigour and complexity; by contrast, Jim Hall's rendition of Piece for Guitar and Strings is bland and folksy. In the first variant on the Monk theme, Schuller has the soloists overlapping in such a way that one player's last chorus coincides with the next player's first; this creates the kind of shifting, multidirectional surface (particularly noticeable when Coleman and bass clarinettist Eric Dolphy are playing together) Coleman achieved on the very significant 1959 *Free Jazz* recording for double quartet.

In contrast, *Abstraction* seems simpler and much less dense, though it is constructed around a central cadenza where Coleman improvises on the basic theme. The piece is cast in ABA form with the final section an exact retrograde of the opening. In serial composition, the music is generated from a non-repeating 'note row' comprising the twelve notes of the chromatic scale deployed in an order which can be inverted or played in retrograde (or inverted and then played in retrograde) in order to generate further musical material but which cannot be fundamentally altered. The 'row' from which *Abstraction* is constructed consists of D F♯ G B F E C♯ C A♯ A G♯. The sequence is not played entire, but distributed through the instruments. The viola plays the first four notes, the first violin the next six and the second violin the final two. The guitar and saxophone are only heard at the start of later transformations, and this enriches the timbral surface of the piece. The sequence of entrances is similar to that heard in baroque fugue and helps give the piece its cumulative impact.

If the opening is almost stark, the central B section, with its free scoring for double bass and saxophone, is extremely rich in texture. Technically, the composed background at this point is a stretto, a narrowing or 'straightening' of the musical material at a point where all the permutations inherent in a fugal or serial process culminate climactically. Coleman listened to the string background several times, before recording his improvised passages. In the variations on Monk's 'Criss Cross' some sequencing errors had been allowed to pass – in line with the old adage that in jazz there are no mistakes, only opportunities – but in *Abstraction* Coleman sounds quite magisterial, and it is difficult for an untrained ear to distinguish what is strictly scored from what is improvised. With that in mind, it is useful to listen to a later (March 1963) concert recording of the piece featuring Eric Dolphy as the saxophone soloist (see *Vintage Dolphy*, below); Dolphy also performed on the 'Jazz Abstractions' sessions. In a sleeve-note to *Vintage Dolphy*, critic Martin Williams contrasted the two approaches by saying that Coleman 'sensed' [the piece], sized it up, and ran a parallel course to it. Dolphy goes inside *Abstractions* [*sic*] and his lines become, spontaneously, an integrated part of it.' It may be that Williams's preferences are showing, for Dolphy works a much more conventional, though tonally much more pleasing, set of 'changes' on the basic material. However beautifully articulated (and timbre has always been an important consideration for Schuller), they lack the closely argued precision of Coleman's statement.

The final section of the work is an exact mirror of the opening, bringing it to a quiet, spare conclusion. The abiding impression of the piece is the one Schuller explicitly intended: that musical time has been extended and compressed; freed from arbitrary internal divisions like barlines; and so constructed as to be 'outwardly fragmentary, but internally cohesive'. This has been the essence of his work since. The most recent of the wonderful concertos for orchestra, *Farbenspiel* (1985), is a dramatic late descendant of the tiny piece of thirty years before, marked by the same formal precision and exuberant, free-handed invention. The slightly earlier Alto Saxophone Concerto (1983) is further than ever from bland jazz pastiche, but it too is deeply marked by Schuller's lifelong desire to tear down fences.

Discographical Information

Other recording: Dolphy, Hall, Raimondi, Kaplan, Rhodes, Rudiakov, Davis, Phillips, Evans (Enja 5045).

Other Schuller: Symphony for brass and percussion (1950; Summit DCD 127); *Seven Studies on Themes of Paul Klee* (1959; Mercury Living Presence 434329); *Duologue* (1983; GM Recordings GM 2021); Concerto for Orchestra no. 3 *Farbenspiel*: First Edition Recordings LCD 003).

Map references: Milton Babbitt, *All Set* (1957; Elektra Nonesuch 79222; Don Ellis, *Improvisational Suite no. 1* (1960; Candid CCD 9004); Ran Blake, *Painted Rhythms* (1977; GM Recordings GM 3008); Anthony Braxton, *Composition no. 96* (1980; Leo CDLR 169).

Further reading: G. Schuller, 'Third Stream Revisited', in *Musings*, New York, 1985.

1960s

The 1950s really ended with the Cuban Missile Crisis and the assassination of John Kennedy. What followed was a great deal less adventurous and forward-looking than is usually assumed. In retrospect, the 1960s wore a nervously chastened and paranoid aspect that was difficult to shake off. Most of the radical music of the decade involved the working-out of ideas and techniques which had been mooted some time earlier. 'Classical' music also had to face up to the challenge of a pop industry of unprecedented scope and resources. The buzz words are 'openness' and 'event'. Chance reigns...

1960 Cathy Berberian premieres her husband Luciano Berio's vocal piece *Circles*.

1961 John Cage's *Silence* is published in the USA. Edgard Varèse's last work, *Nocturnal*, is completed by Chou Wen-chung.

1962 The influential twice-yearly journal *Perspectives of New Music* commences publication.

1963 Peter Sculthorpe joins the music faculty at Sydney University. Death of Aldous Huxley: 'I have music here in a box, shut up, like one of those bottled djinns in the *Arabian Nights*, and ready at a touch to break out of its prison.'

1964 Robert Moog's synthesizer goes on the market, making a greater initial impact on popular music, but also revolutionizing electronic music.

1965 Vagn Holmboe, unarguably the most significant Danish composer since Neilsen, retires as professor of composition in Copenhagen.

1966 Karlheinz Stockhausen visits Japan, studies the music of Noh drama, and writes *Telemusik*. At the same time, Chairman Mao's ultra-purist Cultural Revolution cuts off another potential line of artistic influence and exchange for an entire generation.

1967 Saxophonist John Coltrane dies, having taken harmonic improvisation and rhythmic variation to seemingly impossible lengths. Isang Yun kidnapped in Germany by Korean secret police and sentenced to life imprisonment (later commuted following international pressure) for sedition.

1968 Warsaw Pact troops suppress Alexander Dubček's democratic experiment in Czechoslovakia. London Sinfonietta is founded, and specializes in twentieth-century music.

1969 Four hundred and forty thousand young people convene at Woodstock in upstate New York for the rock festival that lends its name to a generation.

KARLHEINZ STOCKHAUSEN (born 22 August 1928)

Kontakte (1959–1960)

FIRST PERFORMED: Cologne, 11 June 1960
SELECTED RECORDING: Wergo WER 6009 2
 David Tudor (piano, percussion), Christoph Caskel (percussion), Karlheinz Stockhausen, Gottfried Michael Koenig (electronics)
RECORDED: 1960
DURATION: 34' 56"

At first glance, Karlheinz Stockhausen and John Cage might seem to stand for radically opposite tendencies in the development of contemporary music: the American for a sort of jovial mysticism and a relaxed, Rube Goldberg approach to the technicalities of music making; Stockhausen for the cartoon Teutonic virtues of iron discipline, humourlessness, intellectual and technical sophistication. The yogi and the commissar. His music aside, it is somehow hard to picture Stockhausen out picking mushrooms, appearing on quiz shows, or sending up a graduation ceremony, and of the two, it is Stockhausen who still seems radically alien. While it is possible – though hardly desirable – to take Cage as a bit of a joke, the Batemanish Chap-Who-Composed-All-Those-Silent-Pieces, Stockhausen's music is a tougher piece of gristle to get down.

It would be misleading and intellectually dishonest to pretend that such radical differences merely disguise an 'objective' unity of purpose. Cage and Stockhausen have worked from quite dissimilar premises and with very different ends in view. However, they also share an attitude which might loosely be termed mystical, or spiritual, or even, particularly in Stockhausen's case, cosmic. Both have been concerned with the unity of all sound and the need for a new aural discipline, which Stockhausen characterizes as 'immanent concentration on the present, as uninterrupted as possible'. It is, above all, that rejection of interruption that unites them, and it was this that Stockhausen sought in his earliest models, in Messiaen and in Boulez, extending serialism to assert the absolute indivisibility of all sound. In his sympathetically advocated book on Stockhausen, Karl H. Wörner suggests that 'serial thought' – a term he uses in careful preference to 'serialist technique' – requires the mediation of all extremes. If the opposition of black with white is mediated by a sufficiently subtle range of greys, then it is possible to see black 'not simply as an antithesis [in] direct contrast to white, but also as a degree of white itself'. To this Stockhausen has added the Webernian notion of 'principal ideas', in which no necessary element of a structure should be included on any basis other than equal participation.

Since 1977, all of Stockhausen's compositional energies have been directed to a huge operatic cycle known as *LICHT* – or 'Light' – which will, when completed around the turn of the millennium, consist of seven parts corresponding to the days of the week and designed to be performed over seven successive evenings. Its central drama is the journey through the cosmos of a heroic individual called Michael, whose identification as a youthful reincarnation of Stockhausen himself is underlined by the casting of the composer's son, trumpeter Markus Stockhausen, in the central role. The work draws not just on the Catholic symbology that plays such a surprisingly large role in Stockhausen's work as a whole – the early *Gesang der Jünglinge*, from 1955–6, is a wonderful integration of electronic sound and a boy treble singing the *Benedicite* – but also the Kabbalah, the teachings of Sri Aurobindo, and contemporary science fiction.

Whether *LICHT* is the first great music of the twenty-first century or an act of Wagnerian megalomania perpetrated by an artist in irreversible decline (and both points of view have been argued) remains to be seen, but there is a general consensus that Stockhausen's major theoretical and stylistic advances were effected in the 1950s and 1960s. He took major steps in codifying and extending the 'total serialism' of Pierre Boulez and Milton Babbitt, in the systematic use of Cagean indeterminacy, in musical notation, and above all in the development of electronic music, where he forged an influential synthesis between the prevailing style of *musique concrète* and pure electronic sound.

Synthesis is perhaps the key word. *LICHT* is typical Stockhausen, whatever else, as a feat of organization. As with a few other figures of the modern period – Wagner again, Picasso certainly, and at the opposite extreme, even a novelist such as Norman Mailer – understanding Stockhausen is hampered by there being no critical terms available which are larger than those articulated in the work itself or by its creator. Few artists of the twentieth century have theorised and commented on their own work quite so extensively. Stockhausen has sanctioned at least three books of interviews and published six volumes of *Texte zur Musik* (1963–89). He is also deeply committed (in a way that is strikingly different to Cage's attitude) to maintaining control of his own *oeuvre*. In recent years, he has bought back distribution rights to all the influential Deutsche Grammophon recordings of his work and is now issuing them under the imprint of Stockhausen Edition. Though his earlier works were published by the top-drawer publishers Universal Edition, all of his pieces since *Pole* in 1969 have been published by Stockhausen Verlag. With the inception of *LICHT* it is hard *not* to see the headquarters at Kürten as a latter-day Bayreuth.

Stockhausen's self-management has become a model for other creative musicians. At the Huddersfield Festival in 1988, he told me in perfect seriousness that ideally he would prefer it if no performance of any of his works took place anywhere without his supervision. That interview, recorded the night before he directed the 'park music' *Sternklang* (1971) in a Huddersfield sports centre, offered an interesting illustration of his obsessive self-documentation. Crowded into a tiny hotel bedroom with composer and interviewer were two female and one male members of his performing entourage, two of them operating tape recorders for the benefit of the Stockhausen archive. Some observers have been disturbed by the composer's use of his own family – most notably his sons Markus and Simon, a fine saxophone player, but also his companion Suzanne Stephens, a brilliant clarinettist and basset-horn player – as interpreters, almost as if he was some Victorian theatrical dynast, breaking in his offspring to the family trade.

The real Stockhausen is by no means as manipulative or as paranoid as he is portrayed (though, like any superstar, he took pains to point out that the back-up tape machines were also a hedge against mis-quotation). It is one of the central ironies of his career that a composer who has been widely characterized as a control freak should for much of the 1960s have abandoned the notion of formal composition entirely and have regarded himself and his ensemble as a conduit for a proto-"World Music'. Whereas early pieces like *Kreuzspiel* (1951) for oboe, bass clarinet, piano, plus woodblock and three percussion, with its wholly serialized 'crossplay' of pitches, rhythms and durations, might seem the quintessence of absolute codification (and it caused a major fuss on its first performance at Darmstadt), there is really much less difference between it and later, less determinate scores than meets the eye. In *Klavierstücke XI* (1956), the last of the non-*LICHT* solo piano works, the performer is presented with nineteen musical fragments or 'groups' to be played in any sequence. Elsewhere, Stockhausen offers purely verbal formulations which anticipate the deliberately uninflected and content-less works of conceptual and performance art. One of the sections of *Aus den sieben Tagen* (1968), a set of fifteen textual or 'intuitive' pieces for ensemble or voices, is called 'Es', in German an undifferentiated pronoun and also the symbol for E♭. The score consists solely of a much-quoted instruction to the performer: Think NOTHING / ... / Begin to play / As soon as you start to think stop / And try to retain / The state of NON-THINKING / Then continue playing.

If this seems to contradict Stockhausen's own characterization of music as 'thought-form, made audible', it is important to emphasize the difference between the internal armature of thought and outward excrescences such as ideas; the emphasis is deliberately on thought-*form*. It is in this area that he has made his most significant contribution to the development of contemporary music and it is here that he develops the transformational logic of serialism far beyond anything conceived by the Viennese masters. During the late 1950s, the period of *Kontakte*, Stockhausen had developed the notion of 'moments' or 'moment-form'. 'Moments' were conceived as 'individual and self-regulated, and able to sustain an independent existence. Musical events do not follow a fixed course between a determined beginning and an inevitable ending, and moments are not merely consequents of what precedes them and antecedents of what follows; rather a concentration on the NOW'. Moment-form was a logical extension of earlier work on 'points' and on 'groups'; titles like *Punkte* (1952) and *Momente* (1962–4) offer paradigms of these. Stockhausen had attempted to create 'points' of sound with no more absolute relationship between them than between bright stars in the sky, which though they sit in the same plane of vision may be thousands of light years apart. Gradually, though, he rejected the rather abstract pointillism of this method and began to readjust his focal length. The next stage allowed him to work with larger and more graduated constellations of sound, a first step towards the rediscovery of melody. Interestingly, Cage was to derive some of his later pieces from star-maps – the *Atlas eclipticalis* (1961) and the *Etudes australes* (1974–5) – but what interested Stockhausen again was not the indeterminate patterning of cosmic phenomena, but their underlying 'principle of transformation', and it is this principle above all else that unites his output.

Stockhausen's work inhabits a non-Newtonian universe, in which relativity plays a key part. Music no longer progresses from one harmonic and dramatic fixed point to a logical and sequential conclusion; 'a composer is no longer in the position of beginning at a fixed point in time and moving forwards from it; rather he is moving in all directions within a materially circumscribed universe'. That is very much the impression one receives from a work like *Kontakte*. The principle of non-repetition and non-variation is not a surrender to chaos; 'one has the feeling that an immutable and extremely homogeneous continuity is never surrendered. There is a hidden power of cohesion, a relatedness among the proportions, a structure. Not similar shapes in a changing light. Rather this: different shapes in a constant, all-permeating light.'

Light, always. Even Stockhausen's most abstract and apparently secular works are still illuminated by that central, quasi-religious principle. Its essence lies in Stockhausen's perception of time. Lecturing on electronic music in 1971, he quoted the medical biologist Viktor von Weizsäcker as rejecting the traditional notion that 'things are in time' in favour of the subject and relativistic conception that time is in things. What happens in *Kontakte*, most crucially in its taped electronic part, is that small units of sound are accelerated and compressed, a process that changes their timbral and pitch values, and casts the listener somewhat in the position of Einstein's space traveller, observing a continuous sequence of unquantifiable distortions in the time-and-space frame that persists outside the work. These are indefinite only in the sense that their exact values are unlikely to be describable by all but a specialist listener, not at all because they can be thought to be haphazard. Stockhausen works in a highly concentrated way on individual pitches, varying them by microscopic degrees.

Listening to *Kontakte* one is not aware of forms as instants in the passage of time, but rather as simultaneous presents, little quanta of energy that exist for the moment only, making what Stockhausen calls 'vertical incisions' in the fabric of time, rejecting horizontal development and thus leading to a sense of timelessness. The work has none of the carefully prepared climaxes, nor the introductory, dramatic, transitional and cadential stages that are intrinsic to 'classical' – that is, developmental – music. Though the beginning and ending are left open, the piece appears to end quite naturally at a point where the material appears to be used up or at a previously determined duration. For a work of its kind, *Kontakte* is remarkably long, but it appears to be structured quite logically around the exploitation of certain rhythmicized impulses and their associated timbral qualities. The 'contacts' take place between different forms and speeds in different strata of the piece. They are constant, continuous, and appear to resist any deterministic formulation, as would be the case in a serially organized piece.

Kontakte exists in two forms. One is for electronic sounds only, the other with the participation of a pianist and a percussionist. Both have been recorded. The instrumental version is in many respects more demanding, but it is also more viscerally exciting, drawing the listener into a sound-world of startling immediacy and vibrancy. There is a third version, *Originale* (1961) in which the tape piece is fused with a piece of music theatre. Stockhausen quickly recognized the limitations of the tape, and in *Mikrophonie I* (1964, for tam-tam, potentiometers, microphones and filters), *Mixtur* (1964–7, for ensemble or orchestra with sine-wave generators and ring modulators), and *Solo* (1965–6, for instrumentalist and tape feedback), began to utilize real-time synthesis in performance. At the same time, otherwise a relatively unproductive period in Stockhausen's career in terms of completed works, he explored more fully the possibilities of 'moment-form' in *Momente* (1962–4, for soprano, four choral groups and ensemble).

Perhaps the most startling development in his work came in 1970 when *Mantra*, for two pianists, signalled a gradual reintroduction of melodic elements. These had been present, as 'formulae', at the beginning of his career, in *Formel* (1951), but they became a major structural component of his work in the 1970s, notably the *Inori* (1973–4) or 'adorations' for soloists and orchestra, and the short expressive pieces for solo or accompanied clarinet – *Laub und Regen* (1974), offshoots of the zodiacal *Tierkreis* (1975–6), *(Der kleine) Harlekin* (1975), *Amour* (1976), and *In Freundschaft* (1977) – written for Suzanne Stephens. They are also central to the remarkable *Am Himmel wandre ich...* (1972), a setting for two voices of American Indian songs which has the same revelatory, world-spanning quality of electroacoustic pieces like *Kontakte* and *Telemusik* (1966). Vocal music has played a critical part in Stockhausen's output – his first published composition was *Chore für Doris* (1950), an unaccompanied choral piece dedicated to his first wife. *Stimmung* (1968) was written for his second, Mary Bauermeister, and is an excellent measure of his development across those crucial decades, a re-'tuning' of his work in the light of his religious and philosophical preoccupations. These, of course, have led him directly to his *Ring*, the *LICHT* cycle. Stockhausen has prepared concert versions of numerous arias and scenes, numbered like all his work in clearly flagged groups (*Kontakte* for tape is no. 12, the present piece is no. 12½, *Originale* is no. 12⅔, and so on) that constantly underline the totality of his output.

LICHT now commands all his attention. To date, Stockhausen has completed *Donnerstag* (1978–80), *Samstag* (1981–3) and *Montag* (1984–8) and is at work on *Dienstag*; 'Sunday', 'Wednesday', and 'Friday' are still to come and it is anticipated that they will occupy Stockhausen until the turn of the millennium, appropriately enough. On stage, *Donnerstag* is an overwhelming experience, heroic opera with the trappings of a high-tech rock show and an almost ritual concentration. There is a recording of the whole work [DG 423 379 2, since re-licensed by Stockhausen Edition], but a concert version of Act II, *Michaels-Reise*, the trumpeter–archangel's journey round the earth, is a better bet [ECM 1406]. Ironically, it is now more difficult – and expensive – to get Stockhausen's earlier works on record, but vinyl copies of the original Deutsche Grammophon releases are not hard to find and are still of sterling quality, even though the original electronic tapes prepared by Stockhausen in his Cologne studio have begun to deteriorate dramatically and have required restoration.

There is nowadays a hint of tarnish on Stockhausen's reputation. His work is perhaps more talked about than listened to and is just as often guyed as seriously talked about. Stockhausen has had to be the scapegoat (a suitably biblical role) and a rearguard for the European avant garde as it retreats – or temporarily withdraws – in the face of the 'new tonality' and the attendant revivals of realism and narrative in the other arts. Satires like Tony Hancock's movie *The Rebel* suggested that artistic movements like Abstract Expressionism were compounded of luck, gullibility and sheer brass neck. Like Jackson Pollock, Stockhausen was widely perceived as a cynical fraud. A *catalogue raisonné* of the painter's work contains an appendix of known forgeries and it is immediately clear from these pages that Pollock's apparently random gestures concealed a dynamism and internal rhythm that was impossible to imitate. The same applies to Stockhausen, perhaps the greatest composer of the post-war period, but one who is still not fully acknowledged and appreciated by the culture he helped call into being.

Discographical Information

Other recordings: Avery, Schick, Spek (Music & Arts CD 648); Kontarsky, Caskel, Stockhausen (Vox STGBY 638 LP); Wambach, Ardeleanu (Koch Schwann 310020).

Other Stockhausen: *Kreuzspiel* (1951; Deutsche Grammophon DG 2530 443); *Klavierstück XI* (1956; Koch Schwann CD 310009); *Gesang der Jünglinge* (1955–6; Harmonia Mundi DMR 1007–1009); *Momente* (1963–5; Deutsche Grammophon DG 2709 555); *Telemusik* (1966; Deutsche Grammophon DG 137 012); *Stimmung* (1968; 66115); *Aus den sieben Tagen* (1968; Harmonia Mundi 30 899); *Tierkreis* (1975–6; Acanta CD 43201, Jacklin JS 289); *In Freundschaft* (1977; Adda 581047; Bis CD 388); *Donnerstag aus LICHT* (1981).

Map references: John Cage, *Imaginary Landscape no. 2* (1942; Wergo WER 6203); Milton Babbitt, *Composition for Four Instruments* (1948; CRI C 138 LP); Pierre Boulez, *Domaines* (1961; Harmonia Mundi HMA 190.930); Rolf Gehlhaar [personal assistant to Stockhausen, 1967–70], *Polymorph* (1978; Etcetera KTC 1127); Gottfried Michael Koenig [Stockhausen's assistant on *Gesang der Jünglinge* and *Kontakte*, see above], *Funktion Grün/Gelb/Orange/Rot/Blau/Indigo/Violett/Grau* (1968–9; BvHaast 9001/9002).

Further reading: K. Stockhausen, *Texte zur Musik*, Cologne, 1963–89; K. H. Wörner, *Stockhausen: Life and Work*, London, 1973; J. Cott, *Stockhausen: Conversations with the Composer*, New York, 1973; J. Harvey, *The Music of Stockhausen*, London, 1975; M. Tannenbaum, *Conversations with Stockhausen*, Oxford, 1987; R. Maconie (ed.), *Stockhausen on Music: Lectures and Interviews*, London, 1988; M. Kurtz, *Stockhausen: Eine Biographie*, Kassel and Basle, 1988.

KRZYSZTOF PENDERECKI (born 23 November 1933)

Tren ofiarom Hiroszimy (Threnody for the Victims of Hiroshima) (1960)

FIRST PERFORMED: Warsaw Radio broadcast, 31 May 1961
SELECTED RECORDING: Conifer CDCF 168
Polish Radio and Television Symphony Orchestra, Krakow, conducted by Szymon Kawalla
[with: Penderecki, Viola Concerto (1983), Grigori Zhislin; Nancy van

de Vate, Concerto no. 1 for violin and orchestra (1986), Janusz Mir-ynski; *Chernobyl* (1987)]
DURATION: 8' 57"

Despite its forbidding sonority. Krzysztof Penderecki's *Threnody* is one of the most widely known of contemporary works, regularly played in concert and frequently recorded. It has become a kind of modern classic, as starkly beautiful as it is harrowing. Much non-technical commentary on the piece has concentrated on its programmatic intent, and claims to hear air-raid sirens, the murderous whistling of bombs, and the dying screams of Hiroshima's citizenry in its huge string glissandos. It is useful to remember, though, that the piece was written as a technical experiment first and foremost, and acquired its evocative title only after the fact. Even so, Penderecki's memorial, like his later *Dies irae* (1967) for the victims of Auschwitz, is unmistakably sincere and deeply felt. One can only imagine how Penderecki's compatriots, listening to the broadcast premiere a mere sixteen years after the last bombs fell on Warsaw, might have reacted to the sounds coming out of their radios.

Penderecki's artistic coming-of-age coincided with a period of liberalization in Polish life. The October Revolt of 1956 brought to an end a period of near-totalitarian cultural restriction that had lasted long after the ambiguous liberation of 1945. Penderecki was studying with Stanisław Wiechowicz (1893–1963), whose personal commitment to a folkish, quasi-pastoral style was combined with a broadly cosmopolitan understanding of contemporary techniques. After 1956, 'bourgeois formalism' was no longer a cardinal offence, subject to official proscription. It became possible again to think in terms of 'pure' or absolute music, and it is ironic that Penderecki's most programmatic non-vocal piece, apart from an earlier threnody to his other important teacher, *Epitaffium Artur Malawski* (1958, strings, timpani), should have emerged from such a formalist background.

The *Threnody* is scored for fifty-two strings, and represents a radical exploration of tone-colour and pitching similar to but significantly different from that attempted by Iannis Xanakis in the 'stochastic' piece *Metastaseis* (1953–4). In Xenakis's piece, sixty-one strings were deployed according to random number theory to create long, swooping glissandos that would suggest huge, shifting masses of sound rather than linear developments. Though superficially similar, Penderecki's method is less mathematical and, though it is in no way conventionally harmonic or melodic in language, it retains something of a classical linearity. Interestingly, this became a defining feature of Penderecki's music in his later, post-avant-garde period, when in works like the Symphony no. 2: *Christmas Symphony* (1980) he utilized a markedly simpler, almost romantic idiom. Conversely, the String Quartet no. 1, also from 1960, has less in common with classical procedure (even in the fissile and complex manner of late Beethoven) than with the static accumulations of the *Threnody*.

Large sections of the piece call for dense note-clusters, arrayed in bands of sound that contain all the pitches within their given range. With no discernible metre, the music progresses (if that is the right word) by a carefully determined sequence of oscillations between highest and lowest available pitches, as if the bands were being heightened or shortened, stretched or compressed like the sine-waves on an oscilloscope. An electronic music studio was established in Warsaw in 1957; Penderecki worked there for a number of years, writing music for films and the theatre, and he has suggested that it was his own experiments there, working with different conceptions of 'noise' that led him to the cluster effects of the *Threnody*, rather than the example of other composers like Xenakis, Ligeti or even Edgard Varèse (1883–1965), whose *Arcana* (1925–7) for large orchestra and *Ionisation* (1931) for thirteen percussionists, piano and sirens, are often cited as ancestral influences.

The impact of the Warsaw studio is perhaps clearer in *Polymorphia* (1961), where the string players (forty-eight of them, in this case) are asked to imitate electronic sounds by acoustic means, but the later piece signally lacks the tremendous alienating wallop of the *Threnody*. Part of its impact comes from Penderecki's use of innovative articulation devices, like extremes of vibrato and pitchless sound, playing below and even behind the bridge, and on the tail of the violin, and these are evident even in the *St Luke Passion* (1963, soloists, narrator, boys' and mixed choruses, orchestra) with its latter-day evocation of Bach. Throughout the 1960s, like Cage and Stockhausen, Penderecki continued to experiment with unconventional sonic devices, using everyday materials and artefacts like typewriters in a bid to break down the distinction between music and noise.

The first impression of the *Threnody* is apt to be the latter. It is a fearsomely dissonant work with almost no superficial reference points, and a partial or inattentive hearing can leave an impression akin to a sort of cosmetic white noise. However, disciplined performance and respectable recording elucidate a teeming internal structure which is more likely to be intuited than perceived analytically. The *Threnody* builds towards a cathartic climax in which all fifty-two instruments play a huge cluster consisting of individual pitches ranged a quarter-tone apart, creating what Nicolas Slonimsky (ever ready with a polysyllable) helpfully calls 'two octavefuls of icositetraphonic harmony'!

The *Threnody* is a short work, barely nine minutes in length, and consequently a recording favourite, easily dovetailed with other pieces. There is much to recommend the HMV recording, conducted by the composer, but the 1988 Conifer with the finely articulated Polish Radio and Television Symphony Orchestra offers the perfectly logical pairing of Penderecki's own Viola Concerto, a stately, rather sombre work which hovers round a lucid idea in D, taking most of its impetus from the solo part. It also offers a world premiere recording of *Chernobyl*, a later evocation of nuclear disaster by the American Nancy van de Vate (born 1930), now resident in Vienna, which makes full use of Penderecki's dense layering and huge sound masses. Bruno Maderna's recording with the Rome Symphony Orchestra offers a lighter and, in some respects, more lucid reading, but again the main advantage of this pairing is the opportunity to hear Penderecki in the context of his stylistic brethren, Stockhausen most obviously, but also the regrettably under-recorded Henri Pousseur and Earle Brown.

Discographical Information

Other recordings: Rome SO, Maderna (Victrola VICS 1239); Warsaw National PO, Rowicki (Muza PNCD 017); Polish Radio National SO, Penderecki (HMV CDC7 49316).

Other Penderecki: *Polymorphia* (1961; Foyer 1–CF-2308); *Passio et mors domini nostri Jesu Christi secundum Lucam/St Luke Passion* (1963–5; EMI CDS 7 49313); Concerto for violin and orchestra (1976–7; Nuova Era 6705); Symphony no. 2: *Christmas Symphony* (1980; Olympia OCD 239); Viola Concerto (1982–3; Vienna Modern Masters VMM 3010).

Map references: Edgard Varèse, *Arcana (1925–7; Sony Classical SK 45844); Iannis Xenakis, Metastaseis* (1955–6; Chant du Monde LDC 278368); György Ligeti, *Atmosphères* (1961; DG 429 260); Karlheinz Stockhausen, *Mixtur* (1964; DG 137 012); Peter Sculthorpe, *Sun Music* (1965–7).

Further reading: R. Dufallo, interview in *Trackings*, Oxford, 1989.

ELISABETH LUTYENS (1906–1983)

Quincunx (1960)

FIRST PERFORMED: Cheltenham, 12 July 1962
SELECTED RECORDING: Argo ZRG 622 LP
   John Shirley-Quirk (baritone), Josephine Nendick (soprano), BBC Symphony Orchestra, conducted by Norman Del Mar
   [with: Nicholas Maw, *Scenes and Arias* (1962)]
RECORDED: 1969
DURATION: 20′

At the end of her life, Elisabeth Lutyens used to ask mock-innocently, 'Oh, did Schoenberg use the twelve-tone method, too?' Her lifelong and increasingly combative insistence on her own originality – and by implication the philistine stupidity of those who failed to appreciate her music – was one of her more tiresome eccentricities and probably alienated many who might otherwise have been sympathetic.

There was, however, some validity in her claim to have arrived at her distinctive method independently of the Viennese masters. Like Luigi Dallapiccola in Italy and Milton Babbitt in the United States, she was an independent and she came by her best music slowly and experimentally rather than intuitively or by appropriating ready-made techniques. It is perfectly clear, though, that she also absorbed a good deal of serialist theory from her lover and second husband Edward Clark (founder of the North Eastern Regional Orchestra) who claimed an almost apostolic closeness to Schoenberg, Webern and Berg, the dodecaphonic trinity.

'Twelve-tone Lizzie' suffered a double jeopardy. It was hard enough to be a woman and a composer in pre-war England; to compound the flaw with atonality was commercial and critical suicide. She was not a naturally gifted composer. The young Betty Lutyens turned to music because it was the one field of endeavour for which there was no obvious family precedent. Her father was the tame architect of the Edwardian bourgeoisie Sir Edwin Landseer Lutyens, and among her forebears there was the now all but unreadable Victorian novelist Bulwer-Lytton. Atonality was in part, too, a reaction against an upbringing in theosophy, a consuming enthusiasm of her mother's. As a handmaiden to the young Krishnamurti, Betty was required to wear a sari and move in an atmosphere of perfumed spirituality, inconceivable to anyone who knew the tweedy figure of later years, who imbibed whisky, best bitter and bitter gall in equal proportions and was usually surrounded by an aura compounded mostly of cigarette smoke.

In the face of every possible obstacle, Lutyens managed to support herself and her two children by writing music for Hammer horror films – titles like *Blood Fiends, Don't Bother to Knock* and *The Skull* – and for public information shorts. She did also benefit from the patronage of loyal friends, Clark first and foremost who interceded on her behalf with the International Society for Contemporary Music, but also William Walton (Lutyens's 'favourite diatonic composer') and the eminent critic William Glock, a dedicated Schoenbergian, who found himself in a position to assist her when he became Controller of Music at the BBC in 1959. Regardless, she continued to swim against the current. A substantial proportion of her scores now seemed forced, over-wrought, too self-consciously innovative in instrumentation or content and thus fatally time-locked.

There were, however, some impressive pages: a group of chamber concertos and fantasias which called on her enthusiasm for Henry Purcell and contained some imaginative saxophone lines ("Such a *rude*, adolescent instrument', she once said); the cantata *Ô saisons, ô châteaux*

(1946) to words by Rimbaud, fine settings of verse by Dylan Thomas, Salvatore Quasimodo and Pablo Neruda, and more unusual vocal inspirations such as the 1970 *Anerca* for ten guitars and a recitation of Eskimo poetry; there was the motet *Excerpta tractatus–logico–philosophicus* (1953) to texts by Wittgenstein, and there was her own personal favourite *Akapotik Rose* (1966) for soprano, flute, two clarinets, string trio and piano, which used materials by the artist Eduardo Paolozzi and was dedicated to Virgil Thomson.

Her crowning triumph, though, was *Quincunx*, finished at an otherwise fallow time in her career and premiered at Cheltenham in the year of Clark's death. Scored for orchestra, wordless soprano, and baritone, it contains at its centre (and the geometry is literal) a setting of a passage from the seventeenth-century physician and author Sir Thomas Browne's *Urn-Buriall*. The *quincunx* is essentially a square with a central point at the intersection of the two diagonals. It resembles the disposition of spots on the five of a die or suit of cards, though such chance-haunted analogies might have struck her as ironic. Lutyens would almost certainly have known the *quincunx*, even if only subliminally, from her father's architectural library since it was a regular feature of house and garden design, but it had a further, etymological significance. The word means 'five-twelfths', a derivation that contains an obvious reference to her gradual embrace of twelve-note methods.

Quincunx is one of those serial works that strikes the listener as somehow tonally based, an unexpected function of its near-perfect musical geometry rather than of its extreme chromaticism. It is a profoundly poetic work, with a haunting elegiac quality. Lutyens had travelled a long way already from her early, Bartók-influenced romanticism and would travel still further in search of a rhythmic language that would lend vigour to her highly logical but rather brick-built structures. Coming as it did almost exactly half-way through her creative life, *Quincunx* marks a rare point of balance. As Anthony Payne commented in his sleeve-note to the Argo recording, it was an ideal example of Lutyens's furious stream-of-consciousness technique contained within a watertight, but not restrictive, matrix that gave the work form without denying its energies. Ten years before, Lutyens had dedicated her String Quartet no. 6 to the painter Francis Bacon (a drinking-chum in Soho), expressing her sense of kinship with Bacon's rapid, unreflective approach and its relentless foregrounding of unpalatable, often violent imagery.

As befits a work with the *Urn-Buriall* at its core, *Quincunx* is characteristically Jacobean (not at all 'Elizabethan') in its combination of apparently gratuitous violence and considerable philosophical gravitas. As in Browne's extraordinary book, wildly juxtaposed ideas and concepts, few of them chosen for obvious aesthetic delight are strung together by means of a slight, almost meretricious musical argument. Payne rather optimistically talks of Lutyens's 'supple melodic line', but that is an insight that probably comes of having studied the score; *hearing* the work one is much more likely to pick up his subsequent point and recognize the underlying line only at scattered points in the music, and then only half-consciously as something that 'must' be there to keep the whole thing from falling apart. To anticipate the passage she set from Browne, Lutyens's structure on this occasion was genuinely made from 'Cobwebbes', not 'Cables'. There is a wonderfully dusty, aged quality to the music which – much as in John Cage's First String Quartet (1950) – makes it momentarily difficult to identify what century the music is coming out of.

Lutyens's planning of the piece was meticulous and imaginative. The deployment of multiple orchestra groups was still unusual in 1962 (Stockhausen's *Gruppen*, with its three conductors, had been premiered as recently as 1959), and has rarely been used so imaginatively. The image of the *quincunx* permeates the piece utterly. Five orchestral tuttis enclose four passages for single-instrumental groups – in turn, winds, strings, percussion and brass – with the baritone at the centre and the wordless soprano vocalizing as if in echo through the far side of the maze. Lutyens had originally intended the players to be staged in four instrumental groups with the baritone at the centre, but this was eventually ruled out as impractical. To involve the logic still more thoroughly, the orchestral groups themselves each contain five tuttis enveloping four solos. At the centre, almost becalmed, the unaccompanied baritone intones a passage that reflects the surreal calm and dreamy nonsense-wisdom of the piece: 'But the Quincunx of Heaven runs low and 'tis time to close the five ports of knowledge; we are unwilling to spin out our waking thoughts into the phantasms of sleep; which often continueth precogitations, making Cables of Cobwebbes and Wildernesses of handsome Groves.' The effect is much as if Edith Sitwell, Lord Berners and the Virginia Woolf of *Orlando* had suddenly been plonked down in a seminar room at Darmstadt; needless to say, English men and women of that class are genetically selected and bred for their resistance to embarrassment or unease, and the encounter passes off without strain.

There can be no doubt, though, that driving Lutyens throughout her career was an aggressive desire to mess up the politely handsome gardens and façades of an England that was and remains Edwardian rather than (the usual cliché) Victorian in temperament. She had grown up in 'a goldfish bowl' (her own words) and both knew and resented the way roles were assigned and withheld in the grand comedy of English culture. The Establishment – with rare exceptions like Glock – treated her with patronizingly nonchalant disregard as that most embarrassing thing: a *loud* woman who presumed to be clever but declined to be a feminist, insisting on playing the game according to club rules. It is a depressing reflection of the Establishment's success and the partiality of feminist revisionism that at time of writing, only a single piece of Lutyens's music was listed in the CD catalogues. Nor is she often included in concert programmes. If she is to be experienced at all, it has to be on old formats. An early edition of the *Penguin Guide* (worrying about stereo and mono in those days, rather than digital *vs* analogue) praised the Argo recording extravagantly, with a word for John Shirley-Quirk's finely judged performance, and suggested that *Ô saisons, ô châteaux!* and the 1963 String Quintet were equally viable as ways through the 'barbed-wire' approaches to Lutyens's particular sound-world. It would be a pity if her forbidding manner were to be taken too much at face value and she were to be forgotten so very soon.

Discographical Information

Other Lutyens: *Ô saisons, ô châteaux!* (1946; HMV ASD 612); String Quartet no. 6 (1954 [with: *Five Bagatelles* (1962)]; Argo ZRG 5425 LP); *Motet* (1955; Argo ZRG 5426); Lutyens has not (yet) been substantially represented on CD, though a campaign for revival is under way, signalled by the appearance of *Lament of Isis on the Death of Osiris* (1969 [with: Chamber Concerto no. 1]; NM CD 011).

Map references: Ethel Smyth, String Quartet in E (1902/1912; Troubadisc TRO CD 03); Luigi Dallapiccola, *Divertimento in quattro esercizi* (1934; Entr'acte ESCD 6504); Thea Musgrave, Chamber Concerto no. 2 (1965; Delos DCD 1012); Milton Babbitt, *Phenomena* (1970; Neuma 450 74).

Further reading: R. Murray Schafer, *British Composers in Interview*, London, 1963; E. Lutyens, *A Goldfish Bowl*, London, 1972; M. and S. Harries, *A Pilgrim Soul: The Life and Works of Elisabeth Lutyens*, London, 1989.

GIACINTO SCELSI (1905–1988)

Trilogia: *Triphon, Dithome, Ygghur* (1957–1961)

SELECTED RECORDING: Etcetera KTC 1136
  Frances-Marie Uitti (cello)
  [with: *Ko-Tha* (1978 version for six-string cello)]
RECORDED: June 1979 [December 1978]
DURATION: 40′ 20″

One of the most remarkable composers of this century, Scelsi's wider reputation was secured only after his mysterious and fugitive personality was extinguished. There is nothing quite like his work, which admits to no obvious antecedents, belongs to no school, and accords to no identifiable musical system. It has, nonetheless, influenced a younger generation of composers to a quite disproportionate extent, and it is entirely possible that Scelsi's long-term impact will be as great as that of Varèse, or even perhaps of Webern. His admirers would claim that for him.

Though born in La Spezia, and living most of his later life in Rome, Sclesi can hardly be regarded as an 'Italian' composer in any meaningful sense. As a young man, he travelled widely in the East, and his work stands almost entirely outside the Western tradition. It eschews melody and harmony and rarely conforms to any but the most evanescent and subliminal of rhythmic patterns. Through his study of Eastern music, he developed a powerful interest in microtonal structures and in extremes of sonority, and he wrote a wide range of solo works for such improbable instruments as contrabassoon and bass tuba, most of which called for unprecedented and innovative refinements of articulation. Unlike many of his contemporaries, who tended to treat 'extended technique' as a branch of musical theatre, focusing undue attention on the act of bowing, striking or blowing through improbable parts of an instrument, Scelsi appears to have been indifferent to dramatic side-effects. His entire working ethos was based on a rejection of analysis (which has been, whether or not it is overt or obvious, an essential component of the classical tradition) in favour of an absolute concentration on sound as an end in itself rather than as a means to some analytical resolution.

As part of his signature, Scelsi adopted a Zen pictogram consisting of a circle poised above a horizontal line. Inevitably, both his admirers and detractors have been tempted into analysis, suggesting interpretations that range from a rising (or setting) sun (or moon), the stark binary oppositions of computer languages, and even, from more sceptical quarters, a big fat zero. In one perfectly serious sense, the last explanation is the most accurate. Though the pieces on this recording represent an essay in mystical autobiography, Scelsi's music is not concerned with personality or 'expression' in any conventional sense. He regarded himself as a conduit, a spiritual constructor rather than a creator in the romantic sense. He offered no interviews or photo-opportunities, wrote nothing that might be construed as commentary on his work, and preferred to communicate gnomically with a small group of favoured interpreters. That they were mostly women might suggest that neither the Italian nor the Old Adam in him were entirely dead, even that he might regard the performers themselves as his 'instruments', a breach of his own Categorical Imperative. He suggested almost as much in regard to the astonishing *Canti di capricorni* (1962–72), a group of (mostly) unaccompanied pieces devised for the particular vocal characteristics of the Japanese singer Michiko Hirayama. But such relationships are perfectly consistent with Scelsi's philosophy of symmetry and balance, eternal, unresolved interchange between apparent opposites. There is a tense, almost erotic charge to the music.

Scelsi's music began to be more widely appreciated during the final year of his life when the Therwil-based jazz and new music label hat ART released recordings of his Piano Sonatas nos. 9 and 10 performed by the Swiss pianist Marianne Schroeder. Hat ART has continued to promote Scelsi's music, with further releases by Schroeder and the French contrabassist Joëlle Léandre, for whom he wrote and dedicated several solo pieces. Following the recording of the present pieces, he dedicated all his solo cello works to Frances-Marie Uitti.

Uitti is a single-minded explorer and her instrument and has been the recipient of many specially written cello pieces which call not just on her virtuosity, but also on aspects of her extended technique. Her most significant technical innovation has been the simultaneous use of two bows, which allows her to create complex polyphonic effects (literally) single-handed. She has also experimented with instrumental design. In 1978, reacting to Scelsi's intriguing openness to collaborative revision (a different attitude to the like-minded Cage's Zen shrug) she adapted *Ko-Tha* for a six-string cello retuned using wire-wound bass guitar strings. The piece, included on the present recording, relates to the multi-armed Siva/Makhala and his cyclical dance of destruction and creation. It was originally written for amplified guitar, which was to be played horizontally and slapped, scratched and flicked rather than plucked or strummed; the new version gave the piece an added resonance and a far richer array of overtones, effectively reinventing it.

Trilogia stands out a little in Scelsi's *oeuvre*. It is, to some degree at least, a personal testimony, with a clearly specified programme. Most of Scelsi's pieces bear titles which are as hermetic and alien as Xenakis's gutturally poetic Greek. *Trilogia*, though, bears the comforting subtitle 'The Three Ages of Man', and outwardly conforms to the familiar parabola of youth–maturity–age. There are three separate parts, each lasting somewhat over thirteen minutes; the first and last are divided into three movements, while the second is unbroken. The harmonic material is in general quite severely limited. Though most of the work is centred round one or two narrow intervals, Scelsi specifies an enormous range of attacks and dynamic variants, and creates hazy microtonal spectra in which there is a perfect balance between the appearance of great internal activity and functional stillness.

For the opening section of *Triphon*, the cellist is required to fix metal mutes to the C and G strings. Somewhat akin to Cage's 'preparation' of the piano, these create an odd buzzing resonance which Scelsi has likened to the 'rumbling' overtones achieved by Tibetan monks in their chants. The entire trajectory of *Trilogia* is toward final catharsis, and there is no mistaking a tense sexual pressure (perhaps akin to the 'shaking' of American puritan sects) in *Triphon*'s pent-up and unsublimated drama. The opening section becomes quite violent, with tortuous rhythms and loud, snapping sounds from the open strings. The central movement proclaims a hostile energy, and sounds almost like a distorted transcription of Shostakovich's sarcastic wartime marches. This is *loud* music, beguilingly ugly and spectacular, and there is a sense of genuine relief in the final movement of the first piece where the sound takes on a passionate, ejaculatory quality as it negotiates a dramatic exchange of intervals.

The central, single-movement *Dithome* is, appropriately, more sober and calculated. As in the first part, where motifs were echoed on the muted strings, it has a reflexive structure that is intended to express a new triad in which 'Energy', the common stock of youth and maturity, is balanced by 'Thought'. It is, however, not a celebration of reason so much as a dramatic exposé of the limits of reason. Its musical identity is never quite mirrored accurately and tends to dissolve in a shimmer of rapid oscillations. Quarter-tones become increasingly dominant, breaking in on what promises or threatens to become a rational train of thought and the continuous movement ends up pretty much back where it started.

For the cathartic final part, *Ygghur*, Scelsi requires that the cello be substantially returned to B♭, D♭, low B♭, low D♭. In this final part, almost all of the material is derived from quarter-tones and from great swooping glissandos reminiscent of Xenakis's string pieces. The movement is fuelled by the same rumbling oscillations as *Dithome* but these are increasingly accompanied by high harmonics – what European critics evocatively describe as 'flageolet tones' – and by 'shakes' between pitches. The music starts to lose its tonal centredness, and there is a sense of progressive disembodiment as the dynamics are steadily lowered and the overtones take over. *Ygghur* resembles an out-of-body experience. The music seems to float without ordinary structural connections and there is persistent illusion that the sounds are not produced within the body of the cello at all but in the outside air.

It is an ideal response to the confident energy of 'Youth' and 'Maturity'. Written later, it is at once an act of memory (the central movement restates elements of *Dithome* from a lofty, almost transcendent viewpoint) and a dramatic proliferation of perspectives. The score is written on four staves, one for each string, and the tuning allows for bizarre unison effects, which echo moments in earlier parts where he required the simultaneous production from different strings of the same tone, differentiating them only by the presence or absence of vibrato, or of a mute.

Clearly, this is virtuosic music and Utti's responsive performance marks her out as its co-creator. The purely accidental coincidence of an E/F centre in *Triphon* always evokes for me an unexpected echo of Jacqueline Du Pré playing the *Adagio* of Elgar's Cello Concerto. It is obvious, of course, that Scelsi's is music of a radically different order. (The echo only sounds one way.) Its premises and aims are quite different and the intense communicativeness with an audience that affected Du Pré's performances of the Elgar night to night are completely irrelevant here. In the last analysis, analysis itself fails. Scelsi's music requires to be absorbed and internalized; perhaps more than any other single piece in this section, it demands an 'evenly suspended attention'.

Discographical Information

Other Scelsi: *Bot-Ba* (1952; hat ART CD 6092); *Tre pezzi* (1966; Adda 581047); *Canti di capricorni* (1962–72; Wergo WER 60127 50); *Okanagon* (1968; hat ART CD 6124); *Le fleuve magique* (1974; Adda 581189).

Map references: Zoltán Kodály Sonata for unaccompanied cello (1915; Delos DCD 1015); Iannis Xenakis, *Kottos* (1977; Disques Montaigne 782005); John Cage, *Etudes boreales* (1978; Etcetera KYC 2016).

ALBERTO GINASTERA (1916–1983)

Piano Concerto no. 1 (1961)

FIRST PERFORMED: Washington, DC, 22 April 1961
SELECTED RECORDING: ASV DCA 654
    Oscar Tarrago (piano); Oquesta Filarmonica de la Ciudad de Mexico, conducted by Enrique Bátiz
    [with: *Estancia* – Ballet Suite (1943); Harp Concerto (1956), Nancy Allen]
RECORDED: 1989
DURATION: 25' 42"

The premiere in Washington of Ginastera's First Piano Concerto was somewhat eclipsed by the first performance, just over a week later, of his extraordinary *Cantata para América mágica* (1960). A setting of quite spurious 'pre-Columbian' texts, scored for dramatic soprano, percussion and orchestra, the *Cantata* caught the imagination of a public who may well have been primed for it by a current popular vogue for a statuesque Peruvian singer called Yma Sumac, whose 'Inca' antecedents and source materials bore no closer examination than Ginastera's, but whose five-octave soprano was dramatic in the extreme. The *Cantata* created a furore only to be matched by that which attended Ginastera's opera *Bomarzo* (1967, not to be confused with the 1964 *Cantata Bomarzo* which used an identical libretto), and it helped to cement his reputation in the United States. In 1971 the new Kennedy Center in Washington opened with the last and gentlest of Ginastera's operatic trilogy, *Beatrice Cenci*, completing the cycle that had begun in 1964 with the young Placido Domingo's interpretation of *Don Rodrigo*; a fourth opera, *Barabbas*, was never completed.

Ginastera enjoyed an awkward relationship with the Perón government in his native Argentina and on more than one occasion had had to look to the United States for support. He had tussled with Perón as early as the end of the war, but had eventually been permitted to travel and to work with Aaron Copland at Tanglewood, an association anticipated in the vibrant ballet suite *Estancia*. Ginastera's appointment as director of the National Conservatory in La Plata was rescinded on Perón's orders, but he re-entered the musical establishment after the dictator's overthrow, too late perhaps to prevent a steady disenchantment. After divorcing his first wife, the pianist Mercedes de Toro, he married the cellist Aurora Nátola (who later premiered the fine 1979 Cello Sonata) and emigrated to Switzerland, where he died in 1983.

His relationship with the Argentinian authorities came to a head for the last time over his second opera. Three months after its Washington premiere *Bomarzo* was suppressed by the authorities in Ginastera's native Buenos Aires on grounds of gross immorality (rape, murder and deformity play a substantial part). The furore has tended to overshadow the opera's considerable formal inventiveness. A succession of short scenes and interludes each mimic the classical triangle of complication, crisis and dénouement, giving the piece a microstructure that perfectly suits its adventurous modifications of serialism. Ginastera also incorporates elements of chance into the choral parts, and the result is a vivid, intensely erotic dramatic experience (which I remember blushing furiously over in the dark at the ENO in 1976), with none of the drabness that afflicts serial operatic writing. It is, though, probably as well that no recording is available. To hear Ginastera at his most effective on disc, we need to turn back a few years.

The turn of the 1960s had seen him transform himself from a nationalist composer, with an almost sentimental attachment to Argentinian folk themes, into a major international figure whose work nonetheless retains deeply rooted and ineradicable Latin American qualities. Early pieces, such as the *Danzas argentinas* (1937) for piano, are attractive but slight, and some of the earliest orchestral scores, including two symphonies and an 'Argentinian' concerto, were subsequently withdrawn, though the early ballet *Panambí* (1935) contains in a series of miniatures many of the concerns and techniques that came to fruition in the work of his maturity.

Prominent among these were a whirling, almost trance-like rhythmic sense, ultimately derived from Manuel de Falla (1876–1946), a highly personal use of thematic series of varying intervals, and an ability to invent classical forms with new energy. Nicolas Slonimsky sees a connection between Ginastera's work on *Don Rodrigo* and Alban Berg's use of classical forms in the opera *Wozzeck* (1917–21), but many of his innovations were undoubtedly arrived at independently and they seem to me to be most fully integrated in the First Piano Concerto. Ginastera was a superb pianist and his writing for the instrument is always powerful, demanding and thoroughly pianistic. Like its successor (1972), which began with a series derived from the dissonances at the opening of the last movement of Beethoven's *Choral Symphony*, much of the material in the first movement is derived from a serial chord and an underlying note-row. This is treated freely rather than strictly, generating a powerful cadenza in which the soloist and orchestra vie almost aggressively for prominence. Then there follow ten variations and a coda (actually an eleventh variation) which returns to the opening cadenza for its material; all packed into less than nine minutes.

The Piano Concerto no. 2 was unusual in that the piano part in the second movement was for the left hand only, possibly a deliberate echo of Ravel's Piano Concerto in D (1931). The First is in every sense a two-handed work, calling on considerable dynamism from the soloist. This is less immediately evident in the quiet but vital scherzo, to which Ginastera affixed the title 'Allucinante'. Here absolute control is called for as soloist and orchestra frame three separate internal divisions within another introduction and coda (this is a very frequent characteristic of the microstructure of Ginastera's works). The rhythms are light, fast, almost stippled, and though there are no direct quotations from folk forms, the music is meant to suggest the mystical and hallucinatory elements in the indigenous culture of Argentina.

The slow third movement is altogether more stately, in classical ternary form with the last of three sections a repetition of the first. It leads to a powerfully emotional climax that dies away on a mysterious string chord and a soft, almost whispered declaration from the soloist that recalls the secret knowledge of the previous movement. The finale, marked *Toccata concertata*, restores the brash, almost brutal dialogue of the opening movement, and here Oscar Tarrago really comes into his own, abetted by a very immediate and upfront recording. It was Hilde Somer, featured on the alternative Phoenix recording (see below) who premiered both of Ginastera's piano concertos, and her interpretation is nicely judged, but let down by a rather heavy-handed response from the Vienna Philharmonic Orchestra. Ever resistant to discussing his compositions in terms of structure or method, Ginastera said that 'a work which speaks only to the intelligence of man will never reach his heart', and suggested that the essence of the piece was that it should establish a 'flow of attraction between public and artist, independent of its structural implications'. Bátiz, himself a gifted pianist, has a firm instinct for larger cycles of rhythm, and allows the movements to develop organically, rather than with Maerzendorfer's somewhat lock-stepped precision and two-dimensional sound.

Discographical Information

Other recording: Hilde Somer, Vienna PO, Maerzendorfer (Phoenix PHCD 110).

Other Ginastera: *Panambi* (1936; RealTime RT 2003); *Danzas argentinas* (1937; ASV DCA 865); *Pampeana no. 3* (1954; Dorian DOR 90178); *Milena*: Cantata no. 3 (1971; Phoenix PHCD 107); *Popol vuh* (1975; RCA Red Seal 09026 60993); Cello Sonata (1979; Newport Classic NPD 85511).

Map references: Manuel de Falla, *El amor brujo* (1915; London 433908); Béla Bartók, *Dance Suite* (1923; Mercury Living Presence 432017); Silvestre Revueltas, *Sensemayá* (1938; Sony Classical SMK 47544).

LEJAREN HILLER (born 23 February 1924)

Piano Sonata no. 5 (1961)

FIRST PERFORMED: New York City, April 1969
SELECTED RECORDING: Orion ORS 75176 LP
    Kenwyn Boldt (piano)
    [with: Piano Sonata no. 4 (1950), Frina Arschanska Boldt (piano)]
RECORDED: 1975
DURATION: 26'

Lejaren Hiller began his professional life as a research scientist and to some extent has remained one. He regards composition as an essentially modest experimental process rather than as a grand philosophical endeavour; the putting together of interesting combinations and formulae rather than the construction of all-embracing aesthetic unities. His reputation has been correspondingly low-key; which is a pity for his work is lively, humane and constantly interesting, and deserves to be more widely known.

Though he found time for composition study under Milton Babbitt and Roger Sessions at Princeton University, Hiller's training was in chemistry and it may be that the habit of experimental combination and recombination has had an impact on his way of thinking musically. Hiller likes to try the unexpected, even the exotic; who else in the late 1970s would have thought of writing for devil's fiddle and harpsichord, as he did in *Diabelskie skrzypce*? Or of putting together piccolo and *berimbau* (a South American single-stringed instrument with a gourd sound-box) as he did in *An Apothesis of Archaeopterix* the following year? Trade-offs between mathematics, physics, even engineering, and music have tended to be much more common, but Hiller has an instinct for organic coherences that seem to elude even more intuitive composers.

He spent the first few years after his doctorate working in industry, joining the chemistry faculty at the University of Illinois in 1952. Six years later he transferred to music, and since 1968 has been Frederick B. Slee Professor of Composition, co-directing the influential Center for the Creative and Performing Arts with his fellow-composer Lukas Foss (born 1922). More than 75 per cent of Hiller's output has been for piano or other keyboard instruments. The two main exceptions are electronics and music for string quartet, and his best-known work combined the two. In 1956, in collaboration with Leonard Isaacson, Hiller completed the first instrumental score ever to have been wholly devised on an electronic computer. The *Illiac Suite* for string quartet was generated in collaboration with Leonard Isaacson, using the ILLIAC digital computer designed at the University of Illinois. Cast in four sharply contrasted movements, it is a fairly schematic work, not much more than a set of technical exercises with virtually no sense of organic development. The opening movement relates randomly generated numbers to a two-octave C major scale and then subjects the resulting sequences of notes to the basic rules of Renaissance counterpoint, with which the computer had been programmed. These are used in a more complex configuration in the second movement, and in both cases the results are mildly pleasing and certainly unmechanical. The third movement is largely concerned with rhythm, while the last extends the serial language Hiller had experimented with in his earlier piano piece *Twelve-tone Variations* (1954).

Later in his career he was to make more sophisticated use of information technology, co-writing the impressive *Computer Cantata* (1963) with Robert Baker and an IBM machine, and collaborating with Ramon Fuller on significant technical analyses of works by Berg, Webern and earlier figures. His appetite for collaboration reached its peak at the end of the decade when he worked with John Cage on the composition and realization of *HPSCHD* (1967–9), a piece for one to seven amplified harpsichords (hence the vowel- and semi-vowelless title) and one to fifty-one electronic tapes. The piece (on which the British composer Gavin Bryars also worked) represented an interesting conjunction of chance and electronic elements.

Hiller's *own* work – the emphasis is slightly artificial, because he stamps his personality even on the experimental and collaborative projects – has always involved an element of theatre. He has devised dramatic fantasies for voice, instruments and electronic elements, a substantial body of theatre and film scores, and perhaps his major work of the 1970s was the six-hour *Midnight Carnival* (1976) a huge, participatory piece for the city centre of St Louis, Missouri. His sense of drama has also worked on a much smaller scale, permeating some of the instrumental pieces. The Sonata no. 4 for piano (1950, also on the above record) satirizes some of the aesthetic poses of the avant garde. Like the *Illiac Suite*, its four movements are to some extent parodies of specific piano styles; Hiller softens the blow slightly by describing them as 'fantas[ies] on ... well-known style[s] of pianism', successively nineteenth-century romantic, modern popular, neo-classical, and folkish. In the second movement, he pokes fun at a 'legitimate' or 'serious' performer coming unstuck over two ultra-basic themes, a blues in C and a D♭ pop tune, which she (in this case) treats with furrowed intensity and solemnity. It is a mild joke but an effective one, with a sting in its tail.

The scherzo also develops two different themes in opposition to one another, in this case a neo-classical theme and a bland show tune, but it is the finale that shows off one of Hiller's most characteristic effects, a deliberately extreme opposition of pitch and dynamics. The movement restores some of the 'pop' material and the cheerfully antagonistic tonality of the second movement, starting *ppp* at the top end of the keyboard (an effect that reappears in a different context in Sonata no. 5) and gradually building in intensity as the pitch descends, fading away again after middle C until the lowest notes are again played with great quietness. The final pages restore the basic tonality of the 'classical' first movement, which had opened in gentle F major, only to throw itself off-beam by constantly reverting to material from the introduction in its own $\frac{5}{4}$ main section. The effect of the piece as a whole is of having one's leg gently pulled while a quite sophisticated musical message is smuggled past; the essential privacy of Hiller's language is somehow protected by the humour.

With that in mind, Hiller's assurance that the Sonata no. 5, written just over a decade later, is 'by comparison ... a perfectly straightforward piece' should be taken with caution. It is certainly less stylistically capricious, more academic in tone, and mostly unironic. It is, though, not without its unusual and striking features and, along with the *Twelve-tone Variations* which are its ancestors, it is one of Hiller's most impressively unified works. Like the 1954 piece, the Sonata no. 5 is serial but not strictly orthodox. The first movement is derived from what is called an 'all-interval' note-row; that is, a sequence of the harmonic scale in which all the possible gaps between notes are represented, from minor second (a semitone) right up to major seventh (which is only a half-step short of an octave), though not, of course, in sequence. After a brief *Andante tranquillo* introduction, the main part of the first movement begins with a statement of Hiller's row. Beginning on low C, it runs C A♭ D F G B♭ F E♭ E A F♯. This is not a strict series because $C_\sharp$ is omitted, and F repeated. Hiller's intention was to lend an essentially atonal piece a suggestion of a tonal centre, and here and elsewhere it tends to gravitate towards an untroubled, almost pastoral F major tonality.

The main *Allegro agitato* develops three principal subjects (two is the norm) recapitulating each in reverse order and then closing with a coda that restores material from the quiet introduction. A much less effusive and upfront player than his wife, Kenwyn Boldt brings an air of quiet concentration and a subtle command of tone-colour that recalls his own interest in non-Western music. This is even more strongly evident in the long 'Interlude' which follows. Marked *Lentissimo*, the slowest indication in classical music, this astonishing twelve-and-a-half-minute section is written entirely for the highest keys on the piano, and conveys an impression of almost total stasis, comparable to similar effects in Cage's music, or markings like *Infiniment lent* in Messiaen's *Quatuor pour le fin du temps*. Again, Boldt's touch is light and airy, suggesting a very controlled technique that calls on little or no arm-weight.

The next two movements together take up less than half the time. The fast Rondo is almost brusque and sounds curiously fractured. It follows a strict development of thematic outlines but disrupts the tonality with a sequence of chance elements, anticipating some of the procedures in *HPSCHD*. The very brief epilogue again contrasts two classes of material and suggests that (as in the opening movement) there is a third subject at work as well, a tonal bias that never quite surfaces. The dominant of these became the basis for two of the keyboard pieces in *HPSCHD*. The rhythms are $\frac{10}{8}$ and, in the main development, an awkward $\frac{7}{8}$, and Boldt plays with curious internal divisions which are very redolent again of Indian *raga* music.

It would be pointless to claim the Sonata no. 5 as an overlooked masterpiece. It is, by and large, a modest work by a generally uneffusive composer, but it is clearly not quite as innocently straightforward as Hiller liked to claim, and poses interesting questions about how tonality (and thus atonality) are actually perceived, about the workings of musical time, and about received perceptions of musical structure. An exclusive diet of grand masterpieces would be cloying and, ultimately, dull. The by-ways are often every bit as attractive.

Discographical Information

Other Hiller: *Illiac Suite* (1956–7 [with: Isaacson, *An Avalanche* (1969)]; Wergo WER 60128); *HPSCHD* (1967–9; Nonesuch H–71224); *Metaphors* (1989; New World NW 394).

Map references: Leon Kirchner, String quartet no. 1 (1949; CRI SD 395E); Mario Davidovsky, *Synchronism no. 5* (1969; CRI CD 611); Charles Wuorinen, *Archae-*

opteryx (1978; Koch International Classics 3–7110); Milton Babbitt, *It Takes Twelve to Tango* (1984; CRI CD 521); Leon Kirchner, *Music for Twelve* (1985; Elektra Nonesuch 79188).

Further reading: C. Gagne and T. Caras, in *Soundpieces: Interviews with American Composers*, Metuchen, NJ, 1982; S. Husarick, 'John Cage and Lejaren Hiller: HPSCHD', in *American Music*, vol. i/2, 1983.

IANNIS XENAKIS (born 29 May 1922)

ST/4 – 1.080262 (1962)

FIRST PERFORMED: Paris, 1962
SELECTED RECORDING: RCA Red Seal RS 9009
   Arditti String Quartet: Irvine Arditti, Lennox Mackenzie (violins), Levine Andrade (viola), Rohan de Saram (cello); with Geoffrey Douglas Madge (piano)
   [with: *Mikka* (1972; violin); *Mikka 'S'* (1976, violin); *Kottos* (1977, cello); *Ikhoor* (1978, string trio); *Dikthas* (1980, violin, piano); *Embellie* (1981, viola)]
RECORDED: 1982
DURATION: 12' 19"

Explaining the title will take us some way towards understanding the piece. 'ST' stands for 'stochastic music', '4' relates to the number of performers (in this case a string quartet), '1' indicates that it is the first such piece for these forces, and the last six digits give the date on which the piece was composed, 8 February 1962. 'Composed' is no more helpful at this stage than the as yet unexplained first term in the sequence, for like the other pieces in the group – *ST/10* and *ST/48* – and some of Xenakis's later work, the score was worked out on a computer. Inevitably, this has led to a widespread conviction that Xenakis's music, with its gnomically guttural one-word titles is *all* machine-generated and thus forbiddingly mechanistic. A close look at almost any of his works exposes the injustice of such a view.

   Xenakis is the twentieth century's closest equivalent to the totalizing intellect of a Leonardo or of the Ancient Greeks. He seems unaware of any conflict between the 'Two Cultures', the polite and the scientific. He has devised principles of organization which draw more from mathematics and science than from any prevailing musical orthodoxies and schools and has generated a body of music that is both utterly modern and systematic and quite primitive in its impact, like entering a large and alien building whose origin and purpose is not clear; the relevance of the analogy will become clearer. So overwhelming are some of the large-scale orchestral pieces, and so incompletely do they transfer to record, that it is perhaps best to approach Xenakis's major works by way of the chamber pieces. If massive pieces like *Metastaseis* (1954), *Pithoprakta* (1955–6) and *Terretorkh* (1965–6) can be properly called 'architectural', then the shorter works resemble ante-chambers, fragmentary details, humanized furnishings. (It is very much part of Xenakis's philosophical background that the smaller is proportionally related to the whole by a complex but demonstrable set of transformations.) The Arditti Quartet, whom Xenakis has declared the 'best in Europe', have comprehensively recorded and re-recorded the chamber pieces for strings and though the CD option below has much to recommend it, the original performances for RCA are vivid, sensitively recorded, and thoroughly approachable.

Xenakis's life story is remarkable. He was born in Romania of Greek parents and returned to Greece for his education, which combined a preparatory course in engineering with music study. After the defeat of the Axis in Greece, in which he played a part as a member of the Resistance, Xenakis became political leader of a nationalist cell (named, ironically, after Lord Byron) who opposed British interference in Greek politics. During a violent demonstration just before Christmas 1944, he was gravely wounded by a shrapnel splinter that tore through his mouth, palate and left eye. Most subsequent portraits of the composer are right profile or show the left-hand side in deep shadow, hiding a huge, trenched scar that lends his face the appearance of damaged statuary. An exception is a joyous, full-face photograph taken at the Parthenon in 1974, after the fall of the colonels' junta, marking Xenakis's first return to Greece for a quarter of a century.

Xenakis recovered slowly from his wounds, but was placed under sentence of death following renewed Resistance activity. In 1947, using a forged passport, he escaped to France, subsequently adopting French citizenship. Here his musical studies began in earnest, at the Ecole Normale under Darius Milhaud and Arthur Honegger, at the Conservatoire National Supérieur under Olivier Messiaen, who became his sponsor. At the same time, though, Xenakis was architectural collaborator to the controversial Le Corbusier with whom he was to work (the division of credit has never been clear) on such projects as L'Unité d'habitation at Nantes-Rèze, the magnificent Couvent Sainte Marie de la Tourette, at Eveux, the Sports and Cultural Pavilion in Baghdad, and the Philips Pavilion at the Brussels World Fair in 1956, for which Edgard Varèse composed his *Poème électronique*.

Commentators often find it difficult to reconcile careers that seem to be made up of two apparently unrelated strands: painters who compose, poet–physicians, the relation between Noam Chomsky's linguistics and his politics. It was once said that architecture is frozen music. In so far as the analogy holds up at all, Xenakis's music is flowing architecture, in which the grid-like interrelations of verticals and horizontals, elevations and ground-plans, have been replaced by organic aggregates derived from natural processes and in which the linearity of most Western music is replaced by huge *masses* of sound.

Xenakis was convinced that the serialism of the Darmstadt school was a dead-end; even worse, 'it was a kind of Fascism' that attached an almost mystical significance to just one organizational possibility. With twelve-note composition, the scale had become neutral, with no ordering hierarchy of tonics and dominants as in tonal music; the development of electronic technology underlined the redundancy of dividing the octave into twelve semitones. But by imposing a system of twelve notes, the serialists had smuggled in a different sort of hierarchy. Following Anton Webern, Karlheinz Stockhausen had tried to reintroduce an element of hierarchy into the note-row by establishing sub-groups around certain selected pitches, but this seemed absurd to Xenakis. Xenakis shared with the Darmstadt composers – Boulez and Stockhausen primarily – a conviction that Schoenberg had placed too much emphasis on pitch, but was sceptical about their experiments in the direction of 'total serialism' or 'integral serialism', in which every other parameter of the music – timbre, duration, dynamics – was derived from serial procedures.

In the Swiss journal *Die Gravesaner Blätter* (Xenakis had studied under the conductor Hermann Scherchen (1891–1966) in Gravesano), he published an article entitled 'The Crisis of Serial Music' in which he instinctively sided with Messiaen against the Darmstadt composers. Messiaen, he believed, had solved the problem of serialism's inherently static quality without surrendering to an equally restrictive system. The problem, as Xenakis saw it, was that serial composition was restricted to a highly linear polyphony which was heard as no more than a 'heap of notes'. Serialism derives its material from a row which, despite being strung out in a linear sequence has to be perceived as a totality, as one might perceive a painting. If the essence of music is movement in time, then serialism denies itself one of music's defining characteristics.

Xenakis sought an 'escape route from the linear category of musical thought' and a means of composition in which the independence of all notes would be complete. He rejected the notion that music was a language, arguing that the 'sub-structure of music is much closer to the categories of space and time, [and that] music is purer, much closer to the categories of the mind'. The reference to Chomsky above was not entirely incidental for there is a clear parallel between Chomsky's Cartesian linguistics and Xenakis's desire to create a music of radical philosophical purity.

The Gravesano article offended the new music establishment and for the next few years the outsider Xenakis found it difficult to have his work performed. He continued to submit articles to the journal setting out the basic principles of a 'stochastic music'. It is probably easier to define this approach in terms of its alternative title, which is 'probabilistic music'. Xenakis was interested in natural processes – blood clotting, wind, the formation of clouds, the action of water or sand, the growth and arborescence of a tree – in which the behaviour of individuals is considerably less significant than the behaviour of aggregates or masses, and probabilities are more significant than rigidly verifiable rules.

Where the serialists were largely concerned with static geometries of sound (however complex the actual figuration), Xenakis was interested in dynamic change. The most distinctive sound of Xenakis's new music was the glissando, a continuous slide between pitches. It was by no means a new device, and other composers with markedly different philosophies like Stockhausen and Ligeti were quick to adopt it, but only Xenakis used it as a main structural principle. The essential shift was from deterministic music (in which everything conformed to a narrow set of rules) to indeterministic music in which the range of possible events was only governed by the rules of statistical probability. Stockhausen was experimenting with 'statistical' chords in 1955 and showed signs of a switch of emphasis from pitch relationships to qualities like volume, intensity, 'attack', sound-colour, timbre, and absolute pitching. Xenakis, unencumbered by the Darmstadt composers' almost mystical adherence to serialist technique, went very much further, making the *texture* of the music its essential substance rather than a secondary characteristic. This was something Varèse had anticipated in the 1930s when he stated that the roles of colour and timbre would be 'completely changed from being incidental, anecdotal, sensual or picturesque', becoming 'agents of delineation' like the areas of colour on a map. Though Varèse was unquestionably an influence, it is clear that Xenakis was already thinking along such lines when he attended rehearsals for the premiere of Varèse's *Déserts* in December 1954; he had already written, though not yet seen performed, his own first major piece *Metastaseis* (1953–4) for sixty-one instruments. Over the next few years he gradually devised a technique and a philosophical underpinning which allowed him to generate the texture of a piece of music according to such mathematical constructs as probability theory and Poisson's Law, which made provision for rare and apparently haphazard events within a probabilistic continuum.

Put thus, it all sounds off-puttingly arid and cerebral. Heard cold, *Metastaseis* can sound like an undifferentiated 'heap of notes', but it soon reveals a seething field of action analogous to that of natural and organic processes. Xenakis himself has rejected the notion that he was much affected by Le Corbusier's architectural ideas and has said that the origins of *Metastaseis* – which means 'transformation' – lie in the experience of a huge anti-Nazi demonstration in Athens:

> hundreds of thousands of people chanting a slogan which repro- duces itself like a gigantic rhythm. Then combat with the enemy. The rhythm bursts into an enormous chaos of sharp sounds: the whistling of bullets; the crackling of machine guns ... Taken uniquely from an aural point of view ... these sound events made out of a large number of individual sounds are not separately per- ceptible, but reunite them again and a new sound is formed which may be perceived in its entirety. It is the same case with the song of cicadas or the sound of hail or rain, the crashing of waves on the cliffs, the hiss of waves on shingle.

That is perhaps the best guide to listening to Xenakis's music: to approach it as if it were a *single sound event*, rather than attempting to relate its separate components back to some initial point of source, like the note-row in a serial piece, or according to some preconceived order of symmetry. *Metastaseis* begins with a single pitch from which all the instruments radiate, as from a primal atomic event, in a cloud of separate articulations. In *Pithoprakta* (1955–6) for fifty instruments, Xenakis developed the principles of continuous transformation still further, but introducing a much richer timbral language, signalled at the outset by having the string players pat the bodies of their instruments in a pointillist effect. It was further evident in his extensive blending of pizzicato and bowed passages; he also introduces a whole repertoire of non-standard articulation devices, notably *col legno* (playing with the wood of the bow: either *frotté*, stroked, or *frappé*, struck), playing below the bridge (*sul ponticello*), modified bowing without accents, high har- monics and modifications of pizzicato effects. In the same piece he also extended the conjunction of statistically average events and 'rare' or sta- tistically improbable events to create brief dramatic episodes and rapidly change the trajectory of the music.

Xenakis had for some time recognized that the enormous tedium of realizing probability calculi for his scores was strictly unnecessary given the development of fast electronic computers capable of undertaking such functions in minutes and with much less possibility of error. Xenakis was aware of Lejaren Hiller's experiments (q.v.) in the United States with Leonard Isaacson and the ILLIAC computer at the University of Illinois, a collaboration that yielded *Illiac Suite* (1956) for string quartet, the first ever computer-generated musical score. He had no qualms about the validity of using computers, believing that 'human creative thought gives birth to intellectual mechanisms which are merely sets of constraints and choices ... Every rule or repeated con- straint is part of the mental machine. *A musical work can be analysed as a multitude of little machines.'* (The last statement chimes with Le Corbusier's famous definition of a house as 'a machine for living' and has proved to be equally controversial.)

Still completing *Achorripsis* (1956–7) for large ensemble, Xenakis had become convinced that computer-assisted composition depended on breaking down the process into sequential steps, a basic series of 'minimum rules and logical constraints necessary for producing a musical work'. In practical terms, the only part of the process which would require to be done manually, given the absence of automatic transcribers, was the final transcription of the score into traditional notation. In the event, the only practical problem was actually being granted computer time to carry out his ideas, but in December 1961 the research head of IBM allocated the composer one hour on the 7090 computer. Xenakis set out nine distinct compositional 'machines' devised to determine: (1) *duration* of a given musical sequence; (2) the *density* of sounds relative to the instruments involved; (3) available *timbre*-classes, i.e. types of sounds; (4) *timing* and succession of attack; (5) specific instrument; (6) *pitch*; (7) rate or gradient of glissando, if any; (8) *duration* of note; (9) *intensity*; at which point the cycle returns to (4) to determine the next note, returning to (1) when the musical sequence is completed.

This is how *ST/4* and *ST/10* (essentially the same piece), and the contemporaneous quartet *Morosima–Amorsima* (1962, piano, violin, cello, double bass) were generated. The musical material is spread very evenly (that is, probabilistically), but with occasional irruptions from the class of 'rare events' defined by a Poisson distribution. Textures are again more significant than the succession of pitches, since it is the timbre of four instruments (arco, pizzicato, glissando, *col legno*, *sul ponticello*, etc) that changes most rapidly, creating a 'screen' of musical detail across which 'particles' emerge and disappear, collide and are destroyed, like molecules in a hypothetical gas. The effect is, of course, highly abstract, though it should be said that Xenakis intervened quite substantially, generating (by his own estimate) 25 per cent of the finished score and there is one odd moment when the cello takes a long downward march in fixed intervals.

Computer composition has remained an essential but not an exclusive component of Xenakis's work over the last thirty years. In recent times, he has helped devised his own UPIC system (Unité Polyagogique Informatique du CEMAMu) at his Centre d'Etudes de Mathématique et Automatique Musicales, which allows direct computer composition by means of an electromagnetic pen on a sensitive pad. A horizontal line indicates a held note at the pitch determined by its position on the 'page'; lines are repeated in parallel for polyphonic effects; a gradient gives a glissando; and a wavy line replicates the 'random walks' and particle motions with which Xenakis was experimenting in pieces such as *Mikka* (1972) and *Mikka 'S'* (1976), a linked pair of solo violin pieces also on the RCA set.

Committed to change as an aesthetic principle, Xenakis has dramatically altered his approach since the early 1960s and now writes in an altogether more intuitive (one might say, more conventionally composerly) way, reserving technology like the UPIC largely for pedagogical work. The very beautiful *Embellie* (1981) for viola solo was written without computer assistance and points to a more cohesive and expressive approach in his scores of the last decade.

The 2 December 1954 premiere of Varèse's *Déserts* had been significant as the first ever stereophonic broadcast, and Xenakis became deeply interested in the spatial distribution of sound, a device familiar from Stockhausen's *Gruppen* (1956), Bruno Maderna's *Quadrivium*, and the American radical Henry Brant's spatially separated pieces. In the mid-1960s, Xenakis experimented with spatial separation, notably in *Terretektorh* (1965–6) and *Nomos gamma* (1967–8) for eighty-eight and ninety-eight instruments respectively, dispersed through the audience in each case. Following his work on the Philips Pavilion, he devised a series of 'Polytopes' (at Montreal, Persepolis, Cluny), ambitious *son et lumière* shows with multi-channel sound and sophisticated versions of the 1960s 'light show'.

The element of drama has always been central to his work. The early orchestral pieces have an abstract impact comparable to that of a *Gagaku* orchestra. The chamber pieces, including later string quartets like *Tetras* (1983, recorded by the Arditti Quartet, below) manage to combine dazzling technical sophistication with the stressed, personal quality of quartets by Beethoven, Janáček or Bartók. Though *ST/4* appears at first to lack that element of 'expressiveness', it conveys almost perfectly the image of a creative individual who stands *beyond cultures*, and whose resources are the eternal verities of mathematics and philosophy and whose country is music itself.

Discographical Information

Other recordings: Helffer, Arditti String Quartet (different personnel) [with: *Herma* (1960–1), *Nomos alpha* (1966), *Mikka* (1972), *Evryali* (1973), *Mikka 'S'* (1976); *Kottos* (1977), *Ikhoor* (1978), *Dikthas* (1979), *Mists* (1980, Helffer), *Embellie* (1981), *Tetras* (1983), *Akea* (1986)] (Disques Montaigne 782005); Quatuor Bernède [with: *Atrées* (1962), *Morsima–Amorsima* (1962), *Nomos alpha* (1966)] (EMI CVC 2086 [HMV S ASD 2441 in USA]).

Other Xenakis: *Metastaseis* (1954) and *Pithoprakta* (1955–6; Chant du Monde LDC 278368); *Nuits* (1968; Arion ARN 68084); *Kraanerg* (1968; Etcetera KTC 1075); *Mycenae-Alpha* (1978; Neuma 450–74); *Pléiades* (1979; Harmonia Mundi HMC 905185); *Mists* (1980; Adda 581241).

Map references: Edgard Varèse, *Déserts* (1954; Attacca Babel 9263); Karlheinz Stockhausen, *Gruppen* (1955–7); Krzysztof Penderecki, *Threnody for the Victims of Hiroshima* (1960); György Ligeti, *Atmosphères* (1961; Deutsche Grammophon 429260).

Further reading: I. Xenakis, 'The Crisis of Serial Music', in *Die Gravesaner Blätter*, 1 (1955), and *Formalized Music*, Bloomington, Indiana, 1971; B. A. Varga, *Iannis Xenakis* [interviews], Budapest, 1982; N. Matossian, *Xenakis*, London, 1986, rev. 1990.

RONALD STEVENSON (born 6 March 1928)

Passacaglia on DSCH (1962)

FIRST PERFORMED: Cape Town, 10 December 1963
SELECTED RECORDING: Altarus CD 9091 (2)
  Ronald Stevenson (piano)
  [with: Prelude, Fugue and Fantasy (1959); Recitative and Air (1974)]
RECORDED: 1989
DURATION: 80'

In the summer of 1962 Dmitry Shostakovich worked fast and hard on the work that was to spark off his last serious clash with the Soviet establishment. The Symphony no. 13 in B♭ minor, also known as *Babi Yar*, contained a setting for bass voice of 'unpatriotic' lines by Yevgeny Yevtushenko. The young poet's references to Russian anti-Semitism were guaranteed to attract the unwelcome attention of First Secretary Nikita Khrushchev, who was beginning to think better of a post-Stalinist atmosphere of cultural tolerance and pluralism; a fortnight before the symphony's premiere, Khrushchev 'declared war' anew on formalism and treasonable satire in Russian art. Despite the attentions of men in raincoats, the premiere went ahead and was a success. However, the work has rarely been performed in Russia since and Yevtushenko's text was only published in bowdlerized form (the poet realistically consented) in the journal *Novy mir*.

As soon as the score was complete, around the end of August 1962, Shostakovich had flown off to Scotland, to attend the Edinburgh Festival, a lull before the storm that preceded the first performance. At a small ceremony in the George Hotel, attended by the poet Hugh MacDiarmid and others, he was presented with a copy of a new piano score, dedicated to himself, by the thirty-four-year-old Ronald Stevenson, a self-declared 'Scottish composer and admirer of Soviet achievements'. The Passacaglia is a heroic achievement, comprising nearly eighty minutes of concentrated music and probably the largest single-movement work in the literature. Perhaps because it has rarely been risked as a concert piece, demanding exceptional stamina and stylistic versatility, it remains comparatively little known, but nonetheless it is a milestone in piano writing.

In particular, it is a descendant of the titanic *Opus clavicembalisticum* (1930) by the Anglo-Parsee-Spanish-Sicilian Kaikhosru Sorabji (1892–1990) and the *Fantasia contrappuntistica* (1910; rev. 1912) by Ferruccio Busoni (1866–1924) but it also draws on the great keyboard cycles by Bach and Beethoven, and also on Shostakovich's own Twenty-four Preludes and Fugues (1950–1). At the end of his address to Shostakovich, Stevenson had said that the Russian composer gave hope to young Western composers because he had 'preserved the lineage of the great masters'. In a sense, that is precisely what the Passacaglia is intended to do, drawing together all the music of the world (both historically and chronologically, and geographically or synchronically) into a single collective movement. It is the kind of all-embracing, dialectically extreme work that Hugh MacDiarmid had striven (and largely failed) to create in verse, and in his valuable National Library of Scotland study of Stevenson, Malcolm MacDonald perceptively heads a chapter on the Passacaglia with a quotation from MacDiarmid's 'In memoriam James Joyce' that captures the spirit of the piece: 'brooding over all the world history of the dance, / Review with the mind's eye, all the forms, / Passecaille, chaconne, sarabande'.

Shostakovich's name is imprinted in every bar of the work; quite literally. Just as Busoni had constructed the *Fantasia* out of variations on Bach's name (in German notation, B–A–C–H is B♭–A–C–B) so Stevenson had taken a lead from Shostakovich himself in the Symphony no. 10 in E Minor (1953) and the C minor String Quartet no. 8 (1960) and created a similar motif from the initial letters of Shostakovich's name in its German transliteration. Like the chaconne, another of the forms in MacDiarmid's 'world history of the dance', the passacaglia maintains a continuous, unvarying ostinato or 'ground bass'. DSCH yields D, Es or E♭, C and B, and this four-note figure, repeated with what are called octave transpositions up the scale, and then played in retrograde, generates a brief theme that runs in the left hand throughout the entire work. (DSCH is also the basis of Recitative and Air on the same Altarus recording, a piece conceived as a seventieth birthday tribute for Shostakovich, who unfortunately died before it was performed.) There is a strong element of display in passacaglia or *passecaille*, with its underlying meaning of 'promenade' or the Scottish *stravaig* (*extravagare*), and Stevenson's work is a literally extravagant exploration of world music, taking in the European classical tradition from Bach to Shostakovich, touching on African rhythms and the microtonal effects of Highland *pibroch* music for the bagpipes.

In his address to Shostakovich, Stevenson had identified himself as a

Scottish composer. He was, in fact, born in Blackburn, Lancashire, but of impeccably Celtic (Scots and Welsh) ancestry, and the knotted Celtic brooch, with its never-ending loops and repetitions (which can be likened to the undivided structure of the Passacaglia) is a central image in his work. Nicolas Slonimsky identifies him as a 'Brythonic' composer, referring to the old north British kingdom into which Blackburn and Hugh MacDiarmid's birthplace in Langholm would both have fallen. As a description, it is a piece of elegant pseudo-historical nonsense, but it rather neatly pegs the spirit of wilful perversity and cultural uni-lateralism that Stevenson shares with MacDiarmid. The poet swerved between internationalist Communism and Scottish nationalism, quoted obscure Baltic political philosophers and wrote in 'Synthetic Scots', rejoiced in terms like 'syzygy', and located himself 'whaur extremes meet'; his favourite image of himself was a volcano, pouring out lots of ash and hot air, but also the raw, molten magma of creativity. Ste-venson had been similarly volcanic (and that is the word one auto-matically reaches for when hearing his piano-playing on this recording), writing theoretical articles for the press, a capacious history of Western music (1971) that frequently misses the mark but never fails to provoke, and a huge body of music on every scale, from the enormous Passa-caglia down to tiny pieces that MacDiarmid might have characterized as 'tit's eggs'. In spirit at least, he is unmistakably Scottish.

The one specifically Scottish element of the Passacaglia was actually written last, just before the premiere. It occurs on the Altarus recording at the very beginning of the second CD (the work is too long for a single disc and is slightly awkwardly divided) and is based on a seven-teenth-century lament by the legendary Patrick Mhor Mac Crimmon called 'Cumha na Cloinne (Lament for the Children)'. This is the fifth of seventeen sections divided up into three main parts – 'Prima', 'Altera' and 'Tertia' – but played without breaks. The range of reference is astonishing. The piece opens with a relatively conventional sonata *Allegro*, which is nonetheless kept open-ended and supplies material for later variations. This is followed by a waltz, then the first of four 'Episodes', then a suite of dances culminating in a Chopin-like polo-naise. The *pibroch* section, itself a further 'Episode' of arabesque varia-tions, and a gentle nocturne, brings the first part to an end.

The mood changes dramatically in the middle section with the apoc-alyptic sounds of 'Fanfare, Forebodings/Alarum, Glimpses of a war-vision' and a set of variations on a theme that mimics the intonation of '*Mir, Khleb i Zemlya*', the famous Bolshevik slogan 'Peace, Bread and Land'. In the former part, Stevenson attempts to give musical expres-sion to a Soviet poster of the Communist hammer beating a swastika into the shape of a sickle, a connection reinforced by the vigorous action of piano hammers against metal strings.

Stevenson extended the language of the instrument considerably in the central part of the piece. The version given at the premiere in Cape Town, where the composer was teaching in 1963, differed somewhat from the MS presented to Shostakovich. The *pibroch* section was new, but Stevenson also greatly revised the 'Pedal-point' section marked 'To Emergent Africa'. After watching a Bantu drummer, he rewrote the passages intended to suggest 'drum rhythms' in a much more dramatic and literal way, instructing the pianist to reach inside the piano and strike the strings directly, a device already used in the earlier 'Reverie-Fantasy', but here in order to create huge, thunderous effects. These, and other heterodox devices like depressing 'silent' keys (thereby creating different overtone environments for surrounding notes), are not inventions of Stevenson's but they are used with great dexterity.

The 'drumming' section is immediately followed by the virtuosic 'Etudes' which mark the work's central episode, built up as throughout over the same unremitting seven-bar theme. This is followed by a set of variations in the same C minor as Shostakovich's Eighth String Quartet, where the DSCH motto made its most significant appearance. And that brings the huge central part of the Passacaglia to a close. 'Pars Tertia' follows seamlessly. It is a slow, stately tribute to Bach, a complex triple fugue using materials from the opening sonata *Allegro* and, for the first time since then deriving thematic material directly from the ground bass. The second theme of the fugue aligns Bach and Shostakovich, German and Russian, using the BACH and DSCH mottos side by side, while the third part introduces a theme from the plainchant 'Dies irae' and is marked '*in memoriam* the six million', the Jews who died at Auschwitz, Belsen, Treblinka and Babi Yar.

Almost miraculously, Stevenson manages to keep his most intense and emotionally complex writing for the final pages of the piece. Reverting to the neo-baroque style which is his native idiom, he constructs a new theme from the ground, allowing it to grow organically and rationally until the work seems raised to an entirely new level. The effect is not so much 'transcendental', music viewed *sub specie aeternatitis*, but as of a music that springs from its own internal logic and from the union of humanity and 'science' that is its essential subject matter. To one passage, Stevenson appends one of the most remarkable markings in the whole of contemporary music – 'con un senso di spazio gagarinesco', 'with a perception of space like Gagarin's' – a reference to the first Soviet cosmonaut who in 1961 had orbited the earth without, in his own words, seeing God anywhere.

At the conclusion of his chapter on the piece, MacDonald states that 'If nuclear or environmental Armageddon were indeed to wipe out human civilization, and one copy of one work by Ronald Stevenson were to be all that survived the disaster to show (musically literate) explorers what one twentieth-century composer was capable of, that work would have to be the Passacaglia'. A generous, but oddly qualified, claim, and one which must remain true until Stevenson or other hands complete the orchestration of his massive choral symphony *Ben Dorain* (begun 1962). In a liner-note for the Altarus recording of Passacaglia, the Canadian musicologist Paul Rapoport suggests that it may be best to ignore the piece's internal divisions, the better to experience the work's suspension of chronological time. It is perhaps unfortunate that even on CD technical limitations render it impossible to hear the piece without a break. Perhaps one of the new or hitherto uninvented formats will oblige ... Stevenson himself partially restores the sense of chronology in a 'pedal-point-in-prose' when he likens the trajectory of the work to a human life, with its physical climax at around thirty-five minutes (= years), and, we might add, a philosophical climacteric around seventy, when the music suddenly attains a new level of 'maturity'.

Stevenson claims only to have recognized the parallel after playing the piece some twenty times over two decades. It is still not performed often enough, though the Altarus recording has to be adjudged a completely authoritative performance. Stevenson made a limited edition album of the music at Cape Town, but the only other LP version I have encountered is by the great British virtuoso John Ogdon, who gave the British premiere of the Passacaglia in 1966 and recorded it for EMI the following year. Before his tragically untimely death in 1989, Ogdon also recorded Sorabji's long-neglected *Opus clavicembalisticum* (which includes a passacaglia section of eighty-one variations over a ground bass) following its revival by Sorabji advocates Michael Habermann, Yonty Solomon and Geoffrey Madge. Together, the two works are among the classic piano works of the century.

Discographical Information

Other recordings: limited (100) edition made by Ronald Stevenson, University of Cape Town, 1963; Ogdon (HMV ASD 2321/2).

Other Stevenson: *Heroic Song for Hugh MacDiarmid* (1967; Altarus CD 9043); *Beltane Bonfire* (1990; Olympia OCD 264).

Map references: Ferruccio Busoni, *Fantasia contrappuntistica* (1910–12; Centaur CRC 2036); Kaikhosru Sorabji, *Opus clavicembalisticum* (1930, revived 1982; Altarus 8014); Dmitry Shostakovich, Twenty-four Preludes and Fugues (1950–1; ECM New Series 1469/70); Dmitry Shostakovich, String Quartet no. 8 (1960; Teldec 2292 44919), Symphony no. 13: *Babi Yar* (1962; Memories HR 4101).

Further reading: 'Ronald Stevenson writes about his *Passacaglia on DSCH*', *Listener*, 9 Oct. (1969); M. MacDonald, *Ronald Stevenson*, Edinburgh, 1989.

LOU HARRISON (born 14 May 1917)

At the Tomb of Charles Ives (1964)

FIRST PERFORMED: 1964
SELECTED RECORDING: Gramavision GR 7006 LP
   Members of the Brooklyn Philharmonic Symphony Orchestra, con-
   ducted by Lukas Foss
   [with: John Cage, Henry Cowell, Lou Harrison, Virgil Thomson, *Party
   Pieces* (1944–5, 'sonorous and exquisite corpses'); Leo Smit, *Academic
   Graffiti* (1962, rev. 1982), Carol Plantamura (soprano), Smit (piano);
   Vladimir Ussachevsky, Divertimento (1980–1, electronic valve, tape,
   chamber orchestra)]
RECORDED: 1983
DURATION: 3' 40"

Modern American music gathers at the tomb of Charles Ives, half
respectful, half guiltily aware of only having understood him too late.
Recognition was squeezed into the last decade-and-a-half of his life,
long after he had given up active music-making. Ives retired from both
the insurance business and music in 1930, after suffering a catastrophic
heart attack exacerbated by diabetes. Slowly, critics, conductors and
performers began to understand what he was about. His masterpiece,
the Sonata no. 2 for piano (*Concord Sonata*) was eventually performed
entire in New York City in 1939, almost twenty-five years after its completion, and two decades after Ives published it privately. The Second
Symphony (1897–1902) was premiered in 1951, the forbidding Fourth
(1910–16) not until 1965. The tone poem *Central Park in the Dark* (1898–
1907) was given at Columbia University in May 1946, a matter of weeks
after the premiere of the Third Symphony, under Lou Harrison's direction. Just to underline the slow response rate of the American musical
establishment, the Third Symphony, which had been written between
1901 and 1904, was awarded the Pulitzer Price for 1947.
   Ives died in 1954 and things thereafter seemed to move in decade
leaps. For many of us the Ives centennial in 1974 represented a first
opportunity to hear his music in any bulk in the concert hall. A decade
later, and two after its completion, Lou Harrison's memorial piece
became the motto work of an influential festival of American music at
the Almeida Festival in London that helped to locate Ives firmly in the
longer historical continuum, and tracing his lineage in outsider figures
like Carl Ruggles (1876–1971), Wallingford Riegger (1865–1961), Henry
Cowell (1897–1965), John Cage (1912–92), Conlon Nancarrow (born
1912) and Harrison himself.
   Harrison's career has been fairly chequered and he has spent a good

deal of time in non-musical pursuits, including working in an animal hospital and as a florist (both perfectly logical callings for a man of his sympathies). As a young man, he had made contact with Cowell (a pioneering spirit in the synthesis of Eastern and Western musics, and author of two concertos for *koto*, among other things); through Cowell he managed to make contact with Ives and established sufficient *bona fides* as an admirer and kindred spirit to persuade the older man to employ him as an editor. While working as a critic on the *New York Herald-Tribune* and for Minna Lederman's relatively short-lived but influential *Modern Music* (published 1924 to 1946), he prepared the Third Symphony and other Ives scores for performance. Just before *Modern Music* folded, he wrote about the 'mindful personal cultivation' of Ives's career, its wholeness and dedicated amateurism: 'he assembles the data of his observed surroundings and tells the tale, not without tenderness, of what he and his friends were like and where they lived'. That was all the *Party Pieces* (see above) were about. Making 'exquisite corpses' is a little like playing Consequences. In the artistic version, one player draws a head, folds the paper and passes it to his companion who draws a torso; and so on until the paper is unfolded and a grotesquely mismatched player is revealed. In the version made by Cage, Cowell, Harrison and Thomson, each player wrote a bar and two notes, before folding the paper at the barline. They are slight pieces, edited for performance by Robert Hughes, but an interesting record of a friendship.

Despite his rather erratic CV, Harrison managed to gain a reasonably orthodox modern training. He briefly studied with Schoenberg in Los Angeles and was at one time close to Virgil Thomson (though not to his music). During the war, though, while working as a dance accompanist, he had experimented with Cage on new sonorities. Like Harry Partch, he had a strong research interest in non-tempered scales and oriental rhythmic patterns (Harrison is still considerably underrated as a theorist), as well as in unorthodox instrumentation.

A large proportion of his output has been for non-Western forces, often used in non-authentic, macaronic combinations that reflect Harrison's use of Esperanto in his titles: *Simfony*, *Koncherto*, the text to *La koro sutro* (1972) for chorus, gamelan. One apparent exception is the 1985 Piano Concerto, premiered and recorded by the jazz pianist Keith Jarrett, who has given Harrison's reputation a significant market boost, but even here the musical language is basically Esperantist, drawing on a broad spectrum of world music. The solo part is nonetheless a long way removed from Harrison's earlier enthusiasm for 'tack pianos', in which drawing-pins were fixed to the hammers of upright instruments, creating a sound somewhere between a Cagean prepared piano and clavichord.

Perhaps his most important single musicological experience was a trip to the Far East in 1961, after which he increasingly used oriental exotica in his chamber and orchestral scores: *p'iri, changgo, jaltarang, suling, xiao*, instruments associated with the Korean court orchestras (for which he presented a piece, *Moogunkwha, se tang ak*, in Seoul in October 1961). From the mid-1970s, Harrison concentrated very largely on the construction of Sudanese and Javanese gamelan orchestras, grouped under the generic subheadings *gending, lancaran, lagu* and *landring* and mostly dedicated to friends and sponsors.

Closely related to his gamelan work has been his enthusiasm for a class of instruments comprising a flat sound-box and mallet-struck pitched strings and which includes the zithers, dulcimers and psalteries. Harrison wrote a small group of works for psaltery alone, the *Sonat per psaltero* (1961), the *Wesak Sonata* (1963) and the later *The Garden at One & a Quarter Moon* (1969), but it is its use alongside dulcimers and orchestral strings that gives *At the Tomb of Charles Ives* its distinctive sonority. The piece evokes a spirit of almost mystical calm. It is very brief and its gestures are remarkably sparse. The main musical material is derived from a Tibetan folk theme which Harrison uses in much the same way as a *cantus firmus* in plainsong, a main theme in the tenor consisting of even-valued notes. Harrison upsets the symmetry slightly, by displacing the secondary material slightly. This lends the piece something of the quality Shakespeare describes as 'brok'n music' (*cantus fractus*), and which is perfectly appropriate to a mourning piece. It is difficult to get to grips with its technical properties and sound-production, not least because it is so brief and evanescent, over almost before it has properly begun.

Harrison wrote a similar *Threnody* (1979), scored for violin and Javanese gamelan, for the Mexican composer Carlos Chavez, but to the best of my knowledge it has not been recorded. Perhaps surprisingly – or perhaps not, given the unusual instrumentation – Lukas Foss's performance of it with the Brooklyn Philharmonic Symphony Orchestra is the first and so far only one on record. A composer himself (born 1922), he is respectful of the score and leaves it virtually unadorned. The vinyl recording is quiet and rather understated and calls for a degree of meditative concentration. Despite Jarrett's sponsorship, Harrison has still not been admitted to major league status in American music. Like the Ives memorial, the works below are of unmistakable merit and it would be good to hear European orchestras take them up.

Discographical Information

Other Harrison: *Elegiac Symphony* (1941, rev. and premiered 1975; MusicMasters 7021); *Two Pieces for Psaltery* (1961, 1969; Phoenix PHCD 118); *La koro* *sutro* (1972; New Albion NA 015); Piano Concerto (1985; New World NW **366).**

Map references: Carl Ruggles, *Sun-Treader* (1932; DG 429860); Henry Cowell, *Ostinato pianissimo* (1934; Thorofon CTH 2003); John Cage and Lou Harrison, *Double Music for Percussion Quartet* (1941; Hungaroton HCD 12991); Wallingford Riegger, *Dance Rhythms* (1955; CRI CD 572); Thea Musgrave, Chamber Concerto no. 2 (1966; Delos DCD 1012).

Further reading: L. Harrison, *About Carl Ruggles*, New York, 1946, and *Music Primer: Various Items about Music to 1970*, New York, 1971; P. Garland, 'Lou Harrison: A Quick Glance across the Years', in *Americas: Essays on American Music and Culture, 1973–80*, Santa Fe, New Mexico, 1982.

BERND ALOIS ZIMMERMANN (1918–1970)

Die Soldaten (1958–1960, revised 1963–1964)

FIRST PERFORMED: Cologne, 15 February 1965
SELECTED RECORDING: Teldec 9031 72775 2
    Mark Munkittrick (Wesener), Nancy Shade (Marie, his daughter), Milagro Vargos (Charlotte, his daughter), Grace Hoffmann (his aged mother), Michael Ebbecke (Stolzius), Else Maurer (his mother), Alois Tremi (Obrist Graf von Spannheim), William Cochran (Desportes, a Hainault nobleman serving in the French army), Guy Renard (Hauptmann Pirzel), Karl-Friedrich Dürr (Eisenhardt), Klaus Hirte (Haudy), Raymond Wolanksy (Mary); Johannes Eidloth, Robert Wörle, Helmut Holzapfel (three young officers), Urszula Koszut (Gräfin de la Roche), Jerrold van der Schaaf (her son, the young Graf), Karl-Heinz Eichler (her servant), Jürgen Bolle (a young ensign), Jörg Geiger (a drunken officer), Peter Flottau, Hans Tübinger, Uwe Rohde (three captains), Chorus of Staatstheater Stuttgart (officers and ensigns), Staatsorchester Stuttgart, jazz group: Eckhart Bauer, Florian Dauner, Karo Höfler, Georg Maier, Lothar Schmits, tapes: Andreas Breitscheidt, conducted by Bernhard Kontarsky
RECORDED: September 1988 and April 1989
DURATION: 120'

We live, in an Alexandrine age. The late twentieth century is a vast memory palace, a mnemonic hall of mirrors in which it is possible to sustain the illusion that all of history is simultaneously present, all of its art and culture simultaneously available and equally valid. It is an illusion fed by the collapse of distinctions between 'high' and 'low' art, and by the proliferation of technologies like the phonograph and its descendants, by film and video, television, cheap books: all the appurtenances of what the critic Walter Benjamin called the 'age of mechanical reproduction'.

It is also, of course, an age which has given birth to and nourished frightening technologies of destruction and control, and the totalitarian ideologies of Fascism and Marxism–Leninism. In 1940, believing himself about to be denied refuge from the Nazis, Benjamin committed suicide on the Spanish border. Thirty years later, on 10 August 1970, Bernd Alois Zimmermann took his own life at Grosskönigsdorf near Cologne. The composer had long suffered from manic–depressive swings and had discovered that his sight was failing. He had described himself as 'a very Rhenish combination of monk and Bacchus', a phrase that helps explain the curious dynamic of *Die Soldaten*. His last major works were the 'lingual' *Requiem für einen jungen Dichter* (1967–9) which used texts drawn from the works and lives of writers who had killed themselves, while the 'ecclesiastical action' *Ich wandte mich und sah an alles Unrecht das geschah unter den Sonne* (1970) is a bleak contemplation of 'all the oppression that is committed under the sun'. Both had the air of musical suicide notes.

Zimmermann's second opera, a variation on the Medea theme, was never completed. *Die Soldaten*, however, is his greatest achievement and is one of the major musical works of the twentieth century. It inhabits the same emotionally alien world as Alban Berg's *Wozzeck* (1917–21), a connection that is underlined by Zimmermann's use of a story written in 1776 by Jacob Lenz, who was in turn the subject of a remarkable short novel by Georg Büchner's play *Woyzeck* (1837) that Berg took his libretto. For Zimmermann, soldiering and the impact of militarism on civil society were basic metaphors for a world gone seriously awry. His own life was profoundly marked by a period of wartime service in the *Wehrmacht*, during which he took part in the occupation of northern France and Belgium (*Die Soldaten* is set in French-speaking Flanders); his repeated insistence that he never fired a shot is a measure of the deep guilt he felt about the experience.

Zimmermann belonged to no identifiable musical school, and considered the concept of style as 'an anachronism'. He wrote in a densely chromatic language that drew on a huge range of past musics; he called it 'collage'. Its most distinctive characteristic is quotation, often in significantly dramatic contexts, as when Marie's seduction in *Die Soldaten* is accompanied by the chorale from Bach's *St Matthew Passion* which describes the betrayal of Christ. Zimmermann also liked to yoke wildly heterogeneous musical and sonic elements together; in addition to a huge orchestra, *Die Soldaten* calls for a jazz combo and a pre-recorded tape of machine sounds, cries, prayers shouted through megaphones, and military commands.

For Zimmermann, the eternal soldier in man represented the destructive element, and the debasement and prostitution of sexual love – 'mechanical reproduction'? – a direct function of a world under arms. His moral philosophy presupposed a world held together not by goodness but by sin. It is approximately the same formula as Bertolt Brecht's question-and-answer: 'Denn wovon lebt der Mensch? ... Den Mensch lebt nur von Messetat allein!' – 'What lets mankind keep going? ... Man lives by sin alone!' As well as being highly individualistic in his musical language, Zimmermann was a man of enormous general culture. He drew his conception of collage from surrealist painters like Max Ernst and Kurt Schwitters, and read widely in philosophy and aesthetics, drawing ideas from St Augustine, from Henri Bergson and from the phenomenology of Martin Heidegger and Edmund Husserl. The most important of these was his conception of the *Kugelgestalt* – 'sphericality' – of time. The notion of time as a continuum of simultaneous presents was one he found in the Augustinian *Confessions*:

> there are three kinds of time, the present of the past, the present of the present, and the present of the future. For these three are in the human soul and I do not see them elsewhere. The present of the past is memory, the present of the present is one's opinion, and the present of the future is one's expectation.

The dynamic that held together past (both Eden and the Fall), present, and future (the expectation of redemption) is what keeps human nature in flux, in transit between the monk and the beast. For Zimmermann, every dramatic action existed on each of those levels simultaneously. His original plan for *Die Soldaten* involved twelve separate stages as well as such modernist devices as film and tape to convey that simultaneity by collapsing sensation, memory and the hope of redemption into a single scena.

He considered the empiricist belief in a narrow factitious present separating two huge abstract un-realities as a 'nightmare' and posited the idea of 'inner time' in which musical memory – and, of course, memories of past music, stored in the 'card index' of the unconscious – opened up the mind to a hugely expanded present which Zimmermann believed was already implicit in the everyday data of our 'Alexandrine' age. As he wrote in his essay 'Intervall und Zeit' (a distinction that marked his rejection of chronological time):

> One cannot avoid observing that we live in harmony with a huge diversity of culture from the most varied periods; that we exist simultaneously on many different levels of time and experience, most of which are neither connected with one another, nor do they appear to derive from each other. And yet, let's be quite honest – we feel at home in this network of countless tangled threads.

Perhaps only Luciano Berio has made an equal effort to harmonize the buzzing confusion of the modern world which we inhabit with such apparent insensitivity and complacency.

The principle of simultaneism is central to *Die Soldaten*. There is no vague, rear-of-stage 'business' while the main action takes place on the apron. Quiet accompaniments are every bit as significant as shouted vocal passages (and few operatic works make such demands on both singers and orchestra in the matter of dynamics alone). Successive movements are given the names of early musical forms – 'Ciacona', 'Ricercar', 'Toccata', 'Nocturne', 'Capriccio' – often quite out of character with their dramatic function and emotional temperature. The abiding impression is of a stylistic telephone exchange in which equivalence or equidistance between all musical styles, high and low, sacred and profane, ancient and modern, is rigorously preserved and to which Lenz's rapid, jump-cut scenes (reminiscent of *Woyzeck* or even Arthur Schnitzler's episodic *La ronde*) were particularly appropriate. Zimmermann called it 'total theatre'.

If the music is pan-stylistic, the ideal staging would be not just 'in the round' but as if the spectator–auditor were placed at the centre of a huge globe (Zimmermann knew his Shakespeare, too) round whose inner surface the action took place. (Interestingly, Karlheinz Stockhausen attempted something rather similar in the *Donnerstag* section of his *LICHT* cycle, a work which shares many of Zimmermann's philosophical and religious concerns.) Inevitably, there were going to be problems. The Cologne Opera commissioned the piece in 1958 when Zimmermann was already under way with his score. The designated conductor Wolfgang Sawallisch and his administrative colleagues very quickly decided that however suited Zimmermann's first version might be to some 'theatre of the future', it was unworkable in a conventional proscenium opera house with a limited orchestra pit. The conductor on this recording, Bernhard Kontarsky, likens the size of orchestra – 100 players – to that specified by Stravinsky for *The Rite of Spring* or Richard Strauss for *Electra*. The problem lay in the number of bulky keyboard and percussion instruments Zimmermann required; these would almost have filled the pit on their own. The Cologne board were also daunted by a score that called for *six* high tenors (beyond the resources of most opera houses), ten speaking parts and a corps of dancers.

During 1963 and 1964 Zimmermann prepared a much-simplified score, accepting the need to contain the spectacle on a single stage. The published score, which was issued a year after the Cologne premiere, replaces the multiple staging and 360° spectacle with a single stage on several levels, and this has been the basis for subsequent performances. Many observers have argued that the work actually *gains* from a more restricted, less dispersed presentation. It is idle to speculate about how much Zimmermann's disappointment contributed to his final decline, but it is possible to attempt a leap of identification with the composer's rapidly failing sight and say that *Die Soldaten* still works astonishingly well as a recorded work. The original production, produced by Hans Neugebauer and conducted by Michael Gielen, can be heard on a radio recording issued on vinyl by Wergo (see below). It is undoubtedly powerful. The absence of visuals throws the score and the singing into focus in a way that could not have been possible had it been mounted in the original futuristic version. Gielen's Berg-isms are occasionally apparent but never intrusive. The main shortcoming is, inevitably, sound quality, which is rather patchy. The Teldec recording on two CDs balances a huge orchestral sound with closely miked vocal passages, allowing the singers to convey the tiny modulations of mood and address that Zimmermann called for, often within a single phrase. What emerges when the elaborate stage mechanism is set aside is a virtuosi-cally detailed score in which the music is layered and textured with consummate skill. Zimmermann's gifts as a 'pure' composer are yet to be fully recognized, and this recording, paradoxically perhaps, is an ideal place to start.

The time sequence of *Die Soldaten* is given as 'Yesterday, Today, and Tomorrow'. The action opens in Wesener's house at Lille. After a violent, martial overture, dominated by the throbbing drum beat which sets a pulse for much of the next two hours, the merchant's two daugh-ters are discovered sewing and writing. Marie is ploddingly mis-spelling a letter of thanks to Madam Stolzius, her hostess on a recent visit to Armentières, occasionally helped by Charlotte, who guesses that Marie has fallen in love with young Stolzius. The sisters quarrel, and Charlotte is left alone to ponder that even in 'loving, hating, striving, shivering, hoping, fearing to the marrow', life would be 'ein Quark' (mere trash like the frippery she is sewing) did not such antagonisms bring it to bitter life.

Thus ends the first 'strophe'. The scene switches to Armentières, where Stolzius is nursing a headache, brought on, his mother guesses, by his love for the unsuitable Marie, who is distracting him from a valuable contract for uniform cloth. Already Zimmermann has estab-lished the all-pervasiveness of militarism and its relationship to a tawdry aestheticism. The scene returns to Lille. As Baron Desportes pays court to a sceptical but flattered Marie, they are interrupted by Wesener, who refuses to allow the young nobleman to take the girl to the theatre, turning on her coarsely. It is here, though, that Zimmer-mann's ability to communicate rapid modulations of emotion and to suggest underlying strata of meaning by allusion and quotation come into effective play. Wesener imitates the wagging tongues that would greet Marie's appearance on the Baron's arm, and then cloyingly declares that she is his 'einzige Freude', his sole pride and joy. As the girl flounces out, the accompaniment hints at *Fidelio* and repeats earlier, less specific, references to Verdi.

The pace quickens as the scene returns to Armientières and the military. Haudy, Pirzel, and the chaplain Eisenhardt are arguing about the respective merits of comedy theatre and the sermon, with occasional interruptions from Pirzel, the young Graf de la Roche, Major Mary, and the three officers, who provide a kind of satirical chorus. Against the chaplain's view that the theatre is not educative and merely serves as an opportunity for officers to seduce young women, Haudy brashly insists that at the theatre one can at least enjoy oneself and that 'a whore will always become a whore'. The chaplain angrily responds that whores are made, not born. This is an exchange that will come back to haunt the characters in the final act. Back in Lille, Wesener is becoming used to the notion of a Baron as a son-in-law and reads with some satisfaction a love-sonnet Desportes has sent to Marie. He advises her to hedge her bets and not give up Stolzius until she is sure that Desportes's suit is certain and sincere. In a troubled night-piece that subtly incorporates elements of striptease (and a tiny quote from *Salome*), Marie reveals that she still loves the draper but longs to improve her station in life. As the storm builds up outside, violent crashes from the brass and percussion, she exposes her bare breasts fatalistically to the lightning.

The second act opens in Madame Roux's cafe in Armentières. Zimmermann meticulously notates and choreographs a complex, noisy scene, giving precise instructions for the arrangement of tables on the various stage levels. The soldiers order rounds, trade insults and bitter misogynistic talk, and pester a silently complacent Andalucian waitress/dancer. Pirzel and Eisenhardt enter, the latter complaining about the soldiers' unkind treatment of Stolzius. After his departure with the Colonel, the atmosphere becomes more unrestrained. The three cadets execute a polyphonic dance in celebration of army life; their boot-taps and stamps 'must be executed with the precision of a percussion band'. At the same time, Zimmermann has the drinkers tap out further rhythmic complexities with teaspoons on saucers and glasses, and with the flat of their hands on table-tops, just as they do to attract the (silent) landlady's attention. A jazz group – clarinet, trumpet, guitar, double bass – appears and pounds out a wild accompaniment to the Andalucian's dance, which collapses as Eisenhardt and the Colonel return with Haudy, who has pledged to protect his friend Stolzius from the insinuations of the soldiers. When the young draper appears on the scene, they treat him with exaggerated consideration before returning to the attack with sly hints about Desportes and Marie. Deeply offended, he staggers off, and as Haudy roars furiously at his tormentors – 'You bloody arseholes!' – the scene collapses in tumult.

A noisy intermezzo leads directly to the house in Lille, where Marie is reading a reproachful letter from Stolzius. She shows it to Desportes, who sneers at his rival's impertinence. Marie is obliged to admit their engagement. Desportes tries to dictate a letter and Marie repeatedly holds him off, smearing his face with ink. His anger and her obstinacy gradually give way to a romantic chase, and the seduction is complete, signalled by erotic references from a variety of nineteenth-century sources in the accompanying score. At this point the stage darkens and divides into three distinct areas. With the lovers visible in the background, Wesener's old mother sings a deep-toned lament for the 'rose of Hainault', while above her Stolzius's mother spits out her contempt for the soldiers' whore not good enough for her son, who intervenes feebly as he moons over the fateful letter. In the background, Bach's chorale acts as a sort of ghost score. As his mother's anger mounts, Stolzius leaps to his feet, swearing a slow but exacting revenge, singing hysterically and then breaking off in a distracted mutter, a passage demanding the finest control from the singer. This, the end of the second act (and of the first CD) is the central moment of the opera. Zimmermann's synchronization of wildly dissimilar vocal lines and multiple stage levels is quite breathtaking and the modulation from giggling farce to bleak impending tragedy is done with consummate control and skill. There can be few more powerful scenes in the operatic canon.

Act III begins in Armentières, with Eisenhardt and Pirzel still locked in their dialogue of the deaf. The chaplain tries to break in on his companion's daft philosophizing with the complaint that it is impossible to step beyond the town gate without finding a soldier making love to a girl. To a sarcastic reaction, the young captain replies that in military life 'alles mechanisch, / alles, alles mechanisch', a conclusion underlined by the militaristic throb of the accompaniment, which carries over significantly into the next scene. Here, a much-changed Stolzius applies to and is accepted by Major Mary as his batman. After a single bar of silence, the scene switches to Wesener's house and Charlotte scolding her sister's inconstancy; with Desportes (and, so they believe, Stolzius) absent, Marie has already taken up with Mary. As she preens in a looking glass, Charlotte hisses 'strumpet' at her. Shocked and offended, Marie folds her hands over her breasts, an echo of her gesture during the thunderstorm in scene 5. The connection is underlined when Mary is received with elaborate good mornings which recall Desportes's gallantries in the third scene (except this time Marie takes the leading role) and the lover's exchange coy banter about last night's 'fireworks'. These are explicit indications that the trajectory of the opera is a reverse of the first half, with an unmistakably tragic tilt. The sisters briefly notice that Mary's batman, standing unrecognized backstage, bears a striking resemblance to 'a certain person', and then exit.

An elaborate orchestral *Romanza* follows, dominated by silvery percussion effects, deceptively light in touch, but with dark undercurrents. It signals the start of the opera's second night-piece, as the Gräfin de la Roche anxiously waits up for her young son. Suddenly, we seem to be at the beginning of a new opera altogether. There is an elaborate and impassioned duet, which despite its dark, serial scoring, harks back to eighteenth-century and romantic models. The young Graf has apparently been caught in an ambiguous clinch with Marie (again!) after dinner, and the Gräfin is disturbed by the girl's steadily worsening reputation. Her son insists that she is more sinned against than sinning, and the Gräfin agrees to take her in as companion and ward. The magnificent vocal writing continues in the next scene, when the Gräfin grandly reassures Marie and makes her offer of assistance. There is a stunning female trio, with Charlotte gratefully in attendance, and the scene ends.

Any thoughts of having stumbled unawares into an opera of an earlier period and idiom are dispelled by the violent dislocations of the final act's opening scene, which is played as if Marie's nightmare suddenly breaks through into actuality, gradually collapsing time and place in its later stages until all locations are one (the stage-world) and all time-frames simultaneous. The pace of action almost defies description. After the sinister, martial thuds of the prelude, the coffee house erupts in a frantic version of the drunken choreography of scene 6, while Marie's degradation unfolds on three separate film screens. Desportes is in prison for debt and has rejected Marie. She is surprised with Major Mary in the Gräfin's garden and flees. Desportes writes to his gamekeeper that he has found a woman for him. Desportes reappears at a nightmarish party, dancing the Twist. The gamekeeper's motionless eyes fix on his prey. As characters mill around in noisy confusion, officers' voices on the loudspeaker repeat the opera's ironic moral crux: 'Shall those who suffer injustice tremble while only sinners enjoy happiness?' The Andalucian dancer reappears. We see Stolzius buying poison. Eisenhardt repeats his insistence that 'A whore will never become a whore unless she is made one'. Marie is raped by her nemesis: 'You poor child – I'll revive you.' The singers' onstage doubles dance in a range of styles from the eighteenth century to the present day. The company repeats the officers' grim transvaluation of values, and blames Desportes for all their woes; if it was not clear before, the nobleman is suddenly revealed as a cruelly wanton boy, the philosophical pervert who, like de Sade, aims to overturn God by playing god. The clue was in his name all along.

The remainder of the scene is played as if at a military tribunal, with the external details of Marie's downfall now shown simultaneously on all three screens, and the nightmare (all but the eventual rape, which takes place out of sight) unfolding onstage. The central question 'Shall those who suffer injustice tremble / while only sinners enjoy happiness?' is repeated obsessively. The last but one scene is set in Mary's room at Armentières, where the major is dining with Desportes, waited on by Stolzius. Desportes talks sourly of Marie and explains the 'reception' he prepared for her at his house; having had her, the gamekeeper will make an honest woman of her. Mary says *he* would have married the girl gladly, had the young Graf not got in the way, at which point Stolzius serves up a soup laced with rat poison. When Desportes collapses in agony, Stolzius grasps him by the ears and screams 'Marie! Marie! Marie!' in his dying face. Mary runs him through (though in some versions Stolzius takes poison) and the young man dies with a final sad lament on those who ruin woman's lives.

The final 'Nocturne' takes place on a poplar-lined road stretching back into infinity on the banks of the Lys. Artillery and steel-helmeted soldiers move across the background to a tape of amplified voices and mechanical sounds. As Eisenhardt intones the *Pater noster*, a miserable beggar woman stops the distraught Wesener and asks him for money. He brushes her off but then, remembering his daughter's plight, though failing to recognize her standing in front of him, he makes the ultimately ironic suggestion: that she try her luck with the endless stream of soldiers. The young officers and the jazz musicians drunkenly chase the Andalucian dancer out into the street, then halt as if struck by lightning and, like automata, join the eternal procession. Marie sinks to the ground in despair and as Eisenhardt reaches '*et ne nos inducas in tentationem / sed libera nos a malo!*' the opera ends with the inexorable tread of the soldiers' march.

There are many levels on which *Die Soldaten* can be 'read'. There is, for instance, a persistent but almost subliminal reference to the Crucifixion, for Zimmermann the ultimate act of capricious cruelty played out by soldiery against mankind. There is the infinite regress of trees beneath which the soldiers march at the end, the betrayal chorale during the seduction scene, many other musical allusions, the whole notion of time being constantly betrayed and redeemed throughout the Creation. However, the piece does not yield to straightforward thematic analysis. Zimmermann's 'spherical' structure is highly resistant and enormously dense. Following any one idea (either textual or musical), one finds that it is constantly varied, multiplied, inverted and repeated at different levels or in apparently redundant synchronizations. It is a work that must at first be absorbed and assimilated whole.

The sheer scale and complexity of *Die Soldaten* prices it out of the repertoire of most opera houses. It has rarely been seen in Britain, and the production that I remember from the Edinburgh Festival in 1972 was (I am now inclined to think) less than satisfactory. Bernhard Kontarsky, who acted as répétiteur on the original Cologne production, has made a magnificent job of it with the Staatstheater Stuttgart. Opera on record is always a tricky business and transfer of an opera as powerfully visual as *Die Soldaten* would seem to involve fatal compromise at almost every level. However, the basic plot line is as straightforward as in any classical opera, and the devastating immediacy of the recording gives the work a power which moves it, quite appropriately, to an interior stage that seems to require no direct visual or dramatic support. Something is lost, of course, but something else is gained, a vivid concentration on Zimmermann's magnificent score. In my view, *Die Soldaten* is one of the half dozen greatest musical works of the last fifty years.

Discographical Information

Other recording: Gabry, Synek, Jenckel, Ridder, Nicolai, Kelemen; Gürzenichorkester Köln, Gielen (Wergo 60033 3LP).

Other Zimmermann: Sonata for unaccompanied viola (1955; CRI ACS 6017); *Requiem für einen jungen Dichter* (1967–9; Wergo WER 60180).

Map references: Alban Berg, *Wozzeck* (1917–21; Deutsche Grammophon 435705); Sylvano Bussotti, *Songs from La Passion selon Sade* (1965; Wergo WER 60054); Philip Glass, *Einstein on the Beach* (1975; Sony M4K 38875); Karlheinz Stockhausen, *Donnerstag aus LICHT* (1978–80; Deutsche Gammophon 423 379).

Further reading: C. Dahlhaus, *The Sphericality of Time: The Musical Philosophy of Bernd Alois Zimmermann*, Düsseldorf, 1978.

MILTON BABBITT (born 10 May 1916)

Relata I (1965)

FIRST PERFORMED: Cleveland, Ohio, 3 March 1966
SELECTED RECORDING: New World Records 80396 2
   The Juilliard Orchestra, conducted by Paul Zukofsky
   [with: David Diamond, Symphony no. 5 (1947–64), conducted by Christopher Keene; Vincent Persichetti, *Night Dances* (1970), conducted by James DePriest]
RECORDED: 1990 [1990, 1989]
DURATION: 16′ 4½″ [*sic!*]

"Babbitt is perhaps the most complex composer ever.' Qualified though it is, John Rockwell's claim is a startling one. Even so, it is hard to think of a rival contender. In the 1960s Stockhausen's music was considered to be the ten-minute egg of hard-boiled modernism, but set against the American's ultra-rigorous technique, Stockhausen seems, if anything, rather easy-going. Pierre Boulez has sometimes been held up as the real inventor of post-Webernian 'total serialism', but Boulez too can seem like an exponent of carefree Gallic impressionism when put alongside Babbitt.

But Babbitt's what? The music or the theoretical and analytical writings that ran parallel to it? It is mainly as a theoretician of new music that he seems so unapproachable, but even in that role unapproachability may to some extent have been thrust upon him. His most notorious article was a piece entitled (though not by Babbitt!) 'Who Cares If You Listen?', published in *High Fidelity* in 1958 and ever afterward a cherished reference point for those who wanted to demonstrate the avant garde's mandarin indifference and even hostility to the 'listening public'. Babbitt was reportedly upset by the title, which was a sub-editor's eye-catching extrapolation from a rather more measured piece, but there is no doubt that it has captured more attention down the years than the bulk of his compositional output.

Even a declared admirer like Benjamin Boretz could declare – in James Vinton's *Dictionary of American Music* – that Babbitt's theories rather than his scores are 'the principal substance of [his] creative accomplishment'. It is a hard claim to duck. Babbitt's compositions are curiously little known outside America and rarely find their way on to concert programmes. There is, however, much recorded music currently available, much of it on the composer-led CRI label, and Babbitt seems an almost quintessential illustration of my underlying point about contemporary music moving out of the concert hall and into the recording studio. The travails surrounding *Relata I* suggest why.

Babbitt has a wide-ranging intellect and has been much influenced in his musical career by mathematics, which he taught and researched at Princeton and in Washington during the war. Though he had studied music at New York University and had taken composition lessons with Roger Sessions, he was writing little music at this time. His main contribution was a learned disquisition on 'sets' in Schoenberg's twelve-note system, the first properly organized examination of the subject and the source of most of the terminology – 'pitch class', 'aggregate', 'combinatoriality' – used in subsequent analysis of serialist music. His own *Composition for String Orchestra* (1940) owed everything to the Viennese master and, like the abortive Symphony from the following year, was subsequently withdrawn, presumably as being insufficiently individual. *Relata I* was to be his first fully acknowledged orchestral score.

In the later 1940s, Babbitt developed his conviction that the non-pitch elements of a musical work – the time intervals, timbres and dynamics

– should be subject to the same deterministic operations as the pitch material. This led him to develop what came to be known as 'total serialism'. In works like the deliberately neutral *Composition for Four Instruments* and *Composition for Twelve Instruments* (both 1948), he showed how this could be achieved by subjecting rhythmic classes and aspects of the sonority to transposition, inversion and retrogression, the same procedures that would have been applied to pitch alone in a classical twelve-note composition. It has been argued that at this point the idea of 'composition' comes to a dead halt, because with total serialization a piece of music is defined absolutely by certain *pre*-compositional decisions that leave no room for expressive freedom or variation. (This was a charge often levelled at Stockhausen, who moved beyond the total serialization of works like the 1951 *Kreuzspiel* to 'conceptual' scores which seemed to devolve total responsibility for acoustic aspects of the work back onto the performer.) The notion of absolute control was undoubtedly one of the reasons that Babbitt so warmly embraced the idea of computer composition (I have quoted him on another of them below), but it is clear that Babbitt did not regard such procedures as anything like the creative abdication or *felo-da-se* that his critics believed them to be.

In 1957 he returned to his early interest in jazz with a gently punning sextet for saxophones, brasses, and a rhythm section called *All Set*, which blended the advanced combinatorial logic of his concert pieces with a curiously attractive and rather winsome swing. It compares favourably with a piece I have already looked at on p. 91, (*Abstraction* by Gunther Schuller, who also plays a part in the realization of *Relata I*) and is far from off-putting. At the same period, Babbitt was also working on vocal composition, still the most underrated aspect of his generally undervalued output. Songs such as the William Carlos Williams 'The Widow's Lament in Springtime' (1950) and the wonderful cycle after Stramm called *Du* (1951) combine a very strict synchronization of the music and text with a genuine expressiveness. As late as 1982, with a setting of John Hollander's 'The Head of the Bed', he was still producing memorable vocal scores. (In her book *New Vocal Repertory*, soprano Jane Manning discusses the early *Three Theatrical Songs* (1946) but omits any of the later pieces as 'too difficult', though recommendable to singers of 'outstanding musicianship'; a nice example of the slightly back-handed praise Babbitt tends to attract.)

These notwithstanding, Babbitt's most important compositional work has been instrumental. In the two decades between *Relata I* and the Piano Concerto of 1985, he has issued only half a dozen orchestral scores. These are *Correspondences* (1967) for orchestra and tape, a 'sequel' *Relata II* (1968), *Concerti* (1974–6) for violin, small orchestra and tape, and *Ars combinatoria* (1981) again for small orchestra. *Without* a qualifying 'perhaps', *Relata I* is certainly the most complex composition covered in this book. It is a bogglingly difficult work whose internal structure consists of up to forty-eight simultaneous instrumental lines, each subject to a rate of change that defies the perceptions even of musically literate listeners. In purely auditory terms, even Xenakis's 'stochastic' pieces place less demand on concentration and memory. Interestingly, it is a work about which Babbitt has written at length, in an essay for R. S. Hines's 1970 book *The Orchestral Composer's Point of View* (and subsequently reprinted in the analytical journal *Perspectives of New Music*). For anyone but a specialist, the central musicological section should be marked *heare bee dragones*, but the essay as a whole is valuable for the light it sheds on Babbitt's attitudes to composition and analysis, and for the occasional sidelights it offers on the piece itself and its performance. John Rockwell had suggested that Babbitt's weighty prose style might even include an element of self-parody, but while the composer is perfectly capable of humour (and is known as a warm and witty raconteur), it has to be conceded that his notoriously prolix and polysyllabic style contains a recognition that verbal language lags a long way behind the complexity achievable in the scores; to that extent, the suggestion that Babbitt's theoretical writing may be paramount is nonsense. Explication of his music demands 'concepts that have not yet been generally or completely or accurately formulated and for which we do not yet have therefore reliable abbreviational verbal characterizations'.

He claims for himself no 'privileged access' into the workings of the piece, suggesting that the 'composer's point of view' has 'no absolute value' in elucidating what is going on. *Relata I* was written at the high-point of the New Criticism in America, when W. K. Wimsatt's and Monroe Beardsley's *The Verbal Icon* was *the* humanities textbook, the 'words-[or notes]-on-the-page' the only legitimate object of study, and 'The Intentional Fallacy' the chief critical whipping post. The twin dangers, Babbitt suggests, are on the one hand the notion that the composing musician is a kind of *idiot savant* whose creative acts have a sort of 'ineffable untranslatability', and on the other the danger of falling into a sixteenth-century conviction that music is a repository of arcane numerological secrets that are known to a small freemasonry of experts.

At this point, it is tempting to impersonate the police lieutenant in *Dragnet* and snap 'Just give me the facts.' By Babbitt's own account *Relata I* lasts exactly sixteen minutes, four-and-a-half seconds, and consists of 516 non-repeating bars of music. Though the work was 'mentally formed and preliminarily sketched' in late 1964, the main impetus for writing came from a Koussevitzky Foundation commission to write a piece in memory of Serge and Natalie Koussevitzky. It is scored for a full-sized orchestra that is broken down into timbral groups consisting of three woodwind trios, four brass quartets, a sextet of registrally distinct percussion instruments, and two string sextets, one plucked, one bowed. There is percussion in the opening and closing bars which anticipates and then recalls the main pitch and time markings and the overall structure of the piece. The basic tempo is moderate but local changes of speed in the attacks give an appearance of extraordinary variety. Though he claims no privileged insight, Babbitt's suggestion that the piece falls into six parallel sections is borne out by most listeners. In each section there is a full ensemble followed by smaller subdivisions according to the instrumental groupings and subclasses already suggested. The 'twelve pitch class series' is divided into two overlapping 'hexachords', which are not chords at all but scales. Ever-present, but rarely explicit, its relationships are nonetheless 'the most incorrigibly incontrovertible auditory correlates of the acoustical event and ... the progression from these minimal units through structural strata to the totality is founded on extensive interactions of differentiation and association inter- and intra-dimensional, ... [They] demand musical experience and developed memorative capacity for their perception.' Which is to say that not only does *Relata I* demand a highly developed awareness of pitch relationships, durational values and timbre, it also imposes a heavy burden on the listener's ability to remember what had gone before. To repeat what may now be too insistent a burden, it is a work curiously appropriate for recorded performance and excessively difficult and unrewarding from the concert platform.

Indeed, in the same essay, Babbitt discusses at some length the difficulties he encountered over the first performance of the piece. *Relata I* was to be included in a programme of modern music by the Cleveland Orchestra which also featured Sergey Prokofiev's *Scythian Suite* (1914). It was George Szell who, as overlord of the Cleveland Orchestra, took on Pierre Boulez as deputy first conductor to take care of the modern repertoire, a fair indication of his ambivalence regarding contemporary music in particular. The premiere of *Relata I* was conducted by Gunther Schuller, who has already been encountered in these pages as a composer. Schuller is a forward-looking and occasionally adventurous musician, albeit one who has tended to put aspects of his musical life in hermetically sealed compartments. Babbitt clearly has no complaints about the conductor's role in the premiere, but he is far less sanguine about the Cleveland players: 'The orchestra was mechanically and mentally largely unprepared and massively uninterested' in the music. (It is encouraging to find someone who uses more adverbs than oneself.) Coming back to 'the facts', by Babbitt's estimate only 80 per cent of the notes were played *at all*, only about 60 per cent were accurate rhythmically, and only about 40 per cent reflected his dynamic and expressive markings. Even though the situation has improved since 1966, it is profoundly unsettling to speculate on how often such performances may still be happening in contemporary music performance. Premieres, by definition, have no reference points and audiences must judge them on their apparent merits. But how would an audience, let alone a professional critic, react to a performance of the 'Eroica' Symphony or the Academic Festival Overture which lacked one-fifth of its written notes and botched not far off half of its rhythmic markings?

At the time, Babbitt was convinced that the only way forward for contemporary music was the foundation of dedicated contemporary music ensembles sympathetic to new scores and prepared to give them adequate rehearsal time.

> Until, if ever, such an orchestra is formed, few demanding contemporary works will be performed and fewer still will be accurately performed – and the composers of such works who have access to electronic media will, with fewer and fainter pangs of renunciation, enter their electronic studios with their compositions in their heads and leave those studios with their performances on the tapes in their hands.

In the near quarter century that has passed since the Cleveland imbroglio, the situation has improved considerably. The Juilliard American Music Recording Institute, founded in November 1987 within the Juilliard School in New York, is just such an entity, dedicated to distributing accurate performances of twentieth-century American repertoire. Babbitt is listed as a trustee of the Recorded Anthology of American Music Inc board and though the present recording bears no imprimatur from the composer, it has to be assumed that it is a satisfactory realisation.

Though a pioneer of electronic music in the USA (he worked on the Mark II RCA Synthesizer at the Columbia–Princeton Center in the 1950s), Babbitt has shown no serious inclination to retreat into a world of technical literalism and perfectability. The *Ensembles for Synthesizer* (1962–4) are livelier than most electronic music, but Babbitt has never suggested that they constitute a specially privileged representation of his compositional intentions, unblurred by musicianly shortcomings. Ironically, perhaps, he still needs the expressive flexibility that distinguishes humane music from machine sounds. Babbitt likes a pun, and in the late 1980s he produced a sequel to the 1966 *Sextets* for violin and piano (the title refers to structure, not instrumentation). He called the new piece *The Joy of More Sextets*, a reference to a best-selling bedside-table book in which a bearded man and various wild-haired women demonstrated sexual positions as patently unperformable as anything in a Babbitt score. His own reputation to the contrary, the sequel piece was his gentle reminder that making music, like making love, can not be done out of a manual.

Discographical Information

Other Babbitt: *Composition for Viola and Piano* (1950; CRI C 138); *All Set* (1957; Elektra Nonesuch 79222–2); *Ensembles for Synthesizers* (1962–4) [with: *Sextets* (1966) and *The Joy of More Sextets* (1986)]; New World 364–2); String Quartet no. 3 (1970; Music & Arts CD 707); *The Head of the Bed* (1982; New World NW 346–2); *Consortini* (1989; GM Recordings GM 2032).

Map references: Anton Webern, Six Pieces for Orchestra (1913; Deutsche Grammophon 423254–2); Pierre Boulez, Sonata no. 2 (1948; Wergo WER 60121–50); Karlheinz Stockhausen, *Kreuzspiel* (1951; Deutsche Grammophon 2530 443.

Further reading: M. Babbitt, 'Who Cares If You Listen?' in *High Fidelity*, viii/2 (1958), repr. in R. Chase, *The American Composer Speaks* (1966), and in B. Childs and E. Schwartz, *Contemporary Composers on Contemporary Music* (1967); and 'On *Relata I'*, in R. S. Hines, *The Orchestral Composer's Point of View*, Norman, Oklahoma, 1970, repr. in *Perspectives of New Music*, ix/1, (1970); J. Rockwell, 'The Northeastern Academic Establishment and the Romance of Science', in *All American Music: Composition in the Late Twentieth Century*, New York, 1983.

ANDRÉ JOLIVET (1905–1974)

Suite en concert pour flûte et percussion (1965)

FIRST PERFORMED: 1966
SELECTED RECORDING: ADDA MFA 581055
   Pierre-Yves Artaud (flute), Ensemble de Percussions 2E2M: Michel Gastaud, Jean-Louis Forestier, Alain Beghin, Stanislas Skoczinski, directed by Paul Mefano
   [with: *Cinq incantations* (1936, solo flute); *Incantation* (1937, alto flute); *Cinq ascèses* (1967, alto flute)]
RECORDED: 1988
DURATION: 15' 49"

In the summer of 1986, the young jazz musician Wynton Marsalis broke new ground in an already spectacular career by recording three trumpet concertos with the Philharmonia Orchestra in London. He was roundly condemned by jazz purists who objected to his choice of two French composers – André Jolivet and Henri Tomasi – and who considered the 'classical' strand of his contract with CBS an abject surrender to 'white' European values. There was a good deal of loose talk about 'betrayal' and 'sell-out', though this slowly quietened down in the face of Marsalis's formidable musicianship (he topped polls in both jazz and classical categories) and unapologetic self-confidence.

The whole affair was replete with ironies. It became obvious that jazz fans more readily accepted one of their own turning to earlier composers such as Haydn and Hummel, as Marsalis did subsequently, than to modern 'straight' composers like Jolivet and Tomasi, who were the target of quite extraordinarily vitriolic comment in some jazz columns. There is understandable suspicion of supposedly 'jazz-influenced' classical works, most of which blandly co-opt superficial harmonic devices and rhythmic patterns without demonstrating the remotest understanding of jazz's essential nature. Jolivet's Second Trumpet Concerto (1954) is full of unmistakable references – wah-wah effects in the opening, blues passages, striking use of the mute, and even a drum solo! – but his alignment to jazz is much more profound.

In a blindfold test – a discipline much admired by jazz purists – most listeners will guess that the opening or closing movements of Jolivet's *Suite en concert* is an improvisation by one of the more adventurous jazz flautists, Eric Dolphy perhaps, or James Newton. Jolivet's music is unlike almost any other in the period for its full-hearted attempt to get outside the restrictive systematization of the tonal system altogether and restore 'its ancient and primary character as the magic and incantatory expression of human groups'. Jolivet went on: 'Music should be a direct sonorous objectification of the natural and cosmic system.' Though an early admirer of Arnold Schoenberg (he experimented with the twelve-note series in a 1934 string quartet), he remained largely untouched by serialism. Like Tomasi, who directed the very significant colonial network of French National Radio in the 1930s (this was enough to have him dismissed as a colonialist in the *New Musical Express* when the Marsalis recordings were reviewed), Jolivet took a profound interest in ethnic musics. In the summer of 1935 at Blida in Algeria, Jolivet listened to a local musician improvising on flute. The experience strongly affected him. On his return to Paris, he began to write the five *Incantations* (1936) for solo flute, and throughout his subsequent career, music for flute became the cornerstone of his instrumental output.

I have already mentioned Jolivet once, briefly, in these pages. In 1936, along with Olivier Messiaen, Yves Baudrier and Daniel-Lesur, he co-founded La Jeune France, a group dedicated to the replacement of dry and mechanical neo-classicism with a richer and more romantic style that would be more immediately expressive of French culture and values. The year before, Jolivet had founded his own group La Spirale with similar, though less overtly nationalistic, ideals. These were largely the product of an association he had formed as a postgraduate. In 1930, he had studied under Edgard Varèse (1883–1965), whose small but revolutionary body of work is among the most important this century. Varèse, who had returned to France briefly from New York, not only introduced him to African and 'Pan-American' musics, and to the central role they gave percussion, but also to new electronic instruments like the ondes martenot and the Théremin. Varèse's great contribution had been to rethink the organization and production of sound, rather than simply work variations on the tonal system, and it was this that made the greatest impact on Jolivet, who paid posthumous tribute to him in 1968 with a grand *Cérémonial* for six percussion; earlier, he had drawn on some of Varèse's musicological findings in works like the *Hopi Snake Dance* (1948) for two pianos.

Another piano piece, *Mana* (1935), was Jolivet's first entirely characteristic score, putting together slightly folksy melody with a percussive (Jolivet described it as 'combative') impact, and a distinctive though still perfectly legitimate approach to the piano keyboard. Though he put himself on musical iron-rations during the early years of the war, writing in a deliberately stripped-down, almost protestant, idiom, Jolivet continued to experiment boldly with new sonorities. He used the ondes martenot on several occasions, with piano in *Trois poèmes* (1935), setting a pair of them as concertante voices in the orchestral *Danse incantatoire* (1936), grouping one with winds and harp in the mysterious *Suite delphique* (1943, but only premiered in 1948), and writing one of only a handful of convincing concertos for the instrument in 1947. As I have mentioned, he was also drawn to the pure, ringing tones of the trumpet, writing the two concertos in 1948 and 1954 and returning to the instrument at the end of his composing life with the wonderful *Heptade* (1971–2) for trumpet and percussion (another piece that can be recommended to modern jazz fans). Much as *Mana* recalled some of Villa-Lobos's writing for the piano, the vocal orchestra of *Epithalme* (1953) is usefully compared to the Brazilian's 'orpheonic' *Bachianas brasileiras* no. 9 (q.v.).

However, the primeval, 'breathing' sounds of the flute were central to his search for sonorous objects which exist *sui generis*, filled with their own energy, answering to nothing other than their own essential nature. Interestingly, the five *Incantations* come almost simultaneously with what is certainly the most influential flute piece of the century, Varèse's *Density 21.5* (1936), which took its title from the specific gravity of platinum (not titanium, as is sometimes suggested), the material from which the original interpreter Georges Badurier's instrument was made. Varèse's work became the model for virtuosic flute writing and is the clearest ancestor of such ultra-modernist works as Brian Ferneyhough's lip-breaking *Unity Capsule* (1975–6), which ends with a sigh – of weariness or relief! – from the soloist. However strongly affected Jolivet was by Varèse's ideas, he was also working independently and developing a language for flute that is both primitive in impact and highly demanding in articulation. The 1944 *Chant de Linos* for flute and piano (or string trio with harp) is fearsomely difficult.

The *Incantations*, by contrast, are shamanistic utterances, densely knotted but with a touching simplicity that occasionally suggests Messiaen's use of birdsong transcriptions. Like the later *Cinq ascèses* (1967), they have brief texts appended, of which the fourth – 'Pour une communion sereine de l'être avec le monde' – is the essential expression of the composer's aesthetic philosophy. It is tempting to suggest that the *Concert Suite*, which I have chosen from among Jolivet's post-1940 flute works, dramatizes more fully than any of the other works the *non*-meeting of self and modern world. Unlike its predecessor, the relatively conventional Concerto no. 1 for flute and strings (1949), it rarely suggests a mutually intelligible dialogue between soloist and orchestra. The score places almost impossible demands of synchronization and timbral subtlety on the four percussionists, particularly in the last movement, whose initial calm is interrupted by astonishing outbreaks of sound very different in character to the almost military drum-beats that signal the third movement. At the start of the piece, the flautist sounds a rising-and-falling four-note figure that is strikingly similar to that of the final movement of the *Incantations*, 'Aux funérailles du chef pour obtenir la protection de son âme'. The percussionists whisper softly around the edges, but from this point onwards there is a clear and marked separation between the ensemble and the solo part, which develops subtle and ambiguous rhythmic patterns in opposition to the rather conventional structure. In outward form at least, as the title suggests, the *Concert Suite* is much more traditionally centred than either the earlier or later solo works, with their rather unearthly open-air feel.

The second movement is scored for alto flute, which Jolivet had given as alternative instrumentation for the solitary *Incantation* of 1937, and for the *Cinq ascèses* thirty years later; *Incantation* can also be played on ondes martenot or violin (G string only), the latter work was premiered in 1969 on clarinet. The darker sonority and rather minimal percussion accompaniment gives this section a mysterious, searching quality – marked 'habile' or 'stable' – that reflects the composer's interest in examining the minute variations and harmonic subtleties possible even in the 'primordial monody' of 'folk' musics. *Pace* all his protestations to the contrary, there are moments in the *Incantations* which *do* sound like pastiche folk music. The long central section, marked 'Pour que la moisson soit riche qui naîtra des sillons que le laboureur trace' is a piece of synthetic earth-magic, constructed out of an obsessively repeated fragment of melody like a ploughman's whistle. Played with less than total concentration and control, it can sound rather banal, as with all of Jolivet's works. My choice of the ADDA recording is based largely on a full, rich sound and on the superb co-ordination of the percussion quartet, who take the opening two movements at a rather faster tempo than the Kroumata Ensemble (below), who gave the first performance of Jolivet's *Ceremonial* in 1968. Pierre-Yves Artaud's reading of the solo part is both rigorous and convincingly ecstatic. The Brazilian-born Manuela Wiesler, who has recorded a complete Jolivet flute cycle for the Swedish BIS label, is possessed of a lovely tone, but is much less sophisticated in her reading of subtle microtonal variations and tends to give a passage like 'That the harvest of the ploughman's furrows may be rich' from *Incantations*, recorded by her on BIS CD 549, a rather static, plodding feel that may be agriculturally convincing but is musically rather dull.

The *Concert Suite* was dedicated to and first performed by Jean-Pierre Rampal, along with Severiano Gazzeloni perhaps the most significant flautist of the modern period. Artaud is in every way his descendant, with a crystalline sound that modulates very quickly to the more ambiguous, almost *shakuhachi*-like wavering Rampal derived from his study of Japanese music. Wiesler, a pupil of James Galway and Aurèle Nicolet, is more conventionally romantic and some of her phrasing is rather bland. Anyone interested in the solo flute pieces should also try Leendert De Jonge's cycle on Attacca BABEL 9159–2, for a dry, almost academic approach to the same material. There is a further recording of the *Concert Suite*, led by percussionist composer Siegfried Fink (see below for listing), but I have not heard this and cannot pass comment. Until Rampal's long-deleted premiere recording is made available again, the Artaud version will remain definitive.

Discographical Information

Other recordings: Wiesler, Kroumata Percussion Ensemble (Bis CD 272); Fink, Würzburger Percussion Ensemble (Thorofon CTH 2003).

Other Jolivet: *Mana* (1935; Adda 581042); *Chant de Linos* (1944; Koch International Classics 3–7016); Concerto no. 2 for trumpet (1954; CBS MK 42096); *Serenade* (1956; Ottavo OTR C49135); *Heptade* (1971–2; Adda 581225).

Map references: Edgard Varèse, *Density 21.5* (1936; Hungaroton HCD 31526), and *Ionisation* (1931; Hungaroton HCD 12991); Olivier Messiaen, *Le merle noir* (1951; Thésis THC 82012); Brian Ferneyhough, *Unity Capsule* (1975–6).

HANS WERNER HENZE (born 1 July 1926)

The Bassarids (1965)

FIRST PERFORMED: Salzburg, 6 July 1966
SELECTED RECORDING: Koch Schwann 314 006 K3
   Kenneth Riegel (Dionysus/Voice/Stranger), Andreas Schmidt (Pen-

theus, King of Thebes), Michael Burt (Cadmus), Robert Tear (Tiresias), William B. Murray (Captain of the Guard), Karan Armstrong (Agave), Celina Lindsley (Autonoe), Ortrun Wenkel (Beroe), RIAS Chamber Chorus, Chorus Master Uwe Gronostay, Berlin Radio Symphony Orchestra, conducted by Gerd Albrecht
RECORDED: 27–9 October 1986
DURATION: 119' 57"

In May 1961 Hans Werner Henze's opera *Elegy for Young Lovers* (1959–61) was premiered at Schwetzingen. Two months later, it was staged at Glyndebourne with the original, English libretto, which had been written – some of it at any rate – by W. H. Auden, who credited his lover Chester Kallman with 'about 75 per cent' of the actual work. Auden and Kallman had collaborated a decade earlier on Igor Stravinsky's opera *The Rake's Progress* (1948–51), and in the summer of 1962 they amused themselves by translating Carlo Goldoni's libretto for *Arcifanfano, re de'matti* by the eighteenth-century Austrian composer Karl Dittersdorf (1739–99). Though they could thus justifiably claim some solid experience in the medium, what followed when they renewed contact with Henze was rather remarkable.

Auden and Kallman suggested that, given some modernization and some rounding out of character psychology, Euripides' *Bacchae* offered promising material for a grand opera. The story of the Dionysiac cults appealed greatly to Auden – 'Today we know only too well that it is as possible for whole communities to become demonically possessed as it is for individuals to go off their heads' – but again it was Kallman who did much of the work. What was astonishing was the extent to which the two were prepared to dictate to Henze, who was then nearly forty and a composer of established reputation. Auden and Kallman specified not just the text, but details of costuming (the blind prophet Tiresias was, for example, to be habited like an Anglican archdeacon), scenery, choreography, and even music. And they stipulated that Henze should 'make his peace with Wagner' and attend a performance of *Götterdämmerung*, chaperoned by Kallman. What they wanted was a work of symphonic coherence, rather than the song-based operas of the Italian tradition; and that is essentially what, in the summer of 1966, they got.

Born in Gütersloh, mid-way between Hanover and Dortmund-Essen, Henze had emigrated to Italy in the early 1950s, partly to escape feelings of guilt aroused by his bourgeois father's passive acceptance of Nazism, partly in pursuit of a more liberal sexual environment; but also in search of a more sunlit, openly sensuous aesthetic. It is neither fair nor strictly accurate to describe Henze as a man of contradictions. He is a leftist with a marked leaning toward anarchist (or at very least libertarian) principles. He has frequently conceived of musical performance in straightforward agit-prop terms, as when he required that a red flag be hung above the orchestra at the premiere of the oratorio *Das Floss der 'Medusa'* (1968). He has deliberately cultivated ugliness (as in the porcine grunting and squealing required of the baritone in the satirical *Versuch über Schweine* (*Essay on Pigs*) of 1969), at the same time pursuing an almost Hellenic conception of absolute Beauty. Trained in the Darmstadt school of strict serialism, to which he had been introduced by Wolfgang Fortner (born 1907), his first composition teacher, he has created a body of music in which system plays only an incidental (and often negative) role. Even so, these apparent contradictions are so closely interwoven in Henze's make-up as to be inseparable.

The Bassarids predates his more extreme political involvements. The radical student movement, which ultimately sparked off the *Essay on Pigs*, had not yet gathered momentum. Predictably, Henze's attitude to the movement was highly ambivalent, admiring its instinctual radicalism, despising its conformity and swinish ugliness. *'Medusa'* had been intended as a threnody to the bellwether of the student left, Che Guevara, whose dead face, gorgon-like, seemed to have frozen the students into rigid stances, but whose martyrdom and subsequent canonization also represented a latter-day version of erotic religious art.

Chester Kallman was anxious to avoid what he called the 'Glucky Greekiness' of most operatic treatments of the classical world. *The Bassarids* was to aim for the widest range of reference, exploring attitudes to religion from classical times to the present, though not necessarily chronologically or self-consistently. Regarding the title, Auden wrote to Elizabeth Mayer, 'The word *Bassarids* or *Bassariden* really does exist, though to my astonishment it is not in the O.E.D. It means followers of Dionysus of both sexes.' Avoiding the more familiar form of the word or its Latin derivatives helped prevent any hint of 'Greekiness' or bland classicism creeping back in, and sustains its immediacy and relevance.

The central theme of *The Bassarids* is the fatal consequences of any deliberate self-suppression of the sensual, Dionysiac side of human nature. The action is set in Thebes. The city's founder 'Cadmus' has abdicated in favour of his grandson Pentheus, who is cast by Auden and Kallman as a sort of 'medieval ascetic'. It is the new king's first duty to pronounce on the cult of Dionysus, and of Dionysus's mother Semele, daughter of Cadmus, whose tomb is a place of pilgrimage and worship for the Dionysiacs. The crux is whether Dionysus was of unmixed mortal birth or whether, as his followers believe, he was a by-blow of Zeus.

The citizens of Thebes are initially enthusiastic about their new king, for Pentheus is the child of another of Cadmus's daughters, Agave, and of Echion, one of the five Sown Men who sprang up from dragon's teeth at the mythical foundation of Thebes. The new king is fasting in isolation, and there is already a tension in the opening music, which develops in sonata form, between the dry, abstract manner of Pentheus (who will stand for monotheism and restraint in the opera) and the fleshly, rhapsodic manner associated with Dionysus. (It is by no means far-fetched to hear *The Bassarids* as a musical autobiography by Henze; he may not have initiated the project, but he responded to the idea with complete absorption and it reflects almost all his major personal concerns.) The opening chorus is interrupted by a mysterious voice from offstage which calls out 'Ayayalya! / The God Dionysus / Has entered Boeotia!' The music acquires a mysterious quality, and the citizens take up the call and dance away as if tranced.

The androgynous prophet Tiresias is also drawn to the cult, but plaintively admits his lack of physical resolve. Agave (cast by Auden and Kallman as a 'French Second Empire sensual sceptic') is contemptuous of the old prophet's desire to join the dance and pours scorn on the story of Semele's divine coupling, dismissing Dionysus as 'A wine-skin / Emptied with its wine'. With Agave's jibes ringing in his ears, Tiresias limps off to join the ecstatic dancers who are gathering at rear-stage. Cadmus has pleaded for caution, but he is assailed by superstitious fears and nervously ponders the possibility that his grandson may indeed be a god; behind him, the Bassarid chorus continues its sensual hymn. Agave and her sister Autonoe flirt with the Captain of the Guard, who has come to deliver (in a mechanical monotone) the king's inaugural proclamation. Pentheus pronounces anathema on all who believe that the gods lust after mortals and formally denies Dionysus's divinity; he casts his cloak over the flame on Semele's tomb, extinguishing it. Even as the sisters pledge their loyalty to son and nephew respectively, a guitar is heard being tuned offstage, piecing together elements of the note-rows and chords that have made up the first 'movement' (and it seems appropriate to use the word in relation to an opera composed symphonically, rather than in a more straightforward dramatic structure). A favourite instrument of Henze's, it also carries an echo of the guitar in the composer's own *Kammermusik* (1958), a setting of the poems of Hölderlin's madness, and anticipates some elements of the *Royal Winter Music* (1975–6, 1979; after Shakespeare). It grows steadily in intensity, until it is joined by the offstage voice of Dionysus in a throbbing serenade. Agave and Autonoe begin to spin like automata and, hypnotized, dance off to Cytheron, to a mixed accompaniment of ecstatic Bassarids, cynical mutterings from the old nurse Beroe (who is known to be loyal to the old religion of the Great Mother), and the restored vigour and self-confidence of Cadmus.

The old king attempts to reassert his authority at the start of the second, scherzo movement, reminding Pentheus that he only rules by his predecessor's consent. The young king is not disposed to listen, though, and sends his soldiers off to Cytheron to capture as many of the Bassarids as possible. He condemns the new cult – 'Dionysus / Is but a name / For the nameless Nothing / That hates the Light' – but then offers an interpretation of the Dionysian message – 'all is possible, / Wish is deed' – that is all too ironically persuasive. He is accompanied in his aria by the Bassarids' low song of warning and by his nurse's incantation of the old earth-religion; his next act is to take an oath of chastity and abstinence, to which she is called to bear witness.

The prisoners are led onstage: Agave, Autonoe, Tiresias, a silent Woman and her Child (who carries a huge talking doll). With them is a young Stranger, who alone seems free of the trance; he is Dionysus, but is at first taken to be merely a priest of the cult. The Woman and Child are led off to be tortured, while Pentheus summons up family loyalties and calls on his mother to tell what she saw at Cytheron. In a beautiful, brief aria Agave offers what Auden and Kallman described as: 'a Wordsworthian mystical vision of nature': 'Time stopped, I stepped into / A world awaiting me as it ever was'. This is quickly transformed, by a subtle manipulation of both text and harmonic language, into something closer to a romantic–decadent vision: 'flowers opened their old mouths / In songs too slow for sound.'

Beroe has understood who the mysterious Stranger is, but Pentheus ignores her urgent promptings, and once again loses command of a scene dominated by the as yet unrevealed Dionysus, who stands behind Tiresias and delivers a palindromic song of forgetfulness and resurrection: 'I was torn that I be gathered, / I fell who have arisen, / Died I, I live / ... / Live I, I died.' The Captain has learned nothing from the Woman and Child, and seems astonished by their obliviousness to pain. With impotent fury, Pentheus orders that his mother and aunt be confined and that Tiresias' house be demolished. He then turns his attention to the Stranger, whom he still believes to be a minor functionary of the cult. Dionysis is respectful but dismissive, and the movement ends with the familiar tale of his kidnap on the abortive voyage to Naxos, when he conjures vines from the ship's timbers and makes wild beasts appear on deck, terrifying the pirate crew, who jump overboard and are turned into dolphins.

The third movement contained Auden's and Kallman's major addition to the Euripidean text, a comic *Intermezzo* ('The Judgement of Calliope') which is not included in this recording. Its dramatic purpose was to hold up a mirror (literally in the staged version) to Pentheus's buried fantasy life, and it is clearly influenced by the play-within-the-play in *Hamlet*, set in 'a Boucher-like garden, with statues of mythological groups' and sung in heavy couplets to a sequence of popular song-forms that parodies the suite of bacchanalian dances in the previous movement. All this is prefigured, though, by Pentheus's final loss of self-command. Maddened by the Bassarids' mounting song of triumph, and the Stranger's passive defiance, he orders the Captain to 'Root out his perfumed hair. / Break that smiling mouth / Of its lie. / Lay whips to his pampered flesh.' The music to which his opening pronouncement of Truth and Goodness had been set is now fractured and reversed under a frenzied repetition of 'lies … lies … lies'. Thebes is struck by an earthquake and the cloak is snatched from Semele's tomb. It is by the light of its rekindled flame that Pentheus is shown his own reflection in his mother's hand-glass, a gross charade begun and ended by the Bassarids' mocking laughter.

Almost literally beside himself, with Dionysus as his shadow-self, Pentheus resolves to go to Cytheron and learn the truth for himself. The Stranger warns him that he will be killed, and that he must disguise himself in a woman's clothes. As the king hurriedly departs, Beroe comes forward to plead for him, calling on the loyalty due her as Semele's nurse; in desperation, she speaks the god's name, 'Spare him, Dionysus', to which he replies with an obdurate 'No'. Pentheus returns in one of Agave's dresses and is greeted by Dionysus as 'a true daughter of Cadmus'. The voices of god and king merge as they leave the set hand in hand, while Beroe and Cadmus lament the fall of Thebes.

As the scene dissolves into night, Pentheus is discovered perched in a tree, watching, echoing and finally anticipating the Bassarids and Maenads in their hymn to Dionysus. There is a moment of absolute silence, during which Pentheus disappears. The Maenads sing an invocation to their god, whose voice informs them that there is a stranger in their midst. The solemn processional breaks up into a hunting pack, the famous 'Hunt of the Maenads', and the music acquires a baying Wagnerian urgency, with the 'Ayayalya' chant pantingly syllabized. Pentheus is picked out by a sudden ray of light (intended to recall the reflection from Agave's mirror) and the pack fall on him. The last sound to cut the darkness is his death-scream.

The final movement of the two-hour 'symphony' is an elaborate passacaglia, constructed out of a magnificent forty-three-note theme and then developed in a sequence of prime numbers and asymmetrical rhythms. Cadmus and Beroe are still keeping watch in Thebes, while the Maenads sing their song of triumph. Agave enters, bearing aloft the head of her son, which in her trance she believed to be that of a lion. Cadmus has regained his authority and balance and slowly brings her to her senses, the partial restoration of rationality signalled by a more balanced pulse in the accompaniment. Her frenzy gives place to more seemly grief as her son's mangled remains are brought onstage and reassembled by Beroe, as first Autonoe, then Tiresias, and the Bassarids all disclaim responsibility for the violence. It is Agave again who articulates what seems like a philosophical conclusion: 'The strong gods are not good.' At this point, the Bassarids launch into a rather complacent hymn – 'O let my ways be lowly / And all vain thoughts eschew / The gods alone are holy, / And what they will, they...' – only to be interrupted in mid-measure of Dionysus, who proclaims his divinity from Semele's tomb, banishes Agave, Autonoe and Cadmus, and orders Thebes to be burned to the ground. As the royal family depart, he declares that vengeance has been his only motive, and he calls up Semele from the underworld, whence she appears in her new apotheosis as Thyone. The final tableau is set against a sky of intense Mediterranean blue. Thebes is a blackened shell, and as the Bassarids sing quietly of unknowable mystery the figure of Tiresias appears and stretches out his hands to two huge fertility idols, representing Dionysus and Thyone, which stand on Semele's tomb. As he sinks to his knees, vines descend and encircle both the giant figures and the scorched rubble.

It is an enormously powerful moment. However, one of the strengths of *The Bassarids* is that its dramatic force is so wholly sustained by the symphonic structure that it loses very much less than most operas by transfer to record. It is a work that, appropriately, plays out on an interior stage. There had been misgivings about the Schwetzingen set for *Elegy* (Kallman dismissed it as 'God-awful left-over faggot chic by a German heterosexual'). By contrast, *The Bassarids* is much cleaner-edged, almost monolithic. Never previously recorded, its huge, single-act format works far better on CD than it could possibly have done on three or possibly four LPs; the absence of the dumb-show 'Judgement of Calliope' represents no serious loss, and the relentless logic of the structure means that there is little need for separately cued arias (the CDs demarcate only the four movements). As Pentheus, Andreas Schmidt might seem to have less presence than Dietrich Fisher-Dieskau would have brought to the part (Auden was highly enthusiastic about the young Greek baritone Kostas Paskalis, who sang in the premiere) but the very one-dimensionality of his performance is in perfect keeping with Pentheus's rigidly Apollonian nature. By contrast, Karan Armstrong and Robert Tear are subtly modulated as Agave and Tiresias, and Kenneth Riegel's Dionysus touches just the right middle ground between seductive beauty and arrogant evil. Both orchestra and chorus are skilfully deployed.

The Bassarids is one of the finest operatic works of the century, one whose synthesis of the Italian and Wagnerian traditions is a perfect correlative of its exploration of the Dionysian and Apollonian strains in culture and society. Its 'modernization' of Euripides is never jarring, just as Shakespeare's anachronisms are rarely visible, and Henze's undeniable triumph has to be shared with his two unlikely collaborators as well as with all the musical ancestors on whom he refused, even in the moment of his hottest revolutionary fervour, to turn his back.

Discographical Information

Other Henze: String Quartet no. 1 (1947; Wergo WER 60114/5); *Kammermusik* (1958; Koch Schwann CD 310004); Symphony no. 6 (1969; DG 429854 [complete symphonies]); *Royal Winter Music* (1975–6, 1979; Audiofon CD 72029); *Orpheus Behind the Wire* (1981–3; CRI 615).

Map references: Christoph Willibald Gluck, *Orfeo ed Euridice* (1762 [for 'Glucky Greekness']; Erato 2292 45864); Wolfgang Fortner, *Intermezzo* from *Die Bluthochzeit* (1956; RCA Red Seal 09026 60827); Igor Stravinsky, *The Rake's Progress* (1959–61; Sony M2K 46299).

Further reading: H. Carpenter, *W. H. Auden: A Biography*, London, 1981; P. Heyworth, interview with Henze, 'I Can Imagine a Future', in the *Observer*, 23 Aug. 1970; (in German) P. Petersen, *Hans Werner Henze*, Hamburg, 1988.

HARRY PARTCH (1901–1974)

And on the Seventh Day Petals Fell in Petaluma (1963–1964, 1966)

FIRST PERFORMED: Los Angeles, 8 May 1966
SELECTED RECORDING: CRI CD 700, *The Music of Harry Partch*
  Gate 5 Ensemble of Sausalito (original instruments), conducted by the composer
  [with: *The Letter* (1943); *Castor and Pollux* (1952); *The Bewitched*: Final Scene and Epilogue (1955); *Windsong* (1958)
RECORDED: 1967
DURATION: 35' 36"

California usefully symbolizes the farthest edge (on the continent itself) of America's 'manifest destiny'. To a New Englander like Robert Frost, the Pacific sunset conjured up a 'night of dark intent', full of ambiguities, and Californian artists, perched uneasily on the Pacific rim, have been obliged to look East and West simultaneously. Many of them, particularly in the generation that came of age before or during the Second World War, rejected the aesthetic values of the 'Eastern' establishment (the music schools of New York, Boston and Philadelphia) and turned their attention to the culture of the orient and, rather more slowly, of the hitherto neglected American hinterland. Composers such as John Cage, Lou Harrison and LaMonte Young began to study Eastern (that is, oriental) culture in some detail, adopting non-Western procedures and, in some cases, instrumentation.

Inevitably, there were also figures who approached 'orientalism' (in Edward Said's negative sense) in a much less radical way, looking to the East for a little exotic coloration. Alan Hovhaness (an Easterner who subsequently moved to the far West) studied under Bohuslav Martinů at Tanglewood, but seems to have caught nothing more than the profusion bug; having allegedly destroyed *one thousand* youthful works, Hovhaness had amassed over 350 opus numbers by his seventieth birthday in 1981, and has continued unabated, producing music of surpassing dullness. It combines semi-mystical 'Eastern' hokum with Orthodox and Western Church music, and routine 'classical' form and stands as a hefty warning of the superficiality and bland eclecticism that lies in wait even for more adventurous experimenters and that seems a particular pitfall of West Coast culture.

Perhaps because music is a more thoroughly mediated art form – requiring manufactured or crafted instruments, expert performance, ultimately the technology of recording – it has produced fewer genuine 'outsider' figures than the other arts. Even given a quite radical reappraisal in the later twentieth century of Western harmony and rhythms, surprisingly few composers have rejected Western instrumentation and tried to match a new music with new performative means. The obvious exception is, of course, electronics which allowed composers to create complex pitch-clusters, microtonal slides and other effects not readily available on Western instruments. There have been other, more individual responses and importations. John Cage's prepared pianos of 1946–8 are perhaps the best-known example. Conlon Nancarrow's restriction of his compositional output to works for player pianos was a reflection of his isolation in Mexico from qualified performers, but also of his desire for a music beyond the reach of human performance (the Australian Percy Grainger had aimed at something similar, and in his later years collaborated with the technician Burnett Cross on a 'free-music machine', remarkably like a pianola in basic function); Lou Harrison began writing for gamelan orchestra; the legendary 'Moondog' (born Louis T. Hardin, in 1916) overcame blindness to become a highly idiosyncratic composer, combining jazz with Palestrina (though he rejected the indiscipline of the former), and playing invented instruments as a busker; several other composers have experimented with incidental and usually coloristic use of non-Western instruments.

Nobody, though, took such a radical line as the Californian Harry Partch. Born within six months of the new century, Partch is one of its most individual and remarkable figures, and created a body of work which is completely *sui generis*. He spent the Depression years hoboing around the United States, gathering materials, and observing at first hand the way folk and (in the correct sense) popular musics made use of home-made and adapted instruments. At the same time, he was reading omnivorously in folklore and the occult. Partch destroyed a substantial amount of apparently conventional early work (more of a loss, I suspect, than Hovhaness's bonfire) when his researches into tuning and instrumental design led him to question the most basic premises of Western musical practice. He began by adapting existing instruments, lengthening the fingerboards of violins and violas (a device adopted by the contemporary Australian improviser/composer Jon Rose), and his first work in the new style was a group of settings of lyrics by Li Po written in the early 1930s for voice and adapted viola. At the same time, he had begun to work through an almost visceral rejection of equal temperament (the system on which all Western harmony is founded) by returning a cheap parlour organ to a forty-three-note division of the basic octave, according to Ptolemaic 'just intonation'. He set out the main theory involved in a 1949 essay *Genesis of a Music*, which was revised just before his death, at a time when Partch was again making a substantial impact on young composers.

All Partch's mature output was for instruments he had designed and constructed himself. In addition to 'adapted' fiddles and guitars and the retuned organs (which he christened Chromelodeons), he devised a large family of tuned idiophones (instruments whose sound is determined solely by its material structure – metal, wood, whatever) which were based on the marimba, the Tibetan singing-bowl and ceremonial gongs. Some, like the Marimba Eroica, were of extreme sonority. Others were made of unfamiliar materials like light bulbs (Mazda Marimba) and Pyrex (the Cloud Chamber Bowls). After 1930, Partch wrote music almost exclusively for instruments he had himself invented and constructed, only occasionally using more conventional forces.

In *Genesis of a Music*, he defined his aesthetic 'trinity' as 'sound-magic, visual beauty, experience-ritual'. The first and last elements are perhaps most clearly seen in *Delusion of the Fury: A Ritual of Dream and Delusion* (1963–9), his last major composition, whose premiere in Los Angeles in 1969 brought Partch belated attention. It is a shambolic work that suggests a rather wayward, straggling processional, and it overdoes the *faux-naïf* gestures by which Partch liked to set himself apart from orthodox concert music. There is a good quality, composer-supervised recording [CBS M2 30576] which also contains a valuable booklet with colour photographs of all Partch's important instruments, but not, alas, the ritual costumes which are integral to the piece.

Delusion loses a great deal of its impact without the visual component and does seem rather unfocused on record. However, the booklet usefully underlines the third element in Partch's trinity. There is no mistaking the sculptural properties of instruments like the Quadrangularis Reversum, the Eucal Blossom (which are respectively large and small marimbas made of spruce and bamboo) or of the toadstool-like cone gongs. All Partch's instruments are featured in the slightly earlier *And on the Seventh Day Petals Fell at Petaluma* and, from a purely musical point of view, this more abstract piece is the most satisfactory point of entry to his work. It is recorded in respectable stereo (the other items on the disc are mono) and transfer to CD has considerably brightened the ringing overtones of the instruments.

Partch has explained that the title, far from being abstruse word-play, refers to the circumstances of the work's composition. Petaluma is a town about forty miles north of San Francisco, an area Partch – the eternal gypsy – considered home and to which he had returned after an absence of six years. The work was begun in 'the time of falling petals', presumably autumn, for there is a ripeness to the music that confirms the rather grand, self-consciously biblical detachment of a phrase like 'On the seventh day...' The piece, which runs for just over thirty-five minutes, consists of two dozen brief, mostly one-minute duos and trios exploiting the subtle coloration of Partch's forty-three-note scale and bright, staccato rhythms that run in long, looping sequences. Though the individual performers are not specified (the Gate 5 Ensemble of Sausalito was a group dedicated to Partch's instruments and music) it seems likely that Danlee Mitchell and Linda Schell, his two most committed interpreters, are involved. The performers are clear, resonant and absolutely confident, and repeated hearings remove any impression of blur, or haphazard 'free' playing, which might result from the unfamiliarity of Partch's harmonics.

Studio synthesis converts the last eleven one-minute sections into quartets, quintets, and a final septet that underlines the numerological significance of the title and brings the piece to a close in softly glowing showers of sound. The suggestion is of completeness, peace, rest.

It is rather difficult to assess Partch's significance. As a radical individualist, he is an archetypal American culture-hero. Though he was clearly an important role model and tutelary presence for younger composers and musicians, he had no academic post and no formal pupils, and direct 'influence' (which is always a rather questionable construct anyway) is rarely clear. Some innovations which have been attributed to Partch may well have arisen independently elsewhere as independent manifestations of a more general *Zeitgeist*. Microtonal scales and the use of non-standard instrumentation are now *relatively* commonplace, but fewer composers have gone nearly as far as Partch, and perhaps only the Alabaman Ezra Sims (born 1928) has stuck with microtonal music so doggedly.

It is perhaps best to see Partch as a figure somewhat apart, and simply to identify a number of other North American composers who seem to share in different combinations his methods and concerns. Sims's eighteen- or twenty-four-note octave (set within a total chromatic of seventy-two notes; conventional Western tonal music uses the diatonic scale set in a chromatic of twelve notes) is similar to Partch's but at once more academic and more playful. Some of Henry Crumb's ritualistic vocal works suggest a kinship with Partch, while the Canadians Henry Brant (born 1913) and R. Murray Schafer have composed large-scale ritual pieces in similar forms to *Delusion of the Fury*. The combination of advanced harmonic thinking, experimental performance techniques and popular materials surfaces in work by the extravagantly named Curtis O. B. Curtis-Smith (born 1941), a composer with almost no European reputation, who uses a distinctive 'bowed-piano' technique to achieve microtonal effects. Lucia Dlugoszewski (born 1921, 1925 or 1934, depending on your source) has extended Partch's concept of music-as-sculpture ('ladder harps', 'timbre pianos' and the like), as has the New Zealand-born Annea Lockwood (born 1939).

Partch's naughty-uncle standing with the young (even rock fans seem to have been turned on by him) suggests connections with figures as diverse as Robert Ashley (born 1930) and Harold Budd (born 1936), both of whom have combined popular-cultural forms with non-European techniques; Ashley writes densely cross-cut video operas, Budd has largely abandoned concert music for the recording studio. And so on, and so forth. As with John Cage, it is difficult, once you set out to map it, to find the boundaries of Partch's influence. The sad thing is, perhaps, that he is more often identified *as* an influence than enjoyed as a composer. His music is beautiful and deserves to be heard on its own terms.

Discographical Information

Other works by Partch: *Yankee Doodle Fantasy* (1944; Newport Classic NPD 85526); *The Bewitched* (1952–5; CRI CD 7001); *Revelation in the Courthouse Park* (1960; Tomato R2 70390); *Delusion of the Fury; A Ritual of Dream and Delusion* (1965–6; Columbia M2).

Map references: Conlon Nancarrow, Studies for Player Piano (undated; Wergo WER 6168); John Cage, *Three Dances* for two prepared pianos (1945; Attacca BABEL 8949); Lucia Dlugoszewski, *Tender Theatre Flight Nageire* (1970; CRI SD 388); Henry Brant, *Ghost Nets* (1988; AmCam ACR 10303); Hal Willner, *Weird Nightmare: The Music of Charles Mingus* (1992; Columbia COL 472467).

Further reading: W. Zimmermann, *Desert Plants: Conversations with 23 American Musicians*, Vancouver, 1976.

LUCIANO BERIO (born 24 October 1925)

Sequenza III (1965–1966)

FIRST PERFORMED: Radio Bremen, 1966
SELECTED RECORDING: Wergo WER 6021 2
    Cathy Berberian (soprano)
    [with: *Sequenza I* (1958), Aurèle Nicolet (flute); *Circles* (1960), Berberian, with Francis Pierre (harp), Jean-Pierre Drouet, Jean-Claude Casadesus (percussion); *Sequenza V* (1966), Vinko Globokar (trombone)]
RECORDED: 1967
DURATION: 7' 09"

An Italian comic strip from the 1960s. An alien craft moves through the galaxy searching for a new world to call home. The crew are shiny-skinned, hairless and sexually undifferentiated, their eyes as wide and innocent as dinner-plates. They glide wistfully past balls of seething gas, skirt icy moons, look sadly down at planetary surfaces chewed by volcanos and dust storms. And then, when their hope is almost exhausted, they spot the Earth. From a high orbit they monitor a rich eco-system, varied mineral deposits, nitrogen and oxygen, carbon and the rarer elements. They gather excitedly at the portholes, pointing down-wards at Eden. And then their captain switches on the sonic scanner. A fantastic hubbub: rock music, gunshots, opera, engines, car horns and police sirens, random shouts and fragments of verse, angry dictatorial voices, the screams of horror films and the grunts of porn flicks. The tiny figures recoil in shock and regretfully sail on, taking with them cures for cancer, the secret of interplanetary travel, and the key to universal peace. We were simply *too loud*.

Since the 1950s, Luciano Berio has been the most dedicated orchestrator of our century's noise. Though he was born a full generation after *Futurismo* lost its impetus, he is unmistakably its heir – on the right side of the ideological blanket this time. Far from worrying about the fate of art in an age of mechanical reproduction, the Italian Futurists espoused an aesthetics of the machine, elevating the motor car and the tannoy, the strip mill and the electrical generator to the status of musical instruments. In reaction, Berio has tried to re-humanize and reanimate musical culture. Some have found his dramatic work in particular disturbingly death-obsessed. He was born just early enough to witness the Fascist convulsion at first hand. Much of his artistic life has been directed to the central questions of 'post-modernism': how can the voice continue to sing when so many voices have been silenced? how do you continue to tell stories when all the stories have been told? His opera *Un re in ascolto* (1979–83), co-written with the fabulist Italo Calvino, is intimately and explicitly concerned with listening. Confronted by the century's life-denying oppression he has cast himself as the story-teller who stays the knife just as long as the king's attention is diverted by the tale. Berio is our Scheherazade.

Like his countrymen Luigi Nono, whose opera *Prometeo* is subtitled '*Tragedia dell'ascolto*', it has been Berio's aim to help us listen anew. He has restored a sort of linguistic purity to the tired generic terminology of the nineteenth century. Many of his titles are deliberately neutral – *Opera, Sinfonia, A-ronne, Coro* – while others, like the series of single-instrumental *Sequenze* (1958–88), are presented as essays in musical language rather than as conventionally expressive works. Collectively, they represent a dedicated purification of musical resources. *Opera* (1969–70) restores the original (plural) meaning of 'works'; it has no coherent narrative line but is an open-ended meditation on a number of elements relating to death and the frailty of human endeavour (including, interestingly enough, the sinking of the *Titanic*; see Gavin Bryar's piece, p. 200). Slightly earlier and considerably more successful (*Opera* had an abortive production in Santa Fe and little has been heard of it since), *Sinfonia* restores the primitive meaning of 'sounding together' which was gradually lost from classical symphonic writing. Incorporating material from an earlier voice-piece *O King* (1967–8), this remarkable work is a 'symphony' of eight semi-singing vocalists and a text drawn from Claude Lévi-Strauss and Samuel Beckett, and the mournful apostrophe to Martin Luther King. The orchestral accompaniment is complex but remains largely in the background. There is some confusion about the date of *O King*; if it *is* a threnody to the murdered civil rights leader, then it cannot have been written and performed as such in 1967 when King was still alive, as Berio expert David Osmond-Smith appears to be suggesting in his book. The exact occasion no longer matters, for *O King* has now been absorbed into the larger work. It is an important piece, nonetheless, for it marks an early and somewhat simplified stage in Berio's attempt to reconstruct modern music from verbal and phonetic relationships (with carefully indicated expressive markings) rather more than from the vertical pitch-steps and horizontal rhythmic coding that constitute the classical inheritance. In contrast to the usual comforting nonsense offered to beginners in opera, the words in Berio do actually 'mean something', even when they appear as jumbled 'nonsense'.

In works like *A-ronne* (1974–5), a radiophonic phantasy to an abstract poem by the composer's friend Edoardo Sanguineti, meaning has been stretched surreally. Berio hooks directly into the chaotic buzz of the modern world and the whirling gamut – the title means 'A–Z' – of its broken-off messages and interrupted communications. (*A-ronne* is perhaps his most literal version of what the aliens heard over their scanners.) He does something similar with the street-scene *Cries of London* (1973–5). It was premiered at the Edinburgh Festival, prompting one Morningside lady to sniff sharply and mutter: 'Aye, that's what London sounds like to me'. *Cries* was influenced by Berio's work on Sicilian street shouts and though it is a minor piece (nicely recorded, however, by Swingle II on Decca 425 620 2 with *A-ronne*) it illustrates his lasting interest in the simplicity of diction and purity of melodic line associated with vernacular forms and anti-forms. So, too, does *Folk Songs*.

Undoubtedly Berio's best-known and most accessible work, this 1964 piece has been surrounded by misconceptions. Berio never considered the eleven songs it collages to be authentic representations of folk materials. The first two, 'Black is the colour' and 'I wonder as I wander', were actually written by the American composer John Jacob Niles (1892–1980), who suffered throughout his career from the casual assumption than his works were non-copyright. Two more songs, 'La donna ideale' and 'Ballo', were written by Berio himself in student days. The other romantic misconception that sticks to the piece is that the *Folk Songs* were made as a posy for the composer's wife, the American-born soprano Cathy Berberian (1925–83). By 1964, Berio had separated from Berberian and was living with the brilliant young psychologist Susan Oyama. 'La donna ideale' may have been a betrothal present, but both *Folk Songs* and the extraordinary *Sequenza III* were written for Cathy *after* the marriage ended; a minor point, but a significant one.

Berberian was one of the most significant musical performers and collaborators of the century. Benjamin Britten wrote some of his most effective music for his lover and companion Peter Pears. Berberian, who wrote scores of her own, has to be seen as a co-composer, providing Berio with an unparalleled vocabulary of vocal devices and inflections which enabled him to resist the inertial tug of harmonic composition and orthodox serialism. The divorce may have been the gateway to a fuller artistic partnership. Until her untimely death, she lent his music and that of many other composers a hugely, almost explosively dramatic presence. Ash-blonde, heavily kohled and wearing one of her vivid purple dresses, Berberian had her audience softened up with sheer physical charisma before she sang a note. If she then proceeded not to sing in notes but in bizarre onomatopoeic sound-effects, as in her own comic-book *Stripsody* (1966), no one had any power to resist.

Apart from the student songs, Berio had written for her such earlier pieces such as *Opus Number Zoo* (1950–1), the Joyce settings of *Chamber Music* (1953), the 'racconto mimico' *Allez Hop* (1952–9), the tape pieces *Thema (omaggio a Joyce)* (1958) and *Visage* (1960–1), and the e.e. cummings lyrics of *Circles* (1960), all using Berberian's voices as his lead

lead instrument. She collaborated on the development of *Folk Songs*, recalling her own Armenian ancestry in 'Loosin yelav' the third piece, and transcribing the closing Azeri love song from a badly scratched shellac record, without knowing more than a word or two of the language. She also brought her unsurpassed diction to dialect songs from Sicily and Sardinia and to a pair of Auvergnat melodies of the sort collected and orchestrated by Joseph Canteloube (1879–1957). Berio considered his work on the transcriptions to be analytic rather than authentic representation. Though the *Folk Songs* occupy a relatively accessible and lyrical environment they are nonetheless musically challenging and illustrate many of his central concerns. *Sequenza III* is a more obviously demanding work. The *Sequenze* (nos. I–XI) were solo pieces written for flute, harp, voice (III), piano, trombone, viola/cello, oboe, violin, clarinet/alto saxophone, trumpet, and guitar. Though they occasionally called on other sound sources, as in VII for oboe, and in X (which has the trumpeter playing notes into an open piano while an assistant silently depresses keys to alter the resonance), they are intended as virtuosic exercises for single voices. To some extent, they are related to the pure sound experiments of Berio's enigmatic countryman Giacinto Scelsi, but they are more rigorously structured, less instinctively radical than Scelsi's instrumental pieces. In *Visage* Berio had dispensed with language material altogether (except for the self-referential word 'parole', a joke much like having mime Marcel Marceau say 'Non' in Mel Brooks's otherwise *Silent Movie*), and had asked Berberian to experiment with other vocal sounds, lending them 'meaning' by virtue of expression, vocal gesture and expressive coloration. This is essentially what she was required to do again in *Sequenza III*, except that a brief text was included. Berio asked the poet Markus Kutter to give him 'a few words for a woman to sing'. The text, which expands the request to express 'a truth allowing us to build a house without worrying before night comes' is never heard as such, but is broken down into phonetic units and scored according to Daniel Jones's international phonetic alphabet. A significant tool for vocal composers, i.p.a. provided a taxonomy of vocal sounds according to the means and location of articulation, which might be on the lips as in 'p' or 'b', on the alveolar ridge ("t' or 'd'), or back on the palate; the sounds might be made by stopping and sharply releasing air from the lungs (as in the 'plosives' above) or by allowing it free egress through the nose; finally, consonants might be voiced (like all the vowels) or unvoiced (like the first of each of the pairs above) according to whether the vocal chords were made to vibrate or not.

The system gave Berio a notational language as complex and as fruitful as any existing musical system. He was able to manipulate very precisely designated vocal sounds with the kind of accuracy a composer would demand of pitch markings. Patterns of sound are established, inverted and used in retrograde, much as a serialist composer might use melodic cells. What really distinguishes *Sequenza III*, though, is the huge range of expressive marking. The Italian radio corporation had banned *Visage* on the grounds that some of Berberian's grunts and sighs sounded too explicitly sexual. In the later piece, there is the same impression of an underlying psychological process, but one that is changing with almost psychotic speed. In his fine book on Berio, David Osmond-Smith gives as an example one of the ten-second 'bars' of which the piece is constructed; within that short time-frame, the expressive markings run 'bewildered – tense – tender – tense – wistful – tense – tender – languorous', frequently varying from note to note. In addition, the singer is required to utter unvoiced whispers, conventional sung tones, and, most disconcertingly of all, bursts of laughter. In opera, laughter is usually indicated by a brief 'Ha ha ha', underlined with a little stage business, and it is remarkable how alien a sound it is in a vocal score; a suitably bizarre reference point for anyone who doubts this, is Elvis Presley's fabled breakdown in the middle of 'Are You Lonesome Tonight' during his drug-and-nappy period, when he forgets the words and fills already embarrassing gaps with an embarrassed giggle.

The point of *Sequenza III* is not to suggest psychological states or any underlying narrative. The effect is as abstract and synthetic as spinning the dial on a night-time radio and sampling at high speed the disjunct signals and intervening noise of a civilization in overdrive. Berberian's performances were definite and should not be missed. However, the British mezzo-soprano Linda Hirst has also included *Sequenza III* on a set of *Songs Cathy Sang*, see below. Recorded in the studio and at a memorable London concert, the set includes a rather light-voiced version of *Folk Songs*, John Cage's 1948 *Aria*, Henri Pousseur's *Phonèmes pour Cathy* (1966) and Berberian's own *Stripsody*. Hirst has been a member of the vocal groups Swingle II (responsible for an excellent reading of *A-ronne* and *Cries of London*) and the electroacoustic vocal group Electric Phoenix, who made a definitive recording of Pousseur's Berio-like *Tales and Songs from the Bible of Hell* (1979) on the Wergo label [WER 60094]. What all these pieces share is a desire to restore music's collective function, to restore a little humanity to the increasingly mechanised buzz, to insist on listening as a radical discipline and not the most passive form of entertainment. *Sequenza III* is like a coded message for other civilizations, a recognition that we are as lost as they are but willing to be saved: *a few words for a woman to sing a truth allowing us to build a house without worrying before night comes.*

Discographical Information

Other recordings: Berberian [with: *Due pezzi* (1951); *Chamber Music* (1953–4); *Différences* (1958–9); *Sequenza VII* (1969); Holliger, members of Juilliard Ensemble] (Philips 426662 2); Hirst, London Sinfonietta, Masson [with: *Folk Songs*; John Cage, *Aria* (1948); Henri Pousseur, *Phonèmes pour Cathy* (1966), Cathy Berberian, *Stripsody* (1966] (Virgin Classics VC 7 90704 2).

Other Berio: *Sequenza I* (1958; Attacca BABEL 9158–1); *Epifanie* (1959–62; RCA 11530/1); *Laborintus II* (1965; Harmonia Mundi HMA 190.764); *Chemins II* (1967 [based on *Sequenza VI*]; Sony Classical SK 45862); *Sinfonia* (1968–9; London 425832–2); *O King* (1970; Delos D/CD 1011); *Points on the Curve to Find...* (1973–4; as for *Chemins II*).

Map references: Luigi Dallapiccola [Berio's teacher at Tanglewood], *Canti di prigonia* (1938–41; Elektra Nonesuch 79050–2); Hans Werner Henze, *Chamber Music* (1958; Koch Schwann CD 310004); Cathy Berberian, *Stripsody* (1966; Wergo WER 60054–50); Henri Pousseur, *Tales and Songs from the Bible of Hell* (1978; Wergo WER 60094); Joan La Barbara [pioneer of 'extended' vocal technique and, incidentally, the wife of electronic composer Morton Subotnick], *October Music: Star Showers and Extraterrestrials* (1980; Elektra Nonesuch 78029–4); Carlo Mario Giulini [Berio's teacher] conducting Stravinsky's *Firebird* suite (1919 version, recorded 1990; Sony Classical SK 45935).

Further reading: R. Dalmonte and B. A. Varga, *Luciano Berio: intervista sulla musica*, Bari, 1981, trans. by D. Osmond-Smith as *Two Interviews*, London, 1985; I. Calvino, 'Un re in ascolto', in *Sotto il sole giagura*, Milan, 1986, trans. as *Under the Jaguar Sun*, New York, 1988; D. Osmond-Smith, *Berio*, Oxford, 1991.

PETER SCULTHORPE (born 29 April 1929)

Sun Music I, II, III, IV (1965–1967; II revised 1969)

FIRST PERFORMED: I, London, 1965; II, Sydney, February 1969; III, Sydney, 1967; IV, Montreal, 1967
SELECTED RECORDING: EMI Australia OASD 7604 LP
Melbourne Symphony Orchestra, conducted by John Hopkins
[with: *Small Town* (1963, rev. 1976)]
RECORDED: 1976
DURATION: 36'

Music critics, like their colleagues in other fields, are inclined to use a rather categorical shorthand in defining national characteristics. Nordic music is routinely described as 'cold' and ascetic; music from the Latin countries as 'fiery' and passionate; while the English are, or used to be, mostly 'pastoral'. Painters may limit their palette and subject matter according to the scene outside their studio windows, but composers very rarely do; they deal with much more abstract and readily universalized stuff.

The earliest settlers in Australia liked to see their new home as a 'boundless garden', an Augustan nobleman's greenhouse brought out of doors, but they could not quite overcome a brooding awareness of the parched hinterland. The Australian wilderness has not (yet) disappeared or been internalized as the American frontier has, and it remains physically, almost intractably, present in Australian art and culture; one thinks of novels by Patrick White and David Malouf, the work of artists like Sydney Nolan and Russell Drysdale. In music, even apparently programmatic titles can be misleading. The hot, brassy sounds and shimmering percussion of *Sun Music* may seem to convey the same harsh and inhospitable landscape as White's 1957 novel *Voss*, but like Krzysztof Penderecki in the rather similar *Threnody for the Victims of Hiroshima* (1960; q.v.) Sculthorpe did not initially intend to write a programme piece. In so far as such an intention developed subsequently, it has a strikingly universal cast. For Sculthorpe, the sun is an abstract symbol of life and of destruction in an eternal cycle; it is a sun that shines equally on Australia, Japan, Polynesia and Mexico.

Born in Tasmania, Sculthorpe is probably the first Australian composer to reach a genuinely international audience. In the late 1950s, he studied at Oxford under Egon Wellesz (1885–1974) and Edmund Rubbra (1901–86), but he was already dissatisfied with European academicism, and had satisfied himself that serialist methods represented a blind alley. Unlike compatriots such as Don Banks (born 1923) and Malcolm Williamson (born 1931), Sculthorpe had no desire to emigrate permanently to the United Kingdom. Instead, he set about writing a distinctively Australian music, and he did so by re-conceiving Australia as an Asian country rather than as a detached outcrop of the motherland. There are hints in some of his earliest mature scores of the phenomenon known as 'Jindyworobakism', a mostly literary branch of the new Australian nationalism that sprang up during and after the Second World War. The Aboriginal word means something like 'repossession' and the writers associated with the movement attempted to re-establish a significant relationship with the real, physical Australia by importing Aboriginal words into their work. The experiment rarely went further than that.

For a composer, of course, linguistic nationalism can only penetrate as far as his titles. Attempts to combine European forms with native or Aboriginals elements were mostly unsuccessful, though *Corroboree* (1946), a ballet by John Antill (born 1904) and the integration of didjeridu with a 'European' wind quintet (1971) by the Austrian-born George Dreyfus (born 1928) suggested some paths forward. The most important work of Sculthorpe's consciously Australian phase was a 1954 string trio *The Loneliness of Bunjil*, which made use of strange glissando effects, repetitive rhythms and a very limited harmonic and melodic range.

Even without the title, it sounds slightly alien. In the same year, Sculthorpe wrote an austere Sonatina for piano, which extends this new approach even further, constructing the music out of the narrowest harmonic intervals (seconds and thirds are very common), set over a pounding, repetitive bass pattern and unusual syncopations; Roger Covell describes the effect very evocatively as 'spectral automatism'. Indications like 'Briskly: hard and percussive' in the third movement (Sculthorpe's near-contemporary Larry Sitsky – born 1934 – follows the same convention) recall a practice of the Australian pianist–composer Percy Grainger (1882–1961), who rejected Italianate markings in favour of 'blue-eyed English'; but with the exception of two fine arrangements made in 1989 Sculthorpe generally steers away from Grainger's weird jollity and faintly sinister Aryanism. The Sonatina comes from a new and very different sound-world.

Though he also wrote some charming theatre music, in the Copland-influenced style of *Small Town* (above), arranged from the radiophonic piece *The Fifth Continent* (1963), Sculthorpe's scores at this period give off a sense of anguished isolation. The 1960 Sonata for viola and percussion is almost unbearably bleak, and though it lacks a programmatic title, it is impossible to avoid associations of parching heat and exhaustion. Five years earlier, Sculthorpe had begun an important sequence of pieces called *Irkanda*, an Aboriginal word meaning 'faraway place' or hermitage, and somewhat similar to the Scottish poet Hugh MacDiarmid's favourite Gaelic term *aonach*. The first of these, *Irkanda I* is for solo violin. The only external influence that is evident, in the rhythms and assemblage of melodic materials, is Bartók, who had the kind of universalizing musical intellect that Sculthorpe admired and needed. *Irkanda IV* (1961) placed the solo violin against percussion and strings, and Sculthorpe has rearranged the piece without the soloist and also for chamber forces; *Irkanda II* (1961; withdrawn, but included in Sculthorpe's String Quartet no. 6 of 1964) and *Irkanda III* (1961, for string trio) were both withdrawn and then partially absorbed into the very important String Quartet no. 6 (1964–5).

All this suggests one of the incidental difficulties in dealing with Sculthorpe's work-list. He has withdrawn and reworked a number of scores and, more confusingly, has re-used titles. *Sun Music* was not initially conceived as an integral sequence but drew in pieces written for other occasions. Sculthorpe had first used solar imagery in a 1958 song cycle to words by D. H. Lawrence; *Sun* was subsequently withdrawn, but the catalogue still lists a *Sun Song* for mixed vocal quartet from 1976. A 1966 vocal piece called *Sun Music* was renamed and replaced by the orchestra piece *Sun Music II* heard on the above. It was derived from a piece that had been previously called *Ketjak*; based on a Balinese monkey dance, it was inserted when *Sun Music* was to be staged as a ballet and a more strongly rhythmic movement was called for to modulate the rather slow and static quality of the sequence. It was the last of the scores to be put in place. *Sun Music III* was originally written as *Anniversary Music*, a commission to mark the Australian Broadcasting Corporation's two decades of Youth Concerts, and it replaced an earlier movement for strings only in which harmonic stasis was taken to lengths that even the composer recognized were impracticable. Like its predecessor, *Sun Music IV* was written while Sculthorpe was Harkness Fellow and composer-in-residence at Yale University. (As a footnote, it is interesting to note that Sculthorpe's autobiography-in-progress is to be called *Sun Mist*.)

In *Sun Music* the very personal style of the Sixth Quartet, which had been occasioned by the death of a friend, is set aside in favour of a much more formal and ritualistic sound. Roger Covell suggests that Sculthorpe's latent interest in non-Western musics was wakened by his new experience as a teacher at the University of Sydney, where he was called on to give courses in ethnomusicology. He has intensively studied the music of the Pacific rim and has used elements of Balinese music in particular in his scores since this period. Sculthorpe's response to Asian music is probably more intuitive and less academic than that of fellow-composer Richard Meale (born 1932), who went to California to study ethnomusicology at UCLA in 1960 before returning to Australia as planning officer of the Australian Broadcasting Commission.

Meale's approach is also more synthetic than Sculthorpe's, whose first overt use of Asian forms was in *Sun Music III*. Here, Sculthorpe adapted passages of traditional *gender wayang* music, but there is a thoroughly 'Asian' feel to the sequence as a whole. The opening movement is fearsome, a huge, very static exploration of instrumental sonority that is quite clearly influenced by electronic music and close kin to orchestral experiments like the 'stochastic' works of Iannis Xenakis, or Krzysztof Penderecki's *Threnody for the Victims of Hiroshima*. As in the later movements, Sculthorpe works in dramatic contrasts, using stabbing brass figures over protracted string textures that crunch together long sequences of quarter-tone intervals until the sound is very alien indeed. Again, it is difficult not to attach images to the music, but they are monolithic and abstract rather than subjective, a sense of enormously powerful sources. The movement has an overwhelming impact, even on record, that lends itself very little to detailed analysis. It simply has to be experienced.

Sun Music II/Ketjak is perhaps less overtly experimental than the choral piece with percussion which it replaced. Sculthorpe again mingles huge brass shouts, whistles and siren effects from the strings with a great array of percussion, playing in rhythms somewhat reminiscent of the Indian *tala* exploited by Olivier Messiaen, but drawn from

Balinese dance. The rhythms are less frantic than the rice-pounding *ketungan* that appear in the rapid pizzicato passages of Sculthorpe's String Quartet no. 8, but vibrantly powerful nonetheless. Uniquely in the series, pitches are only specified in a rather notional way. Where the original *Sun Music III* was for strings only, *Anniversary Music* reintroduces woodwinds, vibraphone and percussion to create passages of intense mystery. The main material is developed by oboe over strings and uses a five-note scale that unites an Asian influence with the Bartókian scores of earlier years. The pulse is again very slow and stately and there are moments towards the middle of the movement which recall some of Sibelius's slow movements or Bartók's 'night music'.

The final movement restores many of the sound-effects of *Sun Music I* and introduces a new one: Sculthorpe asked the string players to draw a finger sharply down the back of their instruments, creating a 'bird-like' (I would suggest a bat-like) squeak. There are the same whirls of sound, punctuated by brass and percussion but the tone reintroduces the indication 'Angoscioso' – anguished – which had signalled the mourning music in the Sixth Quartet. There are faint echos of Bartók's Concerto for Orchestra near the beginning and even despite its resolute refusal to move forwards the music does suggest something like the symphonic impact of Bartók's structurally non-symphonic piece.

Sun Music represents an intriguing non-generic compression of Sculthorpe's abiding concerns. Though the string quartets (which have been taken up by the high-profile Kronos Quartet) are more immediately exciting, it is *Sun Music* that offers the most complete picture of Sculthorpe's evolving method. In place of a tonal approach to harmony and large-scale melodic variation or polyphony, he has developed a music which depends largely on variations of tone-colour, rhythmic repetition with a heavy emphasis on percussion, and very limited melodic resources. In larger structural terms, *Sun Music* seems to anticipate the distinction Sculthorpe made explicit in his first opera *Rites of Passage* (1972–3) between 'chorales' and 'rites', two levels of musical activity and significance that lead to a symbolic 'rebirth'. Corresponding to these levels are the alternations of self-revelation and shrouded anonymity that mark his work as a whole. Whether it offers convincing 'pictures' of Australia, aural equivalents to Nolan's and Drysdale's hot landscapes, and to White's solitary agonists, is a largely subjective question; there is a hint of a programme in the Seventh String Quartet (1966), subtitled *Red Landscape*, and Sculthorpe has shown an interest in *musique concrète* and, like David Lumsdaine (born 1931), experimenting, albeit in a modest way, with 'sound pictures' like the 1971 *Landscape I*, which uses a tape-loop of natural sound. It is clear that Sculthorpe's approach has been influenced by considerations other than strictly musical ones, and it has been his ability to step outside himself and look beyond the esoteric disciplines of music-making that has allowed him to create a music so wholly compelling.

Discographical Information

Other recordings: *Sun Music I* only; orchestra and conductor as above (World Record Co S/FRAM 1, reissued as Odyssey 32 160150); *Sun Music III* only; Sydney SO, Heinze (EMI OASD 7547).

Other Sculthorpe: Sonatina for piano (1955; Move MD 3031); *Irkanda IV* (1961; ABC Classics 426481); *How the Stars Were Made* (1971; Southern Cross SCCD 1021); String Quartet no. 8 (1969; Nonesuch 7 79111).

Map references: George Dreyfus, Sextet (1971; Southern Cross SCCD 1024); Malcolm Williamson, Concerto for two pianos and strings (1972; ABC Classics 426483); Don Banks, *Trilogy* (1977; ABC Classics 426 807); Larry Sitsky, Violin Concerto no. 2: *Gurdjieff* (1989; Move MD 3084).

Further reading: P. Sculthorpe, 'Sculthorpe on Sculthorpe', in *Music Now*, i/1 (Feb. 1969); 'Some Thoughts upon the Idea of a Pacific Culture', in *Canzona*, vi/18 (Dec. 1984); 'The Asian Influence upon Australian Music', in proceedings of *The Asian Composers Conference Australia*, 1985; M. Hannan, *Peter Sculthorpe: His Music and Ideas, 1929–1979*, Queensland, 1982.

HARRISON BIRTWISTLE (born 15 July 1934)

Punch and Judy (1966–1967)

FIRST PERFORMED: Aldeburgh, Suffolk, 8 June 1968
SELECTED RECORDING: Etcetera KTC 2014 2CD
  Phyllis Bryn-Julson (Pretty Polly), Jan DeGaetani (Judy/Fortune Teller), Philip Langridge (Lawyer), Stephen Roberts (baritone), David Wilson-Johnson (Choregos/Jack Ketch), John Tomlinson (Doctor), London Sinfonietta, conducted by David Atherton
RECORDED: 1980
DURATION: 105'

Punch and Judy marks, in its way, every bit as significant a milestone in the development of English-language opera as *Peter Grimes* a generation before. Unlike *Grimes*, whose creator was there to witness the sea-change, its first performances were marked by controversy, even scandal. *Punch and Judy* was one of the centrepieces of the 1968 Aldeburgh Festival, an annual event established by Benjamin Britten in the small Suffolk town that had fertilized his own imagination so fruitfully before the war. Britten was so horrified by Birtwistle's piece, both the sadistic violence of the stage action and the harsh, blaring score, that he walked out of the Jubilee Hall.

Grimes had been violent in *its* way, an uncompromised portrayal of the way small (and small-minded) communities react to the unconventional, the different. In Grimes himself, Britten had created an archetypal Outsider figure, capable alike of brutality and poetry, trapped in a society that oscillated uneasily between brutality and hypocritical sentiment. A common initial response to *Punch and Judy* was to ask where the poetry, and the flowing lyricism of Britten's score, had gone. It was a question that the opera's two main creators had both asked and answered.

Adults, stumbling across a traditional Punch and Judy show again after many years, are apt to be startled by its violence, Punch's seemingly gratuitous beatings and murders, and the rather token nature of the eventual nemesis. This was not quite the first problem that Birtwistle's librettist had to contend with in his preliminary research. Quite simply, the traditional materials that he uncovered in the British Museum were too unsophisticated to be used without development alongside Birtwistle's densely layered and ironic music. Secondly, he had the associated problem of how to create convincing musical drama out of a simple record of unpunished malignity, and a character of one-dimensional evil. Britten had to contend with a similar dilemma in transforming Crabbe's sullenly brutal Peter Grimes into a character worthy of operatic treatment, and worthy of Peter Pears's voice. The parallels between the two operas persist.

Stephen Pruslin's solution was paradoxically to strip Punch of the cartoon jollity he had acquired in the Victorian era, but then to counterbalance him with two new characters. He went back to the *commedia dell'arte* conception of Punch described in Enid Welsford's *The Fool* (an influential book coincidentally written in the year of Birtwistle's birth); the original, Neapolitan Punch was a murderous figure with a raptor's nose, carrying a cudgel and wearing a pointed hat and hangman's mask, the last detail providing a sharp resonance in Pruslin's version. The librettist counterpointed this image, and the acts of terror that went with it, by means of Choregos and Pretty Polly. The former is not a puppet at all, but the leader of the chorus in classical Greek drama. The name also carries a hint of his function in Birtwistle's *Punch and Judy*, that of self-limiting *ego* to Punch's promiscuous *id*. That is also essentially the role assigned to Pretty Polly, for whom Punch quests yearningly after each murder.

The violence of this 'tragical comedy or comical tragedy' begins promptly after Choregos's brief Prologue. Here he invokes the blaring trumpets (which, with other winds, dominate the score) and establishes the moral ambivalence of the 'littel play' [*sic*]. It is to be a 'Song of paean' and a 'Singsong of hope', but of 'Hope only for abandon, terror, fear'. What follows is a repetitive, highly ritualized sequence of melodramas, word-games, proclamations, and instrumental 'toccatas' played

wistle's and Pruslin's intentions. Those who walked out early certainly missed the point. In the librettist's words, 'Our aim was the collective generalization of known operas into a '"source-opera" which, though written after them, would give the illusion of having been written before them'. *Punch and Judy*'s primal, archetypal quality is insistently reinforced by echos of other works, the chorales of Bach's *St Matthew Passion*, for instance, or an unmistakable pastiche of the witches in *Macbeth* in the closing chorus: 'The hurlyburly's lost and won'. If it is a 'source opera', it is also a numbers opera. Michael Hall sensitively identifies Judy's Passion Aria, 'Be silent, be silent, strings of my heart', as Birtwistle at his most operatic, and hears Bach again in 'Weep, my Punch / Weep out your unfathomable, inexpressible sorrow'.

The pairing of opposites, the amoral couple and their ideal 'positive', is likened by Pruslin to the 'photographic' opposition of Nero–Poppea with an idealized pairing like Tamino–Pamina in *Die Zauberflöt* or Florestan–Leonore in *Fidelio*. But while these are undoubtedly part of Birtwistle's inherited language, the former especially, it is the symphonic ritual of Wagnerian opera that seems to be the most potent influence. That symphonism surfaces again in *Peter Grimes*, of course, but it is given a far more insistent function in *Punch and Judy*, which is full of repetition and cyclical variation, like the metaphoric prism which shatters at the climax. The score, like the libretto, has a precise internal structure. There are hints of Birtwistle's characteristic opposition of mechanism and lyric pastoralism, the ostensible subject of his *Carmen arcadiae mechanicae perpetuum* (1977), whose instrumentation is similar to that stipulated for *Punch and Judy* which gives a prominent role to the five wind players who sit onstage separated from the remainder of the pit band.

They become actors in a drama which works at a bewildering number of levels. Anyone who saw either the early production at Aldeburgh or the Edinburgh Festival, or the Opera Factory London revival in 1982 will attest to its enormous, almost frightening power. Yet it is so musical a piece that, unlike most operas, it is possible to penetrate very far into it without ever seeing it physically staged. The Etcetera CD and its Decca LP predecessor (see below) documents the cast which gave a wonderful concert version in 1979. The standard of singing, from soprano Phyllis Bryn-Julson, mezzo Jan DeGaetani and baritone Stephen Roberts is of the highest order, as is the accompaniment of the London Sinfonietta, then as now one of the finest new music ensembles anywhere. Roberts is a very different kind of singer from Peter Pears, but his high, light baritone (opposed to David Wilson-Johnson's deeper register as Choregos) has a similarly ambiguous effect, suggesting malice and vulnerability almost simultaneously and thus reinforcing the opera's strange blend of aggression and ineffable mystery.

In the score, Birtwistle asks that the tiny instrumental Toccatas, some-times only a few bars long, sound like a machine 'turned on and off', establishing an opposition between the human and non-human worlds parallel but disturbingly different to that Grimes suggests between his own frantic activity and the slow, inevitable wheel of the heavens. The astrological component runs counter to Punch's journey of self-dis-covery, and this was to become the basic message of Birtwistle's later operas and music-theatre pieces.

By the time of *Gawain*, the opposition is no longer between man and a cold, mineral universe, but, much as *Punch and Judy* had anticipated, between man in his muddled, mixed state and a world of absolute, vital compulsion, represented by the animistic figure of the Green Knight. Birtwistle turned to the Middle English poem *Sir Gawain and the Green Knight* as early as 1963 in his choral piece *Narration: A Description of the Passing of a Year* and it is possible to hear even in this slight piece a pre-echo of the opera with its interlocking cycles of fertility and murder, inevitability and pure chance, organic form and mathematical structure (like the flower and the jewel with which Punch woos Judy). Those who find Birtwistle forbiddingly difficult, adamantine (and without the high moral charge that those who take sides on matters relating to the former friends find in Peter Maxwell Davies's work), are perhaps not attuned to the much simpler and lower level on which Birtwistle's morality operates. He is interested first and foremost in humane solu-tions, not spiritual transcendence, in accommodation to the human point of view expressed by Pretty Polly: 'Spring has come. / Shattering the prism, / Dispelling the eclipse, / Unfreezing the stars.'

Discographical Information

Other recording: same recording originally released on LP as Decca HEAD 24/ 25.

Other Birtwistle: *Carmen arcadiae mechanicae perpetuum* (1967; Etcetera KTC 1052); *Verses for Ensembles* (1968–9; Decca HEAD 7 LP); *Meridian* (1971; NMC NMCD 009); *Endless Parade* (1986–7; Philips 432 075).

Map references: Peter Maxwell Davies, *Eight Songs for a Mad King* (1969; Unicorn-Kanchana DKPCD 9052); Alexander Goehr, *Das Gesetz der Quadrille* (1979; Wergo WER 60093); György Kurtág, *Messages from the Late Miss R. V. Troussova* (1976–80; Erato STU 71543); John Casken, *Golem* (1986–8; Virgin EMI VC7 91204).

Further reading: E. Welsford, *The Fool: His Social and Literary History* (London, 1935); M. Hall, *Harrison Birtwistle* (London, 1984); P. Grifiths, interview in *New Sounds, New Personalities: British Composers of the 1980s* (London, 1985).

HENRI POUSSEUR (born 23 June 1929)

Couleurs croisées (1966–1967)

FIRST PERFORMED: Brussels, 20 December 1968 (radio broadcast)
SELECTED RECORDING: Ricercar RIC 036015
  Orchestre Philharmonique de Liège et de la Communauté française,
  conducted by Pierre Bartholomée
  [with: Jean-Louis Robert, *Aquatilis* (1977)]
RECORDED: June 1986
DURATION: 27' 49"

Though he is still the best-known modern Belgian composer, Henri
Pousseur seems to belong heart and soul to the international avant
garde of the 1950s and 1960s. Stylistically, he is much closer to near-
contemporaries like Pierre Boulez, Karlheinz Stockhausen and Luciano
Berio (with all of whom he worked or studied) than to any discernible
'Belgian school'. Nevertheless, he has dedicated much of his life to revi-
talizing the composition and performance of new music in his native
country. Eugène Ysaye (1858–1931), a violinist first and a composer
only second, was perhaps the last Belgian before him to make a comparable impact on modern music. Pousseur's near-contemporary
Yolande Uyttenhove (born 1925) has yet to be taken up in a big way,
and younger figures such as Jean-Louis Robert (1948–79), also included
on the above recording, have been fated not to make much impact at
all; Pousseur's pupil, Robert was killed in a motor accident while still
developing an individual style, and his death almost seems to symbolize the rather short-circuited history of Belgian composition since the
1930s.

There was, however, a climate of experimentation at the Liège and
Brussels conservatories during the following decade which undoubtedly
made it easier for Pousseur to hold his own in his private lessons with
Boulez, and at the Cologne and Milan electronic music studios where he
worked with Stockhausen and Berio respectively. His teacher André
Souris (1899–1970) had converted around 1925 from Impressionism in
the style of Debussy to a species of atonality; Souris also founded the
influential journal *Polyphonie*, whose brief history (1947–54) coincides
almost exactly with Pousseur's student years at the Liège Conservatory.
This, along with the Sirène group of Jean Absil (1893–1974) and the
later Variation, was the radical wing of Belgian music, as opposed to
the more traditionally minded group centred on Paul Gilson (1865–
1942) and his *Revue musicale belge*, to which composers like co-founder
Marcel Poot (born 1901), Gaston Brenta (1902–69) and other members of
the Groupe des Synthésistes contributed.

Pousseur joined Variation towards the end of the 1950s, and in 1958 founded the Studio de Musique Electronique APELAC in Liège, later absorbed into the Centre de Recherches Musicales. Just as a previous generation looked to Gilson, younger Belgian composers have looked to him; but his influence has been far from parochial or regional. The title of his first major orchestral work *Rimes pour différentes sources sonores*, premiered at Donaueschingen in 1959, gives a clue to Pousseur's central concerns. There is a paradox, though. However committed to the discovery of new 'sound-sources', there is a sense in which Pousseur is not really a composer at all, but a philosopher of sound. He is much less concerned with aesthetic impact than with the articulation of new language-structures within music. Predictably perhaps, he regards Webern as his guiding light; his first signed chamber work was a *Quintette à la mémoir d'Anton Webern* (1955, for violin, cello, clarinet, bass clarinet and piano), a good example of Pousseur's strictly serial period, which reached its climax with *Symphonies* for fifteen soloists three years later. Ironically, it was Webern who helped him move to a point beyond serialism. By 1961 and the string quartet *Ode*, Pousseur was developing a language of free rhythm and relative rather than absolute pitches. Webern's career demonstrated the 'multipolarity' of modern music and its commitment to what Pousseur has called '*an unresolved maintenance of tensions*'.

His own career has been a search for 'rhymes' between the farthest flung extremes of the sonic world, 'from Mozart to the noise of automated industry, from samba to the amplified vibrations of cells and molecules'. Pousseur is very much a social philosopher as well, regarding music as the last remaining integrative and unifying force in a machine age. This is perhaps more easily seen in his vocal and dramatic works. The most notorious of these is the synoptic opera *Votre Faust* (1960–8) on which he collaborated with the French *nouveau roman* writer Michel Butor, and in which the audience decide the outcome. A companion piece, *Echos de Votre Faust* (1969, for mezzo-soprano, flute, cello, piano), brings together texts by Goethe, Góngora, Marlowe, Nerval and Petrarch, somewhat in the manner of Berio's later and better-known *Sinfonia* (1968–9). Pousseur returned to this method in 1979 with the extraordinary *Tales and Songs from the Bible of Hell*, a largely spoken piece using texts by the seventeenth-century composer John Dowland, from his *Lachrymae* ("Flow my teares'), William Blake and Edgar Allan Poe; it has been memorably recorded by the British vocal quartet Electric Phoenix [Wergo WER 60094 LP].

Pousseur has always regarded music as research, and has tended to maximize his output much as an academic scholar will recycle research papers and journal articles from neglected corners and by-ways of a larger project. During the 1960s his attention was largely devoted to

Votre Faust, and he had released a number of short concert pieces (prologues, scenes, interludes) drawn directly from it. He did, however, also want to reuse all the harmonic discoveries the piece contained in a single, homogenous work for orchestra. In 1966, while he was at the State University of New York in Buffalo, he received a commission from the Koussevitzky Foundation at the Library of Congress in Washington, DC, asking for a piece dedicated to the memory of the conductor and composer Serge Koussevitzky (1874–1951) and his first wife Natalie Usškov (died 1942). Intriguingly, the piece was not originally intended for performance, but was to be lodged in the Foundation archives.

Greatly influenced by Butor (who had been at Buffalo in 1962) and particularly by Butor's *Mobile: étude pour un représentation des Etats-Unis* (published that same year), which reinforced Pousseur's own developing sense of America as a 'résumeé (transposed almost plastified) of our planet', a cultural theatre very like that of *Votre Faust*. Pousseur was profoundly interested in the high/low juxtapositions of Pop Art and of free jazz (which operated on principles that stood in the same relation to bebop and swing as serialism did to orthodox tonality). Ever aware of the social determinants of culture, Pousseur was also moved by the astonishing economic disparities and racial tensions of American society (presumably quite alien to a Belgian) and by the Civil Rights movement. All of these factors played a part in *Couleurs croisées*.

There is no mistaking the dramatic underpinnings of the piece. It begins quietly, almost subliminally, but with a gathering mass. A piano announces a firm, declamatory theme derived (as is all the material in the piece) from the Civil Rights song 'We shall overcome'. The music then takes the form of a vast procession, with the song dispersed throughout its length in different tonal dialects and out of synchronization. (Anyone raised on the mass demonstrations of the 1960s and 1970s will know the effect; it used to be said you could always tell when a group of anarchists was passing by, even with your eyes shut, because they had an ideological objection to singing in a common key.) At the centre of the piece, signalled by blarting brasses and great clashes of percussion, is a confrontation with authority which builds to a violent climax before quietly fading away as the instruments fall silent and disperse.

Pousseur describes the piece as a 'symphonic poem with a very marked narrative (the preparation for a conflict, the fight itself, and the consequences of the conflict)', but also identifies it as 'a type of "hyperfugue"' which obeys very strictly programmed rules. There is, therefore, a musical drama every bit as compelling as the programmatic one. The piece constantly mediates between the still-antagonistic methods of serialism and tonality, and uses elements of harmonic organization (mostly implicit) alongside polyphonic melody, and distinctive internal groupings of the orchestra according to timbre, a device common to Webern, the later Stravinsky and composers like Stockhausen. The criss-crossing 'colours' of the piece are thus not just the racial mixes of the protest movement, but also the distinctive stylistic colours of all these schools. Among specific references to America and to the ideals of freedom, Pousseur alludes to Aaron Copland's *Fanfare for the Common Man* (1942, brass and percussion), to free jazz, and to a composer charmingly transcribed as 'Charles Yves', which is as blatant an act of re-colonization as can be imagined!

Couleurs croisées dramatizes Pousseur's own liberation from technical orthodoxy and his determination to open his own eyes 'to all sounds of history, geography, nature and urban reality' and thus contribute 'to the emergence of a new form of civilization, one that is adequate to our contemporary conditions of collective existence'. To some extent, Pousseur's problem has been precisely that articulated by American writers and artists from Emerson and Whitman to Mailer and Roth, Ives to Ornette Coleman, Eakins to Warhol: the danger of being swamped by a reality far richer and more complex than the imagination. Pousseur has often seemed *too* open-eared, too enthusiastically committed to the hubbub, and too obsessively self-revising. He has reworked a great many of his finest scores. There is, for instance, a related 1970 piece for amplified female voice, two to five pianos, and electronics called *Crosses of Crossed Colours* which sets Afro-American and Amerindian texts, but it does not seem to have been recorded and I have never heard it performed. Pousseur seems to have dropped out of the central repertoire of post-war music as far as concert promoters are concerned and is little represented on current record releases. Fortunately there is a respectable body of recorded material in the back catalogue, for he is not a figure who can be overlooked.

Discographical Information

Other Pousseur: *Rimes pour différentes sources sonores* (1959; Victrola VICS 1239); *Trois visages de Liège* (1961; CBS S34–61064); *Votre Faust* (1960–8, opera); *Texts from the Bible of Hell* (1978; Wergo WER 60094); *Traverser la forêt* (1987; Adda 581295).

Map references: Charles Ives, Symphony no. 4 (1910–16, first performed 26 April 1965; Sony Masterworks Portrait MPK 46726); Aaron Copland, *Fanfare for the Common Man* (1942; CBS MK 42265); Luciano Berio, *Laborintus II* (1965; Harmonia Mundi HMA 190.764); Cecil Taylor, *Unit Structures* (1966; Blue Note BCT 84237); Yolande Uyttenhove, Sonata for violin and piano (1980; Studio EMS SB 001).

Further reading: M. Butor, *Mobile: étude pour un representation des Etats-Unis,*

Paris, 1962; H. Pousseur, *Fragments théoriques I sur la musique experimentale*, Brussels, 1970, and 'Webern, de la lettre à l'esprit, une autre mutation', in *Musica/Realta*, i (1980); special Pousseur issue of *Revue belge de musicologie*, Brussels, 1990.

MORTON SUBOTNICK (born 14 April 1933)

Silver Apples of the Moon (1967)

FIRST PERFORMED: see text
SELECTED RECORDING: Nonesuch H–71174
   Morton Subotnick (electronic synthesizer)
RECORDED: 1967
DURATION: 23' 45"

The post-war period saw an accelerating shift in the sociology – or demography – of the arts in the United States. Artists, and composers in particular, began to gravitate in increasing numbers toward university campuses. Teaching, rather than performing or arranging, became the main source of income. Because commercial music was increasingly formulaic and market-driven (unlike commercial graphic art, where much of the creative input was still devolved to the artist), composers of 'serious' music had to rely on the patronage of college fellowships and residencies.

There was also a technological dimension. The fastest developing field in new composition was electronic and electroacoustic music. This involved complex and extremely expensive technology, to which only well-funded academic institutions (and some record companies) afforded access. To remain outside the academy was to be excluded from the most advanced technical means available to composers. John Cage had (predictably) been early in the field with the Project of Music for Magnetic Tape, founded in 1951 at the New York studios run by electronic pioneers Bebe and Louis Barron. The first major presentation of electroacoustic music in the United States was at Columbia University in New York on 28 October 1952, when Otto Luening had premiered three tape pieces, *Invention in 12 Notes*, *Low Speed*, and *Fantasy in Space*, works which hastened the foundation of the Columbia Tape Studio (from 1959, the Columbia–Princeton Electronic Music Center).

With the exception of important projects at the University of Illinois, Urbana-Champaign (the Experimental Music Studio), at Yale (the Electronic Music Studio) and at Ann Arbor (the Co-Operative Studio for Electronic Music), the majority of similar groups were located on the West Coast. By far the most significant of these was the San Francisco

Tape Music Center, which relocated in 1966 to Mills College, a women's campus in Oakland with a strong, innovative music strand and a heavy emphasis on composition. Darius Milhaud and Leon Kirchner had both taught there, and one of their composition studies in 1959 and 1960 had been Morton Subotnick, a promising young Californian who had just graduated from the University of Denver.

Subotnick, with his colleague Ramon Sender (born 1934), founded the San Francisco Tape Center in 1961, and it is Subotnick who largely defines the most progressive line of electroacoustic composition in the United States, and arguably the most sophisticated electronic composi- tions anywhere until the founding of Pierre Boulez's Institut de Recherche et de Co-ordination Acoustique-Musique in Paris in 1977. In the early 1950s there was nothing like the vastly powerful music- making computers devised at IRCAM; electronic music was still very much a poor dependent of the electronics industry, using filters and oscillators primarily devised for industrial and scientific functions. Sub- otnick arrived on the scene at a moment when synthesizers – which tel- escoped the functions of an electronic studio – were gradually changing in function from acoustic analysis (the original function of Harry Olson's pioneering RCA Electronic Music Synthesizer) to composition, and thence to performance.

One of the underlying assumptions of this book is that the rapid development of recording technology in the second half of the twentieth century shifted the centre of gravity of new music away from the concert hall and towards the more private, individualized means of communication suggested by recorded music. At one time, these were apocalyptic agenda. Social theorists and journalists fantasized about a 'private future' in which art would no longer be a shared or communal endeavour but a consumer item to be enjoyed solipsistically, and the fantasy ran beyond home hi-fi systems and television sets, to then unheard-of items like personal stereos, replicable art works, three- dimensional holograms and so on. Needless to say, such hypotheses counted without the tremendous inertia of both the cultural establish- ment and public expectation.

In the context of the mid-1960s what is surprising is not that a com- mercial record company should have commissioned a 'serious' composer to write music specifically for a long-playing record, nor that the music should be electronic, but that the experiment should have been so short-lived. New music recording enjoyed a brief flowering in the 1960s on a scale not seen again until the last few years when, in a dramatically different economic climate, contemporary composition occupied a vacuum left by fading interest in many brands of popular music. There was, however, very little take-up of inventive electronic music, which tended to be polarized into functional or second-order uses (for commercials, film scores, public service films) at one extreme, and avant-garde projects at the other. For the most part, electronic music has only been released on small specialist labels, such as Lovely Records, which was run by Mimi Johnson, wife of the composer Robert Ashley, a founder of the Ann Arbor electronic music project. The exception was Nonesuch Records, a division of the Warner group, during the years when the enterprising Teresa Sterne was artistic co-ordinator. It was she who commissioned Subotnick to write *Silver Apples of the Moon*. It was a considerable commercial success for the company, outstripping later projects like *The Wild Bull* (1967–8, also Nonesuch), *Touch* (1969) and *Sidewinder* (1971). The latter pair were released on Columbia Records, where Goddard Lieberson had sponsored a contemporary Masterworks series; Lieberson's eclectic open-mindedness was to be repaid by the 'pop' success of Terry Riley's *In C* (1964), a recording produced by electronic composer David Behrman (born 1937). A colleague of Subotnick's at Mills College, Behrman realized *Runthrough* (1967, exactly contemporary with *Silver Apples*) on self-constructed circuitry, thus demonstrating that it *was* possible to work, if not independently of, then at least alongside the big commercial and academic corporations.

There is a small but telling irony, given a later generation's obsessive distinction between 'live' and 'recorded' music, that Subotnick, a profoundly dramatic musician, should have been selected to write the first 'original, full-scale composition … created expressly for the record medium' (as the sleeve to *Silver Apples* put it). The irony is compounded somewhat by the piece's afterlife as a favourite for dance groups and choreographers. That was by no means accidental, for between 1961 and 1967 (when he embarked on the series of record commissions for Nonesuch) Subotnick had been music director of the Anne Halprin Dance Company. What distinguishes the piece from most other electronic music of the period, which tended to be one-dimensional, unpulsed, vaguely impressionistic, are its vivid use of counterpoint, its clearly articulated and highly physical pulses, its strong aural imagery (despite having been inspired by Yeats) and, above all, its aura of control and order.

Subotnick overturns most of the clichés of electronic music. Though unfamiliar in timbre, the sounds he uses are far removed from the bleeps, waterdrips and whooshes that became staples of computer music and demonstrate an unprecedented – and rarely equalled – control over pitches, with internal and secondary rhythms, and a convincing dramatic exposition. There has long been a feeling, as John Rockwell discusses in an essay on Behrman in *All-American Music*, that electronic means lend themselves to rather 'introverted' music. Like Subotnick, Behrman may have agreed in principle, but he rejected any suggestion that the results need be robotic soundtracks for a 'private future'. Both men have been largely concerned, as was Robert Ashley in *Purposeful Lady Slow Afternoon* (1968) and elsewhere, with explorations of loneliness or solitude, but Behrman in particular has been anxious to emphasize the way music reconciles the individual and the crowd, privacy with mass consumption. Rockwell quotes him as saying 'Solitude could be a universal treasure in a crowded world', and that could also be an epigraph to Subotnick's work.

By present-day standards, the technology used on *Silver Apples* was far from sophisticated. *Silver Apples* was realized while Subotnick was working at the School of the Arts, New York University, on a synthesizer built to specifications from Subotnick and Ramon Sender by Donald Buchla. Perhaps because Robert Moog's more compact performance systems found early favour with rock bands, the Moog is more widely known. Buchla's original set-up (more powerful and flexible variants were to follow) was studio based, like the original RCA equipment, and of more use to a composer than to a performer. It was a modular system, which is to say that it consisted of separate but integrable devices by which any parameter of an electronic signal (from pitch, intensity and timbre to more technical considerations like 'envelope') could be manipulated by adjusting voltages.

It was not until 1975 that Subotnick was able to create an electronic work that was replicable in 'real-time' as a concert piece. *Until Spring* was another record commission, but the control voltages necessary for a 'live' realization were stored on tape and could be activated in performance. After the mid-1970s, Subotnick became interested again in the integration of electronics and conventional instruments. Much of his subsequent work used what he called 'ghost scores' which used devices like ring-modulators and frequency shifters to subject live instruments to ethereal processing. Works like *Axolotl* for cello and ghost box (1981, versions with ensemble and chamber orchestra) and *The Double Life of Amphibians* sequence (1981) unfolded Subotnick's interest in 'life histories' (the title of a 1977 vocal piece). Animal names and associations are not just for poetic effect. He is profoundly interested in the 'amphibious' nature of electroacoustic music, existing in two realms simultaneously, and he is fascinated by organic processes, such as pupation (a host of 'butterfly' pieces) and symbiosis (as in *The Wild Beasts* for trombone, piano, and ghost score, 1978) but also with the whole question of communication beyond verbal language. There is an implication in much of Subotnick's work of a strong parallel between machine language and animal communication, a level of contact above and beyond the human.

Images of flight in later work always managed to avoid degenerating into the hackneyed 'spacey' effects of SF-dominated electronic music; again, the emphasis is very much on natural processes. *Ascent into Air* for cellos, clarinets, trombones, percussion, pianos and computer (1981) was realized on the 4C computer at IRCAM. *Return: The Triumph of Reason*, a hymn to Halley's Comet (1985–6) made use of MIDI computers, highly 'personalized' systems for the ultimate expression of solitude and resilient individuality. Neither piece is aggressively technological; both celebrate cyclical processes and biological rationality in a very positive, very Californian way and make surprising use of simple harmonic and melodic outlines.

In retrospect, *Silver Apples* is still Subotnick's most representative work, containing in dream-like miniatures many of the themes and methods that will reappear later on. By contrast, *Return* seems like a summation of his past work, awakening echoes of the slow, processional effects in part one of *Silver Apples*, where low-frequency sounds seem to cluster and 'ripen' round a particular tonality. Again, though the surface of the music is complex, mysterious, even moon-struck, the basic materials are relatively simple. There are fragments of melody, broken up in such a way as to suggest distant human memories and remembered speech on the one hand, tiny nuggets of speeded-up machine-information on the other. The cross-chatter sound is highly invigorating but, as in *Return*, it is governed by a logical, revelatory progression that is highly palpable but very difficult to pin down by more usual principles of musical organization. The climax comes at the end of two roughly equal quarter-hour movements corresponding to the two sides of the LP, and is an apotheosis of 'a single silver child-angel in a glittering garden of silver star-fruit', represented by tingling electronic tones and a throbbing pulse that continues to inspire dancers and choreographers.

Discographical Information

Other Subotnick: *The Wild Bull* (1968; Nonesuch H–71208); *The Wild Beasts* (1978); *Ascent into Air* (1981; Nonesuch 78020); *Axolotl* (1982; Nonesuch N–78012); *Return: the Triumph of Reason* (1985–6; New Albion NA 012); *In Two Worlds* (1987; Neuma 450–80).

Map references: Otto Luening, *Low Speed, Fantasy in Space, Invention in Twelve Notes* (1952; CRI CD 611); John Cage, *Fontana Mix* (1958; Columbia MS 7139); Robert Ashley, *Purposeful Lady Slow Afternoon* (1968; Mainstream Sonic Arts Union MS 5010); Charles Dodge, *Earth's Magnetic Field* (1970; Nonesuch H–71250); with the exception of the first these are all LPs and will need to be sought out in record libraries or specialist second hand shops; I think inclusion is justified by their historical importance.

Further reading: R. Norton, 'The Vision of Morton Subotnick', in *Musical Journal*, xxviii/1 (1970).

TŌRU TAKEMITSU (born 8 October 1930)

November Steps (1967)

FIRST PERFORMED: New York City, 9 November 1967
SELECTED RECORDING: Philips 432 176 2
    Katsuyo Yokoyama (*shakuhachi*), Kinshi Tsuruta (*biwa*), Saito Kinen
    Orchestra, conducted by Seiji Ozawa
    [with: *Eclipse* (1966, *shakuhachi* and *biwa*; Viola Concerto: *A String
    around Autumn* (1989), Nobuko Imai]
RECORDED: September 1989
DURATION: 18′ 56″

Throughout his subsequent career Tōru Takemitsu has had to bear the
not inconsiderable weight of being the first Japanese composer to establish a reputation in the West. It is clear from Takemitsu's own published comments that he has found this a burdensome responsibility,
furthermore, that he regards the identification of his work as 'essentially
Japanese' or as a 'hybrid' of 'Eastern' and 'Western' forms more than a
little problematic. Though such a hybridization or *rapprochement* has
been an explicit aim of American composers such as John Cage, Lou
Harrison, and Harry Partch, of Europeans such as Karlheinz Stockhausen, and of translated Asians such as Chou Wen-chung, it is not
part of Takemitsu's project. He has always insisted that his work represents an individual act that is not defined or contained by such broad-
brush characterizations or by the kind of pseudo-philosophy that often
comes with it. Understanding Takemitsu's music demands some understanding of the cultural environment out of which it emerged.

In pre-war Japan, Western music was officially proscribed, with the
occasional exception of some German composers and some martial
music, an influence reflected in the work of Kocsak Yamada. Japanese
culture was intensely nationalistic and isolationist. It is difficult to
underestimate the impact made by Western music on young Japanese
during the period of occupation that followed the atomic bombing of
Hiroshima and Nagasaki, and the Emperor's surrender; with compelling
symbolism, virtually all of Yamada's manuscripts and scores were
destroyed during a huge USAF air raid on Tokyo in May 1945. The jazz
musician Sadao Watanabe (whose father was a teacher of *biwa*, one of
the traditional Japanese instruments featured in *November Steps*) has
spoken of the enormous sense of liberation that came with listening to
American forces' radio. Takemitsu had, if anything, even closer contact
with the Americans, working as a mess-boy in an officers' club in
Yokohama; though it is to be doubted that he heard very much
Debussy there, it is clear that he absorbed a large amount of Western

music very quickly and equally clear that his largely unstructured listening took him much earlier than about 1870.

Though essentially self-taught, he took some lessons with Yasuji Kiyose, a pupil of the influential and much-travelled Alexander Tcherepnin who practised a kind of personalized pan-globalism in his own music. By the turn of the 1950s, he was composing in a manner that combined twentieth-century technique with elements of French Impressionism (an enthusiasm fostered in Japan by the blind *koto* player and composer Michio Miyagi) and an interest in the kind of natural 'found' materials that attracted Olivier Messiaen to birdsong. Most of the early work is for small instrumental groups and for electronics; his first orchestra piece, the *Requiem* for strings, was written in 1957.

At this point in his career, Takemitsu was utterly resistant to Japanese music and instruments, and it was not until 1962 and the score for the alarmingly titled *Seppuku* (film music has always been an important strand of Takemitsu's work) that he first used Japanese instruments as an integral element of his music. The mid-1960s were a period of breakthrough for his music. In 1965, the year of Yamada's death, he began the discussions with composer Toshi Ichiyanagi (who still perhaps claims more attention in the West as Yoko Ono's first husband) and Seiji Ozawa, conductor on the selected recording of *November Steps*, that led to the formation of Orchestral Space, a significant contemporary music festival that aligned Japanese musicians with the most innovative trends in Western music. In 1966, Takemitsu wrote *Eclipse*, a chamber piece for *biwa* and *shakuhachi* that represented his most developed essay in the use of traditional instrumentation in a modern context. The following year, *November Steps* was premiered, significantly in New York City.

To some extent, the work is a 'return-of-the-repressed', a coming-to-terms with Takemitsu's vigorously denied past. Much as Watanabe's father had taught *biwa* (thereby perversely encouraging his son to take up the alto saxophone) so Takemitsu's father had been an enthusiastic amateur performer on the bamboo *shakuhachi* (a memory that doubtless influenced the young Takemitsu to dabble in the acoustically hard and, in the 1950s, inflexible field of electronics). However, it is important not to psychologize *November Steps*; in the same way, while it can be argued that the reversed-out (white-on-black) notation of *Eclipse* and the dramatic lights and darks Takemitsu suggested for the stage lighting, it is clear that the composer's main intention is a formal one.

The *biwa* is essentially a large lute, with a variable number of silk strings, and a distinctive clattering timbre; for *November Steps* Takemitsu specified the five-string *satsumabiwa*. The more familiar *shakuhachi* is essentially a bamboo recorder (rather than a flute, as it is often described) with five finger holes, a deceptively crude instrument which requires considerable virtuosity from the player. Takemitsu's score (particularly in the cadenza) calls for a wide range of fingering and embouchure variations, allowing the player to extend its tonal and timbral range considerably.

The score specifies that the two soloists be ranged front left and right on either side of the conductor, with two widely separated string groups (each with harp and percussion) behind them, and a phalanx of wind players centred at the rear. Takemitsu has frequently made use of spatial separation in his music, but it is perhaps more dramatically and effectively handled here than elsewhere. Though *November Steps* represents Takemitsu's most developed investigation of traditional Japanese music (the 'steps' of the title are the separate sections of the work, a term borrowed from traditional practice) and though the soft, unfamiliar pitching and timbre of the two solo instruments is pleasantly alien, *November Steps* is essentially a Western work, located somewhere between the richly ambiguous harmonic language of Olivier Messiaen and the starker serialist procedures of Pierre Boulez. The *biwa* and *shakuhachi* come from quite different aspects of the Japanese tradition and are only somewhat anachronistically twinned. The two soloists perform essentially a concertante role, doubling or commenting on the instruments in the orchestral groups (at several points, Takemitsu has the right-hand harpist imitate the sound of the *biwa*). There is no obvious programmatic intent. Though many of Takemitsu's works suggest an almost pictorial approach (the 1977 orchestral piece *A Flock Descends into the Pentagonal Garden* is an extreme example), his music is almost always impressively abstract and *November Steps*, named simply after the month of its first performance, is no exception.

Most of the score is in conventional notation, but the last but one of eleven 'steps' is a free cadenza for the unaccompanied solo instruments in which both players play a number of musical cells in whatever order each chooses. These cells are notated very differently; the *biwa* player is presented with a graphic score that gives no indication how specific sounds are to be produced; the *shakuhachi* player is presented with something like Tibetan neumes or medieval tablature, and is much more constrained. The effect is very powerful and, at that point in the piece, quite startling.

There is no doubt that the popularity of *November Steps* is due in part to a taste for musical exotica. However, its persistence is largely explained by the fact that it sits, notwithstanding the accents of the two soloists, very comfortably in the twentieth-century orchestral repertoire. The music is rather violent by Takemitsu's usual limpid standard, and though it is possible to argue that the juxtaposition of extreme violence and lyrical gentleness is 'quintessentially Japanese', the robustness of *November Steps* has little in common with the decadent, sado-masochistic romanticism of a writer such as Yukio Mishima (who, with the film director Akira Kurosawa, is perhaps the only other Japanese artist with a reputation comparable to Takemitsu's).

Takemitsu likes to tell the story that when Kurosawa approached him to write a soundtrack for the movie *Ran*, he suggested that he would like something 'modern'. Takemitsu's dismay had nothing to do with the fact that Kurosawa offered up a European example of what he wanted (*Ran* was, after all, based on *King Lear* and Macbeth), but that the director's idea of a 'modern' score was Gustav Mahler's First Symphony, 'The Titan', written almost a century ago and subsequently marked by the shadow of totalitarianism and war. Takemitsu's loyalty has always been to the new, and that has never had any national, or even Continental, boundaries.

Discographical Information

Other recordings: Isuruta, Yokoyama, Royal Concertgebouw Orchestra, Haitink Philips 426 667 2; Tsurutu, Yokoyama, Saito Kinen Orchestra, Ozawa (Philips 432176).

Other Takemitsu: *Uninterrupted Rest* (1952–9; Decca HEAD 4); *Vocalism Ai* (1956; RCA Victrola VICS 1334); *A Flock Descends into the Pentagonal Garden* (1977; Deutsche Grammophon 423253); *Toward the Sea* (1981; Etcetera KTC 1143); *All in Twilight* (1988; New Albion NA 032).

Map references: Alexander Tcherepnin, Triple Concertino (1931; Thorofon CTH 2021); Chou Wen-chung, *Soliloquy of a Bhiksuni* (1958; Crystal CD 667); Michio Miyagi, *Haru no Umi/The Sea at Springtide* (1955; Crystal CD 316); Karen Tanaka, *Prismes* (1984; Bis CD 490).

BETSY JOLAS (born 5 August 1926)

Points d'aube (1968)

FIRST PERFORMED: Le Havre, February 1968; revised version (recorded here) Geneva, 1971
SELECTED RECORDING: Ades 14.013 LP
   Serge Collot (viola), Ensemble Ars Nova, conducted by Marius Constant
   [with: *J.D.E.* (1966), Ensemble Ars Nova; *Stances* (1978), Claude Helffer (piano), Nouvel Orchestre Philharmonique de Radio France, conducted by Constant]
RECORDED: [April] and June 1978
DURATION: 14′ 45″

Betsy Jolas belongs to perhaps the last generation of women for whom music-making was prescribed as an 'accomplishment', part of the process of social harmonization that led inevitably to marriage. I have already mentioned Elizabeth Maconchy's experience as a student in London, and her single-minded response to it. Jolas, on the other hand, had the great good fortune to be raised in a thoroughly artistic environment. Her father was the distinguished editor Eugène Jolas, founder of *Transition* magazine and first publisher of Joyce's *Finnegans Wake*. Her Scottish-born mother Maria MacDonald was a highly respected translator and amateur singer. The fact that her parents were both literary rather than professionally musical may well have helped Jolas establish her own creative identity. It has been suggested that it also steered her toward vocal music and opera in preference to 'pure' instrumental music. Though compositions for voice are not in the majority in her work-list (there are many more chamber and instrumental pieces) there is throughout her work a strong singing line which is sometimes at odds with the apparent abstraction of her means. This was made explicit in her second 'string quartet', *Quatuor II* (1964), where a coloratura soprano takes the place of the first violin.

Jolas has maintained dual French and United States nationality throughout her adult life, a detail that usefully highlights the distinctive character of her work, neither wholly 'European' nor characteristically 'American' in style. Unlike her near-contemporary Thea Musgrave, another eclectic individualist, Jolas was not drawn to America by cultural attraction, but by sheer force of circumstance. In 1940 the family fled the German occupation and crossed the Atlantic, where Jolas took her degree at Bennington College. She returned to France after the war and studied under Darius Milhaud (himself already straddling the Old and New Worlds), Olivier Messiaen and the pianist and composer Simone Plé-Caussade (born 1897).

If there is such a thing as a 'female aesthetic', it almost always involves an innate or subtly conditioned resistance to hard-and-fast generic or stylistic categories. For a young woman used by her own account to creating her own imaginary worlds and indulging her creativity unchecked by 'correctness' (she gave up piano-playing for composition when she realized that her technique was not sufficiently sound), there was little attraction in systems. Like Musgrave, she was greatly affected by the music of the maverick Charles Ives, on whom she wrote a valuable essay in 1970 for the journal *Musique en jeu*. Jolas has always insisted that each of her pieces works according to its own logic and structure, an internal landscape which appears to her entire, with all the immediacy of a memory or a dream, and which then has to be reconstructed 'in the light of necessary means'. A good deal of Jolas's instrumental work is for solo performance, and gives a sense of having been conceived, not as a series of technical essays, but as an attempt to allow individual instruments to find their own voices. Over two decades (1964–84), she wrote a sequence of eight unaccompanied 'episodes', which can be likened to Luciano Berio's *Sequenze* (1958–88), but which also includes works for instruments still rarely seen in a 'classical' context. The very fine *Episode huitième* (1984) for double bass is now perhaps the best known of the group, having been regularly performed and recorded [Adda 581043] by the French virtuoso, Joëlle Léandre. *Episode quatrième* (1983) for tenor saxophone has been recorded by Daniel Kientzy [Polyart PAR 5303], but *Episode septième* (1984) seems not yet to have been added to the growing list of contemporary recorded pieces for electric guitar (see article on Tim Brady).

There is also in the series a piece for viola (*Episode sixième*, also 1984) which reflects Jolas's particular interest in the instrument that occupies a central position (literally) in *Points d'aube*. Without stretching the point too far, it is interesting to note how the resurgence of the viola as a solo instrument has run parallel to a growing awareness of women's music. Very often, certainly too often to be coincidental, string quartet viola players are female and orchestral viola sections (this is based on a quick, unscientific sample of five European and American orchestras) have proportionately twice as many female players as the first or second violins, and significantly more even than the cellos. Jolas has been strongly drawn to the rich and slightly unfamiliar tone-colour (the viola is, of course, known as the *alto* in France) and has written other significant works for it: an early unaccompanied sonata (1955), which more than stands comparison with works by Bernd Alois Zimmermann (an exactly contemporary Sonata), Peter Maxwell Davies (*The Door of the Sun*, 1975), the Franco-Vietnamese Ton-That Tiet (born 1933, *Terre-feu*, 1981), and Morton Subotnick (*An Arsenal of Defence*, 1982) included on a fine Composers Recordings Inc compilation [CRI ACS 6107]; there are also *Remember* (1971, for viola or cor anglais), a set of four duos (1979) with piano accompaniment, and a full-scale Concerto (1990–1).

Points d'aube and the similarly constructed *Points d'or* (1982) for saxophone and fifteen instruments are not quite anti-concertos (on the contrary, they restore the original etymological sense of struggle between unequal forces), but both refer with gentle irony to the classical traditions of concertante writing. Something similar happens in Jolas's 'piano concerto' *Stances*, also on this recording, where the orchestra intermittently acts as an echo chamber for the piano before taking part in a more even-handed dialogue. In *Points d'aube*, the soloist begins playing seated in the middle of an apparently hostile, certainly not a co-operative or 'replenishing', ensemble, and only gradually establishes the traditional primacy of the soloist, standing and moving front-stage as the piece develops. The effect is not just a theatrical gimmick, though it was, of course, very much part of a late 1960s 'performance' aesthetic;

one thinks of Thea Musgrave's ultra-modern 1967 Clarinet Concerto [Argo ZRG 726 LP], in which the soloist vies with the conductor for control of small orchestral groups, wandering round the platform, peeking at other players' scores, or of Harrison Birtwistle's peripatetic *Verses for Ensembles* (1969). In *Points d'aube*, the device is also audible as the piece gradually develops – or dawns. The soloist alternates between apparently respectful attention to his fellow players and oblique, individualistic sorties that break the piece up into a sequence of brief, discontinuous movements in which the solo line and the 'accompaniment' are by no means exactly synchronized. Musgrave had also used a similar device more satirically in her Chamber Concerto no. 2 (1966), a tribute to Charles Ives, in which the viola (a part for her husband Peter Mark, but here impersonating Ives's 'Rollo', a know-nothing figure of fun) off-puttingly whistles banal variations on the melodic line with the aimless perseveration of the musically illiterate.

The ensemble for *Points d'aube* is an unusual one, consisting of thirteen winds, and its basic sound is one that reflects Jolas's apprenticeship with Milhaud and Messiaen (who chose her to replace him at the Conservatoire Nationale de Musique Supérieure between 1971 and 1974). Though Messiaen's *Quatre études de rythme* (1949–50, brilliantly recorded by Yuji Takahashi on Denon [33CO 1052]) blazed a trail for Boulez's 'total serialism', Messiaen himself did not go far down that road. Instead he developed ideas, such as the famous 'modes of limited transposition', which were ultimately derived from Asian and ancient European sources, and which allowed him to develop a language of great rhythmic complexity and strong tonal colour that aligns his music with that of (the earlier, non-serialist) Stravinsky, Villa-Lobos and, an even odder bedfellow, George Gershwin (1898–1937). The brusquely dissonant smears and 'shakes' which Jolas commands from her eight brasses in *Points d'aube* have a very American, almost 'jazzy' feel, as do some of her low-toned bass clarinet figures and stretched-out rhythmic patterns. The almost antagonistic uncommunicativeness of soloist and ensemble is signalled by a sharp brass clarion in the opening measure, which the violist chooses to ignore, but the background modulates steadily into a more lyrical 'Chinese opera' effect which also surfaces in the chamber opera *Le pavillon au bord de la rivière* (1975) and in the brilliant *Préludes–Fanfares–Interludes–Sonneries* (1983) for wind orchestra. However, Jolas never uses dissonance dramatically and polemically, as, for example, Leonard Bernstein does). Less than a year after *Points d'aube*, she took an unambiguous stand for modernism in the journal *Preuves*: 'Il fallait voter sériel même si'. Jolas's basic language is twelve-note, though with a highly individual slant and a concentration on linear melody that aligns her with Schoenberg. *Points d'aube* is not generated by a single, over-determining note-row, but by a number of melodic fragments which 'melt' together into ever longer melodic sequences as the soloist takes control of his own destiny. This happens, too, in *Stances* where in the final movement the soloist takes the central role, supported much more functionally and deferentially than before by the orchestra. Ten years separates the two pieces, and though they are very different in basic sonority, they are unmistakably by the same hand.

What links Jolas's works, as I mentioned above, is their constant, poetic approximation to song and almost narrative specificity of line. That is evident in the orchestral *Tales of a Summer Sea* and in *Onze Lieder* for trumpet and orchestra (both 1977). It is also explicitly signalled in subtitles like 'Ohne Worte' – 'without words' – for the second of her instrumental 'episodes' (also 1977). Her daring with unusual timbres and sonorities is only possible because the main trajectory of each piece, however different, is so strong. That is already noticeable in her first major work, *La plupart du temps* (1949), settings for mezzo-soprano and piano of poems by Pierre Reverdy, and in the Messiaenic orchestral accompaniments to her choral *L'oeil égare dans les plis d'obéissance du vent* (1961), another untranslatable title; it appears, too, in 'songs without words' like *D'un opéra de poupée en sept musiques* (1982), where she adds electric guitar, two ondes martenot, and *four* electric pianos to a conventional chamber group. When she turns to actual opera, as she did increasingly in the 1980s, the instrumental combinations become even more adventurous. *Le pavillon* is scored for two flutes, cor anglais and three trombones; in 1986 *Le cyclope*, after Euripides, dispensed with the woodwinds and added electric guitar and bass guitar, while in the following year, *Schliemann*, her most ambitious work to date, used a full orchestra with a sound diffusion system that may well have been inspired by that devised by Xenakis for his own archaeological fantasies, the 'Diatopes' and 'Polytopes' (1967–77).

Though much admired in France and America, her two countries of citizenship, Jolas's music seems not yet to have acquired long-term visas for travel elsewhere. Like the Sino-Swiss Tona Scherchen(-Hsiao), daughter of Hermann Scherchen and the Chinese composer Hsiao Sheshien, who is a dozen years younger, she has been marginalized not so much because her work is 'difficult' (which it is not) or harshly dissonant (which it is only intermittently), nor even because she is a woman (which is now very much a plus point in the new, revisionist atmosphere), but because she quite simply belongs to no definable school, national or stylistic. And that seems a pity.

Discographical Information

Other Jolas: *B for Sonant* (1973; Adda 581241); *E.A.* (1990; Adda 581225).

Map references: Thea Musgrave, Impromptu no. 2 (1967; Leonarda LE 325); Tona Scherchen, *Shen* (1968; Philips 6521 030 LP); Joan Tower, *Breakfast Rhythms I* and *II* (1974; Summit DCD 124).

Further reading: 'Entretien avec Betsy Jolas', in *Courrier musical de France*, 1969; B. Jolas, 'Il fallait voter sériel même si', in *Preuves*, i (1970).

GAVIN BRYARS (born 16 January 1943)

The Sinking of the Titanic (1969–)

FIRST PERFORMED: London, 1972
SELECTED RECORDING: Les Disques du Crépuscule TWI 922 2
  Gavin Bryars Ensemble: Alexander Balanescu, John Carney (violas), Gavin Bryars (double bass), Martin Allen (percussion), Roger Heaton (bass clarinet), Dave Smith (tenor horn, percussion)
RECORDED: April 1990
DURATION: 60' 13"

'Pataphysics is 'the science of imaginary solutions', a branch of speculative literature and philosophy devised by the French playwright Alfred Jarry (1873–1907). It deals with closed-room mysteries, narrative lacunae, coincidence and serendipity, associative logic and the absurd. Exponents are required not so much to suspend disbelief as to hang it by the neck until dead. Its underlying philosophy is that set out by Sherlock Holmes: once a process of reasoning has eliminated all likely solutions, then whatever remains, *however improbable*, must represent the 'facts in the case'.

Gavin Bryars has been a member of the Collège 'Pataphysique since 1974; he is also an active member of the Sherlock Holmes Society, and of Oulipopo, a cadet branch of the Ouvroir de littérature potentielle. Bryars's particular gift as an artist has been to follow a given idea to its logical limits, *however improbable* they may seem. It is unwise to define him narrowly as 'a composer'. His undergraduate studies were in philosophy. Up until the mid-1970s, he had worked primarily in an experimental fine arts context and, as a double bass player, in free jazz. His earliest 'scores' were in a conceptual vein closer to performance art than to formal composition. Between 1972 and 1974, he gave up active composition altogether to study the work and ideas of Marcel Duchamp (1887–1968), the self-dramatizing genius of modernism whose classicism, chess-player's lateral intellectualism and sense of radical aesthetic purity have made a substantial impact on Bryars.

His career as a performer began in working men's clubs in his native Yorkshire, but rapidly embraced free (abstract) improvisation. Bryars co-founded the group Josef Holbrooke, which was named after a neglected English composer (1878–1958) of markedly but unsuccessfully populist tendencies. While teaching at Portsmouth College of Art in 1969 and 1970, Bryars co-led the infamous Portsmouth Sinfonia, a 'scratch' orchestra of untrained but deadly serious amateurs whose brief career culminated in an explosive reading of the '1812 Overture' at the Albert Hall. The opposite of a musical snob, Bryars revelled in the unstuffy commitment of the Sinfonia, and was out of sympathy with the stern proletarianism of improvising groups like the (so named) Scratch Orchestra and the Marxist–Leninist–Maoist circle of the renegade avant-gardist Cornelius Cardew (1936–81). A professorial appointee at Leicester Polytechnic (before the 'binary divide' was abolished and university status universalized), he has remained outside the academic freemasonry of contemporary composition in Britain, the exponents of 'squeaky door music' and was an early apostle of a new accessibility. He has stayed loyal to his roots in jazz and performance; like the American Philip Glass (born 1937) and his near-contemporary Michael Nyman (born 1944) he runs a self-named ensemble as an outlet for his own music. He has made no attempt to renounce or withdraw his earlier, more experimental works, and has continued to perform and revise the finest of them, the 1971 piece for ensemble and tape *Jesus' Blood Never Failed Me Yet* and its open-form predecessor *The Sinking of the Titanic*.

The loss of the supposedly 'unsinkable' White Star liner on its maiden voyage in April 1912 presented Bryars with the perfect 'pataphysical 'equation of facts'. Some of these at least are incontestable. The *Titanic* lies 15,000 feet below the Atlantic surface at latitude 41.16 N, longitude 50.14 W, a location established on 1 September 1985, when a salvage company found the wreck. Bryars's interest in the disaster centred on two details in particular. First of all, there was the intriguing conceit that the historical sinking of the *Titanic* was actually a 'realization' of an earlier conceptual piece. Like his friend and sometime collaborator, the artist Tom Phillips, who adapted one in his work-in-progress *A Humument*, Bryars has long been interested in obscure Victorian fiction. In 1898 Morgan Robertson published a novel called *Futility* about a huge liner called (incredibly) the *Titan*, which struck an iceberg in the North Atlantic on its maiden voyage (and in April!) and went down with a substantial proportion of passengers and crew.

Alongside this bizarre example of life mimicking art was a detail that rapidly became part of the mythology of the *Titanic*, enshrined in the film about the disaster *A Night to Remember*. This relates to the junior wireless officer's report that the ship's band had continued to play as the *Titanic* slowly upended and sank. Harold Bride reported hearing them play a ragtime tune and then, as he floated away on his lifebelt, a hymn. This was reported in the press to be the Episcopal hymn 'Autumn', but it seems likely that this was a pressman's mis-hearing of 'Aughton', an altogether more death-haunted theme. Mythology and the movies have further displaced the facts. It is widely believed that the band played 'Nearer My God to Thee' as the *Titanic* went down. This gained currency following the use of that theme by the organist– composer Sigfrid Karg-Elert (1877–1933), one of Bryars's pantheon of forgotten geniuses, during a *Titanic* Memorial Concert at the Albert Hall in May 1912.

The significant element of Harold Bride's testimony, from a 'pataphy-sical point of view, is that while he reported the band continuing to play as the ship settled in the water, *he did not report it as having stopped*. In Bryars's imagination, there remains a quasi-logical possibility that the music simply continued underwater, and the essential sound-material of *The Sinking of the Titanic* is a hymntune slowed up and diffused as it loses contact with chronological time. This gains 'scientific' support by intersecting with a further set of associations. The *Titanic*'s maiden voyage was the first occasion on which wireless telegraphy had been used in marine rescue. Its inventor Guglielmo Marconi, who greeted Bride on his arrival in New York, believed later in his life that sounds never die; they simply become infinitely faint. Water is an excellent con-ductor of sound and, given the conceit that the musicians continued to play below the surface, it is possible to imagine their music diffused eternally throughout the North Atlantic, a detail that chimes with a para-scientific experiment in one of Bryars's sacred texts, Raymond Roussel's strange novel *Impressions d'Afrique*. (Scientists in the 1980s detected a faint after-echo of the Big Bang at the origin of the universe, a detail that reduces the improbability of Bryars's premises by a sub-stantial notch.)

He has left the performance 'score' of *The Sinking of the Titanic* open in order to accommodate new findings and configurations of fact, not least the rediscovery and filming of the sunken ship in 1985. The hypo-thetical possibility of raising the *Titanic* (the film mogul Lord Grade said it would be cheaper to lower the Atlantic) with its 'cargo' of diffused sound sets a logical end-limit to the open-form status of a piece many people felt had been realized definitively by the version recorded in 1972 for the Obscure label. But Bryars has continued to revise it, largely, one assumes, in response to renewed activity in the North Atlantic.

The Disques du Crépuscule version was recorded in live performance in a disused nineteenth-century water-tower (appropriately) at Bourges. The musicians were located round the basement perimeter and the sound was passed through a reverberant upper chamber before being filtered back into the 'auditorium' on the middle floor, thus preserving the metaphorical structure of the event itself. The *Titanic* band was a string sextet, three violins, two cello and a double bass. Bryars has retained the number of musicians, but has significantly revised the instrumentation in order to introduce new sound effects and musical references, most notably a bass clarinet lament for the young Scottish bagpiper who died on the ship and whose posthumous *pibrochaid* diffuses solemnly through the water. The tenor horn has obvious potential for evoking a fog-bound seascape. Percussion mimics specific sound effects reported by survivors, two of whom – Edith Russell and Eva Hart – are actually heard on tape. Woodblocks repeat a distress sequence in Morse code, while the marimba, with its chill, rather static sonority, sounds out the hymn tune, suggesting an interesting (but to Bryars probably unwelcome) parallel with Peter Maxwell Davies's 'sea-piece' *Ave maris stella* (q.v.).

As in his opera *Medea* (1982–4), Bryars has dispensed with violins, preferring the more muted and liquescent sound of violas and his own double bass, which he occasionally octave-shifts during the piece with electronic pedals. This new realization is strongly marked by the sound of his superb (and still unrecorded) concertante piece *By the Vaar* (1987, double bass, bass clarinet, percussion, strings) for the jazz bassist Charlie Haden. The harmonies are kept deliberately static, often using enharmonic repetition of the same notes, and the music consists largely of repetitive, ostinato patterns, characteristically (some have said monotonously) slow in tempo. The music is somewhat similar to the American minimalists but without their mathematical approach to phase-shifting and bravura piling-up of notes; Bryars has always been suspicious of excess 'dots'. A more significant influence has been the music of jazz composer Carla Bley (born 1938) and the jazz trios led by pianist and composer Bill Evans (1929–80), particularly those *c.*1961 featuring the virtuosic young bass player Scott LaFaro, who died in a motor accident aged only twenty-five. In recent years, Bryars has renewed his interest in jazz composition and performance, signing a recording deal with the high-tech German jazz and new music label ECM; *The Sinking of the Titanic* is a rare exception but Bryars and his engineer and co-producer Chris Ekers have achieved a sound which is well up to scratch. He has derived a chamber piece – *Sub rosa* (1986) – from a guitar improvisation by the American Bill Frisell, and has written pieces, such as *Alaric I or II* (1989, two soprano saxophones, alto saxophone, baritone saxophone) for jazz-orientated players, as was *By the Vaar*. He has also discovered new ways of combining the elaborate fabulism of his experimental phase with existing genres, as in the String Quartet no. 1: *Between the National and the Bristol* (1985), in which the four musicians also 'impersonate' composer/string players of the early years of the century.

Even at his most extremely experimental, Bryars rarely shrank from accessibility, arguing that during a period in which 'squeaky door' music was dominant, euphony and even an element of sentimentality could be construed as radical gestures, deliberately eliminating the boundaries of 'serious' and popular music, and the class boundaries of musical literacy and professionalism. *The Sinking of the Titanic* is a work that has, like the eerie hulk shown up in the Taurus International underwater film, stood the vicissitudes of time better than its early history might have suggested. Bryars has poured a considerable proportion of his later musical understanding into the Bourges performance. It gains additional resonance as a memorial to a friend killed in the Lockerbie bombing, betrayed by transport like his predecessors of 1912, but somehow redeemed by the aural transports of this remarkable piece.

Discographical Information

Other Bryars: *Jesus' Blood Never Failed Me Yet* (1971– ; Philips 438823); *My First Homage* (1978; Disques du Crépuscule TWI 027); *Alaric I or II* (1989 [with: *After the Requiem* (1990)] ECM New Series 847537–2); *The Green Ray* (1991; Argo 433847–2); *The Black River* (1992; ECM 437956–2).

Map references: Sigfrid Karg-Elert, Partita op. 37 (1905; CPO 999 051-2); Harold Budd, *Madrigals of the Rose Angel* (1972; Editions EG EGED 30); John White, Symphony no. 19: *The Whistlers and Their Mothers* (1987; Musica Nova 3).

Further reading: G. Bryars, 'The Sinking of the Titanic' ["score'/documentation/ realization notes], in *Soundings* (USA), 1975; P. Griffiths, interview in *New Sounds, New Personalities: British Composers of the 1980s*, London, 1985.

1970s

The 1970s have always unjustly suffered from simple chronology, having to follow the supposedly innovative and forward-looking 1960s. If the new decade appeared to look backwards, it was to a style and philosophy of music that had still not been absorbed into the mainstream, though it was already several decades old. This was the high-water mark of academic serialism, a forbidding orthodoxy that seemed inclined to outlaw anything remotely tonal or comfortably accessible, and sustained by an increasingly mandarin musical establishment. It was also, however, the decade that saw the beginnings of a response to that orthodoxy. 'Minimalism' became a new buzz word and, from the middle of the decade onwards, punk rock and its aftermath exerted a bracing influence on all branches of music...

1970 Karlheinz Stockhausen performs his music in a huge, specially constructed geodesic dome at Expo '70 in Osaka. Steve Reich visits Ghana to study drum music.

1971 Igor Stravinsky dies in New York.

1972 Erhard Karkoschka's *Notation in New Music* attempts (unsuccessfully, as it turns out) to systematise a proliferating range of new notational systems.

1973 Toru Takemitsu organizes annual 'Music Today' festival in Tokyo. The Kronos Quartet is formed in San Francisco; it concentrates on new repertoire and on dramatic ways of presenting contemporary music: a sharp contrast to the London-based Arditti Quartet, equally dedi-

cated to recent and specially commissioned work, but with a much more sober philosophy and image. Pablo Picasso dies.

1974 British critic Michael Nyman publishes *Experimental Music* which in addition to coining a new descriptive category suggests a new teleology for contemporary music, centred on Cage and his followers rather than Schoenberg and Webern.

1975 Dmitry Shostakovich dies.

1976 Over the next four years, Pierre Boulez conducts the centenary *Ring* cycle at Bayreuth. Odaline de la Martinez and Ingrid Culliford found Lontano ensemble.

1977 IRCAM commences activities in Paris. Maria Callas dies.

1978 Peter Maxwell Davies's First Symphony is premiered, a significant moment in post-war British music. Davies had already moved out of reach of the mainland and the metropolitan musical establishment, by making his home in Orkney.

1979   The first 'complete' perfor-

mance of Alban Berg's *Lulu* (the third act reconstructed by Friedrich Cerha) is given in Paris, conducted by Boulez (again). Shostakovich's controversial *Testimony*, 'edited' by Volkov, is published.

GEORGE CRUMB (born 24 October 1929)

Ancient Voices of Children (1970)

FIRST PERFORMED: Washington, DC, 31 October 1970
SELECTED RECORDING: Elektra Nonesuch 7559 79149 2
    Jan DeGaetani (mezzo-soprano), Michael Dash (boy soprano), Contemporary Chamber Ensemble: George Haas (oboe, harmonica), Stephen Bell (mandolin), Susan Jolles (harp), Gilbert Kalish (electric piano, toy piano), Raymond DesRoches, Richard Fitz, Howard Van Hyning (percussion), Jacob Glick (musical saw), conducted by Arthur Weisberg
    [with: *Music for a Summer Evening* (1974), Gilbert Kalish, James Freeman (amplified pianos), Raymond DesRoches, Richard Fitz (percussion)]
RECORDED: January 1971
DURATION: 25' 41"

It has taken George Crumb's reputation some time to recover – in Europe at least – from a tendency to dismiss his work as gimmicky, superficially trendy, rather 'sixties' in orientation. Perhaps only since the release in 1990 of the Kronos Quartet's recording [Elektra Nonesuch 79242] of his *Black Angels* (1970) for amplified string quartet has Crumb begun to be seen again as a major American composer.

Much is always made of the 'dramatic' or 'ritual' properties of Crumb's work. His first major work was the Pulitzer Prize-winning *Echoes of Time and the River* (1967), a set of four 'Processionals' which required some members of the orchestra to march across the stage. In *Lux aeterna* and *Vox balaenae* (both 1971), the performers are masked; in the former piece, the players are also robed, and sit in lotus position round a single candle, singing lines from the Latin Requiem; for the latter, based on recent researches into whale song, the stage should be lit with a deep sub-marine blue, and the masks are intended to 'efface a sense of human projection, ... symbolize the powerful impersonal forces of nature'. This is slightly ironic, and *Vox balaenae* represents something of an exception in Crumb's work, which almost always places considerable demands on performers' ability to 'project' themselves with great individuality and forcefulness. It is interesting to note that among all his experiments with amplification, non-standard performance techniques and instruments, there is not a single purely electronic work.

Nor, significantly, are there any 'aleatory' scores. Crumb leaves nothing to chance, notating every work precisely, with an exact sense of what sounds are required. There is a sense in which his work is all concerned with the confrontation of 'powerful impersonal forces' in various forms, both positive and negative. The bleak siren-sounds and blasts of *Black Angels*, which was subtitled 'Thirteen Images from the Dark Land' and intended as a response to the horrors of the Vietnam War, represent an extreme example, with an unusually direct and programmatic frame of reference; they are also atypical in assigning an unambiguously hostile role to the technological elements. At the opposite extreme, of course, is the non-human but non-threatening music of *Vox balaenae*.

Inevitably, though, the most significant of all the 'impersonal forces' Crumb confronts is that of his own musical training. In 1954 and 1955 he studied under Boris Blacher at the Hochsschule in Berlin; his earliest works, like the impressive orchestral *Variazioni* (1959), were serially organized, but it was already clear that Crumb's instincts steered him toward a latter-day version of baroque practice (there are explicit quotes in *Ancient Voices*) in which ensembles represent dialogues, 'arguments' and reconciliations between highly individualized instrumental voices. In this respect, and with regard to the highly unusual sound-sources and timbres he uses, Crumb has also been influenced very directly by the Appalachian folk music of his youth (he grew up in West Virginia), with its jugs, jaw harps, hammered dulcimers and even musical saws (one of which appears in the second song of *Ancient Voices*).

Crumb's aesthetic is best characterized by his own much-quoted statement (1982) that 'Music might be defined as a system of proportions in the service of a spiritual impulse'. Influenced by medieval and Renaissance numerology, and by such devices as the *quadrivium*, he conceives pieces as balanced systematic wholes constructed out of rich musical imagery, but in which the laws of motion, parameters like timbre, dynamics and pitch are all subject to strict proportional control. This is the philosophical basis for the sequence of piano works known as *Makrokosmos* (Parts I–IV, 1972–9), with its zodiacal structure (I, II) and references to 'Celestial Mechanics' (IV), though the title of the sequence (meaning something like 'the universal whole' or 'the whole of creation') is also an act of homage to Bartók and his piano-book *Mikrokosmos* (1926–39). And it is this concern with control, as well as their different approaches to the 'preparation' of instruments that distinguishes Crumb's from John Cage's aesthetic, on which it nonetheless significantly draws.

If one single artistic influence is dominant in Crumb's career it is his longstanding commitment to the poetry of Federico García Lorca, who was executed by his nationalist captors in 1936 during the Spanish Civil

War. Lorca's untranslatable concept of *'Duende'* represented a perfect conjunction of non-personal forces with the 'spiritual impulse'. *'Duende'* is a kind of mysterious blood-knowledge, owing little to rational argument or familiar constructions of beauty ("sweet geometry'), but by no means anarchistic, reflecting the combination of passion and symmetry found in flamenco, or the systematized violence, spatial and organic balance of the bullfight.

The first piece in Crumb's Lorca cycle was *Night Music I* (1963, soprano, piano/celesta, two percussion), followed by four books of *Madrigals* (1965–9, soprano, ensembles), *Songs, Drones and Refrains of Death* (1968, baritone, electric guitar, amplified double bass, amplified piano/harpsichord, two percussion), *Night of the Four Moons* (1969, contralto, alto flute/piccolo, banjo, amplified cello, percussion), and culminating in *Ancient Voices*. The cycle was first heard as a whole at Oberlin, Ohio, in 1972. A key moment in the development of the sequence was Crumb's first meeting with the brilliant American mezzo Jan DeGaetani (1933–89) at the University of Pennsylvania. Their subsequent relationship was every bit as fruitful artistically as that of Luciano Berio and his wife Cathy Berberian (1925–83). Crumb was intrigued by what he described as DeGaetani's 'enormous technical and timbral flexibility'. In her Lieder recitals and interpretations of such modern works as Schoenberg's *Das Buch der hängenden Gärten* (1908–9) and *Pierrot lunaire* (1912), she had shown an astonishing ability to combine intense lyricism (her *Pierrot* is probably the most romantic version yet attempted) with a profound analytical grasp of microscopic modulations in pitch and rhythm which made her an ideal interpreter of demanding contemporary repertoire. The first two books of *Madrigals* were written with her in mind and mark a significant advance in Crumb's treatment of voice.

For *Ancient Voices*, he grouped together fragments from a number of Lorca poems in such a way as to suggest the 'larger rhythm' of the complete works. He also interpolates two instrumental movements – the second and fifth, 'Dances of the Ancient Earth' and 'Ghost Dance' – in such a way as to underline the original meaning of 'suite' as a sequence of thematically unrelated dance pieces; the third of the songs is also subtitled 'Dance of the Sacred Life-Cycle'. The mezzo-soprano soloist is required to sing much of the time in a demanding wordless *vocalise*, using phonemes that nonetheless manage to sound like an atavistic root-language. She is also asked to sing directly into the strings of the amplified piano, which resonate sympathetically, thereby creating a mysterious backwash of overtones; this effect, coupled with the use of an echoing boy soprano (who sings offstage until the final measures of the last song, 'Se ha lleneda de luces mi corazón de seda', 'It's filled with lights/my heart of silk', which culminates with a fervent prayer for 'mi alma antigua de niño', 'my ancient soul of a child') reinforces the mysterious and atavistic aura characteristic of Crumb's music. The percussionists use a wide variety of antique instruments, including Asian temple bells and prayer stones, and are asked to sing, chant and sibilate at points during the performance, deepening the sense of ritual and magic.

The scoring is typically idiosyncratic, marked by Crumb's 'urge to fuse various unrelated stylistic elements'; in *Black Angels* he had introduced quotes from Camille Saint-Saëns's *Danse macabre* and Franz Schubert's 1824 D minor string quartet *Der Tod und das Mädchen*. At the widest extremes, *Ancient Voices* contains elements of flamenco and the baroque, but there is no self-conscious eclecticism, probably because the timbral language of the piece is so carefully crafted and individualized. There is an imaginative use of folk instruments. In the second song, 'Me he perdido muchas veces por el mar', 'I have often lost myself in the sea', the mandolin player (actually a second musician on this recording) switches to musical saw, introducing the 'pitch-bending' effects Crumb had learned from the virtuoso percussionist–composer John Bergamo. These are also evident when in the fourth song 'Todas las tardes en Granada / todas las tardes se muere un niño', 'Each afternoon, each afternoon, a child dies in Granada', the oboist switches to harmonica, though the oboe itself also produces 'bent' notes, as does the harp and mandolin. Much as he had done in *Vox balaenae*, where the cello is retuned (a technique known as *scordatura*), Crumb has the secondary strings of the mandolin lowered a quarter-tone, increasing a likeness to the sitar he was later to use in *Lux aeterna*.

'Preparation' of this sort inevitably invites comparison with John Cage, who throughout the 1940s had experimented by wedging screws and bolts between the strings of a piano, creating an altered sonority which was nonetheless constant for the duration of the piece. Crumb's use of toy piano in the fourth song may well recall pieces of Cage's such as *Music for Amplified Toy Pianos* (1960), but he avoids the fixities of prepared piano by having the performer press a chisel blade against the strings in the second song, distorting the pitch momentarily. The resemblance to Appalachian hammered dulcimer is further underlined in the instrumental interlude 'Dances of the Ancient Earth', where the harpist threads paper between the strings, altering the timbre very considerably. (A better parallel than Cage might be the Californian composer–inventor Harry Partch, who rejected Western resources and scales altogether, devising his own orchestra of microtonal instruments; but even Partch's instruments are essentially 'fixed' in pitch and timbre, rather than yielding moment-by-moment variations of sound-colour like Crumb's.)

Merely listing these effects in isolation is to run some risk of focusing undue attention on them as self-consciously iconoclastic gestures. Though listening to Crumb's music on record does involve a certain loss of visual or dramatic resonance, it also prevents undue emphasis on purely technical considerations. It is often quite difficult and usually redundant to try to determine what instrument is playing at a given moment. Crumb does not tamper with instruments merely in order to demonstrate that it can be done; in her essay on 'Keyboard music' in volume 6 of *New Grove*, Susan Bradshaw goes out of her way to clear him of the charge of 'gimmickiness'. Crumb uses 'experimental' techniques purely because he requires a particular sound or set of sounds. His understanding of whale music, for instance, is logically related to his wider ideas, just as Messiaen's transcriptions of birdsong were not decorative, but part of his general harmonic and melodic conception; for comparison, and a good example of gimmickiness, it is worth looking at Alan Hovhaness's briefly trendy *And God Created Great Whales* (1970), a proto-New Age work which used the taped song of Pacific hump-backs. Crumb's works are always coherent and logical, classic instances of scores that generate their own highly specific, often unique, musical languages. Probably no other composer has gone so far in this direction as Crumb, and perhaps for that reason it is difficult to find comparative terms of reference for his works. He has stated that music has powers even beyond those of language to 'mirror the innermost recesses of the human soul', and in *Ancient Voices* he goes as far as anywhere in his work toward that aim, creating a music that is utterly without precedent but yet responsive to musical history, fundamentally humane and emotive but yet conscious of the great impersonal forces (death pre-eminently) that command human affairs.

Discographical Information

Other Crumb: Five pieces for piano (1962; Mode 15); *Madrigals I–IV* (1965–9; New World NW 357–2); *Songs, Drones and Refrains of Death* (1962–70; Bridge BCD 9028); *Black Angels* (1970; Elektra Nonesuch 72942); *Vox balaenae* (1971; as for *Madrigals*); *A Haunted Landscape* (1984; New World NW 326 2).

Map references: John Cage, *Amores* (1943; Hungaroton HCD 12991); Harry Partch, *The Bewitched* (1955; CRI CD 7000/7001); Alan Hovhaness, *And God Created Great Whales* (1970; Crystal CD 810); John Bergamo, *Nideggen Uthan* (1986; CMP CD 27).

Further reading: B. Fennelly, 'George Crumb: *Ancient Voices of Children*' in *Notes*, 29, 1972–3; D. Gillespie, *George Crumb: Profile of a Composer*, New York, 1985; R. Dufallo, interview in *Trackings*, Oxford, 1989.

EDISON DENISOV (born 6 April 1929)

Sonata for alto saxophone and piano (1970)

FIRST PERFORMED: Chicago, 14 December 1972
SELECTED RECORDING: Globe GLO 5032
    Arno Bornkamp (alto saxophone), Ivo Janssen (piano)

[with: Florent Schmitt, *Légende* (1918); Paul Creston, Sonata (1939); Paul Hindemith, Sonata (1943); Alfred Desenclos, *Prélude, cadence et finale* (1956); Jacques Charpentier, *Gavambodi 2* (1973)]
RECORDED: October 1989
DURATION: 12′ 03″

The composer Hector Berlioz greeted the invention of the saxophone with barely restrained enthusiasm, claiming that Adolphe Sax's new instrument was 'incapable of mere musical futilities'. The saxophone is the only entirely new instrument of the last century and a half; the patent letter is dated 20 March 1846. It is customary to describe it as a 'hybrid' of the woodwinds and the brass family (which Sax had already revolutionized with a group of saxhorns), but this is rather misleading. Even if a technological development – the wheel, the pencil, the internal combustion engine – seems 'inevitable' it still requires a quite specific and deliberate intervention to bring it into being.

The saxophone is a single-reed instrument, usually, but not inevitably, made of metal, and what distinguishes it from the clarinets and oboes is that it has a conical bore, a fact that explains many of its technical and performing difficulties. It was conceived as a dual-purpose instrument, for use both in military bands, and with a different pitching, in orchestras. It did the French armies, whose quartermaster-generals had been instrumental (!) in commissioning it, no good at all in 1871, and it enjoyed only a rather brief and intermittent vogue in classical orchestras, marred by vehement rejection in some quarters, and falling into disuse after Sax's death in 1894. Its reappearance was, of course, rather spectacular, but it came at some considerable distance from its main intended purpose. Since just after the First World War and with increasing visibility as it replaced the lighter sound of the harder-to-play clarinet, it became one of the main instruments of jazz and popular music. In public consciousness, the saxophone is not a 'serious' instrument at all; it even has something slightly disreputable about it. Arnold Bennett is alleged to have described its sound as 'the embodied spirit of beer', and in the 1930s the *Saturday Evening Post* published a cartoon of its inventor with the half-joking caption: 'Posterity will never forgive you, Adolphe Sax'. Across the Atlantic, the Nazis condemned it as the embodied spirit of 'Judaeo-Negroid degeneracy' and undertook not to forgive anyone caught playing one.

Given that weight of prejudice, it was until relatively recently difficult to recognize that the saxophone had managed to sustain a 'respectable' existence as a concert instrument, and that there was, in fact, a considerable amount of formal, scored music for it. The dominant playing style, that of the French master Marcel Mule, was rather languid and restrictive, and advances in the instrument's performance capabilities

were very largely (though again not exclusively) the preserve of improvising jazz musicians. The sort of multiphonic effects audible in Edison
Denisov's piece came into the instrumental language via the work of
men like John Coltrane and Eric Dolphy.

There were also saxophone virtuosi in the classical field, most prominently perhaps the German–American Sigurd Rascher (born 1907) for
whom Glazunov wrote a Saxophone Concerto in 1934, but it was not
until the 1980s that a very substantial body of writing for the saxophone
began to appear and some earlier master-works to be dusted down. No
one contributed more to the new vogue for 'classical' saxophone music
than the British player John Harle, whose tone and presentation is
peerless, but who clearly prefers euphonious, jazz-tinged scores to more
jaggedly modernistic works. In the latter category the Frenchman Daniel
Kientzy is predominant, having mastered all the main members of the
saxophone family, from soprano to bass. It was he who premiered
Denisov's *Concerto piccolo* (1977) for six percussionists and one saxophonist playing four instruments.

The 1970 Sonata has become something of a test piece for contemporary saxophone players. Harle describes it as 'outrageously difficult' and labours some parts slightly. Arno Bornkamp's version is fleet
and confident, and the sound is much more natural than on Hyperion's
rather intense recording. The piece is in three radically different movements and though there is little evident structural cohesion between
them, it succeeds as an entity. Denisov has always asserted that
personal style is a matter of absorbing and then transcending a multiplicity of received forms. In the Sonata, as in a cluster of solo and
accompanied instrumental pieces over the next five years, he appears to
write a form of musical autobiography, compressing wildly disparate
styles into a piece which only gains coherence by the force of his
creative personality.

Much is always made of the separateness of the Sonata's three movements. Harle suggests that 'it would be a brave composer who presented such a work as "through-composed" ', given the range of musics
it draws on and seems to parody. In fact, each of the three movements
enacts a stylistic journey that brings it into line with each of the others,
eliminating quite basic differences in musical philosophy along the way.
Though it is one of his lighter and more playful pieces, it also directly
addresses Denisov's conviction that music is a profoundly spiritual art.

The opening movement is rather stark and abstract. It uses serial
technique but only in a very non-restrictive way, and the real impetus
comes from the rhythmic interaction between saxophone and piano,
which gradually builds to a dramatic climax. Denisov's technique is
palpably influenced by the Italian composer Luigi Nono, who visited
the Soviet Union as a loyal but maverick Communist in the early 1960s,

shortly after Denisov began teaching at the Moscow Conservatory. Nono's fractured lines and aspects of his 'sonorism' (the use of sonorities for their own sake, regardless of pitch relationships) are evident in the *Allegro* opening, though handled with enough confidence to suggest that Denisov may have been thinking along similar lines independently.

The slow central movement opens with an alien wail like a muezzin's call and plunges the saxophonist into a strange, mystical environment which calls on radical new performance techniques. Pragmatically, it evokes a wild, wasteland landscape, and it may be significant that Denisov was born at Tomsk in Siberia on the edge of the huge expanse of marshlands that stretch northwards from Novosibirsk. He wrote the Sonata for the French virtuoso Jean-Marie Londeix, and part of the intention was to extend the instrument's formal vocabulary into areas that had only been explored by improvising musicians. These include multiphonics (the simultaneous sounding of more than one note), quarter-tones and other micro-intervals, and disturbing slithers from one pitch to the next. Playing virtually unaccompanied (the piano contributes a few brittle harmonies from the top end of the keyboard) the saxophone is quite cruelly exposed. If Denisov's tongue is firmly in his cheek for at least part of the piece, the soloist's tongue is required to make some unprecedented contortions of its own, including 'flutter-tonguing', a technique known to brass and flute players, which creates very rapid tremolo effects.

Emphasizing the radical nature of the technical requirements may be misleading. The *Lento* movement is also hauntingly beautiful, calling on the 'tender, veiled tone-colour' which Berlioz had spoken about so warmly. Its very primitivism seems to belie the complexity of its expressive means. By contrast, the final movement is a bravura workout for both instruments, locked together in a jazzy battle of wills and styles, covering bebop (with its adventurous harmonic idiom) and the 'free jazz' approach of Ornette Coleman and Eric Dolphy. Harle very evocatively describes the movement as 'lip-breaking' and it is here that he sounds least at home with the music. Bornkamp rides it out with great confidence and aplomb, maintaining an admirable evenness of attack. Bornkamp's other repertoire is also rather more challenging than that on Harle's record (which has, in any case, disappeared from the catalogue) and offers a rather longer historical perspective on chamber composition for saxophone.

As an introduction to Denisov, the Sonata cannot be said to be absolutely representative, but it gives an excellent impression of the way in which the composer has combined a multiplicity of styles to shape his own individual voice. His major work to date has been the surreal opera *L'écume des jours* (1981) after a novel by Boris Vian, and here too he uses popular music as an important element in a texture which manages to convey great expanses of musical history in instants of time. The interlocking lines of his earliest acknowledged piece, the 1955 Sonata for two violins, suggest how painstakingly he constructs his counterpoint. Perhaps for the same reason, he was a slow starter as an orchestral writer. After an early, relatively conventional symphony (also 1955) and a more idiomatic *Sinfonietta on Tadzhik Themes* (1958) – perhaps modelled on the *Tadzhik Suite* (1938) by Boris Arapov (born 1905), who was head of the instrumental department at the Leningrad Conservatory – Denisov offered no more orchestral scores until 1970. With the exception of the magnificent Chamber Symphony (1982) and an unnumbered work premiered in Paris in 1988, he has largely avoided symphonic writing in favour of a long and increasingly sophisticated sequence of concerted works. This began with the Concerto for cello and orchestra in 1972 and including works for piano (1974), flute (1975), violin (1978), a small group of double concertos (rather like Schnittke's concerti grossi) for flute and oboe (1979), bassoon and cello (1982), two violas, harpsichord and strings (1984), then for viola alone (1984), oboe (1986), and clarinet (1989). It is worth labouring the list, for it represents a remarkably concentrated exploration of instrumental sound. There is a comparable body of chamber sonatas, both unaccompanied and with piano, guitar or organ, but unfortunately – apart from Two Pieces, again written for Londeix and premiered at Bordeaux in 1974, and the *Concerto piccolo*, first presented at the same festival five years later – Denisov has not written more for the saxophone.

Discographical Information

Other recordings: Harle (alto saxophone), Lenehan (piano) [with: Phil Woods, Sonata; Richard Rodney Bennett, Sonata for soprano saxophone and piano; Dave Heath, *Rumania* (soprano saxophone, piano); Michael Berkeley, *Keening* (also saxophone, piano)] (Hyperion CDA 66246); Delangle, Soveral [with: *Concerto piccolo*; piano and percussion works] (Pierre Verany PV 790112); also EMI C 065 12805; Open Loop XPL 1059; Colosseum Colos SM 640; Coronet LPS 3044.

Other Denisov: *Sun of the Incas* (1964; Mobile Fidelity MFCD 869); Trio (1971; Mobile Fidelity MFCD 917); *Colin et Chloé* (1981, suite from opera *L'écume des jours*; Melodiya SUCD 10–00107); Concerto for two violas, harpsichord and strings (1984; Bis CD 518); Symphony (1988; Melodiya SUCD 10–00060).

Map references: Alexander Glazunov, Saxophone Concerto (1934; EMI/Angel CDC 54301); Jacques Ibert, *Concertino da camera* (1935; chamber orchestra; as above); Giacinto Scelsi, *Tre pezzi* (1961; Adda 581047; Niels Viggo Bentzon, Sonata for soprano saxophone and piano (1985; Steeplechase 32017).

Further reading: S. Bradshaw, 'Edison Denisov', in Tempo, ii (1988).

EMMANUEL NUNES (born 31 August 1941)

Litanies du feu et de la mer, no. 1 and no. 2 (1969, 1971)

FIRST PERFORMED: Paris, 1976
RECOMMENDED READING: ADDA/MFA 581095
  Alice Ader (piano)
RECORDED: January 1988
DURATION: 48′ 03″

Critical pigeon-holing is largely an unconscious business, done auto-
matically and without much reflection. There is a sort of statistical
common sense that helps us get our ears and mind tuned in to what a
new or hitherto unheard piece of music is likely to sound like. Experience tells us what we might reasonably expect from Stockhausen or
Leonard Bernstein, from a work of the 'Darmstadt school' or of
'American minimalism', from a sonata or from a work 'influenced' by
Javanese gamelan; and there is nothing whatever wrong with that,
except that it cuts across certain cherished notions about the meta-
physics of music. How often do we *really* hear a composition emerge
out of the silence and then retreat into the silence again? Do we not
more often perceive it as emerging out of and then contributing to a
background buzz of critical and aesthetic preconceptions? How often
would we want to risk the discomfiting rigours of a 'blindfold test'?
How many pieces of music, even in a self-consciously radical and subversive contemporary repertoire, offer no stylistic clues or generic toe-
holds, no hints of 'national' characteristics?
  Emmanuel Nunes is by no means well known, even to new music
specialists but he deserves inclusion first because this piece is so very
extraordinary and then – and only then – because his work illustrates
some interesting points about the progress of contemporary music
outside the main centres of creative and critical activity, where the
'opinion-formers' are. Given its size, Portugal has made surprisingly
little direct impact on contemporary culture; even highly literate people
might find it difficult to name a single contemporary Portuguese writer
or artist. In music, only Fernando Lopes-Graça (born 1906), Jorge
Peixinho (born 1940), and Nunes, who was Lopes-Graça's pupil at the
Lisbon Academy of Music in the early 1960s, have made any kind of
impact outside their own country in this century. It is ironic that the
main axis of 'Portuguese' musical culture has been tilted towards Portugal's former colony Brazil, with its complex local factors. To illustrate
the extent if not the reason for this isolation, continue the diagonal up
through Europe from south-west to north-east and compare Portugal

with Finland, a country with exactly half the population and a fore-shortened history of independence, but one which has made an enormous contribution to modern music with a long roster of names that would be familiar (even if only as names) to the majority of new-music enthusiasts.

This is not the place to attempt an explanation, but it is interesting to note Lopes-Graça's nineteenth-century-sounding definition of music as 'an equation between the artist and his milieu'. Doubtless influenced by the 'new nationalism' of the Brazilian composers, Lopes-Graça attempted to combine modern compositional techniques with traditional folk music and with a broad, epical understanding of Portuguese culture and myth, particularly Camoes's *Lusiads*. There was a political as well as aesthetic reason for this. Lopes-Graça's adult life was dominated by the military dictatorships of Antonio de Oliveira Salazar and subsequently of Marcello Caetano; between 1928 and 1968, Portuguese artists were quite simply not free to say what they wanted, and only during Caetano's rearguard tenure between 1968 and 1974 did Lopes-Graça and younger artists begin to express themselves without restraint. Denied access to the musicians he required, Lopes-Graça organized amateur choral groups of urban and agricultural workers, of students, even (at greater distance) of political prisoners to perform a 'music of social interaction', somewhat similar to the anti-modernist project of radical English composers Alan Bush (born 1900) and Cornelius Cardew (1936–81), and the American Frederic Rzewski. By combining folk materials and modern techniques, he attempted to subvert the nationalistic official culture of the Salazar years.

I have laboured these points about Nunes's teacher because inevitably the *Litanies du feu et de la mer* do not emerge out of a cultural vacuum. Nor is it entirely redundant to suggest ways in which the work can be thought to reflect certain specific resonances of 'Portuguese culture'. Portugal is a small country on the westernmost edge of Atlantic Europe, separated by language from its larger Iberian neighbour. A colonial power, its political influence has been quite disproportionate to its actual size. To post-Enlightenment Europe, the Lisbon earthquake of 1755 long stood as a warning against complacent rationalism and faith in unruffled progress. To a very large extent, Nunes's work is directly concerned with these questions. Though he had a relatively conventional postgraduate training (Darmstadt, Paris, Cologne) he has always registered a certain sense of isolation, a need to reconstruct music from the ground up, or out of an undifferentiated residue of sound. It is not too fanciful to liken the process to the rebuilding of a devastated city. Nunes destroyed most of his early work; the earliest surviving piece, *Degrés* for string trio (1965) represents a painful rediscovery of all the constituent parameters of music, as if information and communication systems were being slowly restored, clear signals emerging from the disordered 'static' with which the piece begins.

The architectural analogy probably works best. Moving through Nunes's mature output is a little like exploring a futuristic city, where one is unable to determine with confidence the purpose of individual buildings, or the line of former thoroughfares, but finds oneself able to move between locations and levels by unknown or unexpected means. Though individually his compositions tend to be *sui generis*, using a wide variety of instrumental and electroacoustic combinations, since 1973 he has also arranged them in two overlapping cycles, the first untitled, the second known ominously as 'The Creation'. Some of the pieces in the latter cycle, like the three string solos known as *Einspielung* (1979–81), may be played simultaneously in the manner of some of Cage's works; others, like the massive *Tif'ereth* for six orchestral groups (1978–85), are actually cannibalized from earlier pieces. Almost all are concerned with a process of initiation, a kind of technical and spiritual 'apprenticeship', in which processes are examined in the context of a single life-work, their constituent materials and techniques simultaneously flourished and disguised.

It is this last characteristic that makes Nunes so difficult a composer to write about either descriptively or analytically. He really does have to be heard. Nunes is as much a social philosopher as he is an 'artist' in the romantic sense; he resembles the Chinese *wenren*, the 'pioneer-engineers in art'. Like Iannis Xenakis (who was actually trained as an architect), he tends to construct pieces with blocks of sound, rather than as linear developments; both men have shown a close interest in 'group theory' and in the interrelationship between architecture and 'information'. Nunes's pieces tend to be long, resolutely undramatic, and mimic the combination of haphazard fact and positive purpose that is characteristic of human life itself, or of the structure of a large urban complex. That is to say, they are highly logical, almost obsessively orderly and controlled, while appearing to be the opposite.

The *Litanies* are, surprisingly, Nunes's only acknowledged compositions for solo piano. They predate the earlier of the two cycles, but in interesting ways they anticipate the concerns of both, an obsession with pitch relationships and tonal colour in the first, a shift of emphasis toward rhythm, duration and metre in the second. As in his work as a whole, it is virtually impossible to *demonstrate* uniformity, contrast, symmetry or logical progression in the two pieces. Marked respectively '*Vers tendre...*' and '*Se detourner de...*', it remains unclear whether they are intended as separate but thematically connected pieces, or as subsidiary elements of a continuous piece. Nunes makes use of great blocks of sound, vertical aggregations of tones which could be analysed into their constituent parts were such analysis not so patently irrelevant.

Chordal shapes appear in both pieces, but they may be *faux amis*, will-o'-the-wisps. The music constantly 'breaks down' into repetitive patterns, insistently hammered out, obstinately refusing to move forward. There are virtually no indications in the score as to how the notation is to be interpreted, and in this appropriately dry recording Alice Ader resists any temptation to emote or to vary a notably rigorous delivery. The effect is very alienating, very enigmatic, and very troubling for a listener primed for a cathartic climax or a resolution of the harmonic materials.

There is no obvious point of stillness in the centre, between the two parts, but the second piece gradually increases in intensity, with ever deeper chasms of silence between the blocks of sound. This may suggest deceptively that some apocalyptic conclusion is around the corner, but in the event any such expectation is utterly confounded. At the end the music simply crumbles, and nowhere has the awful old pun about *de*-composing seemed more relevant. Nunes appears to be demonstrating the impossibility of any ultimate revelation in the music itself, and as such he sets himself against such mystically inclined composers as Alexander Skryabin (1872–1915), with his mystic chord, and Olivier Messiaen, with his triumphant rainbows and amens and shivering silences. It may be that the title is intended as a specific and ironic echo of Claude Debussy's symphonic sketches *La mer* (Debussy was, after all, a major influence on Lopes-Graça) and his constituent titles 'De l'aube à midi sur la mer', 'Jeux de vagues', 'Dialogue du vent et de la mer' suggest temporality, playfulness, complementary interchange in a way that seems quite lost in Nunes's suddenly startling title: *Litanies of fire and the sea*. If wind and water can engage in meaningful dialogue, making significant patterns out of their conjunction, clearly fire and water cannot, and the final truth of Nunes's work is extinction: the edge of Europe again? Lisbon shaken and in flames? Columbus sailing out over the brink of the known world? All these are possible resonances. A litany is a series of petitions, a recurring formula of desire; it is not to be confused with liturgy, a formulation that suggests at least some of the answers are known, by at least some of the participants. Nunes's music is about the impossibility of final answers, in music as in life, and about the impossibility, as he sees it, of transcendence. Such a radical position can make his creative enterprise seem bleakly despairing, but it actually places tremendous weight on the act of music-making itself, rather than on any imported system of value. Nunes is hard to understand, but he is perennially challenging.

Discographical Information

Other Nunes: *Minnesang* (1974–5) [with: *Grund* (1978)] (Adda 581110); *Degrés* (1965), *Nachtmusik I* (1977–78); Accord 204392.

Map references: Claude Debussy, *La Mer* (1903–5; London 433711); Alexander Skryabin, Piano Sonata no. 9 in F (*Black Mass*) op. 68 (1914; RCA Gold Seal 09026 60526); Fernando Lopes-Graça, *Canto de amor et de morte* (1961; A Voz de Dono 8E 063/40345).

PIERRE BOULEZ (born 26 March 1925)

Rituel in memoriam Bruno Maderna (1974–1975)

FIRST PERFORMED: London, 2 April 1975
SELECTED RECORDING: Sony Classical SMK 45839
  BBC Symphony Orchestra, conducted by the composer
  [with: *Eclat/Multiples* (1966, in progress), Ensemble Inter-Contemporain, conducted by the composer]
RECORDED: November 1976 [December 1981]
DURATION: 25' 19"

It may seem perverse to define Pierre Boulez as a 'difficult' composer and then select what is probably his most accessible and expressive work, deliberately overlooking major pieces like the ground-breaking *Le marteau sans maître* (1952–4) or *Pli selon pli* (1957–62) or ... or what? The problem with Boulez is that he is more 'important' than he is great or even likeable. His influence on contemporary music as conductor, critic and administrator has been enormous, in some respects over-determining, in others (like the authoritarian lockstep he has imposed on much of the modern canon) baleful, but he has somehow never quite seemed as compelling as a composer. It is nonetheless difficult to agree with David Mason Greene's suggestion that Boulez 'is as likely to wind up as a curiosity treated in a footnote [to musical history] as he is as a Moses who led music out of the wilderness – or the doldrums'. A Moses is precisely what he now seems: as the chief propagandist of 'total serialism' which, though stiflingly restrictive, purged contemporary music of much of its nineteenth-century moss; as the reinventor of Wagner (the centenary *Ring* in 1976) for the late twentieth century; as the conductor who gave the French premiere of Alban Berg's *Wozzeck* (nearly four decades late!) and *Lulu* its definite shape; most obviously, as the founder of IRCAM, his own Bayreuth in the heart of Paris.

Perhaps influenced by René Leibowitz, the St Paul of serialism, the younger Boulez took an extreme and often doctrinaire view on most subjects. His first important teachers were Olivier Messiaen, and, a little earlier, the pianist and composer André Vaurabourg (1894–1980), who was also the wife of the Franco-Swiss composer Arthur Honegger

(1892–1955), through whom he may have acquired his taste for machine-like rhythms. It was from Messiaen that he drew the conviction that serialism had to be extended not just to the pitch materials of music but also to parameters like rhythm and intensity. Boulez had been profoundly influenced by Leibowitz's performance in Paris of Schoenberg's op. 26 Quintet for woodwinds (1923–4), but looked on Schoenberg less as a Moses who was not destined to see the Promised Land of full-blooded serialism than as (in Schoenberg's own typology) an Aaron who was content to implement compromised versions of radical ideas. In 1952, and in the face of Leibowitz's espousal of Schoenberg as the bearer of musical truth, Boulez wrote an essay for William Glock's *The Score* entitled 'Schoenberg is dead' (he was, of course), and then set about the artistic canonization of Anton Webern which has played such a crucial role in contemporary music.

Boulez was determined that music should move out of its period of relaxed and open-ended 'expressiveness' and enter a realm of scientific exactitude and precision, in which every single parameter could be defined precisely. It was a determination – the first part, but not the second – that he shared with John Cage (q.v.). Despite similarities of background (both their fathers were engineers, Cage's in a rather improvisational sense) they came out of very different cultural contexts. Just as Cage was pluralistic and libertarian, a representative American, Boulez embodied in extreme form the aggressive integralism of French culture. Oddly, it was another American who staked a claim to have discovered the principles of 'total' – or 'integral' – serialism a year or two before Boulez, but Milton Babbitt (born 1916) was never an ideologue in the way that Boulez was to be.

The works of the late 1940s are forbidding even half a century later. A Sonatina for flute and piano (1946) sounds as if it is in dialogue with Stravinsky, the Second Piano Sonata (1948) with Schoenberg, but in the harsh accents typical of conflict between generations. The *Livre pour quatuor* (1948–9, later revised as *Livre pour cordes*, 1968–9) has a more winning and accommodating sound, as if in respectful homage to both Webern and Messiaen. However, like many works from the period, it prompted an ambivalent reaction from the composer. Parts of it did not see the light of day until 1962; none of it was performed until 1955. Other works of the period – the piano piece *Notations* (1945) and *Polyphonie* (1951) for eighteen instruments – were withdrawn; the Third Piano Sonata (1957–) was given an incomplete performance at Darmstadt (symbolic, for Boulez was not a 'Darmstadt composer') but has never reached a definite form. It appeared that he sought, and found, satisfaction in other directions.

In 1953 he persuaded Jean and Madeleine Renaud Barrault (for whose theatre company he had worked as director of music) to sponsor a series of Sunday concerts of contemporary music. These began in 1954 as the Petit-Marigny concerts, shortly to be renamed the Domaine Musical. That was to be in 1955, the year of *Le marteau sans maître*. This most striking of works was scored for female voice, alto flute, guitar, vibraphone, xylorimba, percussion and viola, and represented both a setting of and a shadow 'commentary' on verses by René Char, one of the least transparent of the Surrealist poets. It was in fact his third Char setting; *Le visage nuptial* (1946) and the radio play *Le soleil des eaux* (1948) had preceded it. But it represented a quantum leap in Boulez's output at the same time as it reflected a new dependence on extra-musical principles of organization. Over the next few years, Boulez began an open-ended series of works for soprano and orchestra dedicated to Stéphane Mallarmé, the *Improvisations* (1957, 1959), *Tombeau* (1959) and *Don* (1960), all of which were subsequently revised and grouped as *Pli selon pli* (1960).

The 1960s saw him move steadily away from composition as his main focus of attention. He taught at Basle and at Harvard. In 1966 he was invited by Wieland Wagner to conduct *Parsifal* at Bayreuth, a trial run for the centenary *Ring* cycle a decade later. In 1967 he became 'first guest conductor' of the Cleveland Orchestra, an ill-fitting off-the-peg designation which meant in effect that he conducted those modernist works which did not appeal to the principal conductor George Szell. He had recently resigned the Domaine Musical to another conductor/composer Gilbert Amy (born 1936) and staged something of a sulk at minister of culture André Malraux's appointment of the 'conservative' Marcel Landowski as inspector-general of L'Enseignement musical. Boulez refused to have his work performed by government-funded orchestras or in Paris at all.

His compositional career seemed to have hit dead water. An ensemble version of *Eclat* (1965) was premiered in Los Angeles, but it was only in 1970 that the extended *Eclat/Multiples* (1965, unfinished) was unveiled, and by then Boulez was dividing his time between the BBC Symphony Orchestra and the New York Philharmonic. He was also considering Georges Pompidou's suggestion (they met to discuss it the day Charles de Gaulle died) of a proposal for a centre of musical research which had originally been floated by the Max Planck Institute. (That was a detail that further soured Boulez's view of the existing French musical establishment.) Since 1974 the Institut de Recherche et Coordination Acoustique/Musique, or IRCAM, has claimed a substantial proportion of his energies.

To go back to 1970, though, it is difficult to overestimate the effect that day-to-day contact with an open-minded and technically adroit orchestra had on Boulez. On his return to Paris he founded the Ensemble InterContemporain, a counterpart to the ambitious London

Sinfonietta. He had maintained contact with William Glock, Controller of Music at the BBC from 1959 to 1973, since the mid-1950s and was offered a much freer hand than under Szell at Chicago. In a memo accompanying a Domaine Musical programme, Boulez had written that he considered conducting one's own works the best possible discipline for a composer; much later he commented on the 'utopianism' of his own early work, its lack of a solid mediation in performance. In 1973, the untimely death of his friend the conductor and composer Bruno Maderna (1920–73) gave Boulez's new-found self-confidence an unexpectedly emotional focus.

The result was *Rituel*, premiered in London two years after Maderna's death. Typically of Boulez, this was no quick outpouring of grief, and not at all an 'occasional' work in any meaningful sense, but a painstakingly worked out score that drew some inspiration from Maderna's own orchestral *Aura*, premiered in Chicago in 1972, and even more on the ambitious *Quadrivium* (1969) for four percussion and four orchestral groups, itself a descendant of Stockhausen's *Gruppen* (1955–7) and *Carré* (1959–60) for multiple orchestras. On the face of things, *Rituel* seems to stand in the line of Boulez's earlier threnodies, the Mallarmé works and the shifting versions of '...*explosante fixe*...' (1971–85), written in memory of Stravinsky. However, *Rituel* is not an open-ended work-in-progress but a formidable feat of technical organization. Conversely, though its structure is essentially simple, it is not an exercise in numerology, but a profound and personal essay that constitutes an almost cathartic reorganization of formal values.

For the first time since *Le marteau sans maître*, Boulez produced a score in which form is seen as emerging from a sequence of related and determining events, creating what Boulez describes (and it is an accurate description of the piece) as a 'sonorous frieze'. Like the Stravinsky memorial, it is based on a simple rule of seven and it is constructed, almost unbelievably for Boulez, on a basically melodic framework, albeit one that is in constant transformation. The work operates by simple accretion and diminution. It is scored for eight unconducted instrumental groups of increasing timbral density: one oboe, two clarinets, three flutes, four violins, a wind quintet of oboe, clarinet, alto saxophone and two bassoons, a string sextet, and a mixed septet of alto flute, oboe, cor anglais, clarinet, bass clarinet and two bassoons; each group has a co-ordinating percussionist who plays a different instrument for each of the seven main sections. There is in addition a large group of fourteen brass that plays homophonic tuttis with the assistance of two percussionists. The brass *tuttis* are the most symmetrical element, increasing from a first appearance with one slow chord (tempos throughout the piece are alternately *Très lent* and *Modéré*) to seven on the seventh. The pattern of accretion is more complex and asymmetrical with the unconducted solo groups, a fact that imparts to the work a more complex internal mathematics of three-against-two, while always preserving the basic rule-of-seven.

The implacable, ritualistic quality of the piece is established by a steady crescendo of sound (accentuated by the absorption of each preceding solo group into the next tutti) and elaboration of tonal material from the original seven-note row. At the centre of the piece is a huge orchestral passage that sounds like a compressed autobiography. Thereafter the solo groups retreat, not in reverse or 'mirror' order, but as they came in, solo oboe first, the mixed septet last, leaving the brass choir to sound the final E♭. This may be (I have not heard it suggested elsewhere) a reference to Beethoven's op. 81a Piano Sonata *Das Lebewohl, Abwesenheit und Wiedersehen* (1809), better known as *Les adieux*, with its plangent imitation of 'horn fifths', which would be poetically quite appropriate; the technique of having instruments gradually drop out of the orchestra is one associated with Haydn's Symphony no. 45 (1772), known as the *Abschiedsinfonie* or the 'Farewell'.

Even listeners who have previously found Boulez desiccated or plain hard will respond to *Rituel*. What makes it important is that it is by no means an 'untypical' or 'uncharacteristic' work. On the contrary, it seems to be the culmination of his attempts to create a music in which the separate elements are all subject to strict control. There is throughout it a feeling of grief held in check, but by no means suppressed, and of humanity and compassion given expression in the most lucidly intellectual terms.

Discographical Information

Other recording: Orchestre de Paris, Barenboim [with: *Messagesquisse* (1977, solo cello, cello ensemble), *Notations* (1978)] (Erato 45493 2).

Other Boulez: Sonatina (1946; Erato 2292 45648–2); *Le marteau sans maître* (1952–4; CBS 73213); *Domaines* (1961–8; Harmonia Mundi HMA 190.930); *Pli selon pli* (1962; CBS SBRG 72770); *Messagesquisse* (1977; Erato 2292 45493–2); *Le visage nuptial* (1988–9; Erato 2292 45494).

Map references: Anton Webern, Symphony op. 21 (1928; Deutsche Grammophon 423254–2); Milton Babbitt, *Composition for Four Instruments* (1948; CRI C 138); Karlheinz Stockhausen, *Kontra-Punkte* (1952–3; Vega C30 A66); Bruno Maderna, *Quadrivium* (1969; Deutsche Grammophon 423246–2); Tod Machover [director of musical research at IRCAM, 1980–4], *Nature's Breath* (1985; Bridge BCD 9002).

Further reading: C. Deliège, *Par volonté et par hasard* [interviews], Paris, 1975, trans. 1977; P. Boulez, *Points de repère* [articles and texts], Paris, 1981, trans. as *Orientations*, London, 1986; W. Glock (ed.), *Pierre Boulez: A Symposium*, London, 1986.

DAVID DEL TREDICI (born 16 March 1937)

Final Alice (1974–1975)

FIRST PERFORMED: Chicago, 7 October 1976
SELECTED RECORDING: Decca SXDL 7516 LP
   Barbara Henricks (soprano), Chicago Symphony Orchestra, conducted
   by Georg Solti
RECORDED: 1981
DURATION: 42' 04"

Few modern premieres have been received with such rapturous acclaim
as that of David Del Tredici's *Final Alice* in October 1976, and the
occasion marked a kind of sea-change in the perception of contemporary 'serious' music. Del Tredici broke the rules. He composed
music that was tuneful, witty, and accessible, music that the public
actually *liked*. What was worse, he broke ranks with the academic establishment and voiced the ultimate heresy: as he put it to Richard Dufallo,
'if you write something atonal, dissonant, chance-filled, you can often
get away with murder. It's more difficult to separate the good from the
bad; standards are not quite so clear.' At last, a member of what had
seemed a closed order, almost a freemasonry, had uttered the very
doubts and suspicions that ordinary people entertained about modern
music. How do we know it's good? Do we just have to take your word
for it?

   Del Tredici has made much of his Catholic background, and it seems
clear that his own sceptical attitude to critical orthodoxy, particularly
that which prevailed in the 1960s and 1970s, was analogous to liberal
suspicion of the Latin Mass and an esoteric priesthood which jealously
guards its occult knowledge and specialist functions. Just as he had
been educated by priests and nuns, Del Tredici had been trained as a
composer in the rigid serialist orthodoxy that dominated American
music schools after the war. Much of his career has been, in the words
of his 1985 orchestral piece, a 'march to tonality', and it is entirely
fitting, given his playfulness as a composer, that his Italian surname
should convey a pun. *'Tredici'* means thirteen, and Del Tredici's career
has been a quest for the 'thirteenth note' that represents a step beyond
strict twelve-note technique. It has become a kind of signature in his
work, appearing verbally at the end of *Final Alice*, where the performers
count up to thirteen in Italian, with a heavy emphasis on *'tredici'*, but
also in complex time-signatures like $\frac{13}{8}$, devices which call into question
the critics' nervous dismissal of Del Tredici as a crowd-pleasing populist
who has turned his back on 'serious' music and excellent promotion
prospects in the serialist establishment to pursue commercial success.

For a decade, Del Tredici worked in an 'advanced' idiom, beginning with the piano *Soliloquy* (1958) and *Fantasy Pieces* (1959–60), and a rather aggressive String Trio (1959), and culminating in the very important *Syzygy* (1966), for soprano, horn and orchestra. This piece was significant in that it marked the beginning of Del Tredici's virtual concentration on music with voice, and the culmination of his first great textual obsession, with the work of James Joyce. Del Tredici has explained that though his basic technical idiom at this time remained serialist, he experienced melody as a virtually unconscious 'return of the repressed'. His musical career had begun as a concert pianist, and his training had, after all, been under the supervision of two of the less doctrinaire senior figures, Roger Sessions (1896–1985) and Earl Kim (born 1920), and so at a more conscious level he was primed for disenchantment with a situation in which the rigorous organization of total – or 'integral' – serialism was yielding results indistinguishable from music generated by chance operations. This was absurd, and absurdity became his theme.

Since 1968, virtually all of his published work has been directly inspired by Lewis Carroll's 'Alice' stories and associated Victorian texts. The perversity of the material and of his whole-hearted concentration on it underlines the cross-grained nature of Del Tredici's challenge, but it also sounds a warning. Del Tredici's Carroll is not just a comfortable bourgeois fantasist; he is also Charles Lutwidge Dodgson, the mathematician and clergyman, whose relationship to the historical Alice Liddell sends awkward ambiguities rebounding through the tales. It is all too easy to overstate Del Tredici's 'accessibility', to put too much emphasis on witty graphic devices like 'The Mouse's Tale' in *Adventures Underground*, where the orchestral part wiggles down the page in imitation of Carroll's original text; many of his structures and devices are extremely complex (how many of the first night audience at *Final Alice* were aware of thirteen-note rows and $\frac{13}{8}$ rhythms?) and his vocal writing from *I Hear an Army* (1964) and *Night Conjure-Verse* (1965, both Joyce settings, both premiered by Phyllis Bryn-Julson) has been awesomely demanding and virtuosic. Equally, his themes have been uniformly ironic and dark, not at all cosy.

Initially, in *Pop-Pourri* (1968) and the *Alice Symphony* (1969, 1976), Del Tredici seemed to be torn between his instinct for melody and a more academic style. Though the basic structure is tonal, the surface is harsh and dissonant and the use of rock and folk groups within the orchestra is not yet entirely successful. In the earlier piece, Del Tredici had asked for two saxophones and two electric guitars, in the *Alice Symphony* two soprano saxophones, tenor banjo, mandolin and accordion, and it is the latter line-up that reappears in *Final Alice* in a sort of concertante role. The score allows for the dramatic parts to be distributed among several sopranos, but at the premiere and in this recording Barbara Hendricks took all the roles. The piece contains five main arias and scenes (though one of each was cut from the recorded version to make it conform to LP length; any eventual CD will presumably restore them) drawing on the trial scene in *Alice's Adventures in Wonderland* (1865) and on verse by William Mee which Carroll parodies in his book; this ironic telescoping is a further element of Del Tredici's project. The music is terse and languid by turns but unmistakably tonal and, except at the height of forensic frenzy in the trial scene ("Contradictory Evidence', and 'Still More Evidence, Arguments in the Jury Chamber'), has almost none of those 'scrims of wrong notes' that crept into the earlier Alice works.

There is one signal advantage in listening to a recording rather than a concert presentation of the piece. Because of the size of the orchestra involved, a huge Straussian shimmer, it proved difficult to guarantee that Barbara Hendricks's wonderfully soft high As would be audible, so Del Tredici specified that the solo voice should be amplified, a device that somewhat compromised the range of vocal characterization and voice-colour that Hendricks brought to her roles. On record this was not a problem. Her voice is well forward without sounding artificially 'close' or intimate, and the orchestra is solidly present without being domineering.

It is difficult to know what to call *Final Alice*. Del Tredici has admitted that he is divided between the utterly different languages of symphonic and operatic music; it could be argued that this is precisely the dilemma he inherited from Richard Strauss (or from Berlioz or Wagner), but in this one he seems to have found a satisfactory point of balance. The later *Child Alice* (1977–81) has been more successful as a repository of shorter concert pieces – including the Pulitzer Prize-winning 'In Memory of a Summer Day' – than as a full-scale work.

Final Alice was originally intended, as the title suggests, to bring the sequence to a close. It would be cynical to suggest that its enormous commercial success persuaded Del Tredici not to kill a golden goose. Though they are divided regarding its legitimacy, both he and the critics still regard the turn to tonality as a daring strategy; for the composer it entails risk rather than complacency, a challenge rather than a retreat. There is no sense in which *Final Alice* represents a capitulation to a reactionary tendency in modern music; instead it poses a major political challenge to the paradoxical conservatism of the old avant garde. It bears all the distinguishing marks of 'post-modernism': playfulness, multiple irony, shifting resolution, a determined collapsing of 'high' and 'popular' forms, an invigorating tension (as in the Joyce pieces) between 'difficulty' and lyrical directness. As such, it is one of the most important works in the contemporary canon. It is difficult to assess Del Tredici's influence on other composers, largely because he has introduced no single technical innovation, but he is unquestionably important for having drawn attention to a considerable appetite for change both among musicians and their audience. Time has already diminished the shock value of his work but not its technical brilliance or intellectual generosity.

Discographical Information

Other recording: 'Acrostic Song' from *Final Alice*; Leonard, The Sixteen, Christophers (Collins Classics 12872).

Other Del Tredici: *Soliloquy* (1958; New World NW 380-2); *Fantasy Pieces* (1960; Desto DC 7110 LP); *I Hear an Army* (1964), *Night Conjure-Verse* (1965), *Syzygy* (1966; all on CRI ACS 6004); 'In Memory of a Summer Day', from *Child Alice* (1980; Elektra Nonesuch 79043–2); *Steps* (1990; New World 80390–2).

Map references: Richard Strauss, *Four Last Songs* (1947; EMI Classics CDD 64290); Luciano Berio, *Epifanie* (1959–62; RCA RK 11530/1–2 LP); John Corigliano, *Poem in October* (1970; RCA Gold Seal 60395–2); Richard Rodney Bennett, *Spells* (1974–5; Continuum CCD 1030); Peter Dickinson, *Stevie's Tunes* (1984; Conifer MCFRA 134).

Further reading: D. Del Tredici, 'Contemporary Music: Observations from Those who Create It', in *Music and Artists*, v/3 (1972); J. Rockwell, 'David Del Tredici: The Return of Tonality, the Orchestral Audience and the Danger of Success', in *All-American Music: Composition in the Late Twentieth Century*, New York, 1983; R. Dufallo, interview in *Trackings: Composers Speak with Richard Dufallo*, Oxford, 1990.

PETER MAXWELL DAVIES (born 8 September 1934)

Ave maris stella (1975)

FIRST PERFORMED: Bath, 27 May 1975
SELECTED RECORDING: Unicorn-Kanchana UKCD 2038
The Fires of London: Philippa Davies (flute/alto flute), David Campbell (clarinet), Beverley Davison (viola), Alexander Baillie (cello), Stephen Pruslin (piano), Gregory Knowles (marimba), unconducted chamber performance
[with: *Runes from a Holy Island* (1977); *Image, Reflection, Shadow* (1982), conducted by Peter Maxwell Davies]
RECORDED: January 1980 [May 1984]
DURATION: 29' 27"

Ave maris stella was the first major product of what Peter Maxwell Davies described as his *'pax Orcadiensis'*. Written when the composer had just turned forty, it marks a significant watershed in his immensely prolific career, leading directly on to the First Symphony (1976) and summarizing many of the concerns of the previous decade. Davies had moved to the Orkneys in 1970, but had only recently occupied the refurbished croft on Hoy that was to become his hermitage. In the circumstances, a Marian plainsong that addresses the Virgin as 'Star of the sea' must have seemed a highly appropriate choice of material.

Davies had a longstanding interest in medieval and Renaissance music, the work of figures such as Guillaume Dufay (1400–74) and the Englishmen John Dunstaple (c.1385–1453), John Taverner (c.1490–1545) and Thomas Tallis (c.1506–85). He had used plainchant in the Marian *Alma redemptoris mater* (1957) for wind sextet, but *Ave maris stella* is his most complex blending of medieval procedures with modern, post-serial composition. The most vivid image of that highly distinctive synthesis and of Davies's approach in general can be found in the most gnomic work of Davies's music-theatre period. *Vesalii icones* (1969), for cello, flute, clarinet, piano, percussion and dancer, recasts the Fourteen Stations of the Cross in terms of Vesalius's engravings for *De humani corporis fabrica*, where the human form is progressively stripped of skin, flesh, sinew, blood and bone in a surreal, secularized Passion. In the piece, Davies anatomizes his own music, introducing parodic quotations from Beethoven and medieval chants, examining the relationships between early and modern musical procedures (as he had done since his first significant pieces, the 1955 Sonata for trumpet and piano and the orchestral *Prolation* of 1958), seeming to lay bare the internal workings of the music at the same time as he preserves its essential mystery; the dancer, after all, remains physically entire.

Davies's music has always presupposed the closest possible contact with its interpreters and performers. In recent years, he has written a sequence of concertante pieces – the *Strathclyde Concertos* (1987–) – for the players of the Scottish Chamber Orchestra, of which he is associate composer and conductor. Previously, he had co-directed (with Harrison Birtwistle) the Pierrot Players, a chamber ensemble based on the instrumentation of Schoenberg's *Pierrot lunaire*. The association inspired *Grand Guignol* music-theatre pieces like *Eight Songs for a Mad King* (1969) and the later, even more intense *Miss Donnithorne's Maggot*. It was written in 1974 by which time the Pierrot Players had transformed into the Fires of London under Davies's sole directorship. He remained the Fires' artistic director until 1987, and the tremendous empathy that built up between them is evident from these unconducted performances of *Ave maris stella* and *Image, Reflection, Shadow*.

That the two pieces represent a companion pair is made clear when the first movement of *Image* echoes the climax of the earlier work. Nonetheless they are very different in mood, an effect accentuated by the switch from a darker, richer analogue to a brighter digital recording for the second piece. Despite its acclamatory title, *Ave maris stella* entirely lacks the bursting, extroverted vitality of *Image*, with its prominent part for gypsy cimbalom. It is, by contrast, a rather inward-looking piece, and its brooding, almost Nordic sound, with uneasy shifts of temporal sequence relative to chronological, biological and historical time, suggests an aural equivalent of an early Ingmar Bergman movie.

Davies has said that on Hoy he feels outside time. The cliffs opposite his croft show the strata of successive geological eras, frozen in what appears to be a moment of arrested collapse into the sea. (At a climactic moment in the writing of the Second Symphony in 1980 a huge slab of rock did actually detach itself and crash down into the waves below!) In discussing *Ave maris stella*, Davis has related its acceleration and compression of pulse sequences to his fantasy of a time-scale in which the rising and setting of the sun was so accelerated as to appear simultaneous and eternal. It may be that Davies had also seen time-lapse photographs of the 'midnight sun' of the sort prepared as tourist posters. Summer nights in Orkney are extremely brief and the cycle of seasons speeded up with the poetic intensity Davies found in the work of Orcadian poet George Mackay Brown.

Ave maris stella compresses the rhythms of a lifetime into a single day, a twenty-four-hour period in which darks and lights alternate. It begins and ends with a becalmed 'night music' reminiscent of Bergman's 'Hour of the Wolf'. Time briefly stands still before the musical colours brighten with the dawn. In the second movement, the clarinet is introduced as if in echo of cock-crow and morning chorus; significantly, it also sounds in the 'death cry' at the very end of the work, a closing gesture which is as affirmative as the opening is ambiguous, and establishes the cyclical nature of the process. The music is essentially elegiac and was written in memory of Hans Juda, a close associate of the Fires of London, who had recently died.

In writing the music, Davies made use of a 'magic square' originally devised as his bookplate in which a sequence of nine pitches and durational values is successively transposed and rotated to create a grid of intervals and rhythmic matrices which significantly exclude certain possibilities in such a way as to give the whole a certain asymmetrical consonance. The sequencing relates closely to Davies's use of Stravinskian note-rows, with less than the full complement of twelve semitones, alongside quasi-Renaissance structures based on limited pitch-classes, a device he may have explored with the composer Goffredo Petrassi (born 1904) while studying in Rome in 1957. Buried in the square, like a name in a letter puzzle, is a sequence related to the Gregorian 'Ave maris stella' chant, but this is only heard explicitly near the end of the piece when the flute sounds it.

In the gentle, almost static opening movement, it is heard transformed as the cello simply articulates the square in sequence from top to bottom. It is joined by the viola, which traces the same course in reverse at a tempo which is 60 per cent of that of the cello, and by the piano which plays the same sequence at a rate ten times faster than the viola and six times faster than the cello. The alto flute, completing the rather sombre sonority, plays more freely while the marimba, given an unprecedented role in the piece as an equal voice (anticipating the use of pitched percussion in the First Symphony), throbs out a quasi-tonal 'pulse' that prefigures the irregular and fading heartbeat of the final movement.

It is hard to see how unconducted players could achieve any satisfactory synchronization of a work whose rhythmic plan was so complex, but Davies assigns a 'pulse-giver' to each movement, so that the players are effectively conducted from within, by one of their own number. The result is a freely organic exposition which stands in sharp contrast to the lockstep favoured by composer–conductors like Pierre Boulez. The basic trajectory of the piece is from C♯ to E, the main diagonal of the square, but this is varied by spiralling sequences, as in the third and fourth movements which take the central B♯ as their point of focus. Davies breaks the ensemble down into smaller units, beginning with the clarinet's powerful statement in the second movement, across which flute and piano weave in an increasingly vital dance of elements. The marimba is dominant in the brisk third movement, setting out a pulsing figure at the height of its potency, but with death-shades in the contrary motion of the other instruments. The very fast and perilously synchronized fourth movement elicits shorter sequences of the sort that are developed canonically in the fifth section, with intervals of a third and a fifth very prominent. The marimba then retraces a course from the central position to the initial C♯ before the ensemble reiterates the main diagonal course.

From this point, the piece becomes ever more poetically resonant, as it appears to gravitate towards, then confounds the tragic implications of what had initially seemed like a tonal centre in C♯. This is forcefully expunged in the final pages, where the marimba reiterates the square's main diagonal, and the palpitating rhythm of its central sections stutters and begins to slow down. The alto flute's exposition of the plainchant is followed by a coda of absolute stillness, cut across by the death-scream / birth-cry of the clarinet, which Davies also perceives as a great wave of light bursting out of the silence.

Ave maris stella may seem to be far from its source material, but it powerfully juxtaposes the 'silence of Mary', with which Davies in his isolated clifftop home felt a profound empathy, and the violently life-giving message of her son. As in his opera *Resurrection* (1987), Davies's stance on Christianity is robustly personal and premised not on abstract doctrine, just as his music is not based on abstract systems, but on a sort of chastened joy and astonishment at the simple fact of being alive.

Discographical Information

Other Davies: Sonata for trumpet and piano (1955; Bis CD 287); *Sinfonia* (1962; Unicorn-Kanchana UKCD 2026); *Seven In Nomine* (1963–5; Collins Classics 1095–2); *Eight Songs for a Mad King* (1969; Unicorn-Kanchana DKPCD 9052); *Vesalii icones* (1969; Nonesuch H 71295); *Turris campanarum* (1971), *Miss Donnithorne's Maggot* (1974; London 430005–2); *An Orkney Wedding – with Sunrise* (1985; Unicorn-Kanchana DKPCD 9070); Violin Concerto (1985; Sony MK 42449); Symphony no. 4 (1989; Collins Classics 11812).

Map references: John Dowland, *Lachrimae, or Seven Teares* (1604; Virgin Classics 59586); Goffredo Petrassi, *Preludio, Arie e Finale* (1933; Bongiovanni GB 5035 2); Harrison Birtwistle, *Secret Theatre* (1984; Etcetera KTC 1052); George Benjamin, *At First Light* (1982; Nimbus NI 5075).

Further reading: P. M. Davies, 'Pax Orcadiensis', in *Tempo*, cxix (1976); P. Griffiths, *Peter Maxwell Davies*, London, 1982; R. Dufallo, interview in *Trackings*, Oxford, 1990.

FREDERIC RZEWSKI (born 13 April 1938)

The People United Will Never Be Defeated! (1975)

FIRST PERFORMED: New York City, 4 November 1976
SELECTED RECORDING: hat ART 6066
   Frederic Rzewski (piano)
RECORDED: October 1986
DURATION: 61' 04"

Few modern composers have explored quite so many compositional styles and philosophies in their careers as has Frederic Rzewski. To some extent this is a by-product of his first career as a concert pianist, specializing in contemporary repertoire (David Del Tredici has made a similar observation about his own performance work); but Rzewski's attitudes as a composer have also been deeply marked by a long-standing interest in philosophy and Greek literature, and his mature work embodies political mythology and ideas of cultural tolerance to an extent unequalled by any of his contemporaries.

He had an orthodox – even mandarin – serialist training at Harvard and Princeton, studying under Walter Piston (1894–1976), Roger Sessions (1896–1985) and Milton Babbitt (born 1916), and working mainly on Wagner. At Princeton he won a Fulbright scholarship and moved his base of operations across the Atlantic, studying with the idiosyncratic Luigi Dallapiccola (1904–75) at Florence, subsequently working throughout Europe as a teacher and recitalist. Rzewski (the initial letter is silent: *zhev-ski*) premiered the revised version of Karlheinz Stockhausen's *Klavierstuck X* in 1962, and over the next two years studied further with Elliott Carter at Berlin, during which time he became interested in the work of Hanns Eisler (1898–1962). During this period he became increasingly interested in improvisation, and in 1966 he co-founded Musica Elettronica Viva with other young American avant-gardists resident in Rome; a rotating membership included at different times composer Alvin Curran (also born 1938), synthesist Richard Teitelbaum (born 1939), trombonist Garrett List (born 1943) and saxophonist Anthony Braxton (born 1945), the last three also composers. In this period Rzewski produced most of his tape and mixed media works, including one that involved amplified sheets of glass, and also a delightful jazz-influenced piece for variable instrumentation called *Les moutons de Panurge* (1969).

But Rzewski was also working extensively with vocal materials, and here his political concerns were increasingly evident. His earliest setting, a modernist *Requiem* (1963) was rearranged four years later to accommodate popular, almost folksy, instrumentation like bull-roarers, jaw harps and radio receivers and other works of the time showed the influence of Dallapiccola's interest in the application of twelve-note techniques to melody. The *Work Songs* (1967–9) were musically indeterminate texts, whose performance required improvisation, as in traditional blues and labour songs. Significantly, shortly after this Rzewski returned to live and work in the United States for the first time in a decade, and the period of five years from 1971 to 1976 sealed his politicization and growing anti-modernism.

His first major political pieces were *Coming Together* and *Attica* (1972), settings of letters from a black inmate (Steven Melville) caught up in the ruthlessly suppressed prison riots at Attica State Penitentiary, upstate New York in September 1971. The earlier piece was probably influenced by Steve Reich's electronic composition *Come Out* (1966), which manipulated a tape-loop of a black man complaining about police brutality. Increasingly, though, Rzewski was interested in the use of folk and popular melodies, writing in a style that he came to describe as 'realist' rather than abstract. As he put it to Walter Zimmerman, this involved 'techniques which are designed to establish communication, rather than to alienate an audience', a desire echoed in a much less engaged and political way by David Del Tredici, but which is very similar to the radical populism of Eisler or, in a more contemporary context, the English composer Cornelius Cardew (1936–81).

Like most people on the left in the early 1970s, Rzewski was moved by the resistance of the South American left, particularly in Chile, against military dictatorship and totalitarianism. In 1975, he created a mammoth set of variations on the Chilean revolutionary song 'Pueblo Unido Jamas Sera Vencido!', written by Sergio Ortega and recorded by the popular Quilapayun (though Rzewski seems to have heard it performed by the exiled group Inti-Illimani). His version of it raises several interesting questions, not least its status as a political text, for Rzewski's variations are clearly modelled on Beethoven's *Diabelli Variations* and intended as a concert piece. On 2 January of the same year as *The People United* was written, Cornelius Cardew gave a concert of 'socialist piano music' in New York City (I have no way of knowing if Rzewski was present or even if he heard about it). Cardew prefaced his performance by pointing to the growing politicization of music and quoted the example of the 'bourgeois pianist' Maurizio Pollini opening a recital with a stern denunciation of American involvement in Vietnam. It has always been difficult to identify clearly the political content of instrumental music (Shostakovich's relationship with Stalin is definitive), and Cardew's example seems to imply that 'political music' is simply music with politics added.

Rzewski's own work marks an impressive response to the problem. As had been the case throughout his career, he had to take a step outside his native environment in order to make it. *The People United* uses the original song as a kind of pre-text; it is always present but it has been lent a universal significance. Rzewski said that the piece 'tells a story which, although it may not translate into words, is nonetheless based on real events'. The theme-and-variations format is handled with impressive formal rigour, according to a rule-of-six. There are thirty-six variations of a thirty-six-bar theme, and the variations are divided into six groups; the sixth variation in each group sums up the preceding five, as does the sixth *group* of variations, while the thirty-sixth and last sums up the piece as a whole. In his notes to the original recording, composer Christian Wolff (born 1934), suggests that *The People United* attempts to *enact* a process of solidarity – the 'coming together' discussed ironically in the 1972 piece of that name – in abstract musical terms, gathering in individual diverse elements and combining them dialectically into a unity which nonetheless preserves their autonomy. At almost an hour, it combines an inexorable logic with the inventiveness of jazz. In later years, both men turned to North American popular and activist songs – as in Rzewski's own *North American Ballads* (1978–9, piano) and the Brechtian *Antigone-legend* (1982, voice, piano), and Woolf's *Wobbly Music* (1975–6, chorus, instruments), *The Death of Mother Jones* (1977, piano) and the similarly-inspired *Hay una mujer desaporscida* (1979, piano) – but no single work has the command of *The People United*.

A rare British concert in November 1992 demonstrated how forceful and committed a performer Rzewski is. His own recordings of this piece and the later *North American Ballads* and *Squares* (1979, also on hat Art 6089) are in many respects preferable to the greater formal polish given them by their original interpreters, Ursula Oppens and (for the *Ballads* and *Squares*) Paul Jacobs. Oppens, who is the dedicatee of *The People United* has an elegance of delivery and easy flow that contrasts sharply with Rzewski's rather staccato approach, and there are differences in the respective pianos used and in the studio acoustics; ironically, the Oppens recording is rather dry, where Rzewski's is bold and resonant, bringing an added dignity to music of determined simplicity and precision.

Discographical Information

Other recording: Oppens (Vanguard VSD 71248).

Other Rzewski: *Les moutons de Panurge* (1969; Opus One 20); *Coming Together* and *Attica* (1972; Hungaroton HCD 12545); *North American Ballads* and *Squares* (1979; hat ART 6089); *Antigone-legend* (1982; CRI SD 548); *De profundis* (1990–2; hat ART CD 6134); Musica Elettronica Viva can be heard on two rare vinyl releases: Mainstream MS 5002 and BYG Actuel 529326.

Map references: Ludwig van Beethoven, Sonata no. 32 in C minor (1821–2; EMI Classics CDC 54599); Luigi Dallapiccola, *Canti di prigionia* (1938–41; Adda 581284); Hanns Eisler, Sonata no. 3 (1943; Ambitus AMB 97862); Steve Reich, *Come Out* (1969; Elektra Nonesuch 79169); Cornelius Cardew, *Thalmann Variations* (1975; Matchless MR 24); Christian Wolff, *Edges* (1968; hat ART CD 6156).

Further reading: W. Zimmermann, interview in *Desert Plants: Conversations with 23 American Musicians*, Vancouver, 1976; J. Rockwell, 'The Romantic Revival and the Dilemma of the Political Composer', in *All-American Music; Composition in the late Twentieth Century*, New York, 1983.

LOUIS ANDRIESSEN (born 6 June 1939)

De Staat (1973–1976)

FIRST PERFORMED: Amsterdam, 28 November 1976
SELECTED RECORDING: Elektra Nonesuch 7559 79251 2
  Schoenberg Ensemble, conducted by Reinbert de Leeuw
RECORDED: February 1990
DURATION: 35' 24"

De Staat is a rare example of successful political music. It is not 'protest' music; nor is it an attempt to glorify any party or political system, like the catch-all symphonic output of officially sanctioned Soviet composers in the Cold War years. Rather, it is intended 'as a contribution to the discussion about the place of music in politics', and draws directly on ideas expressed (with what degree of dramatic irony I have never been able to determine) in Plato's *The Republic*.

In writing the piece, Andriessen confronts a paradox in his own thinking about music. On the one hand, he rejects entirely the notion that abstract musical material is politically or morally coloured. ('There is no such thing as a fascist dominant seventh.') Plato had expressed misgivings about the moral and civic impact of particular musical sounds and modes, notably those associated with soft or 'feminine' qualities, and had proposed that the 'wailful' Mixolydian and Hypolydian modes be banned from the ideal state. Modulation itself he also saw as politically dangerous, because 'any alteration in the modes of music is always followed by alteration in the most fundamental laws of the state'. While rejecting the naivety of this position, Andriessen paradoxically wishes that it were true, that music did, indeed, have such an impact on the social body.

Andriessen was born on the very cusp of the Second World War and inherited a cultural situation (see entry on Theo Loevendie) which demanded radical reconstruction. Like many of his contemporaries, he instinctively turned to jazz and American music – Andriessen is a founding member of the Charles Ives Society – but he also took possession of a more personal musical legacy from his composer father (and first teacher) Hendrik Andriessen (1892–1981). Andriessen senior attempted to heal the breach in the Dutch musical tradition by combining modern atonality and polytonality with medieval and Renaissance modalities. His approach to choral writing was a confident synthesis of the two, and there are hints of it in the vocal parts of his son's work. Louis certainly also came under the influence of his uncle, Willem Andriessen (1887–1964), a brilliant concert pianist who wrote the vivid scherzo *Hei, 't was de Mei* (1912), but the most significant encounters of his student and apprentice years were his two periods of study under Luciano Berio (q.v.) in Milan and Berlin.

Despite the artistic success of *In memoriam* (1971) and *Il principe* (1974), created some years later, Andriessen has not been especially drawn to electronics, perhaps feeling that such élitist appurtenances do not square with his determinedly democratic style. What he did draw from Berio was a strong sense of voice – though ironically he wrote no vocal works between 1959 and 1972, when he began work on *De Staat* – and in particular, a neo-Hellenic confluence of choral and symphonic writing, restoring both words to something like their original significance.

Andriessen has combined composing and an academic career with performance. He is a fine, perhaps underrated pianist, with all of his uncle's formal control, and has been co-founder and keyboard player with two significant contemporary ensembles, De Volharding and Hoketus, both of them named after Andriessen compositions. The first of these (1972, the title means 'Persistence') was a strong piece for winds and piano that drew committedly, as did the later *On Jimmy Yancey* (1973), on his interest in the polytonal possibilities of jazz ensemble. The latter (1977) exploited the interesting timbral potential of panpipes, saxophones and electric keyboards, with bass guitar and congas, in a version of the 'hocketing' melody lines that form a common link between jazz and medieval music.

Andriessen has written little non-dramatic orchestral music since the 1970s. Pieces like *The Nine Symphonies of Beethoven* (1970) for promenade orchestra and ice cream bell (!), and the later *Symfonie voor losse snare* (1978, 'open strings') are openly satirical. *Worker's Union* (1975) for loud instruments is daringly confrontational in a manner that recalls Darius Milhaud (subject of the 1978 threnody *Hymne*) or Stravinsky, rather than Ives. Andriessen has described *De Staat* as a 'polemic' on the traditional symphonic idiom. His gift is for smaller, non-canonic ensembles, often with a particularly uniform sonority: *Dubbelspoor* (1986) for piano, harpsichord, glockenspiel and celesta is an extreme example. The recent *Widow/Song Lines* (1990) for saxophone choir, premiered at Maastricht, continues a line of writing for wind orchestra begun in the 1970s with *Volkslied* (1971, any number of any instrument), *Symphonieen der Nederlanden* (1974, two or more wind orchestras) and *Nederland let up uw schonheyt* (1975, brass band and wind band), tongue-in-cheek anthems which are directly relevant to the ironic nationalism of his meditation on *The Republic*.

De Staat (and it is probably preferable to leave the title untranslated) follows Plato's injunction in excluding violins (as scapegoats for the dulcimers) and flutes. It is scored for oboes, horns, trumpets, trombones, violas, and female voices, all grouped in fours, with two electric guitars, bass guitar, two harps and (not credited on this recording but the basis of a key board reduction of the piece) two pianos. Andriessen's 'contradiction' of the symphonic ensemble is carried over into styles of performance as well. The piece demands a free, big-band sound ("like Count Basie and Stan Kenton'), rather than the precise articulation of a conventional orchestra, and this has frequently hampered concert performance by symphony orchestras whose technique is too 'legitimate'. The Schoenberg Ensemble (modelled on Schoenberg's Society for Private Musical Performance, and augmented for this piece) are chiefly young freelances committed to contemporary repertoire, and they give a much more vivid reading than the original LP version by the Netherlands Winds.

The present recording was made just after a concert series dedicated to the work of Andriessen and Steve Reich, and the most obvious parallel for the music is the work of the American minimalists, Reich, John Adams and Philip Glass. It moves in large blocks of sound rather than with any obvious linear development. The piece begins with mysterious, almost Asian tonalities from the higher instruments. Andriessen has said that the only aspect of the music that is authentically Greek is the use of oboes (*aulos*) and harps and the disposition of four-note tetrachords, a device that explains the instrumental groupings. After several repetitions of the static opening figures, the brass enter with a rapid and threatening $\frac{2}{4}$ building up a tremendous inertial tension that is only released with the first intervention of the four voices, singing their phoneticized Greek.

The juxtaposition of rhythmically and timbrally contrasting sections continues, with occasional brass smears and 'solo' excursions by a lone trumpet spelling out the components of the tetrachord. The rhythms alternate a looped melodic cell, sounding almost as if a gramophone needle has stuck on the opening phrase of a cantabile theme, and savage, motoric figures in the lower register. There is already a tendency for the orchestra to divide into two distinct sections and this is further confirmed when the voices return for their second units. There is, however, no polyrhythmic activity until the coda, when the two orchestral groups play a similar canonic melody independently, returning to the homophonic subject introduced by the voices on their first appearance.

There is certainly more Stan Kenton than Count Basie in Andriessen's conception. He achieves an astonishing density of sound and an aggressively over-determined submersion of individual voices. This may very well reflect the political programme of *De Staat*, but with the exception of the soaring voices and the brief post-coda, the sonority seems ill-adapted to any libertarian conclusion. For Andriessen, the essence of jazz seems to be a tense dialectic between individual and collective statement, and he also seems to make use, as does his friend and sometime collaborator Peter Schat (see below), of the more ambiguous collectivism of rock music and freely incorporates electric instruments. In the work of his pupil, the controversial young English composer Steve Martland (born 1959), this precarious balance has perhaps been lost altogether and some observers have detected totalitarian overtones in pieces like Martland's jarring *Drill* (1987) for two pianos.

Condemning Andriessen for unsubstantiated derelictions in the work of his one-time student is to risk the same fallacy he confronts in Plato: judging music by its putative 'social impact'. Andriessen has created a body of work that asks searching questions about the social construction of music. His superb account of Machiavelli in *Il principe* for two choirs, winds, piano and bass guitar, is implicitly concerned with the relationship between 'residues' and 'derivations', actual political ideas and ideological contrivances. The collaborative opera *Reconstructie* (1968–9), written with Misha Mengelberg, Peter Schat, Jan van Vlijmen (all born 1935), and the pianist and conductor Reinbert de Leeuw (born 1938), was a significant, if ultimately rather ephemeral, expression of the resurrection of post-war Dutch music, making the breach in (musical) history the subject of historical music. In *De Staat* he lifted the argument to a new level.

Discographical Information

Other recordings: Netherlands Wind Orchestra (Composers Voice 7022 LP); also 2-piano reduction, Bouwhuis, van Zeeland [with: Cage, *Three Dances* (1945); Stravinsky, *Agon* (1954–6)] (Attacca BABEL 8949–2).

Other Andriessen: *Triplum* (1963; Composers Voice CVCD 8701); Melody for Flute and Piano (1972–4), Symphony for Open Strings (1978; Attacca BABEL 9267–6); *De Tijd* (1981; Elektra Nonesuch 79291–22).

Map references: Hendrik Andriessen, *Variations and Fugue on a Theme of Kuhnau* (1935; Olympia OCD 504); Ton de Leeuw, *Mouvements rétrogrades* (1957; q.v.); Peter Schat, *Mozaieken* (1959; BFO A 17); Steve Martland, *Shoulder to Shoulder* (1986; Attacca 8953–6).

Further reading: L. Andriessen and E. Schoenberger, *Het Appolonisch Uurwerk* [on Stravinsky], Amsterdam, 1983, trans. as *The Apollonian Clockwork*, Cambridge, 1990; E. Vermeulen, 'Compositions by Louis Andriessen and Peter Schat Incorporating Quotations', in *Sonorum speculum*, xxxv (1969).

HENRYK MIKOLAJ GÓRECKI (born 6 December 1933)

Symphony no. 3: *Symphony of Sorrowful Songs* (1976)

FIRST PERFORMED: Royan, France, 4 April 1977
SELECTED RECORDING: Erato 9275 LP
   Stefania Woytowicz (soprano), South-West German Radio Symphony Orchestra, Baden-Baden, conducted by Ernest Bour
RECORDED: 1986
DURATION: 46'

In the early spring of 1993 a new phrase entered the language of music marketing. Promotion and publicity departments began to talk, wishfully, about 'doing a Górecki', put with the same fatalistic shrug gamblers adopt when putting money on wild outsiders. At the time of writing, an Elektra Nonesuch recording of Henryk Górecki op. 36 Third Symphony featuring soprano Dawn Upshaw and the London Sinfonietta under David Zinman has sold in excess of 300,000 copies, steering

it out of the quiet neglectful backdraw normally reserved for contemporary composition and tossing it – and Górecki – straight into the
frothy floodwater of major popular success. In January 1993 Górecki
topped not just the classical album charts, but the pop charts as well,
leaving high profile groups like REM and U2 bobbing in his wake.
Since then, there has been a full-length presentation of the symphony on
the influential Thames Television programme *The South Bank Show*,
acres of newsprint about the sixty-year-old Polish composer and his
music, and something of a sea-change in industry perceptions of contemporary music and its potential audience.

The whole phenomenon was replete with unanswerable ironies. How
and why did a relatively obscure modern work, of a markedly philosophical nature, manage to garner such an audience? Given that it had
been recorded *three* times already, why did a relatively indifferent performance so dramatically outsell its predecessors and rivals? What did
its success say about the usual glad-handing round of promotional
activity when the composer had so conspicuously failed to emerge from
isolation to give interviews and make personal appearances? Or did it
merely prove the cynical industry conviction that, next to 'tragic death',
'secluded', 'solitary', 'mysterious' and 'enigmatic' are the most effective
marketing tags on offer? Setting cynicism aside, did the *Symphony of
Sorrowful Songs* simply address profound spiritual and aesthetic needs
in a public sated on three-minute pop and un-nourished by forbidding
intellectualism?

So much has now been written about the symphony itself that it is
perhaps more interesting to look at the nature of its success. To some
extent it was anticipated by the smaller but still dramatic market performance of the Estonian composer Arvo Pärt's *Tabula rasa* (1977), and by
The Protecting Veil, a 1987 work for cello and strings by the English
composer John Tavener (born 1944). Tavener, who has written much
music for the Orthodox communion, which he embraced in the 1970s,
found his music in some odd settings following the high chart showing
of *The Protecting Veil*. It was more than slightly jarring to hear work of
such concentrated spiritual intensity played in wine bars (my local routinely followed it with a tape of Les Negresses Vertes), and Górecki's
success has thrown up similar oddities. However, it is interesting to
note that these began well before the appearance of the Elektra
Nonesuch recording. The first recorded version of the *Symphony of Sorrowful Songs* found its way into the credit sequence of Maurice Pialat's
brutal and misogynistic cop movie *Police* and the Erato sleeve featured
Gérard Depardieu gazing stonily at Sophie Marceau through the mesh
of a holding-pen. It may be that Pialat and his colleagues dimly recognized the need for some concluding transcendence, a gesture toward
'higher values' and hopes. Or it may simply be that 'background

musics' are considered to be interchangeable so long as they are tonal, melodic and preferably repetitive.

It has become fashionable to characterize Górecki as a shy, withdrawn mystic, other-worldly and untainted by material or merely intellectual concerns, growing up under the shadow of Nazi invasion and then pitched against the denying secularism of post-war Communism. Arvo Pärt (born 1935), raised to cult status following his adoption by the high-profile jazz and new music label ECM, owes something of his undoubted charisma to the suppression of his work by the pre-*perestroika* Communist regime, to his exile in the West, and to the long compositional silence that divided his 'difficult' earlier work from the more recent 'tintinnabulary' style that has struck such a chord with New Age sensibilities. It is mistaken, however, to see Górecki as an outsider figure in quite the same way. His mystique has been reinforced by two periods of wretched and near-fatal illness, against which his efforts to continue composing seem even more heroic; but his professional life began against a background not of oppression but of significant liberalization and cultural thaw. In his homeland at least, Górecki was far from being an obscure figure. Between 1975 and 1979 he was rector of his own former music school in Katowice, and his first major pieces, like the First Symphony, subtitled *1959*, have all the confidence of a public figure. He resigned the rectorship in protest in 1979, but it was in that same year that he enjoyed his first great international triumph, ironically at a moment of nationalist fervour, when his mass *Beatus vir* was performed at Krakow on the occasion of John Paul II's first return as Pope to his native Poland.

Despite the enthusiasm of critics and musicologists in the West (Adrian Thomas foremost among them), Górecki's international reputation had been slower to develop, and when he was 'discovered' there was a predictable but rather misleading emphasis on his 'Polishness' at the expense of other qualities. In 1961, Górecki had undertaken a period of postgraduate study in Paris. There is a story that he worked under Olivier Messiaen, but this is unfounded and only serves to reinforce a certain image of Górecki by association with another composer saddled with a reputation for other-worldliness. What Górecki did encounter in France was the music of the post-war avant garde, but he seems to have found it artistically and spiritually unsatisfying. The orchestral *Scontri* (1960) were apparently written as a response to Luigi Nono's *Incontri* (1955), with the purpose of showing how Nono's modernist 'encounters' are actually less fruitful than his own deceptively naive 'collisions' of old and new musics.

Unlike Pärt, Górecki seems not to have gone through a period of radical modernism, and has been notably resistant to any notion of 'pure' or absolute music. Almost all his scores have some ritual or revelatory significance and from the beginning, despite conventional exercises in twelve-note composition, his technique was characterized by its recurrent references to 'the olden style'. This is not to make him sound like a drab conservative. When he chooses to shorten the solemn modal melodies and slow tempos that are most typical of his work (and particularly of the Third Symphony) and write in a more consciously upbeat style the result is quite startling. Most people listening cold to the remarkable Harpsichord Concerto (1980) will identify it as a product of American minimalism (it is worth noting that Górecki is only three years older than Steve Reich). Listening to it again, or to Pärt's astonishing *Tabula rasa*, reveals how subtly and radically structured both pieces are, with no sign of the imported devices and structural prefabrication that gives the minimalists their slightly second-hand feel. The Pärt title is a significant one, for what he shares with Górecki is a sense of music being built from deep foundations and from the most basic of materials. It is always tempting to read such titles metaphorically or auto-biographically as reactions to life under totalitarian regimes where whole areas of the cultural past can be 'disappeared' by decree, but in Górecki's case at least the technique responds to and serves more directly musical ends.

Throughout his career, Górecki has remained deeply rooted in the landscape and culture of his native Silesia, a coal-mining region, not the Ruritanian fastness some commentators have tried to portray. He has drawn inspiration from the folk traditions of the Tatra Highlands and from a highly emotional Catholicism, but without ever losing sight of twentieth-century musical language. The material and handling of the Third Symphony represent the culmination of this approach, combining old and folk materials in strict and often complex canons, maximizing musical activity (as in the second of the three 'Sorrowful Songs') within a very narrow harmonic span, and attempting a significant 'collision' of past and present. In externals, this is most evident in his juxtaposition of fifteenth-century religious lyrics with the desperate graffito of a young Polish girl imprisoned by the Gestapo in 1944, but it emerges most strongly in the third movement when Górecki combines simple modes with elements of dissonance in such a way as to compress and accelerate the spiritual drama of the whole piece.

The symphony begins with a dark processional from the double basses, rising by a sequence of simple fifths as the other instruments of a large orchestra slowly enter, gradually building the first arch of a huge symmetrical canon. The opening movement is enormous – Zinman and Kamirski (below) have it at twenty-four and twenty-six minutes respectively, but Bour, who gave the premiere in Royan, stretches the *Lento* marking over half an hour – and dominates the work as a whole. Some recent commentary has made it sound as if the opening movement *is* the symphony, with just the briefest comments on the lyrical components of the succeeding movements. This may be understandable, but it is also misleading. The opening movement establishes the architecture, but it is in the second and third sections that the real drama of the piece takes place.

The canon is taken from a folk melody, one of a collection made by the musicologist Father Władislaw Skierkowski. At the point of maximum intensity it is 'broken' by the soprano. The first of the three 'Sorrowful Songs' is the Świetokrzyski – or Holy Cross – Lament, taken from a fifteenth-century collection known as the Lysogora Songs. Coming at the heart of the movement, it represents the Holy Mother's address to her crucified Son, asking that He share His wounds with her. After this invocation, the eight-part polyphony returns, this time with different shadings and textural effects to its essentially static form. The stepwise descent is not quite a mirror of the opening, but is suffused with echoes of the central prayer. The counterpart gradually simplifies until there are just two parts and these fade to reveal the twenty-four-bar *cantus firmus* in the low strings that underlies the whole movement.

Both emotionally and structurally, Górecki needed to conceive the two remaining movements in such a way as to provide balance as well as contrast. To some extent, they function as a composite. The second movement is marked *Lento e largo*. The metronome marking is only fractionally different from that of the first movement, which is qualified *Sostenuto tranquillo ma cantabile*, but the textural detail and the surprisingly positive mode with which the soprano introduces the second song give it a strongly contrasting feel. It is a setting of four brief lines found scratched and signed by the eighteen-year-old Helena Wanda Błazusiakówna on the third wall of the third cell of the notorious 'Palace', the Gestapo detention centre at Zakopane, a small town in the Tatra Mountains near the Czech border. It runs: 'No, Mother, do not weep, / Most chaste Queen of Heaven / Support me always'; and ends with the Polish version of 'Hail Mary'. The harmonic language is deliberately restrictive, as if it reflects the narrowness of that cell, and the pulse and melodic structure has a recurrent 3×3 pattern that may well be intended to recall its number. The girl's youth and the touching simplicity of her plea are immediately evident in Górecki's use of a light, open mode, and it is here that I take issue with Dawn Upshaw's reading of the score on the best-selling Elektra Nonesuch issue. Where Stefania Woytowicz sings the line here and in the final movement with total simplicity and apparent artlessness, Upshaw 'projects' and supports the leading notes. Her diction is also too deliberate and precise, and there is even a sense in which the London Sinfonietta's much-respected accuracy works against them on this occasion. Woytowicz's three versions vary in small respects, as one might expect, but it is the *quality* of her voice and the quietly understated emotion of her delivery that sets her apart. It was she who premiered the work in 1977 and she can reasonably claim it as her own; it is to be hoped that at least some of the thousands who have bought the Upshaw version will have an opportunity to hear Woytowicz as well.

The final section is again very slow, but this time marked *Cantabile – semplice*. It draws its lyrical material from Adolf Dygacz's transcription of folk material from the Opole region, north-west of Katowice and Krakow. Like the opening section, it is again a mother's lament for her murdered son. This time, though, she does not know where his grave lies, and there is no reason to think that even enough tears to create a second Oder will restore him to life. This is a more secular vision than either of the first two movements. The son is one of the world's 'disappeared'. It is 'God's little song-birds' and 'God's little flowers' that will mark his resting place. The trajectory of the Third Symphony is both into history, away from the Mother at the foot of the Cross to the universal mother bereft of her children, and into music and the imagination. The 'collisions' of ancient melody and modern dissonance are heard for the first time in the closing movement and it is only at the end that the verse melody restores the 'home' tonality of A major, a folksy, almost bucolic key that suggests new growth and even a touch of chastened optimism.

I find it a humane and determinedly unmystical conclusion. The *Symphony of Sorrowful Songs* is clearly a work of profound spirituality, but it is false to its essential drama to assume that it is also a work of mystical transcendence. For all his deeply felt religious beliefs, Górecki is clearly also a man of his time and will accept no ready-made solutions. It is too easy to treat composers such as Pärt and Górecki, and even Tavener, as purveyors of quick consolatory fixes, validated by the composer's own suffering and struggle but requiring no apparent effort on the part of the listener. The *Symphony of Sorrowful Songs* is as 'difficult' a piece as any work of the avant garde, but its difficulty is hidden behind a deceptively consumable exterior. Will Górecki 'do a Górecki' in future? It seems both unlikely and undesirable that he should.

Discographical Information

Other recordings: Woytowicz, Berlin Radio SO, Kamirski (Koch Schwann CD 311 041 H1); Woytowicz, Polish National Radio SO, Katlewicz (Olympia OCD 343); Upshaw, London Sinfonietta, Zinman (Elektra Nonesuch 7559 79282).

Other Górecki: *Beatus vir* (1979; Argo 436835); Harpsichord Concerto (1980; Adda 581233); *Lerchenmusik* (1984–6; Olympia OCD 343; String Quartet no. 1: *Already It Is Dusk* (1988; Elektra Nonesuch 79319).

Map references: Olivier Messiaen, *Chronochromie* (1960; Koch Schwann CD 311015); Arvo Pärt, *Tabula rasa* (1977; ECM New Series 1043); Galina Ustvolskaya, Symphony no. 4: *Prayer* (1984; hat ART CD 6135); John Tavener, *The Protecting Veil* (1987; Virgin Classics 59052).

Further reading: A. Thomas, 'The Music of Mikolaj Górecki: The First Decade', in *Contact*, xxvii (autumn 1983), and 'A Pole Apart', in *Contact*, xxviii (autumn 1984); umpteen press pieces on the Third Symphony.

ERIK BERGMAN (born 24 November 1911)

Bim Bam Bum (1976)

FIRST PERFORMED: Uppsala, 23 April 1977
SELECTED RECORDING: Finlandia FACD 368
  Reijo Ollinen (reciter), Jyrki Malmio (tenor), Ilkka Korpi (baritone), Esa Jokinen (tubular bells, conch, temple blocks, raganella), Pekka Seppänen (prepared piano, flexatone, guiro, reco-reco), Timo Hongistu (flute), Kari Kariluoto (jaw harp), Ylioppilaskunnan Laulajat (Helsinki University Chorus), conducted by Johtaa Martti Hyökki
  [with: *Drei Galgenlieder* (1959); *Loitsuja/Charms* (1983); *Four Vocalises* (1983); three folksongs from Southern Ostrobothnia]
RECORDED: 1987
DURATION: 14' 44"

No composer – perhaps no artist in any medium – has weighed so heavily on the cultural life of his country than Jean Sibelius on Finland. Because of his international eminence (in the early 1930s, American concert-goers voted him the most popular composer *of all time*) and because of his role in giving Finnish nationalism an expressive form, he and his work became, in Keats's image for Shakespeare and Milton, a Great Wall over which Finnish modernists had to clamber or remain within its bounds. Sibelius's dominance was, if anything, reinforced by his physical isolation at Järvenpää (several contemporary composers – including Joonas Kokkonen and Paavo Heininen – still live there, as if to remain close to the Presence) as well as by his decision to release no more music during the last thirty years of life. Silence is a powerful medium. Sibelius's unfinished and unheard Eighth Symphony (he eventually burned the MS) took on an almost mythic significance and his refusal to speak out, even ambiguously *à la* Shostakovich, against the Soviet invasion in 1940 was likened to the silence of God or the Buddha.

At Sibelius's funeral in 1957, and at the request of the family, Erik Bergman conducted the massed ranks of the Academic Choral Society and the Helsinki University Chorus, two groups which expressed the continuity of Finnish choral music. The Academic Choral Society had been founded in 1838, while Finland was under the control of Sweden, Ylioppilaskunnan Laulajat (or YL) in 1883 when Finnish-speaking students at the University of Helsinki broke away to found a more modern- and nationalistically-minded choir. Choral music has been as significant in the development of Finnish music as the symphony and male-voice groups (as in Wales and the Saxon–Nordic glee clubs and barbershop groups of North America) are enthusiastically supported. Sibelius himself wrote many choral pieces, as did Selim Palmgren (1878–1951), Leevi Madetoja (1887–1947) and Kokkonen (born 1921), but the Swedish-speaking Erik Bergman was the first to give the tradi-tional male-voice choir a decidedly modern character.

Bergman was, indeed, the first fully-fledged Finnish modernist. He studied musicology and literature (important background for a vocal composer) at Helsinki University in the early 1930s, before specializing in composition. He spent two years in Berlin just before the war and seems to have shaken off a naive romanticism there ("seems' because no scores earlier than 1944 survive in the catalogue) in favour of a more richly chromatic style. With the restoration of peace, he went to study twelve-note music under Wladimir Vogel (1896–1984) in Switzerland and at Ascona, and took a look at the huge library of plainsong in the Vatican library; elements of Gregorian chant appear as late as the instrumental *Quo vadis* (1983) for cello and piano. He also established a pattern of musicological travel and research that took him to the Balkans and Turkey, Egypt, the Far East, Central and South America. None of these cultures is directly audible in his work as an 'influence', but they encouraged him to work quickly through a basically serial period and to develop his characteristic synchronization of precise rhythmic values with improvisation.

There was a strong measure of rhythmic complexity in *Rubaiyat* (1953) for baritone, male chorus and orchestra (written for the choral group Muntra Musikanter, which he conducted from 1951 to his retire-ment in 1978), but the first really significant modernist pieces were for orchestra. *Tre aspetti d'una serie dodecafonica* (1957) is as tentative as it sounds, but *Aubade*, written the following year, uses serial technique to define every part of the music. Bergman soon extended this to vocal writing, the *Drei* (see above) and *Vier Galgenlieder* (1959 and 1960) and the beautiful *Fåglarna* (1962, see below) for baritone, chorus, percussion and celesta, after words by his wife Solveig von Schoultz. The latter piece anticipates one of the most intriguing and effective aspects of *Bim Bam Bum*, the use of percussion instruments to support the choir. Bergman was strongly attracted to the 'fantastical grotesqueries' of the German poet Christian Morgenstern, who evokes a world somewhere between Lewis Carroll and Edward Gorey. Bergman had set the two groups of 'gallows-songs' in 1959 and 1960, using a speaking chorus for the first time in order to make Morgenstern's words and nonsense syllables ("Kroklokwafzi? Sememoni! / Seiodrontro – prafriplo: / Bifzi, bafzi, hulalemi') precisely audible.

In *Bim Bam Bum* he uses a reciter and a solo voice for the same reason, but again the attraction is the sheer musicality of the sounds Morgenstern produces. The sequence actually consists of four songs of which the title song is the first. Like 'The Whalefish and the Flood' and 'Der Rabe Ralf' (which Keith Bosley translates nicely as 'The Crow Called Phelps') in the *Galgenlieder*, they address the childlike consciousness which Bergman valued in the poet and which balances playfulness with a shiver of horror. 'Bim Bam Bum' is cast as a dialogue between bell-sounds, 'male' and 'female'. It is perhaps as well not to make too much of the song's slight narrative content, except that it represents a semi-serious comment on singing styles and religious preferences as well. The 'she-clang BIM' has broken faith with the lovelorn BAM, who flies 'birdlike through the night ... in Catholic regalia'; she, it seems, has fallen for BUM's – or BONG's – more assertive, 'Evangelical' sound; these are Bosley's versions of the German. The three syllables which punctuate the song are delivered as long notes, set alongside quieter 'beats' and soft vocal textures, a device Bergman borrowed from Joonas Kokkonen and which later figured in one of his own rare chamber pieces, the aptly titled *Silences and Eruptions* (1979) for winds, percussion, piano and string quartet. The tiny drama is heightened with tubular bells and the cracked sonority of a prepared piano; there is an aural pun on 'Vogelflügel' (birdflight) and 'Flügel', an alternative German word for the wing-shaped pianoforte. Broken-winged, it plays a mournful accompaniment to the bells, and reflects the deliberately strained falsetto of the tenors' 'chimes'. In the second song, the dominant sound is 'The Sigh'. Bergman uses a breathy flute and whiney flexatone to suggest the fragility and triviality of conventional romantic passion. The sigh skates over moonlit ice below a dreamlike castle, but its hot breath and 'sweet fever' dissolve the treacherous surface and it disappears below. Love is brought down to earth and then drowned.

The next step is the boldest of all. Bergman follows Morgenstern into an alien element. The 'Fisches Nachtgesang' contains no words and only unpitched sounds, just a graphical representation of (fish) scale-like shapes which Bosley 'translates' into the symbols for metrical quantities, x and /. It is a bold stroke. Bergman converts a mild typographical joke into an alien and 'untranslatable' musical environment that is perfectly placed in the middle of a sequence about love, loss and illusion. In addition to flute and prepared piano, he adds the burbling sound of a conch and the twanging of a jaw harp. In the last song, the location and emotional temperature of the drama changes again to the ironically 'Philanthropic' (Morgenstern's original title) perspective of 'Ein nervöser Mensch', whose bucolic idyll is interrupted by the insect chatter of percussion instruments. The joke is that Bergman has conveyed the 'nervous' urban man's un-ease with the natural world by means of a Lappish *joik*, a traditional song-form that usually conveys complete identification with nature. 'A Nervous Man' does, though, give the drama of *Bim Bam Bum* a satisfying moral roundness and depth, suggesting a return to the 'middle' realm of everyday human affairs. Significantly, the final song is scored for the 'mature' baritone voice, rather than the tenor.

Though it is handled comically, the sequence utilizes the same themes as the earlier and more obviously lyrical *Fåglarna* (see below), in which a single baritone flies ahead of 'the flock', plunging into the mist and cloud to express its belief in light and the mysterious joy of a shared destiny. The speaking chorus evokes a background of clattering wings and confused cries until the vibraphone signals the end of darkness, and the whole flock descends into common day and perpetual light. *Fåglarna* is also perhaps a more concentrated and expressive work, but *Bim Bam Bum* is no less profound for its lighter touch. Though the piece was written for The Orphei Drängar in Uppsala to commemorate the semi-millennium of the university there, it has become a central item of YL's concert repertoire and their performance is absolutely authentic. The London Chamber Choir (below) were actually the first to record the piece, and though the pairing with *Fåglarna* and *Nox* (1970), a rather Berio-like synopsis of texts by Arp, Eliot, Eluard and Quasimodo for baritone and mixed chorus with flute, percussion (and a very Sibelian cor anglais), the YL performances are 'state of the art' modern choral singing and should not be missed. In Thomas Mann's *Doktor Faustus*, Adrian Leverkühn says: 'The human voice may be abstract ... but it is an abstraction like that of the naked body.' Bergman's vocal music conveys something like that combination of abstraction and nakedness.

Discographical Information

Other recording: Walmsley-Clark, Varcoe, Potter, New London Chamber Choir, Wood [with: *Fåglarna* (1962), *Nox* (1970), *Hathor Suite* (1971); Walmsley-Clark, Endymion Ensemble] (Chandos CHAN 8478).

Other Bergman: *Concertino da camera* (1961; Ondine OCD 774–4); *Silence and Eruptions* (1979; Ondine OCD 774–2); Violin Concerto (1982; Bis CD 326); *Lament and Incantations* (1984; Simax OSC 1052); *etwas rascher* (1985; Capria CAP 21435); *Der sjungande trädet / The Singing Tree* (1988; Ondine ODE 794–2).

Map references: Jean Sibelius, *Laulu Lemminkäiselle* (1896; Ondine ODE 754–2);

Einojuhani Rautavaara, *Ludus verbalis* (1960; Bis CD 66); Joonas Kokkonen, *Requiem (in memoriam Maija Kokkonen)* (1981; Bis CD 508).

Further reading: various, *Erik Bergman: A Seventieth Birthday Tribute*, Helsinki, 1981.

THEA MUSGRAVE (born 27 May 1928)

Mary, Queen of Scots (1975–1977)

FIRST PERFORMED: Edinburgh, 6 September 1977
SELECTED RECORDING: Novello NVLCD 108
  Ashley Putnam (Mary, Queen of Scots), Jake Gardner (James Stewart, Earl of Moray), Jon Garrison (Henry Stewart, Lord Darnley), Barry Busse (James Hepburn, Earl of Bothwell), Kenneth Bell (David Riccio), Francesco Sorianello (Lord Gordon), Carlos Serrano (Cardinal Beaton), Robert Randolph (Earl of Morton), Pietro Pozzo (Earl of Ruthven), Gloria Capone (Mary Seton), Nancy Boling (Mary Beaton), Ann Scholten (Mary Livingstone), Pamela Scott (Mary Fleming); Edward Bogusz, Robert Crutchfield, Ryan Fletcher, Bruce Frazier, W. Bernard Ham, Wayne MacDonald, Charles Oliver, Keith Savage, Carlos Serrano, Richard Weston (Lords of the Congregation), the Virginia Opera Association Orchestra and Chorus, conducted by Peter Mark
RECORDED: April 1978
DURATION: 130′

Thea Musgrave's second choice of faculty at the University of Edinburgh was – in the context of the late 1940s – rather more controversial than her first. She had originally matriculated to study medicine, a male bastion already breached by Elizabeth Garrett Anderson (and by two world wars), but she subsequently switched to music and declared a strong interest not in such safely 'feminine' pursuits as piano playing or singing, but in composition. Since graduating, she has produced more than a hundred highly distinctive scores, most of which sufficiently combine experimental daring with enough simple humanity to suggest that she might well have been an equal success as a physician.

  Musgrave has been resident in the United States since 1973, having married the violist and conductor Peter Mark two years earlier, and America has figured as largely in her music as in her life. After graduating, she undertook further study as the Conservatoire National Supérieur de Musique in Paris under Nadia Boulanger (a confrontation of two strong personalities it would have been interesting to observe); there she met Aaron Copland, an association continued at Tanglewood in 1959 where she also made contact with the cerebral but pawky

Milton Babbitt. After extra-mural teaching in the University of London (perhaps just as well she remained outside its institutional walls), she visited the Soviet Union as a delegate of the Composers' Guild, and spent a year as a visiting professor at the University of California, Santa Barbara, about as far as it is possible to go culturally within the English-speaking world from her birthplace in Barnton, Midlothian.

It would be hard to imagine two composers more different than Copland and Babbitt, but Musgrave managed to draw sustenance from both. In the early 1950s, she was already experimenting with Copland-esque synthetic 'folk' melodies, as in the lovely *A Suite o' Bairnsangs* (1953) to poems by Maurice Lindsay, but after Tanglewood (and discussion with Babbitt, presumably) she began to underpin a growing interest in quite extreme chromaticism and free tempos with serial organization. Pieces like *Triptych* (1959), a free setting of Chaucer's 'Merciles Beaute' for tenor and orchestra, might in other, more parochial hands have descended to Britten-and-water. Musgrave found that she was able to combine serialism with Bartók's folkish chromaticism and implicit tonal centres to create something that still sounded as if it were derived from traditional Scottish music. Her 1961 setting for tenor and guitar of the ballad 'Sir Patrick Spens' is a case in point, as is *A Song for Christmas* (1958), her first explicitly serial piece, written to putative verses of William Dunbar. Even here, there are identifiable tonal shadings, and Musgrave's tenor settings were always singable – as Peter Pears recognized – even when her instrumental music had become very angular.

She had been much affected by the work of Charles Ives (who died during her final year in Paris), and her second Chamber Concerto (1966) for small ensemble is dedicated to Ives's memory. Musgrave described this work, and others of the period, beginning with the aptly named *Colloquy* (1960) for violin and piano, as 'dramatic–abstract', by which she meant that while its presentation was dramatic, it was so in a non-programmatic, non-narrative way, 'an extension of the concerto principle' and a restoration of the original implication of struggle rather than bland concord. Perhaps because of her carefully sustained balance of tonal and non-tonal language, strict and free tempos, Musgrave's music has always seemed inherently dramatic. It is surely no coincidence that her first important teacher in Edinburgh was the exiled Viennese Hans Gál (born 1890), whose most important works were the operas *Der Arzt der Sobeide* (1919), *Die heilige Ente* (1923 – David Mason Greene translates this as *The Sacred Duck!*) and *Das Lied der Nacht* (1926). It is not clear whether or how closely Musgrave studied these scores, but her own operatic writing has the same qualities of tight narrative focus – particularly evident in the Dickensian evocation of *A Christmas Carol* (1978–9) – and a characteristically dreamlike associationism. Her first and second operas, *The Abbot of Drimock* (1955) and *The Decision* (1964–5) were again written to librettos by Maurice Lindsay, but it was with *The Voice of Ariadne* (1972–3) that she really hit stride. Adapted from a Henry James story, 'The Last of the Valerii', its aura of atavistic dread easily bears comparison with that of Britten's *The Turn of the Screw* (1954). The score includes a prominent tape part whose effects she reduplicates by conventional means and in a more elegiac vein for Mary's mist-shrouded arrival in her new kingdom. Perhaps Musgrave's most remarkable development of such atmospheric effects, which had begun with a dance score for Scottish Ballet Theatre's *Beauty and the Beast* (1969), was with her radio opera *An Occurrence at Owl Creek Bridge* (1981), written after Ambrose Bierce's hallucinatory short story. *Ariadne* also marked her first association with the work of Amalia Elguera, on whose play Musgrave's *Mary, Queen of Scots* is based.

It is by no means a conventional or stereotypical portrait of the tragic queen. Elguera's play is called *Moray*, and the main protagonist is Mary's half-brother James Stewart, the Earl of Moray. Musgrave shifts the focus back towards Mary. Though she frequently refers to the ways in which the queen has been turned into an unhistorical icon, her main concern is to humanize and fill out a much-romanticized figure. Where Elguera has the male characters execute complicated political steps round the figure of the young queen, Musgrave has her join the dance and even set its rhythm, literally in the ballroom scene at Hollyrood, when she defuses an explosive situation by leading Bothwell into a lively reel. There are some oddities in the *dramatis personae*. John Knox, who blew the loudest whistle against the 'monstrous regiment of women', does not appear. He was apparently included in a first draft and is mentioned several times, though with nothing like the *frisson* that attends a reference to another offstage presence, Queen Elizabeth of England; when James speaks her name, again in the ballroom scene, a chill descends on the room. The Catholic Cardinal Beaton who confronts James in the first scene is an invention (though there was also an historical Beaton, who died in 1546, fifteen years before the action of the opera). Musgrave's Beaton has written to Mary in France advising her to throw in her lot with the lowlander Hepburn, Earl of Bothwell, and to beware of her brother's rampant dynastic claims as the bastard son of James V.

This is how the opera begins. As Beaton is robed, his attendant monks sing versicles from Psalm 43 which plead for deliverance from the unjust and deceitful man. James enters from the darkness, exactly on cue. Beaton greets him with caution, but with some affection, as 'my son'. When James angrily rejects the address, the old man's anger boils over and he accuses his one-time protegé and potential successor of disloyalty to both his half-sister and his Church. James produces the letter

Beaton has written to Mary enjoining her to place her trust in Bothwell. The cardinal responds that whatever Bothwell's ambitions, the crown is not among them. Startled, James repeats the word – which according to a stage direction 'flashes and sparkles' between them – obviously aware that he has tripped himself with his memory of a sister who had once said, 'Most of all I love / My brother James, / Who might have been my King.' He makes a vaunting speech, setting himself above all talk of crowns and sceptres, then summons Morton and Ruthven to arrest the cardinal, who is dragged away screaming 'God have mercy on you James Stewart, / And on your sister!' James burns the letter and then, alone on stage, confirms his arrogant sense of destiny: 'Only I shall stand beside the Queen / ... / For this, God sent her back to me; / For this, God made her widow of France.'

Shivering string chords and an unevenly tolling bell mark the link with the second scene, which unfolds upstage on the misty quay at Leith. Mary is first seen swathed in long black veils; her first husband, the Dauphin, is not long dead, but she has also been abruptly separated from her beloved France. Offstage 'voices from her lost kingdom' bid her adieu with lines from Pierre Ronsard's 'Elégie, à Marie Stuart'. Singing her famous motto 'En ma fin est mon commencement' (which Ashley Putnam enunciates rather oddly) she turns to face Scotland, in an aria that is, typically, lyrical but also emotionally fraught and bereft, with the same missed-heartbeat rhythm of the tolling bell: 'No-one and no-one and no-one. / Like a wave I reach / The shore...' Bothwell and the waiting soldiers, still hidden in the mist, are enchanted by the sight of her and sing a low refrain as she expresses her friendliness. Eventually Bothwell breaks the spell and steps forward, explaining that the country is fogged by the fires of rebellion sparked by her half-brother James. Explaining that she has entered a hard world, explicitly a man's world, Bothwell grasps her by the arm: 'Am I then your prisoner, Lord Bothwell?' Again on cue, James enters, just as Bothwell gallantly responds, gazing at her, 'No! It is I who am held captive'.

Mary greets her brother with affection, but challenges him on Beaton's imprisonment. As the men jostle and argue for primacy, the man of action is outflanked by the cunning pretender. Mary takes command, and seems to dispense with Beaton, settling on him as the fomenter of discontent. As the sun burns away the mist, the people gradually come forward to greet their new queen, who processes into her capital with James at her side, attended by the semi-legendary Four Marys – Seton, Beaton, Livingstone and Fleming – who were to be her companions and confidantes on Scotland, and with Bothwell, Morton and Ruthven in her train, temporarily reconciled.

The lighting changes in another slow dissolve, and the crowd sing a long, complacent 'Peace Chorus', summing up the quiet year that has passed since Mary's arrival; this is interrupted by Lord Gordon (another fictional device) with the news that Beaton is dead on James's instructions. The crowd's sceptical response is witnessed by Morton, the 'gimlet-eyed' chief of the Douglas clan (a chequered bunch, I regret to say). Morton asserts that neither Scotland nor Mary will need Beaton: 'We are followers of Knox; / Knox and James.' Gordon's lonely fears are thrown into stark relief as the stage brightens for the ballroom scene, leaving him sombrely silhouetted as Mary, no longer in her black weeds, dances a pavane with her cousin Henry Stewart, Lord Darnley (Mary's father and Darnley's mother were both offspring of Margaret Tudor, though by different husbands). Standing on the sidelines are Bothwell and his soldiers, their discomfort with the ways of the court audible even through the offstage band's lively music. Mary's Italian-born favourite, later her French secretary, David Riccio is in attendance. As he accompanies the musicians on a tambourine, the queen dances with the Four Marys. Morton and Ruthven break in on Darnley's rapt gaze, draw him aside and sarcastically flatter him as James takes brief advantage of the queen's ear to warn her it is unseemly to dance so much with the 'vain and ambitious' Darnley. She angrily brushes him off and, as the musicians take up a *Branle simple* and *Branle gai* (see Stravinsky's *Agon*) and a *Danse royale*, continues to flirt with her young kinsman, offering him a rose from her corsage but gently putting down his arrogant suggestion that the 'rose and thistle' be united.

All the while, Bothwell has become increasingly impatient and finds himself briefly James's ally in their suspicion of Darnley. He encourages his soldiers to take up their song again. They mount a vigorous reel, based on Dunbar's 'Of a Dance in the Queen's Chamber', that gradually crowds out and silences the courtiers' dance. For each verse a new dancer occupies the centre of the ring, impersonating a character from the song, one of whom is a 'Mistress Musgrave / Who might have lernit all the lave [rest]'. The refrain, 'A mirror dance might no man see', is conventional enough, but must also refer to the serial inversions and reversals by which Musgrave maintains tension in the accompaniment. The tension in the ballroom evaporates unexpectedly when Mary, instead of taking offence, catches Bothwell by the hand and sets him in the ring, while she claps time. She and then James take their turn and the whole court enters into the spirit, all except the outsiders Darnley and Riccio, who do not know the steps.

Both, though, are quickly restored to their talents, the young Englishman with a glass of wine, Riccio with a romantic song which becomes an accompaniment to mixed thoughts about the queen's growing attachment to Darnley. This is beautifully done and conveys something of the youthful awkwardness and headlong romance of their courtship; Darnley was, after all, only nineteen when he married her, the same age

Mary had been when she returned to Scotland. James interrupts them rudely and breaks off the song with the name of Darnley's patron Elizabeth, spoken too loudly for anyone's comfort. As Riccio nervously carries on, Bothwell sneers about 'foreign intrusion' and, goaded past endurance, grabs a sword to skewer Darnley, who dances just out of reach. In a fury, Mary banishes him, and in a repeat of James's speech at the end of scene 1, accompanied this time by a clattering percussion figure, Bothwell predicts that the day will come when Mary will need him again and then she will be in his power. James watches him leave with his men and the first act ends with a silent gesture of disgust.

The seasons change. Mary has now married Darnley and Riccio has been appointed secretary. Act 2 begins in an antechamber at Hollyrood, as the Lords of the Congregation wait impatiently for Mary, muttering about the unsuitability of her consort, who is known to frequent the Edinburgh taverns and whorehouses. They jeer and assault Riccio, then fall icily silent as Mary and Darnley enter. He is insulted, she calm. When she explains that she has sent for James, her husband's anger is redoubled. It is clear he is drunk, and that her gentle equanimity is that of a woman well used to sudden swings of temper in the man she loves (and whose child she is, we learn, now bearing). After a last tender look, she leaves him to his maudlin self-pity – 'Always alone!' – in which state Morton and Ruthven find him, softened up and mawkishly susceptible to their flattery. They call him king, while the Lords gathered offstage shout their alarm. Morton and Ruthven persuade Darnley that he is only third in the queen's affections, turning him against his one-time ally Riccio, goading him to action with '*En avant Darnley!*' In a frenzy, the young consort is led away by his tempters, leaving the stage to the newly arrived James, whose passion is as cold and hard as Darnley's was sodden.

The end of the first CD could have been better placed for Mary's entrance at the end of her half-brother's soliloquy – 'She has killed my love / All tastes of ashes / Even her love of me. / Now all I seek is power. / I shall rule!' – marks another of those powerful changes of emotional temper which Musgrave manages so well. She pleads with James to help her, echoing the words – 'Vanquish the mist' – with which Bothwell welcomed her to Scotland. It is a significant recollection, underlined by the accompaniment which reverses, then explicitly repeats, the music of the second scene, and it slowly dawns on Mary that James's vaulting ambition is more than a contrived political rumour. They argue back and forth in a storm of passion which is one of the high points of twentieth-century opera, and worthy of comparison with half a dozen classical warhorses. James barely keeps his temper under control, but the estrangement of brother and sister is complete. Mary recognizes that she cannot rely on any of the three men, husband, brother and banished suitor, who court her and in a sudden reversal, marked by an ambiguous harmonic consolidation, turns the opera's central thematic motif into a statement of resolve: 'Alone, alone, I stand alone / .... / This is my kingdom / And I must stand alone. / I shall rule, I alone, / And after me, my son.'

The scene shifts to Mary's supper room, where Riccio is again playing his mournful (and now dangerously prophetic) song of Orpheus, whose end Mary has yet to hear. As the courtier and the Four Marys finish a verse, Darnley staggers in, with Morton and Ruthven still hissing encouragement from the shadows. James stands hidden on the balcony above. Now quite beside himself, Darnley brutally stabs Riccio to death, only coming back to reality when he slithers in the blood on the floor (blood which miraculously survives in the parquet of Hollyrood House for the edification of many generations of tourists and school parties). James's triumph seems complete and, as the scene dissolves again to the Council Chamber, a faction of troubled Lords led by Morton asks him to assume power. As a crowd grows outside, buzzing with evil rumour and pleading for the queen's intercession, Ruthven bursts in to say that Mary has disappeared. Still resisting the suggestion that he declare himself Regent, James moves to the window to address the crowd. Shedding oniony tears at the death of Riccio, he tells the Scots that their queen has deserted them, a charge again denied by the heroic Gordon. There is, though, better proof to come, for Mary then reveals herself in the midst of her people, from where she accuses Morton and Ruthven, and James himself, of plotting Riccio's murder. As the hostile Lords accept their banishment, the crowd returns to the 'Peace Chorus' of the third scene, repeated now with a rather more desperate and uncertain air. As they sing, Mary reiterates her claim to rule alone, the two melodies clashing more than ambiguously as the curtain falls on the second act.

The dénouement is relatively brief. As Act III begins, Mary has given birth to her son and is still weak from childbed. She puzzles why Darnley has not come to see the boy, and then sings a tender lullaby, first with Mary Seton and then alone. It is a rare moment of intimacy and one of Musgrave's finest tunes. Gordon, fated to be a kind of operatic fax machine, breaks in again to announce that James has raised an army and is marching on Edinburgh. Mary refuses to be panicked into flight and renews her lullaby. At this point, Mary Seton ushers in Bothwell. 'A beautiful woman needs / A strong protector': the soldier comes directly to the point, condemning Darnley and eagerly taking up her wish to be protected from James. She is too weakened to resist any further, and Bothwell sweeps her off her feet and into an adjoining chamber. A brief orchestral interlude suggests that the seduction is complete. James comes in through a secret doorway, enters the bed-chamber and discovers the couple *in flagrante*. Bothwell taunts him and Mary beats helplessly at her brother with her fists. Gordon reappears yet again with the news that Darnley has been murdered by an unknown hand. Mary is compromised, and no less under suspicion of her husband's assassination than the other two who fight back and forth until Bothwell is wounded and manages to escape.

It is not entirely unfair to suggest that Musgrave's dramatic invention fails her slightly in the first half of Act III. The pace of events is too rapid, too much is dependent on events offstage, but while such elisions are characteristic of classical opera, here they disrupt the ordered, inevitable motion of the opening act and the development *too* much to be convincing. There is even an element of bedroom farce in the seduction scene and its aftermath. But Musgrave has a last card to play, a beautifully sequenced finale in which Gordon's role as *deux ex machina* casts Mary into the ultimate solitude of exile and separation from her child. Left briefly alone, she soliloquizes about the dark and her innocence of harm to Darnley. Gordon returns to overhear the last couple of lines and confirms that the crowd, now audible outside, believe that she is a murderess and are calling for her abdication. Mary calls for her child, poignantly asking 'Who will cradle him? / And who will teach him / To face the world and its cunning?', but is persuaded by Gordon that the boy has already been sent into exile. James's voice can also now be heard outside, calling the people to war. Mary makes a last attempt to plead her innocence from the balcony and is drowned out by cries of 'Whore!' Resigned to imprisonment, she appears at the top of the ramp, dressed in black as in her opening scene, unnoticed by James, Ruthven and the soldiers. As the portcullis descends behind her, signalling the end of her reign, her cry of farewell attracts their attention and they turn to watch. Morton enters with Mary Seton and the child but as they move towards James, Gordon rushes at the usurper and stabs him to death. Trapped beyond the portcullis, Mary can only scream in horror and reach out toward her dying brother and her heir, who is snatched from Mary Seton's arms by the *quondam* ruler of Scotland, Regent Morton. It is a poignant conclusion, and an appropriately ambiguous one.

Flawed though it is, *Mary, Queen of Scots* is a beautifully sustained invention. Its historical veracity is frequently shaky, but Musgrave's careful avoidance of overblown set-pieces like the fictitious but much-dramatized confrontations with Knox and Elizabeth, or the final ascent to the headsman's block, means that she is able to maintain some distance between a convincingly historical Mary (however fictionalized) and the conventionalized romantic icon. The music further removes the narrative from bathos, having at its heart the queen's own cyclical motto: 'In my end is my beginning.' Exile to exile, solitude to a dramatically different solitude, out of history but not yet quite into the pages of romance. It is a measure of Musgrave's sceptical intelligence that she attempts no final apotheosis, whether from the balcony at Hollyrood or on the block at Fotheringay. Mary is a woman first and last, and a queen first and last, and her passions as a lover and then as a mother cut across the neat packaging that makes her a warmer-blooded foil to her cool English cousin Elizabeth.

The Novello CD is a live recording from the successful Virginia Opera production of *Mary, Queen of Scots* directed by the composer's husband. As live recordings go, the sound quality is decent if a little noisy in places. I have some doubts about the singing. Ashley Putnam's articulation is rather uncertain in the second and third acts, with awkward caesuras in places where Musgrave surely did not intend them. A few American pronunciations intrude – 'Scatland', 'Scattish', and a hint of 'Stooart' – but the libretto is admirably clear (most listeners will soon dispense with the booklet) and unimpeded by Musgrave's sensitive scoring. Of the principals, Jon Garrison as Darnley stands out, a romantic, vulnerable tenor who occasionally manages to sound stronger than Jake Gardner's baritone James. As Riccio, Kenneth Bell uses the under-exploited bass-baritone range, and gives the song of Orpheus a curious sweetness which is perfectly balanced by the quartet of Marys, two sopranos and two mezzos. Carlos Serrano seems a little wasted as Beaton, disappearing after the first scene and only thereafter lending his vibrant baritone to the collective Lords of the Congregation.

Mary, Queen of Scots is unaccountably omitted from *Kobbé's Complete Opera Book*, though surely it is a more significant piece than Oliver Knussen's *Where the Wild Things Are* (1980), which gets full coverage. Musgrave's perspective on Mary's story is less inherently dramatic than Donizetti's in *Maria Stuarda*, but it earns its considerable dramatic force scene by scene, only faltering slightly as the patiently accumulated tension collapses a little too quickly. A British revival (and of *The Voice of Ariadne*) is long overdue, and it still seems outrageous that Musgrave's later opera *Harriet, a Woman Called Moses* (1981–4) has not been properly mounted in the United Kingdom. An important role model for a new generation of young women composers in the 1970s, Musgrave continues to exert an influence on contemporaries such as Nicola LeFanu (born 1947, see entry on Elizabeth Maconchy) and the much-admired Judith Weir (born 1954).

Discographical Information

Other recording: [same production] (Moss Music Group MMG 301 [USA]; Fono FSM MO 301 [continental Europe]).

Other Musgrave: String Quartet (1958); *Triptych* (1959; HMV ASD 2279 LP);

Colloquy (1960; Argo ZRG 5328 LP); Chamber Concerto no. 2 (1966; Delos DCD 1012); Clarinet Concerto (1968; Argo ZRG 726); *Pierrot* (1985; Crystal CD 742).

Map references: Gaetano Donizetti, *Maria Stuarda* (1834; Decca 425 410); Nicola LeFanu, *Same Day Dawns* (1974; Chandos ABR 1017 LP); Judith Weir, *The Consolations of Scholarship* (1985; Novello NVLCD 109).

Further reading: D. L. Hixon, *Thea Musgrave: A Bio-bibliography*, London, 1984.

ALFRED SCHNITTKE (born 24 Novmber 1934)

Concerto grosso no. 1 (1976–1977)

FIRST PERFORMED: Leningrad, 21 March 1977
SELECTED RECORDING: Deutsche Grammophon 429413 2
   Tatiana Gridenko, Gidon Kremer (violins), Yuri Smirnov (harpsichord, prepared piano), Chamber Orchestra of Europe, conducted by Heinrich Schiff
   [with: *Moz-Art (à la Haydn)* (1977); *Quasi una sonata* (1987)]
RECORDED: 1991
DURATION: 32′ 13″

Concerto grosso was an orchestral form of the baroque period, a common ancestor of the classical solo concerto and the symphony. Bach's 'Brandenburgs' and the late eighteenth-century *sinfonia concertante* represent transitional stages, and slightly different evolutionary paths, but the line of descent is still obvious. The concerto grosso differs from the modern concerto in using a small instrumental group instead of an individual solo player. The *concertino* or 'little ensemble' serves as a multiple soloist, alternating with the 'grand ensemble' of the whole orchestra, whose function is to 'replenish' the solo group; hence the alternative designations 'tutti' and 'ripieni'.

   The concerto grosso fell into desuetude during the nineteenth century, having been overtaken by the highly developed symphonic forms worked out by Haydn and Mozart. It has, though, staged something of a revival in the twentieth century. If Scott Fitzgerald is correct and an artistic generation is defined by a 'revolt against the fathers' then it is likely that artists will feel greater kinship with the period-before-last than with the language and styles of their immediate predecessors. The revival of interest in medieval and baroque forms was in part an expression of modernist alienation from the watertight self-confidence of the nineteenth-century orchestra and its associated forms. It also reflects an ironic – or what later became known as a 'post-modern' – attempt to collapse all musical styles, high and low, serious and popular, ancient and modern, into a single, multi-faceted compositional esperanto.

The most significant early twentieth-century experiment with the baroque concerto grosso was Max Reger's op. 123 *Konzert im alten Stil* (1912, the year of *Pierrot lunaire*). The title recurs with Henryk Mikolaj Górecki (in the Three Pieces for orchestra from 1963, written 'in the olden style'). Elements of Renaissance and baroque music also appear in works by György Ligeti, Peter Maxwell Davies (q.v.v.), Arvo Pärt (born 1935) and the defiantly tonal post-avant-garde works of the Slovak Ladislav Kupkovič (born 1936); the violin concerto *Offertorium* (1980–6) by Schnittke's compatriot Sofiya Gubaydulina is derived from a theme in Bach's *Musical Offering*.

Like Reger's Górecki's language is resolutely *un*ironic, and expresses a deep-seated nostalgia for musical and cultural consonance. Rather than reflecting the moral fractures and philosophical uncertainties of modern life, these composers create a kind of healing or consolatory counter-magic; and this is perhaps one explanation for the unprecedented market success of recorded works by Górecki and Pärt in recent years. By contrast, Davies and Schnittke have confronted the ambiguous relationship of music and modern society much more directly. Both combine older forms and techniques with modernist distortions and elements of phase effects as the strings play out of strict synchronization. The opening motif quickly rises to an almost hysterical climax. This signals the start of an antiphonal – that is, alternating – sequence in which rhythms and pitches are neither tonally or metrically centred, giving the music a disconcerting headlong tilt. The *Recitativo* is constructed over stately, organ-like chords from the lower strings in a slowly circulating rhythm that cuts short the violinists' rhapsodic entries by bringing each figure back to its starting point. Far from being a skittish show-piece, the *Cadenza* features some of Schnittke's most impassioned pages, and a nervous pizzicato middle section. It leads directly into the brilliant pastiche of the *Rondo* which logically ought to bring the music to its conclusion, as it would in an orthodox classical piece. But the coda repeats the prepared piano's naive octaves, framing the whole work and immediately casting doubt on the 'seriousness' of the foregoing music. In other contexts, it might be possible to suggest that Schnittke intends an oriental, or even more specifically a gamelan, sound; in the context of this piece, it seems appropriate to have the continuo player (it was Schnittke himself at the Salzburg Mozarteum performance in 1978) pick out a tune on a 'broken' and tuneless instrument. The melody conveys just the vaguest hint of the 'Internationale', the Communist Party hymn, which plays a significant role in the 1985 piece *Ritual*, written in memory of the victims of the Second World War, and also of the old Tsarist anthem, but these are subliminal and possibly accidental.

Schnittke extended his satirical side further in *Moz-Art (à la Haydn)* (1976, 1977, 1980, 1990). The orchestral *(k)Ein Sommernachtstraum* (also from 1985, the year of his illness) is a sardonic companion piece to the deeply felt *Ritual*. Marked 'not after Shakespeare', it develops the stylistic play in order to make terms with a culture in which the kaleidoscopic simultaneity of styles virtually occludes 'serious' music, reducing it to a branch of entertainment. (This may already be the fate of Górecki and Pärt.)

Schnittke has defined his own approach as 'polystylistic'. It draws on the widest possible spectrum of styles and, still more obviously, of moods. His music can be subversively witty one moment, exhaustingly passionate and emotional the next. Though strangely rootless, its very eclecticism of manner is what marks it out as archetypally Russian, despite Schnittke's unusual background. Born in the German-speaking Volga Republic (his surname betrays non-Russian descent), he was raised in Vienna and received his first musical training there at the end of the war. He moved on to the Moscow Conservatory in 1953 and subsequently joined the faculty. During his first year as a teacher, he encountered the Italian modernist Luigi Nono (q.v.), an occasion that fostered his growing interest in the Western European avant garde. His experiments in serial form set him in sharp opposition to the Soviet musical establishment, and for a significant proportion of his creative life he was denied opportunities to hear his work adequately performed. The First Symphony (1969–72) was considered too *outré* for Moscow or Leningrad audiences and the premiere was exiled to Gorky, not being heard in the capital for a further decade.

The effect of this critical isolation was twofold. Schnittke was forced to make his living writing music for films, a discipline that encouraged his innate theatricality and responsiveness to contrasts of mood. Lack of official recognition also made him particularly dependent on sympathetic interpreters (Peter Maxwell Davies has also been close to his performers, but not, of course, in such an atmosphere of constraint) and this in turn has inspired Schnittke to write a great many scores with prominent solo or concertante parts. Players of international standing like violinist Gidon Kremer and violist Yuri Bashmet have contributed substantially in bringing his work to the attention of a wider public. Things have improved dramatically in recent years and the post-*glasnost* thaw in cultural relations has made Schnittke an international figure, recognition only marred by wretched health following a serious heart attack and stroke in 1985.

The Concerto grosso no. 1 is dedicated to Kremer. In instrumentation, it follows very closely the model of the baroque *concertino*, which usually consisted of two violins, a cello, and a harpsichord continuo; which played a figured bass. The most obvious innovation is, of course, the use of the Cagean 'prepared piano', which lends a strange off-pitch chiming effect to the opening *Preludio* and closing *Postludio*. In between, there are four main movements, each in a contrasting style: *Toccata*, *Recitativo*, a brief *Cadenza* for the soloists, and a *Rondo* which despite strong hints of tango rhythm is the most obviously neo- or pseudo-classical of the four. One distinctive characteristic of the composition, though something of a private joke, is that in it Schnittke has incorporated music from a number of his own film scores, notably a 1976 feature known as *How Tsar Peter Got the Black Man Married*, a title that doubtless loses something in translation. These appear to have no function other than to provide the composer with musical *objets trouvés*, and the work as a whole gives off a strong sense of having been put together under some internal pressure with tag-ends of music from other times and places.

The *Toccata* begins comfortingly enough with baroque figures that only sound slightly off-pitch until the *ripieno* begins to introduce bizarre internal mirroring and pervasive sense of deception and unreliability that was already evident in the Concerto gross. Schnittke's later essays in the form (from 1981–2, the vintage but near-fatal year of 1985, and from 1988) have less immediate appeal than the first, but they represent a fascinating non-linear history of classical form; by 1988, the Concerto grosso no. 4 is also identified as the Symphony no. 5, completing the stylistic equation.

The Swedish BIS label are engaged in a long-term project to record all of Schnittke's mature output and the performance by Bergqvist, Swedrup, Pöntinen and the New Stockholm Chamber Orchestra is very good. It is, though, unwise to pass over Kremer and Tatiana Gridenko, whose fluency in this repertoire is unparalleled. The Russian Melodiya recording is paired with a fine version of Schnittke's First Cello Concerto, conducted by another of the composer's sponsors, Gennady Rozhdestvensky. The Deutsche Grammophon version is well ahead for sheer brilliance of sound and wins a vote on that alone.

Discographical Information

Other recordings: Kremer, Grindenko, Moscow Philharmonic Society Soloists, Bashmet (Melodiya SUCD 10–00067); Bergqvist, Swedrup, Pöntinen, New Stockholm CO, Markiz (Bis CD 377).

Other Schnittke: Sonata no. 2 for violin and piano: *Quasi una sonata* (1968; Ondine ODE 800); Symphony no. 1 (1974; Melodiya SUCD 10–00062); *Requiem* (1974–5; Bis CD 497; String Quartet no. 4 (1984; EMI Classics CDC 54660); Symphony no. 5 (Concerto grosso no. 4) (1984; London 430698).

Map references: Max Reger, *Konzert im alten Stil* (1912; Colosseum COL 34.073); Henryk Mikolaj Górecki, *Three Pieces in the Olden Style* (1963; Koch Schwann CD

311041); Arvo Pärt, *Perpetuum mobile* (1963; Bis CD 434); Sofiya Gubaydulina, *Offertorium* (1980–6; Deutsche Grammophon 427336); Peter Schickele/P.D.Q. Bach, *Grand Serenade for an Awful Lot of Winds and Percussion* (unknown, but very old indeed; Telarc 80307).

THEO LOEVENDIE (born 17 September 1930)

Six Turkish Folkpoems (1977)

FIRST PERFORMED: Rotterdam, 1977
SELECTED RECORDING: Etcetera KTC 1097
   Rosemary Hardy (soprano), Nieuw Ensemble: Harie Starreveld (flutes), Arjan Kappers (clarinet / bass clarinet), Ernestine Stoop (harp), Herman Halewijn (percussion), Angel Gimeno (violin), John Snijders (piano), unidentified cellist, conducted by Ed Spanjaard
   [with: *Strides* (1976, piano solo); *Music for Flute and Piano* (1979); *Venus and Adonis* (1981, soprano and five instruments); *Two Songs* (1986, mezzo-soprano, eight instruments; from opera *Naima*); *Back Bay Bicinium* (1986, seven instruments)]
RECORDED: 1990
DURATION: 14′ 37″

Theo Loevendie's first major concert piece was not written until he was nearly forty, a fact that has unshakeably tagged him as a 'late developer'. However, long before he began formal musical study at the Amsterdam Conservatory, he had been a professional jazz musician and leader of a successful touring ensemble. Inevitably, many of his earliest works were for his own instrument. *Scaramuccia* (1969) is for clarinet and orchestra, and there are several other, smaller scale works for clarinet, most notably *Music* (1971) in which Loevendie creates a convincing role for the unwieldy bass clarinet. In this he was perhaps influenced by the American jazz multi-instrumentalist Eric Dolphy, who made his last official studio recording at Hilversum in the Netherlands, shortly before his tragically early death in 1964.

   This at once raises the troublesome question of the extent of Loevendie's debt to jazz in his 'serious' music. The title of his opera *Naima* (1982–5) might seem to make reference to one of saxophonist John Coltrane's most celebrated themes, but in fact the only one of Loevendie's post-Conservatory scores to make explicit use of jazz is the piano piece *Strides* (included on the above), with its echoes of James P. Johnson and Fats Waller. Like Louis Andriessen and Ton de Leeuw, Loevendie was instinctively suspicious of serialism, which took root in the Netherlands after the war. His own music sets exclusively harmonic organization at something of a discount and places considerable emphasis on melody and rhythm, and on the timbral characteristics of individual instruments. His first pieces for large ensembles were influenced by Duke Ellington's practice of integrating instrumental solos into the fabric of a piece as part of its essential structure. *Confluxus* (1966) for jazz band and symphony orchestra was very much concerned with the integration of two sometimes antithetical approaches.

There is, though, always a danger of misunderstanding what precisely a 'jazz influence' might mean to a composer's work. It is of the essence that a successful jazz solo sounds *logical* as well as spontaneous. Even when his technique is quite strict, Loevendie's work is characteristically very immediate, almost improvisational in impact; but it is so because of, not despite, a high degree of control. As in a solo by Charlie Parker, rhythmic daring and decorative exuberance are not just free-floating, but are directly indebted to the robustness of the original melody, its harmonic underpinning and metrical 'code'; Loevendie has even traced back his fondness for powerful ostinato figures to a compulsory training in Morse during his national service. In later years this was systematized into what he called his 'curve' technique, in which the various melodic components of a piece are generated by expanding or contracting, but in exact proportion, the given intervals of a basic 'curve', which remains constant throughout the piece. (This technique makes an interesting comparison, beyond the accidental verbal echo, with Luciano Berio's pitch cycles in the 1974 work *Points on the Curve to Find . . . .*)

If the 'jazz influence' is too deeply embedded in his aesthetic make-up to be visible on the surface, it is also advisable not to be misled by titles like *Six Turkish Folkpoems*. A trip to Turkey with his ensemble in 1955 made an enormous impact on Loevendie but it did not simply provide him with a suitcaseful of musicological souvenirs. Instead it confirmed the very same technical preferences and resistances that determined his response to jazz. Turkish folk music is not impelled by harmonic changes but by heterophony (where two or more performers simultaneously generate variations on a common melodic line) and a marked concentration on instrumental timbre.

Loevendie had completed no vocal music before 1977 (though he had been working on *The Nightingale* for narrator and seven instruments since 1974), and the *Six Turkish Folkpoems* were as much of a surprise as they were an immediate success. None of his works has been so widely recognized. It is worth emphasizing that the title does *not* specify 'folk-songs' (as in Berio's great work of that name from 1946–7, which shares essentially the same instrumentation) but 'folkpoems'; the texts are authentic folk literature, but the music is Loevendie's entirely, without a hint of pastiche. He drew his six *mâni* (quatrains with a simple but flexible AABA rhyme scheme) from a collection of over 3000, describing them as 'typical specimens of folk art; their content is extremely concrete and linguistically pure without the intellectual niceties or Arabic and Persian words which frequently occur in literary art'.

The melodies are pungent and highly coloured, but also extremely simple, even austere. In the manner of Middle Eastern singing, the vocal line is often quite elaborately decorated while the basic musical material is generated from a simple tetrachord (a four-note chord consisting of D, E, F and G) of a sort common in Turkish music. However, the rhythmic structure of the songs and the cycle as a whole is not derived from Middle Eastern sources at all but from African polyrhythms (perhaps via jazz again) and from Loevendie's interest in the isorhythms typical of the Ars Nova of fourteenth-century France. As in the motets of Guillaume de Machaut (*c*.1300–1377) and others, these provided common rhythmic phrase patterns or *talea* (usually in the tenor, rather than the bass) which would recur throughout the piece. By displacing these relative to a repeated melodic pattern, a count of twenty in the first as against sixteen in the latter, Loevendie is able to desynchronize an essentially simple structure and refocus attention on the timbral properties of the instruments. By grouping the six songs into three groups (I, II–III–IV, V–VI) he is able to carry over these effects into the larger structure of the cycle, thus greatly increasing its sophistication.

In later years, as the Etcetera recording demonstrates, Loevendie was to make considerable further strides in these directions. In 1980, he adapted music originally written for a staged production of Shakespeare's non-dramatic *Venus and Adonis*, using an ensemble originally conceived as a hybrid of Middle Eastern and Renaissance consorts. The Nieuw Ensemble, which has been a highly significant and well-backed focus for new repertoire ever since, premiering works by Brian Ferneyhough, György Kurtág, and Pierre Boulez (q.v.v.), is unique in its pairing of non-sustaining plucked instruments with bowed strings and winds. *Venus and Adonis*, which prominently features guitar (or *darbuka*) and mandolin alongside Loevendie's trademark bass clarinet, can almost be regarded as a companion piece, as should the two songs from *Naima*, which derive their texts from Shakespeare again and from his near-contemporary Thomas Campion. Rosemary Hardy's voice is lighter and not so resonant as Dorothy Dorow's on the Olympia version of the piece (below), most obviously in the long, ululating vowel sounds of the first song, but Ed Spanjaard's reading of the instrumental score is impeccable. It is also valuable to follow Loevendie's isorhythms through the less crowded texture of the 1979 *Music* for flute and piano. While Loevendie does in some regards mark the culmination of '400 years of Dutch music' (the subject of the Olympia series), like most of his more interesting contemporaries he is best looked at as a figure to whom national or nationalistic qualities simply do not adhere. He is individual without being excessively idiosyncratic, and his work needs to be examined from the inside and in detail, rather than with a ready reckoner of historical or stylistic generalities. The Etcetera collection is the ideal place to begin.

Discographical Information

Other recording: Dorow, members of Het Residentie Orkest, Bour (Olympia OCD 506).

Other Loevendie: *Scaramuccia* (1969; Donemus DFAVS 7374/4); *Music* (1971; Gaudeamus 72001); *Timbo* (1974; Donemus CV 7802); *The Nightingale* (1974–9; Donemus CVS 1981); *Strides* (1976; Etcetera KTC 1097); *Naima* (1985; Donemus CVS 1986/5); *Duo* (1987; Attacca BABEL 8945).

Map references: Guillaume de Machaut, *La messe de Notre Dame* (mid-14th century; Editio Classica 77064 2 RG); Hendrik Andriessen, *Variations and Fugue on a Theme by Johann Kuhnau* (1935; Olympia OCD 504); Eric Dolphy, *God Bless the Child* (bass clarinet solo recorded live in Europe 1961; *Stockholm Sessions* Enja 3055; see also *Last Date*, recorded in Netherlands, EmArCy 5101242); Louis Andriessen, Symphony for Open Strings (1978; Attacca BABEL 9267 6).

R. MURRAY SCHAFER (born 18 July 1933)

The Crown of Ariadne (1979)

FIRST PERFORMED: Toronto, 11 May 1979
SELECTED RECORDING: Centredisques CNC DC 41/4292
    Judy Loman (harp, percussion, pre-recorded tape)
    [with: three works for harp with Orford String Quartet: Schafer, *Theseus* (1983, also with soprano); Pierick Houdy, *Quintette* (1984); Raymond Luedeke, *The Moon in the Labyrinth* (1984)]
RECORDED: 1992
DURATION: 19' 35"

Who can resist a composer whose work-list includes scores for orchestra and snowmobile, twelve trombones and small lake, or an ensemble of fog horns? R. Murray Schafer's work is so varied and abundant as to refute any attempt at classification or generalization, but at its core is the passionate drama of alienated man's reintegration with the natural environment. It has the epical quality one associates with young countries, and Schafer is perhaps the first Canadian artist – in any medium – with the breadth of vision to put his country's rich cultural resources on a world stage.

Not often enough, so far. Schafer premiered a major multi-media work in Europe in 1989 (significantly or not, it was in Liège, rather than in one of the more obvious centres), but he is still too little known outside Canada. In the United Kingdom, he is even now probably best known for a fine book of interviews with British composers, published in 1963. To some extent, this is due to his own reclusive habits; with the exception of a brief sojourn in Switzerland in the mid-1980s, he has lived in rural Ontario (not at all like living in rural Berkshire, or even upstate New York) since 1975. If isolation has narrowed his access to the established networks of concert promoters, publishers and critics, it has allowed Schafer to develop the kind of totalizing intellect and imagination people automatically liken to Leonardo's. Schafer is not just a composer, but a writer, dramaturge, scientist and linguistician; two of his most beautiful works, *Snowforms* (1981) and *Sun* (1982) consist entirely of unaccompanied vocalizations of single words – the Eskimo homonyms for snow, and the word for sun in thirty-six languages. His perceptions of a relatively unshaped physical and cultural environment have encouraged him to develop a highly theatrical, almost shamanistic approach which accounts for a large proportion of his work.

Since 1966, he has been engaged in a huge, twelve-part work called *Patria*, a dense, atavistic ritual, part of which, *The Black Theatre of Hermes Trismegistus* (*Patria IV*, 1988) was the work mounted in Liège. Some of the more extravagant devices in *Patria* had been tried out earlier. The appearance of a large SnoCat alongside the orchestra during *North/White* (1973) is a *coup de théâtre*, but no more gimmicky or out of place than Vaughan Williams's wind machine effects in the *Sinfonia antartica* (no. 7, 1949–52). During the early 1970s, Schafer directed the World Soundscape Project. This was not a mystical indulgence but a serious scientific enterprise with the aim of studying 'the tuning of the world', as he described it in a 1977 book of that name. Many of his works have been for carefully specified *plein air* settings which make use not just of natural acoustics but of the unique dramatic properties of the Canadian wilderness. *Sun-Father Sky-Mother* (1986) is a piece for solo voice in a mountain setting near both water and forest. It derives from the as yet unfinished epilogue to *Patria*. The prologue, known as *The Princess and the Stars* (1981) is perhaps Schafer's most remarkable single piece to date. It begins an hour before dawn on a mountain lake to a backing of amplified water sounds. As light breaks, singers, sound poets and dancers are revealed in canoes on the water. Accompanied by wind players hidden in the trees they enact the creation of the world as understood by the Huron tribes. A later section, *Ra* (1983) is based on the *Egyptian Book of the Dead* and involves (literally) a participatory audience of seventy-five. Other parts are less obviously mythic. The earliest to be completed was *Patria II: Requiems for the Party Girl* (1972) followed by *Patria I: The Characteristics Man* (1974), later renamed *The Wolf Man*. *Patria III: The Greatest Show* (1988) is set in a gigantic fairground and uses the dances in *The Crown of Ariadne* (see below) in a shadow-puppet show. *The Princess and the Stars* somewhat resembles a 1984 work, *Bran(d)t ann de Amstel*, by Schafer's fellow-countryman Henry Brant (born 1913) and also the huge millennial cycles projected by Karlheinz Stockhausen, in the *Licht* operas (1977–2000), and by Anthony Braxton (born 1945), whose comparable operatic sequence, the twelve-part *Trillium Dialogues* (1985– in progress), was first staged in San Diego in 1985, and who has spoken about (but not so far received funding for!) multi-orchestra works to be performed on orbiting space stations.

To see *Patria* as the sum of Schafer's output, which would be understandable given the emphasis he has placed on it in recent years, and to take at face value his definition of his own role as an 'acoustic designer' rather than a composer, is to miss the unique straightforwardness of his inspiration. He has shown some resistance to generic composition throughout his career and even parodied the romantic orchestra repertoire in *Son of Heldenleben* (1968) for orchestra and tape. There are, for instance, no symphonies, and Schafer only undertook a cycle of string quartets rather reluctantly. As an example of how his acoustic research has fed back into his music, the Second String Quartet, subtitled *Waves* (1976), makes direct use of his work on wave forms and patterns and is virtually free of conventional developmental procedures. In recent years, though, Schafer has written a sequence of impressive concertos, for flute (1984), harp (1987) and guitar (1989), and these, like the increasingly personal string quartets, show the expressive side of Schafer's musical temperament in a way that it is possible to appreciate on record.

The selection of *The Crown of Ariadne* is not made *faute de mieux*. It is in every way a characteristic Schafer piece, a suite of delicate but strongly pulsed dances which combines a dramatic programme with an unusual instrumental sonority. It is a concert version of some of the music in *Patria V*, also known as *The Crown of Ariadne*, a version of the Theseus myth which Schafer has reworked over the past decade. It is, of course, related to *Theseus* for harp with string quartet, also included on this recording, and at least in part to *La testa d'Adriane* (1977) for soprano and free-bass accordion, which has also been recorded. The harp has deep-rooted associations with epic literature – Homer, Virgil, the *Beowulf* poet, Lord and Parry's anonymous Balkan bards – which would appeal to the mythographer and anthropologist in Schafer. In addition to tackling some unprecedented articulations, Judy Loman, who premiered Schafer's Harp Concerto in 1987, is required to play an array of percussion instruments, including ankle bells and wood blocks.

These are used to give the music a more pointed rhythmic contour than the harp alone might allow. The most distinctive of the new articulation devices Schafer introduces is the use of the tuning key directly on the strings, to produce weird, indefinite pitches. Whereas at the end of *Theseus* he has a soprano voice calling out the single word 'Ariana', in *The Crown of Ariadne* the harpist is required to sing through a tube on to the strings, creating a further array of harmonics.

The piece begins quietly with a soft arpeggio first on harp then on chimes, signalling Ariadne's wakening. Percussion is also used to suggest certain programmatic aspects of the suite and there is a gently sun-kissed quality to the opening piece. 'Ariadne's Dance' is more vigorous and more explicitly rhythmic, albeit in subtly divided rhythmic cells that may suggest the Javanese background of the puppet play in *The Greatest Show*. This movement is sharply counterpointed in the next two parts, the forceful but never deliberately grotesque 'Dance of the Bull', with its lower-pitched and rather lonely sounds, and the pointillistic 'Dance of the Night Insects', a much longer and more detailed movement which establishes a mysterious, expressionistic atmosphere. The final movement is the longest of all, incorporating a 'Sun Dance' which is accentuated by bright, brassy percussion, and the 'Labyrinth Dance' of Theseus and Ariadne. Here the mazy, deceptive world of the Minoan Labyrinth is conveyed by a pre-recorded tape of open-tuned harp sounds, through which the dancers move towards a carefully ambiguous 'escape' into the outer air.

Fortunately a good deal of Schafer's music has been recorded in recent years. The Orford String Quartet, who perform sensitively on *Theseus*, have covered the cycle of quartets to date on Centredisques [CMC CD 39/4090]. On the same label there are excellent versions of an early instrumental piece Concerto for harpsichord and eight winds (1958). The Canadian Broadcasting Corporation, an enlightened body who sponsored Schafer's first mixed-media work *Loving* as long ago as 1966, have recorded the vocal sequence *Adieu, Robert Schumann* (1978) for alto, piano, orchestra and tape, and the orchestral *Dream Rainbow, Dream Thunder* (1986). There are obvious constraints on regular perfor-mance of Schafer's more extravagant works but his concert music alone would seem to guarantee him a significant place in the history of late twentieth-century music; and if, as seems likely, Canada becomes one of the leading cultural centres of the next century, he will increasingly be recognized as an important ancestor figure.

Discographical Information

Other Schafer: Concerto for harpsichord and eight winds (1958; Centrediscs CMC CD 3488); *Dream Rainbow, Dream Thunder* (1986; CBC Records SMCD

5101); Concerto for flute and orchestra (1984; CBC Records SMCD 5114); *Le cri de Merlin* (1987; Chandos CHAN 8784).

Map references: Henry Brant, *Angels and Devils* (1947; Centaur CRC 2014); Alexander Brott, *Ritual* (1942; CBC Enterprises SMNCD 5044).

Further reading: R. Murray Schafer, *The Tuning of the World*, Toronto, 1977, and *The Thinking Ear: Complete Writings on Music Education*, Toronto, 1986; S. J. Adams, *R. Murray Schafer*, Canadian Composers Series, 4, Toronto, 1983, and 'Patria': The Greatest Show on Earth?', in *Journal of Canadian Studies*, xxiii (spring/summer 1988).

1980s

This was the decade that saw 'classical' music become fashionable again. Record corporations needed to do something to promote the decade's single most significant technological innovation, the CD. They did so by trying to make the classical repertoire 'sexier' – young performers, wearing more casual (and in some cases, fewer) clothes – but also by getting behind 'new music' on a scale that had not been seen since the early 1960s. The dominant musical style was probably Minimalism, itself ideally geared to a young and relatively untutored public, but the decade also saw the emergence of the New Complexity, a restatement of rigour and control...

1980   Robert Simpson resigns from BBC, in disagreement with the corporation's handling of new music in the Proms and elsewhere.

1981   Violinist Gidon Kremer establishes the Lockenhaus Festival in Austria. Radical British composer Cornelius Cardew is killed in a hit-and-run accident.

1982   Stravinsky's centenary is celebrated. Renewed interest in his work all over the world encourages a resurgence of neoclassicism and of tonality.

1983   Olivier Messiaen's only opera, *Saint François d'Assise*, is performed in Paris. Centenary of Anton Webern's and Edgard Varèse's births.

1984   A major year for opera, this saw Berio's *Un re in ascolto*, the second part of Stockhausen's huge *LICHT* cycle, and the completion (with *Akhnaten*) of Glass's 'portrait' trilogy, as well as Michael Tippett's *The Mask of Time* for chorus and orchestra and Harrison Birtwistle's dramatic-abstract *Secret Theatre*.

1985   Paul Griffith's collection of interviews *New Sounds, New Personalities* identifies an established generation of British composers.

1986   The digitally encoded compact disc revolutionizes music recording.

1987   Centenary of Heitor Villa-Lobos begins a slow resurgence of European interest in Latin American music.

1988   John Cage is appointed Charles Eliot Norton Professor of Poetry at Harvard, some fifteen years after Leonard Bernstein. The

Solidarity movement in Poland achieves sweeping gains following martial law.

1989 Herbert von Karajan, principal conductor of the Berlin Philhar-monic Orchestra (and still at this point the most-recorded conductor of all time), dies at the age of eighty-one.

LUIGI NONO (1924–1991)

Fragmente – Still, an Diotima (1979–1980)

FIRST PERFORMED: Bonn, 2 June 1980
SELECTED RECORDING: Deutsche Grammophon DG 415 513 2
  LaSalle Quartet: Walter Levin, Henry Meyer (violins), Peter Kamnit-zer (viola), Lee Fiser (cello)
RECORDED: December 1983
DURATION: 38'

If any single musical work justifies the purchase of a CD player, it has to be Luigi Nono's extraordinary string quartet. It is a work of utter concentration, fragile almost to the point of evanescence, and radically subjective. More than half of its substance is pure silence, and the ticks and scratches to which vinyl recordings were constitutionally vulnerable seemed ruinously loud on the original LP issue. It is the kind of music that should probably be listened to on headphones in pitch darkness and in great stillness; getting up to change sides somehow scarred the mood.

The piece is remarkable on its own terms, but it stands out prominently in the work-list of a composer who has written very few chamber pieces (only a dozen or so in forty years) and who has long espoused a political philosophy that rejects 'subjectivism' as a bourgeois vice. Nono was on the national committee of the Italian Communist Party from 1975 until his death and had been an active member since 1952. Though Italian Communism has generally embraced Trotsky's acceptance of high art as consistent with revolutionary logic, it is hard to imagine the composer of *Fragmente – Still, an Diotima* grinding away at the Dialectic. During the 1960s, he organized factory and trade union debates and devised a number of informal or 'portable' works intended for performance in the workplace. He also created a sort of music theatre with the polemical immediacy of poster-art. This began with *Intolleranza 1960* (revised and re-dated a decade later) which was an extended protest against Fascism, war and the nuclear arsenal, and the structural antipathies that sustained them. It sparked a near-riot at its premiere in Venice in 1961. Nono extended the approach in the synoptic *A gran sole carico d'amore* (1972–4), which used texts by Marx, Lenin,

Gramsci, Castro, Guevara, Brecht and Mayakovsky. He toned it down somewhat in non-dramatic vocal works like *Ein Gespenst geht um in der Welt* (1970–1), with its text from *The Communist Manifesto*, and the choral *Simao la gioventu del Vietnam* (1973) but he never turned his back on a method that afforded him considerable theatrical and ideological purchase and it culminated in the massive 'aural drama' of *Prometeo* (1981–5), in which Nono's political and aesthetic concerns attained a new apotheosis.

Fragmente – Stille, an Diotima is a transitional work, part of Nono's desire to effect changes in the nature and social construction of listening itself; *Prometeo*'s subtitle, *tragedia dell'ascolto*, made this explicit. If the piece has historical antecedents, they can be found among the late quartets of Beethoven. In his dedication of the score to the LaSalle Quartet, Nono makes the connection clear by affixing the phrase 'mit innigster Empfindung', 'with the deepest feeling', which was used as an expressive marking in the mysterious and inward slow movement of Beethoven's op. 132 String Quartet in A minor (1825).

From the modern canon, the piece draws heavily from 'intimate pages' for quartet by Bela Bartók, Leos Janáček (1854–1928), and Alban Berg (1885–1935). More than any other single work, it recalls the alien emotional world of Berg's extraordinary *Lyrische Suite* (1925–6). There is some suggestion that his music-theatre works also drew something from Berg's opera *Wozzeck* (1917–21) but Nono had a more direct *entrée* into the world of the Second Viennese School. He had received a relatively conventional and neo-classical musical training under Gian Francesco Malipiero (1882–1973) at his home-town conservatory in Venice, but after studying law had gone on to receive advanced instruction in twelve-note technique from the conductor Hermann Scherchen (1891–1966) and from the Italian conductor and composer Bruno Maderna (1920–73), who became his greatest supporter. His first success in the modern idiom were the *Variazioni canoniche sulla serie dell'op. 41 di A. Schoenberg* (1950), made on his first visit to Darmstadt. In 1955, the year of the ground-breaking *Incontri* for small orchestra, he married Schoenberg's daughter Nuria.

Nono was never an orthodox serialist and it is interesting to speculate on the exact nature of the artistic dowry Nuria brought him. In later years, he devised a technique he called 'sonorism', which deployed sonorities for their own sake, not relative to pitch relationships. He also frequently subordinated strict musical argument in the interests of dramatic effectiveness. It may be that family connection lent Nono an unequalled insight into the most neglected (and most personal) aspects of Schoenberg's work, the impassioned drama of *Moses und Aron* (1930–2, third act begun 1951 but unfinished), the coded politics of *Ode to Napoleon* (1942, piano, string quartet, reciter; after Byron) and the sense of betrayal and loss in the anguished post-war *A Survivor from Warsaw* (1947, narrator, chorus, orchestra).

The essential thrust of Nono's 'aural drama' was to engage with a realm where Schoenberg's more intellectual approach ultimately failed him: to externalize that which has been internalized, and to lay bare the secret world of the emotions. Nono's intention, influenced by residual religious pieties as well as by political beliefs, is to give suffering a form which is not merely formal or contrived, which is aesthetically coherent but at the same time not arbitrarily extracted from the broader continuum of experience. Such an aim is clearly at work in a 1976 piece for piano and tape, dedicated to Marilisa and (the pianist) Maurizio Pollini. The title *... sofferte onde serene...* has a mysterious fragmentary quality, heightened by the strange word order ("suffered waves serene'), which signals a new inwardness and minimalism in Nono's work. Like the title and like the later *Fragmente*, the piece itself sounds like a small segment out of something much larger, moving in and out of focus in a dreamlike sequence of aural associations. The effect is both painful and redemptive, locating suffering against a vast, impersonal backdrop. The sounds, in contrast to earlier works, are very small, mostly quiet, and interspersed with silence.

In *Fragmente – Stille, an Diotima*, Nono takes the approach a step further. The subtext (and subtext it remains) is the idealized love of the 'mad' poet Friedrich Hölderlin for Susette Gonthard, the wife of his employer in Frankfurt. In the ecstasy of meeting 'Diotima', as he called her, Hölderlin wrote to his friend Neuffer: 'there is a being in the world on whom my spirit can dwell, and will dwell for thousands of years, and still see how all our thought and understanding blunder before nature. Loveliness and nobility, calmness and vitality, and spirit and temperament and form are blissfully united in this being.'

Hölderlin sublimated his passion in verses to 'Diotima', which Nono transcribes at fifty-two points round the score. These are not for recitation, and are not intended as programmatic markings, suggesting parallels between musical structures and specific emotions. They are offered as 'silent songs' (somewhat akin to the 'air from other planets' vocalized in Schoenberg's Second String Quartet) by which the performers may harmonize themselves with the emotional temper of the piece. The intention is a work of pure sound, much as Hölderlin's fragmentary utterances strive to break out of the inertia of language.

Hölderlin saw 'Diotima' as a representative of 'der Menschen alte Natur', man's ancient nature, an ancient Greek translated into barbary. In much the same way, Nono synthesizes ancient and modern, telescoping Diotima with Our Lady (and the Judaic *Shekhinah*) in a sort of aesthetic simultaneity. One of the work's underlying codes is the famous 'scala enigmatica' – C D♭ E F♯ G♯ A♯ B C – used by Giuseppe Verdi (1813–

1901) in the 'Ave Maria' of the *Quattro pezzi sacri* (1888–97), his last group of works. Verdi had combined and extended choral variation that had so intrigued Elliott Carter (q.v.) with the motet style of Palestrina (1525–94), thereby establishing a long continuum in Italian music. By adopting Verdi's 'enigmatic scale', Nono carries that tradition on a further two generations. He also copies the framing device by using the melody of a renaissance *chanson* by the Flemish composer Johannes Okeghem (*c.*1410–1496), an erotic lament called 'Malheur me bat', 'ground down by bad luck', which he had analysed under Maderna's tutelage in 1946. Like most of the musical material, it emerges as if 'from the ether' and is only just audible in the viola part in the closing pages.

Audibility is of the essence. Nono's dynamic instructions are very precise and range from *p* – *piano* or 'soft' – down to a barely detectable and (I think) unprecedented *ppppp*; only Morton Feldman (q.v.) has dared to work at length in anything approaching this register. As with many of Feldman's works, *Fragmente* seems unsuited to the vagaries of concert performance. Sounds of such fragility can only be produced by the lightest bow-weight and require almost superhuman control. Nono also makes use of high harmonics, *col legno* effects and notes produced high on the fingerboard or down close to the bridge of the instruments. The LaSalle Quartet gives a dedicated and definitive performance, executed 'mit innigster Empfindung', and communicating the same hushed combination of loveliness and nobility, calmness and vitality, spirit and temperament and form, which Hölderlin found 'blissfully united' in his unattainable ideal. *Fragmente – Stille, an Diotima* violates the very tradition it seems to extend by rejecting any logic of development in favour of a music as evanescent and fleeting as mist. For some it will seem *too* insubstantial, but like Hölderlin's poetry it repays close study as it gradually unfurls a secret world of pure sound which seems to exist behind and beyond the haze and bustle of everyday reality.

Discographical Information

Other Nono: *Composizione* no. 1 (1951; Arkadia CDMAD 027.1); *Il canto sospeso* (1955–6; Sony Classical SK 53360); *La lontananza nostalgica utopica* (1989; Deutsche Grammophon 435870); *Como una ola defuerza y luz* (1971–2; Deutsche Grammophon 423 248).

Map references: Ludwig van Beethoven, String Quartet in A minor op. 132 (1825; Teldec 9031 76457); *Anton Webern, Langsamer Satz* (1905; Deutsche Grammophon 419994); Alban Berg, *Lyrische Suite* (1925–6; Disques Montaigne WM 789001); Gian Francesco Malipiero, String Quartet no. 6: *L'arca di Noè* (1947; ASV CD DCD 457); Bruno Maderna, *Widmung* (1967; Adda 581259).

Further reading: G. Pone, 'Webern and Luigi Nono: The Genesis of a New Compositional Morphology and Syntax', in *Perspectives of New Music*, x/2 (1972); and disappointingly little else worthwhile in English.

EINOJUHANI RAUTAVAARA (born 9 October 1928)

Angel of Dusk (1980)

FIRST PERFORMED: Helsinki, 6 May 1981
SELECTED RECORDING: Finlandia FACD 009
   Olli Kosonen (double bass), Finnish Radio Symphony Orchestra, conducted by Leif Segerstam
   [with: *A Requiem for Our Time* (1953), brass of Helsinki Philharmonic Orchestra, conducted by Jorma Panula; *Cantus articus* (1972, concerto for birdsong and orchestra), Klemetti Institute Symphony Orchestra, conducted by Pertti Pekkanen, sound effects recorded by Einojuhani Rantavaara)]
RECORDED: at premiere
DURATION: 26' 53"

Charles Villiers Stanford once memorably described the double bass as a 'rogue-elephant'. Composers since have given the instrument an appropriately wide berth. Of all the modern string family, it is by far the least employed. In the eighteenth century, there was a flourishing literature of solo and concerted works for the bass and its relatives; Haydn even flattered his patron with a rash of pieces for the odd and unwieldy baryton. In the nineteenth century, though, there was a marked decline of interest, and the double bass retired, along with the once-prominent bassoon and the tuba, to the orchestral back four. Even in the present century, apparently hungry for 'new' sounds and eager to experiment with extremes of sonority, there has been only a very slow revival, and this has largely been restricted to virtuosic solo pieces for the small number of technically progressive and adventurous bass players working in the classical field; one thinks of pieces like Iannis Xenakis's *Theraps* (1975–6) and Luciano Berio's *Psy* (1989), or of the English composer Michael Finnissy's (born 1946) marvellous *Alice I* (1970–5), all of which were written for the brilliant Italian bass player Fernando Grillo. There have been, proportionately, more innovative bass players in jazz and improvised music, one of whom, the French-woman Joëlle Léandre, has made a substantial crossover impact with scores by Giacinto Scelsi, Betsy Jolas and Sylvano Bussotti (born 1931), and with her own bass/vocal compositions.

   However, whereas the once overlooked viola is now firmly established in the repertoire of concerted works (see essay on Betsy Jolas), concertos for double bass and orchestra are still something of a rarity, avoided even by the hyper-active Danish composer Niels Viggo Benzton (born 1919) who can usually be relied upon for an exception to prove any rule. Two double bass concertos of exceptional quality did appear in the 1980s. In so far as she is known at all to Western audiences, Joanna Bruzdowicz (born 1943) is recognized for a fine Olympia recording [OCD 329] of her violin and double bass concertos (1976, 1982, the latter dedicated to and performed by Grillo), which are paired with her Polish compatriot Krzysztof Penderecki's Symphony no. 2 (1979–80). Bruzdowicz writes in a flowing classical idiom, with modernist and personal inflections, and her use of the bass as a solo instrument is unmistakably traditional.

A pupil of Aare Merikanto (1893–1958), and a nephew of the fine soprano Auliikki Rautawaara (1906–90, often so spelt), Einojuhani Rautavaara also began his career as a classicist, but from the early 1950s he began to import elements of modern Russian symphonic language, and later, of free twelve-note technique. The former came from Shostakovich chiefly, but also from Prokofiev. There are powerful echoes of Stravinsky in Rautavaara's first major work, the piece for brass orchestra *A Requiem in Our Time* (1953), which is included on this CD compilation, but it is Charles Ives and Shostakovich again who dominate Rautavaara's Symphony no. 1 (1956, substantially revised and reordered 1988). It is worth looking at the First Symphony by Rautavaara's pupil Kalevi Aho (born 1949) whose opening movement was orchestrated from a student string quartet at Rautavaara's suggestion and bears strong indications of a Shostakovich influence. The serial strand is evident in Rautavaara's Second Symphony, written shortly thereafter (1957), and reaches its culmination in the Fourth, *Arabescata* (1963), but already in the Second String Quartet (1958) and in the Third Symphony (1961) there are signs of an orderly tactical retreat from ultra-modernism. The language is more lyrical, implicitly if not wholly tonal, marked by open counterpoint and what has been seen as Brucknerian development. In recent years, Rautavaara has continued to develop a highly personal voice, defined by an unironic post-modern synthesis of classical and modernist elements. It is perhaps most clearly seen in his opera *Vincent* (1987), based on the life of Van Gogh and premiered in Helsinki in 1990. The essential thrust of the score is a troubled, almost schizophrenic opposition of figure and ground; 'characters' emerge out of the background texture, change coloration and outline, and are reabsorbed. This has been a component of Rautavaara's large-scale writing since the late 1960s, particularly of the concertante writing which began to figure in his output around that time; it plays a central part in the series of 'Angel' pieces begun in 1978 with *Angels and Visitations*, continued with the Double Bass Concerto, and with *Playgrounds for Angels* (1981) which, with the unrelated *Serenade* (1982), revives an interest in writing for brass orchestra.

For all its apparent eclecticism (and it *is* an appearance rather than a fact) Rautavaara's music has always been highly personal and emotionally focused, its models chosen for their 'existential' qualities rather than for purely formal values. His *Canto III* (1972) for string orchestra, which follows the first two concertos, for cello (1968) and piano (1969) respectively, is subtitled *A Portrait of the Artist at a Certain Moment*. The sense of self or rather of identity that it conveys is fugitive and rather mysterious, an effect Rautavaara sustains in the *Cantus arcticus* (1972), written for the first graduation ceremony at the new University of Oulu and also included on this recording. (There is an even better version on the Ondine label [ODE 747], paired with the Fourth and Fifth Symphonies and conducted by the most consistent of Rautavaara's interpreters, the Leipzig Radio Symphony Orchestra under Max Pommer.) This extraordinary 'concerto' for taped birdsong and orchestra is by no means a gimmick, nor is it an example of bland nature mysticism, like Alan Hovhaness's once-fashionable *And God Created Great Whales* (1970). The score requires orchestral instruments to imitate the microtonal variations of bird calls (an opening section called 'The Bog' evokes the eerie cry of the curlew-like whimbrel) while the pitches of taped bird calls are manipulated to evoke a 'Melancholy' duet in the short central section or the startling cumulative sound of swans migrating in the final part. Strict literalism is only partly to the point, because what is conveyed by Rautavaara's mysterious integration of 'solo' and orchestral parts is nothing other than the birds' identity with their environment, both physical and musical, and with one another. The haunted isolated sounds of the opening section give way to a synthetic dialogue (the piping *tsee-ree* of shore larks slowed down many times) and thence to the electronic congregation of the swans.

Something of the same drama – isolation toward integration – takes place in *Angel of Dusk*; enough, certainly, to confirm a sense of continuity with *A Requiem in Our Time* and the concertos, in which Rautavaara dramatizes his own technical progress. The Finlandia recording, made at the premiere, is rather noisy, particularly on CD, but it is also unquestionably atmospheric. The opening movement quickly establishes a self-assured quasi-tonal theme from the bass, marked by the same double-stopping as in the unaccompanied opening measures of the earlier Cello Concerto. It also has certain significant details in common with the Concerto no. 2 for cello (1969) by the Leningrad-born (1939) Boris Tishchenko, in its remarkably sonorous original scoring for soloist, forty-eight cellos, twelve double basses and percussion. Whether or not Rautavaara knew the piece when he wrote *Angel of Dusk*, the connection seems to reaffirm his interest in a modern Russian idiom. As the opening movement advances, it is continually interrupted by aggressive brass-dominated figures based on the same serially disposed germ-cells that are dotted about in the *Requiem*. As the movement proceeds, the bass's opening theme is gradually absorbed and apparently silenced by these figures. The Angel's 'First Appearance' hardly seems conclusive. It certainly does not prepare one for what follows. The second part is an astonishing 'Monologue' for the soloist, who emerges out of the background with one of the richest inventions for the instrument this century. The part was written with the direct collaboration of Olli Kosonen. Again, it recalls the vivid opening of the Cello Concerto. Dark, bowed figures are punctuated by a resonant solitary plucked note and by a pattern briefly slapped out on the body of the instrument. Kosonen employs other 'extended' devices, like slapping the wood of his bow against the strings, playing in high harmonics or drones and drawing a finger up the string to create steadily darkening slides. Throughout this section of the piece, there is virtually no intervention by the orchestra, which only re-emerges after about six minutes with wailing string glissandos, peremptory calls from the trumpets, and sudden clatters of percussion. At the next break in the monologue, the soloist begins a long, singing passage which takes the instrument up into the middle cello register, strongly reminiscent of Zoltán Kodály (1882–1967), another Slavic composer who has made a discernible impression on Rautavaara. For the first time, he appears to take the orchestra with him in a relatively conventional accompaniment, but there are still violent outbreaks – and a whooshing surf effect – which suggest, correctly, that the end is still some way off. The bar-length suddenly doubles as the music acquires a new sense of direction and the bass's ostinatos become the accompaniment to further restless figures from the orchestra, again punctuated by assertive percussion. At the climax, the soloist is joined by a vibraphone (which has already contributed distant tingles of dissonance) in a passage of Bartókian night-music. With a fragmented and re-ordered version of the opening theme, the piece comes to an entirely appropriate close, in which a substantial measure of ambiguity remains. Who is the Angel? Does he only appear with the onset of darkness, or does he bring it down? Is he benign or sinister? Wounded or whole? Is his 'Last Appearance' a farewell or a reconciliation? Rautavaara is too subtle a technician and too sophisticated a musical poet to write orthodox 'programme' music, and it is perhaps best not to impose too fleshly an identity on the Angel of Dusk, who seems in every way evanescent and shadowy, as angels ought to be.

Discographical Information

Other Rautavaara: Symphony no. 1 (1956; Ondine ODE 740); *Ludus verbalis* (1960), *Monologues of the Unicorn* (1980; Bis CD 66); *Annunciations* (1977), *Playgrounds for Angels* (1981; Chandos CHAN 8390).

Map references: Zoltán Kodály, Sonata for cello (1915; GM Recordings 2031);

Kalevi Aho, Symphony no. 1 (1969; Bis CD 396); Boris Tishchenko, Concerto no. 2 for cello (1969; Koch Schwann CD 311 119); Joana Bruzdowicz, Double Bass Concerto (1982; Olympia OCD 329); Betsy Jolas, *Episode huitième* (1984; hat ART CD 6014).

Further reading: Kalevi Aho [composer, see below], *Einojuhani Rautavaara as Symphonist*, Helsinki, 1988; Mikko Heiniö [composer, see below], 'A Portrait of the Artist at a Certain Moment', in *Finnish Music Quarterly*, ii (1988); both are in English.

ARIBERT REIMANN (born 4 March 1936)

Unrevealed (1980)

FIRST PERFORMED: Berlin, 3 September 1981
SELECTED RECORDING: Classic Produktion Osnabruck cpo 999 031 2
    Richard Salter (baritone); Kreuzberger String Quartet: Ilan Gronich, Friedegund Riehm (violins), Hans Joachim Greiner (viola), Dietmar Schwalke (cello)
    [with: *Variationen* (1979), David Levine (piano)]
RECORDED: May 1986
DURATION: 39' 45''

Few contemporary composers have been more thoroughly steeped in vocal music and the art of song than Aribert Reimann. His father was a choral conductor, and at the age of nineteen Reimann was appointed assistant répétiteur at the Studio of Städtische Oper in Berlin. He served a long apprenticeship in classical Lieder as accompanist to the baritone Dietrich Fischer-Dieskau, under the influence of whose voice many of Reimann's songs and vocal roles were later created, most notably the aged king in the 1978 opera *Lear*, the *Tre poemi di Michelangelo* (1985), and the Byron settings of *Unrevealed*. The experience also contributed to Reimann's writing for piano, either as a highly idiomatic vocal accompaniment for vocal works such as the two cycles after Eichendorff called *Nachtstück* (1966, 1978), and the remarkable *Neun Sonette der Louise Labé* (1986), or as a solo instrument, as in *Variationen*. The pairing of *Variationen* with *Unrevealed* confirms my rather contentious preference for the CPO recording over Dietrich Fischer-Dieskau's reading (see below). Richard Salter brings more open-hearted passion to the part, though it is well worth hearing Fischer-Dieskau, both for comparison, and for a fine performance of the 1989 piece *Shine and Dark* for baritone and piano.

For *Unrevealed*, Reimann chose the less familiar accompaniment of a string quartet, an instrumentation that immediately recalls Arnold Schoenberg's String Quartet no. 2 op. 10 (1907–8) with its soprano setting of a Stefan Georg poem and wistful F$_\sharp$ minor tonality. Earlier in his career, Reimann had written settings of troubadour verse – *Trovers* (1967) – and of Rilke – *Denn Bleiben ist nirgends* (1968) – in an amalgam of speech and singing related to the *Sprechstimme* or *Sprechgesang* used by Schoenberg to underline the alienated, 'moonstruck' quality of *Pierrot lunaire* (1912); in the third movement of *Unrevealed*, he attempts something rather different, calling on the baritone to speak a prose text with a nervous, breathless recitation. Reimann's first scores were Webernian and quite strict in construction, but this changed in the mid-1960s to a more relaxed interpretation of serialist technique, one that admitted a degree of repetition for dramatic emphasis (useful in vocal setting) and using often subliminal tonality to unify passages made up of quite separate rhythms and textures. Clusters of sound, little coded sequences of chords, punctuate a rather free rhythm, and this helped Reimann considerably in his approach to setting English words with their strong, uninflected endings, a notoriously difficult task for the vocal composer.

The texts he uses in *Unrevealed* are far removed from conventional love poetry, for they relate to Lord Byron's incestuous affair with his married half-sister Augusta Leigh. Reimann took his title and epigraph from a diary entry of Byron's – 'Dear sacred name, rest ever unrevealed' – which Byron had in turn adapted from Alexander Pope's *Eloisa to Abelard*, an earlier treatment of forbidden love. The tone of the music is, appropriately, one of containment, concealment and separation. Reimann sets four Byron texts, two sets of 'Stanzas' and an 'Epistle' to Augusta in an ABAB rhyme scheme, together with a letter dated 17 May 1819, written to her after their separation and his final departure for Greece. The trajectory of the cycle is from relatively conventional declaration of love *contra mundum* in the first of the 'Stanzas' ("When fortune changed – and love fled far, / And hatred's shafts flew thick and fast, / Thou wert the solitary star / Which rose and set not to the last'), to the impassioned misgiving and reassurance of the second, with its almost obsessive repetition of 'though' and other conditionals, to the hectic unrepentance of the letter in the third, to the philosophical resolve of the 'Epistle' in the final movement, where Byron reiterates his love and the music moves full circle: 'The tie which bound the first endures the last!'

Reimann has identified the piece as a 'piece for baritone next to a string quartet which stands by itself in its four movement form', and this appears to distinguish it from a more typical song cycle. Reimann had demonstrated in the Rilke settings, in *Lear* and the later operas *Die Gespenstersonate* (1983, after Strindberg) and *Troades* (1985, after Euripides) how adept he was at combining voice with very powerful orchestrations (*Lear* calls for huge forces, with augmented brass and percussion), and in *Unrevealed* again he manages to sustain a near-perfect balance between verbal and musical audibility and comprehensibility. The piece opens with a sequence of chords that reappears throughout the work at significant moments in the text, varying in pitch and intensity, but always suggesting a coded declaration that contrast sharply with the rather nervous and reticent music that surrounds it. It may be useful to hear in the string quartet not just echoes of Byron's anguished and passionate voice (most noticeable in the coda for solo viola with which the work ends) but also whisperings of society's scandalized but never openly expressed reaction to relationships like Byron's and Augusta's. There are, surely, some indications of this in the first movement, but such reactions are cancelled out by Byron's firm assurance of his confidence at the end of the penultimate stanza – 'Thy soul, though soft, will never shake' – which is supported by a robust confirmation from the cello. (This last detail resembles a device in the subsequent *Solo* for unaccompanied cello (1981), where low tones emphasize an unrelated lyrical movement in the higher register.)

Reimann's interest in subtle and flexible rhythmic synchronization is evident in the long second movement, which begins with a sweeping passage from the strings before launching into the second set of 'Stanzas'. The baritone part is unusually notated, with durations shown by horizontal lines and with no stems on the notes; he had also used graphic notation in 1975 for *Variations* (an orchestra piece, not to be confused with the piano work paired here with *Unrevealed*) to indicate quarter-tones. The stanzas are longer, more repetitive; there are extra beats, and Richard Salter brings a new sense of urgency to the words. The opening 'code' reappears, with a darker timbre, at the words 'And when winds are at war with the ocean, / As the breast I believed in with me, / If their billows excite an emotion, / It is that they bear me from *thee*', and ushers in another restless passage of equal lines from the strings.

The third movement is brief, as the baritone hurriedly recites Byron's letter to Augusta, over strings played pizzicato and with the wood of the bow; again the chord sequence signals a change of direction and a switch of mood as he repeats the saying that 'absence destroys weak passions – and confirms strong ones – Alas! *mine* for you is the union of all passions and of all affections – '. On the strength of that robust declaration, the final movement begins with solo voice, gradually supported by calm passages from the quartet and a steady, almost subliminal 'revelation' of the same chordal code that marks the musical and emotional centre of the first three movements. This last movement is the longest of all, more than twice the duration of its predecessor, and it is the most musically developed, ending with unison passages and a tender coda from the solo viola.

Unrevealed is a work of tremendous expressive subtlety. As in *Lear*, the *Hölderlin-Fragmente* for soprano and orchestra (1963), the *Six Poems by Sylvia Plath* for soprano and piano (1975, premiered at the Edinburgh Festival and recorded on the Wergo label [WER 60097]), the Strindberg and Euripides operas, Reimann shows an ability to compress tremendous amounts of emotion into small compass without strain. In that respect, he is perhaps closer in spirit to Robert Schumann than to Franz Schubert, and it is therefore no accident that in the later 1980s he should have turned to Schumann's op. 135 *Gedichte der Maria Stuart* (1852, arranged by Reimann 1988) and written the beautiful *Sieben Fragmente: in memoriam Robert Schumann* (also 1988); or that he should have felt such a kinship with the poet Eichendorff, who was one of Schumann's main sources. The ability to convey mental distress and profound emotional alienation without either mawkishness or banality is a very remarkable one. *Unrevealed* is both cathartic and healing, an essay in reconciliation between the isolated artist and his community, the outsider and those who stigmatize him.

Discographical Information

Other recording: Fischer-Dieskau; Cherubini Quartet (Orfeo 212901).

Other Reimann: *Six Poems by Sylvia Plath* (1975; Wergo WER 60097); *Neun Sonette der Louise Labé* (1986; Wergo WER 60183).

Map references: Robert Schumann, *Dichterliebe* op. 48 (1840; Philips 416352); Michael Nyman, *The Man who Mistook His Wife for a Hat* (1987; CBS MK 44669); Reimann's accompaniments for Fischer-Dieskau include Lieder by Schubert, Berg, Schoenberg.

Further reading: R. Dufallo, interview in *Trackings*, Oxford, 1989.

LEONARD BERNSTEIN (1918–1990)

Ḥalil (1981)

FIRST PERFORMED: Jerusalem, 23 May 1981
SELECTED RECORDING: Deutsche Grammophon 415 966 2
   Jean-Pierre Rampal (flute), strings and percussion of the Israel Philharmonic Orchestra, conducted by the composer
   [with: *On the Town: Three Dance Episodes* (1945); *Three Meditations from 'Mass'* (1977–8, cello, orchestra), Mstislav Rostropovich; Divertimento for Orchestra (1980)]
RECORDED: May 1981
DURATION: 16' 04"

Leopold Stokowski used to express irritation that his admirers talked about coming to 'see' him conduct: 'Apparently they listen with their eyes rather than their ears.' The complaint must be considered a shade disingenuous coming as it does from a conductor who played straight man to Mickey Mouse in Walt Disney's *Fantasia* (1941) and appeared with Deanna Durbin – and ninety-nine others presumably – in *100 Men and a Girl* (1937). Stokowski's attitude to the classical repertoire was rarely self-effacing and usually controversial. Though he had little of his countryman Thomas Beechman's bandmaster–martinet vices, his concert performances were grand theatrical productions with the conductor at their centre.

Leonard Bernstein was in many ways Stokowski's heir, a forceful larger-than-life personality who found it difficult to conceive of himself as a servant to the music. Oscar Levant complained that 'Lenny' used music as an accompaniment to his conducting, which was quintessential *maestro* stuff with tossed hair, grandiloquent gestures and facial calisthenics. Though less obviously iconoclastic than Stokowski when it came to the classics, Bernstein rarely let himself be upstaged, and kept his wagon firmly hitched to whatever social and political star was in the ascendant. (It should be remembered that Tom Wolfe coined the phrase 'radical chic' after a party at the Bernsteins' given in support of the Black Panthers.) Bernstein also belongs to a small and rather problematic group of conductor–composers (or composer–conductors; the order of priority is especially problematic in Bernstein's case) who have spent a more than incidental amount of time interpreting the music of others. One thinks first of Pierre Boulez and of his successor at the Domaine Musical, Gilbert Amy (born 1936), both of whom are probably thought of as composers first and foremost, and then of musicians such as the American Gunther Schuller, and the Finns Leif Segerstam (born 1944) and Esa-Pekka Salonen (born 1960), and the Anglo-Scot Oliver Knussen (born 1953) who are probably thought of (however *they* apportion the emphasis) as conductors-who-compose, with the implication that they are the musical equivalent of Sunday painters.

Bernstein falls into an intermediate category. Though much of his straight music is still not well known, scores like *On the Town* (1944) and *West Side Story* (1957) are among the most widely recognized in twentieth-century music, in any genre, and this is the source of an interesting problem. Recognition for the others has been lost in the double glare of his dazzling gifts as a communicator and the huge success of *West Side Story*. Great popular artists always stand in some danger of being identified with 'untypical' works, but Bernstein has been the object of a rather one-dimensional and reductive critical press that has focused on his conservatism and sometimes aggressively affirmative Americanism (which some listeners detected in the synoptic *Songfest*) at the expense of much understanding of the artistic and emotional price he has had to pay for such stances.

Though in the 1970s he conducted premieres of many advanced contemporary pieces, including Milton Babbitt's fiendishly difficult *Relata II*
(1968), he remained essentially unsympathetic to twelve-note composition, which he regarded as an aberration and tended to use as an
expression of agony and despair, in opposition to the natural language
of tonality and diatonicism. That is essentially the programme of the
Second and Third Symphonies, and it is the central drama of *Halil*. The
one generalization that does make sense of Bernstein's music is that it
is, like the man himself, essentially dramatic and divided. Bernstein
called his collected Charles Eliot Norton Lectures *The Unanswered
Question* (1976), a title borrowed from Charles Ives, but also profoundly
expressive of his own conviction that music was a branch of moral and
philosophical enquiry, a means of resolving contradictions.

A Jew raised in Protestant America, a romantic in an era of stern
experimentalism, generous and capricious, cheerfully macho on the
podium, he gave the full orchestra an unmistakably 'masculine' sound,
but was sexually ambivalent in his not very private life. He came of age
at a moment of supreme irony for an American Jew, with the Great
American Way seemingly triumphant throughout the world and some
millions of his own race dead in Europe or huddled on refugee ships.
He was a star at the Kennedy White House (and wrote a *Fanfare* for the
inauguration) who was marked for ever by the events in Dallas. There
is a dark thread twined through the work. *West Side Story* is, of course,
a tragedy, or at least is based on a tragic source. His comic operetta
Candide (1956, revised 1973) is derived from Voltaire's cynical and jolly
demolition of the Enlightenment. Bernstein's First and Second Symphonies bear subtitles, *Jeremiah* (1942) and *The Age of Anxiety* (1949, after
Auden) respectively, that convey something of their brooding seriousness. The First contains a mezzo-soprano part derived from Jewish
liturgical music and the Third, *Kaddish* (1963, revised 1977) is based on
the mourning prayer. It falls into two parts, an agonized opening
movement in which Bernstein extends the twelve-note elements he had
introduced in the Second, and a gentle diatonic lullaby. It also includes
vernacular texts in which Bernstein argues with God. To his friends and
detractors, this was either a good joke against himself or a further
symptom of his supreme arrogance. The posh term for it is theodicy.

Bernstein was always concerned with the need to explain the
presence of evil in the world, which is a more modest and less hubristic
project than justifying the ways of God to man. *Kaddish* (significantly
the first of his works to be premiered in Israel, as *Halil* was to be) can
be seen as a formally conservative work in its apparent rejection of
modernist language. However, it is suffused with Bernstein's version of
the archetypal American myth: the belief that society can be restored to
an Edenic simplicity. It is no coincidence that the work Bernstein valued

most from his entire output is the significantly entitled *A Quiet Place* (1983), a work of great musical and emotional complexity, written in the aftermath of his wife Felicia Montealagre Cohn's prolonged illness and death. The first American opera to be mounted at La Scala in Milan, incorporating the earlier *Trouble in Tahiti* (1951) as a flashback, it is Bernstein's masterpiece, far more deeply interfused with his artistic personality than *West Side Story*, which bears the mark of several other hands.

In the same way, and despite the jolting surprise of the opening twelve-note melody, *Ḥalil* is pure Bernstein; within a very few measures a melody rises up out of the slightly bleak, semi-serial chords which is unmistakably from the same hand that wrote 'Maria' and 'Tonight'. He described it as 'formally unlike any other work I have written', but immediately recognizes that its concentration on the 'struggle' between tonality and non-tonality is typical; here, though, the struggle is integral to the musical argument, and this saves *Ḥalil* from slipping toward the rather schematic two-part drama of *Kaddish*. The piece is described as a nocturne for flute, percussion and strings, but is far removed from the dreamily one-dimensional night-music one associates with John Field, or even Chopin. Though it has something in common with Bartók's 'night music' in the Second Piano Concerto (1930–1), it is the troubled spirit of Arnold Schoenberg which pervades the whole structure.

Bernstein's title (the opening sound is palatalized like the 'ch' in Scottish 'loch') is Hebrew for flute and *Ḥalil* is dedicated to Yadin Tannenbaum, a gifted young Israeli flautist whom Bernstein never actually met, but who was killed in the Yom Kippur War in 1973. There is no mistaking the undercurrent of violence in the piece, particularly towards the end, where the soloist in this recording, Jean-Pierre Rampal, takes the flute into its metallic upper register. These passages represent the most complete disruption of the opening twelve-note melody, which is divided into an opening call of four notes that seems to identify the young Israeli's open-hearted self-confidence, a more ambiguous three-note motif that descends a semitone as it is repeated, and then a two-note cadence that anticipates the ultimate destination of the piece.

Bernstein subjects the melody to retrogression which (I am guessing) may have less to do with orthodox twelve-note procedures than with the 'Hebrew manner' of singing or playing, that is, from right to left on the page, marked *Canite more Hebraeorum* in early and baroque scores. It seems entirely possible that in *H.alil* Bernstein is demonstrating his solidarity with the fellow-Jew rather than the proto-serialist in Schoenberg; at one point he almost certainly refers to a well-known retrograde canon in the eighteenth part of *Pierrot lunaire*. Most of *Ḥalil* proceeds by continuous variation of the two basic motifs, with their ambiguous downward shift pointing both formally to the finale and expressionistically to the tragic theme. Bernstein's own description of the piece is as 'ongoing conflict of nocturnal images: wish-dreams, nightmares, repose, sleeplessness, night-terrors – and sleep itself, *Death's twin brother'*, and it manages to convey both that turbulent succession and its quiet, fearfully accepting conclusion. At the centre of the piece, there is a martial section in which the percussion play a large part and over which the flautist enters with a forceful cantabile passage apparently intended to suggest Tannenbaum's buoyant patriotism at the moment of his country's greatest danger. There is unmistakable brutality in what follows, with anguished breath noises from the flautist, before a quiet, almost folkish simplicity is restored (Bernstein marks the flute part 'childlike'). There is a final apotheosis before the quiet ending, which is cast in the same unsymphonic D♭ as Debussy's *Clair de lune* and other piano pieces, but which for strings presents profound ambiguities.

Bernstein made no very considerable formal innovations in his music and there is no single stylistic device or manner associated with his name. His music is in the fullest sense personal. How much of it will survive now that its most charismatic interpreter is gone? *West Side Story* is now a recognized modern classic; the *Candide* overture and some concert versions of dance pieces are solidly established in the repertory; *A Quiet Place* merits regular revival. It seems unlikely that the symphonies or the theatre piece *Mass* (1971, represented on this disc) will ever be as prominent as Bernstein's presence once made them. Of the concert music, *Ḥalil* is perhaps the best memorial to a man who stood at the far-from-still centre of the twentieth century and its music, looked back and (more fearfully) forward, drew conclusions that were entirely his own, and asked unanswerable questions that continue to resonate.

Discographical Information

Other Bernstein: Symphony no. 1: *Jeremiah* (1942), Symphony no. 2: *The Age of Anxiety* (1949; Deutsche Grammophon 415964–2); *Candide* (1956, rev. 1973 and 1989; Deutsche Grammophon 429734–2); *West Side Story* (1957; Deutsche Grammophon 415253–2); Symphony no. 3: *Kaddish* (1963, rev. 1977; Deutsche Grammophon 423582–2); *Chichester Psalms* (1965; MCA MCAD 6199); *Mass* (1971; CBS M2K 44593); *Songfest* (1977; Deutsche Grammophon 415965); *A Quiet Place* (1983; Deutsche Grammophon 419761); *Arias and Barcarolles* (1989; Delos DE 3078).

Map references: Arnold Schoenberg, *Pierrot lunaire* (1912; Elektra Nonesuch 79237–2); Walter Piston [Bernstein's teacher], Concerto for flute and orchestra (1971; CRS CD 8840); Béla Bartók, Piano Concerto no. 2 (1930; Philips 426 660–2).

Further reading: L. Bernstein, *The Unanswered Question*, Cambridge, Massachusetts, 1976; and *Findings*, New York, 1982; J. Peyser, *Bernstein*, New York and London, 1991.

MORTON FELDMAN (1926–1987)

Untitled composition for cello and piano (1981)

FIRST PERFORMED: Middleburg, Netherlands, July 1982
SELECTED RECORDING: Attacca BABEL 9160 3
  René Berman (cello), Kees Wieringa (piano)
RECORDED: 1990
DURATION: 72' 08"

As with his friend John Cage, the essential component of Morton Feldman's music is the silence on which it is inscribed. A typical Feldman score is quiet and almost motionless, its constituent sounds all but unrelated. Its nature can be gauged by comparing the deliberately uninflected title of the piece above with the dense poetic underpinning of Luigi Nono's profoundly subjective string quartet *Fragmente – Stille, an Diotima* (see above), which it superficially resembles in matters such as dynamic range. But where Nono prescribed detailed variants on standard performance technique, radically altering the timbre and attack of classical instruments, Feldman almost entirely abandoned rhetoric in favour of undifferentiated 'washes' of sound colour which occupy musical time in much the same way that colours occupy space in a canvas by Mark Rothko.

Feldman was initially more influenced by visual artists than by other composers. In 1971 he wrote a moving choral piece for the ecumenical Rothko Chapel in Houston, and he has dedicated works to Jackson Pollock (1951, a film score), Franz Kline (1962, soprano, horn, piano, tubular bells, violin, cello), Willem De Kooning (1963, horn, percussion, piano, violin, cello), and Philip Guston (1984, flute / alto flute, percussion, and piano/celesta), as well as to the writers Frank O'Hara (1973) and Samuel Beckett (1987, a very late work), and to a former pupil and fellow-composer *For Bunita Marcus* (1985). Dedications of this sort are as typical of Feldman's output as neutrally categorical titles like *Orchestra* (1976), *Piano* (1977), and the untitled piece under consideration here.

Feldman's interest in the visual arts was reflected in his pioneering use of graphic notation. At a time when he was working through a minimalistic non-serial counterpoint and his own version of Varèse's and Cage's conception of 'organized sound', Feldman devised a system, initially for the *Projection* series (1950–1, I–V) in which pitch range and rhythms were indicated only very loosely. Relative pitch was indicated by small squares or oblongs of varying length (to indicate durations) placed within three tiers of boxes approximating high, medium and low registers. In *Projection I*, for cello, the performer is also instructed whether to play pizzicato (P), with the bow (A, for arco) or in harmonics (a diamond sign), but exact pitch, dynamics and expression are left unspecified. This allows the performer a certain very limited gestural freedom, somewhat like being given a restricted palette and carefully demarcated canvas.

(There is an excellent section on graphic notation in Reginald Smith Brindle's brief but quite demanding survey *The New Music: The Avant-Garde since 1945* (Oxford, second edition 1986), in which he gives examples of graphic scores by Cathy Berberian, Berio, Earle Brown, A. Buonomono, Sylvano Bussotti, Cage, Cornelius Cardew, Franco Donatoni, Roland Kayn, J. Levine, Ligeti, Anestis Logethetis, and Stockhausen (a list that incidentally reflects Smith Brindle's close involvement in the Italian scene); for anyone interested in following contemporary scores there is also a valuable appendix giving new notational symbols and markings.)

In the mid-1950s, Feldman abandoned graphic notation to return to strict specification of sounds. This, though, robbed the music of the plastic quality that he sought, and so with two significant piano pieces from 1957 he returned again to elements of freedom, allowing the music (not the performer!) to determine its own course, both vertically in the pitches and horizontally in the rhythms. The device was also successful for large-scale pieces; *Atlantis* (1958) for seventeen instruments is written to a graph in which each box represents a time unit and the numeral in each box represents the number of notes (or chordal components in the case of harmony instruments) which can be played within the period. Throughout most of his subsequent career he moved more freely between non-determined pitches and strict notation, always concerned with sustaining his definition of music as a 'totally abstract sonic adventure'.

As in *Piano (Three Hands)* and Piece for Four Pianos, the two transitional works from 1957, much of his output related to the co-ordination and synchronization of instruments and instrumental groups. This was handled explicitly in the (strictly notated) orchestral piece *Of Time and the Orchestral Factor* (1969) and in sequences like *Instruments* (1974–9, I–IV), which followed on from *Durations* (1960–1, I–IV) and *Vertical Thoughts* (1963, I–V). Feldman is essentially concerned with the nature and continuance of sound. The main innovation in his work after 1979 has been its extended duration. In a written footnote (1980) to an earlier interview, John Cage described having heard Feldman's ninety-minute String Quartet no. 1 (1979), a work which confirmed his earlier impression that Feldman's music 'continues rather than changes', a very different temporal matrix to that suggested by Elliott Carter's string quartets (q.v.). Cage also describes Feldman's music as 'erotic' as well as tranquil, a characterization that has to be seen in the context of Cage's rather special, non-aggressive interpretation of Eros; and he makes a further point which is relevant to the music's status as a recorded artefact (though not as an 'object') rather than a concert experience: the piece 'would have given the same impression if instead of captive the audience had been in a different architectural situation permitting at any point in time or space exit and entrance, that is, at home'.

In the 1980s, Feldman's scores pushed at the boundaries of performability, not because of their 'difficulty' but because of their sheer length. A strict realization of the Second Quartet (1983) would occupy nearly six hours. At just over seventy minutes, the *Untitled composition* is relatively short, but it immediately establishes the irrelevance of formal boundaries by beginning *in media re* with no harmonic or thematic benchmarks. The implication is that this music pre-dates its own performance and that it scarcely requires a listener to give it meaning or coherence. It persists with a studied sensuousness (which is presumably what Cage means by erotic) and is quite removed in intention from the fragmentary glimpses of ideal form that Nono offers in his string quartet.

The piece is notionally divided into nine movements – of which the middle three are more than ten minutes in length – but these have no structural significance whatever and the divisions seem quite arbitrary. It follows what Feldman described, *à propos* Bunita Marcus, as a 'non-developmental development', a process (in her own words) 'where nothing ... seems to be developing, yet the emotional experience of the piece is moving ahead ... a music where everything is internal and subconscious; where nothing seems to be happening at all, and you are changing inside'. The key to understanding is to focus on the silences rather than the sounds, like looking *away* from a star at dusk.

As with earlier Feldman pieces, it involves a substantial degree of repetition, often of very narrow pitch intervals. An excellent example of this, and of Feldman's ensemble co-ordination is the 1970 piece *Madame Press Died Last Week at Ninety* in which a solo flute repeatedly sounds the 'cuckoo' cadence of a minor third (ornithologists and musicologists will argue about this) over a strangely unresolved background of muttering chords. In the *Untitled composition*, similar devices recur, and the level of repetition invites the necessary and necessarily sudden switch of attention from the actual sounds to the spaces in between, as in one of those black-and-white puzzle pictures of two profiles and/or a vase, or an Escher painting of birds-and-fish in continuous visual rhythm. The cello is played *con sordino* – muted – and with minimal vibrato throughout, and its part has the neutral colourless quality associated with playing in harmonics. Like many contemporary composers, Feldman has been drawn to the viola (the piece that immediately followed *Madame Press* is called *The Viola in My Life*) with its middling pitch-range and slightly vague sonority; that is very much the sound he achieves in the higher cello parts. The piano is not 'prepared' but it plays with a flat, almost muffled sonority. The tempos are very slow, and are often so elaborately coded that they can only be intuited over long periods of time. It is a purely subjective response, but repeated listenings to these very concentrated performances by René Berman and Kees Wieringa suggest a kind of meta-order.

It is probably misleading to see the abandonment of indeterminacy and the recurrence of (implicit) harmony in Feldman's later work as a backward step. There are signs that Feldman's almost trance-like music – particularly those pieces released on CD by the Swiss hat ART label – has acquired a 'New Age' appeal. It would be a mistake to assume that this is a cynical posthumous misrepresentation of Feldman's 'real' intentions. Along with John Cage, few artists worked more consciously to bring about the New Age than Morton Feldman. What Cage identified as erotic in his music is a blissful sensuousness that is very much in keeping with present-day needs, a kind of safe-sex for the ears. The later scores are outwardly less 'adventurous' than the spikier work of the 1950s, but they can still be aesthetically challenging.

Discographical Information

Other Feldman: *Piano (Three Hands)* (1957; Etcetera KTC 2015); *The King of Denmark* (1964; Mode 25); *Rothko Chapel* (1971; New Albion NA039); Crippled Symmetry (1983; hat ART 6080); *For Bunita Marcus* (1985; hat ART CD 6076).

Map references: Earle Brown, Music for Cello and Piano (1954–5; hat ART CD 6101); Anestis Logothetis, *Katarakt* (1978; Thorofon CTH 2003); John Cage, *Etudes boreales* (1978; Etcetera KTC 2016).

Further reading: W. Zimmermann, interview in *Desert Plants: Conversations with 23 American Musicians*, Vancouver, 1976, and [as ed.] *Morton Feldman Essays*, Kerpen, Germany, 1985; C. Gagne and T. Garas, interview in *Soundpieces: Interviews with American Composers*, Metuchen, NJ, 1982.

ELLEN TAAFFE ZWILICH (born 30 April 1939)

Symphony no. 1: Three Movements for Orchestra (1982)

FIRST PERFORMED: New York City, 5 May 1982
SELECTED RECORDING: New World Records NW 336 2
   Indianapolis Symphony Orchestra, conducted by John Nelson
   [with: *Prologue and Variations* (1983); *Celebration* (1984)]
RECORDED: November 1984
DURATION: 17' 21"

Ellen Taaffe Zwilich was just pipped for last place in American *Grove* by two scant lines on 'Zydeco'. She claims priority, though, in other, more significant regards. Zwilich was the first woman ever to receive the Pulitzer Prize in music, awarded in 1983 for her First Symphony. (The present recording also won the Arturo Toscanini Music Critics Award.) She had come to public notice in 1973, when Pierre Boulez premiered her *Symposium* for orchestra at the Juilliard School in New York City, and she was later (1975) the first woman to be awarded a doctorate in composition by that school, a remarkable comment on prevailing trends.

Zwilich grew up in Florida and began her musical studies there, inspired by a meeting with the veteran Hungarian piano virtuoso Ernst von Dohnányi (1877–1960) who was composer-in-residence at the State University at Tallahassee. She had been writing music from the age of ten, including pieces for high school bands, but she has been ruthless with her juvenilia, withdrawing everything written before the age of thirty-two. The earliest pieces to survive are two settings of Herman Hesse – *Einsame Nacht* (1971) and *Im Nebel* (1972) for baritone and also respectively, with piano accompaniment – and though her vocal works have not attracted anything like as much attention as her orchestral scores, she has also written effective settings of Georg Trakl, Sandör Petofi and the American poet A. R. Ammons.

Zwilich trained as a violinist, and though she studied composition at Juilliard under Roger Sessions and Elliott Carter, her education as a composer is deeply marked by her experience as a performer (rounded out by a season working as an usher at Carnegie Hall). In 1969 she married a fellow-violinist Joseph Zwilich (he died prematurely a decade later), and for seven years she worked under Leopold Stokowski in the American Symphony Orchestra. Zwilich has said that the First Symphony 'was written with great affection for the modern orchestra, not only for its indescribable richness and variety of color, but also for the virtuosity and artistry of its players'. She has always been far more concerned with the individual 'voices' and textures of individual instruments within the orchestra than with the mechanical elaboration of abstract structures. Consequently her writing is always clear and uncluttered, carrying across the vivid articulation of chamber pieces like the Sonata in Three Movements (1973–4) for violin and piano (written for her husband), the glorious Clarino Quartet (1977) for four trumpets, and the fine String Trio (1982). The same virtues pervade the Second Symphony (with its prominent cello parts) and the series of concertante works written in the late 1980s, for trombone, and more unusually, bass trombone, flute, and oboe. In all of them, she favours long rather lyrical lines, usually derived from very simple initial ideas or mottos from which all the material develops organically. Use of repetition over a harmonically fixed background recalls elements of American minimalism, which was the currently fashionable style, but probably derives from the work of earlier American symphonists like Roy Harris and her teacher Sessions.

The 1989 Concerto for bass trombone, strings, timpani and cymbals represents perhaps the most developed incorporation of percussion into a large-scale work (she had attempted something similar on a smaller scale five years earlier in the Chamber Concerto) but elements of tuned and unpitched percussion, bell sounds most particularly, have always been an integral part of Zwilich's writing. They are prominent in the First Symphony which opens *sotto voce* with violas, harp and a whisper of cymbal sounds. Virtually all the symphony's material is compressed into the first dozen bars and is based on the interval of a minor third, which is repeated and layered, accelerated and arrested as the cellos and flutes take it up, to create a flexible motto that generates the main *Allegro* section logically but by no means unpredictably. Brass and side-drums step in to reinforce echoes of Shostakovich (though Brahms is also in evidence), and the movement perfectly demonstrates Zwilich's desire to combine 'modern principles of continuous variation', her 'organic' approach, 'with older (but still immensely satisfying) principles, such as melodic recurrence and clearly defined areas of contrast'.

The movement ends very quietly, as it began, and there is an almost imperceptible transition to the slow second, which assigns a highly significant role to the vibraphone and orchestral bells. The basic interval of a third is reiterated, but is converted into a chord, which gives the second movement more of a tonal quality, albeit unconventionally so, than the first. Low strings huddle behind the opening vibraphone sounds, casting intriguingly dark shadows over an essentially celebratory movement. Zwilich does much the same thing in the test-piece *Celebration* (1984), written for the opening of the Circle Theatre, home of the Indianapolis Symphony Orchestra, where these recordings were made, but in the First Symphony the contrast of light and dark is more sophisticated and the affirmative nature of the music more carefully wrought and sought after. She takes a chance by giving the most positive and singing theme to the tuba, evidence of her love of deep brass sounds, and its sonority picks up strong echoes of the bells and the brief punctuation (again Shostakovich-like) of thirds and fourths from the piano.

The final movement is a briskly unconventional rondo, the traditional finale of classical symphonies. Breaking with classical practice, Zwilich progressively transforms the recurrent refrain and dispenses with the usual contrast of keys in the intervening episodes. This gives the movement (which is the shortest of the three) a nervous, harmonically tense quality, underlined by sharp, almost peremptory rattles of percussion, and the ending on big brassy chords is as dramatic and surprising as it is ultimately logical. Zwilich's music is remarkably 'pure' in that it seldom suggests a programme or underlying emotional current. The First Symphony, with its neutral, almost bland, subtitle, is no exception. The piece's interest and unmistakable excitement come from the music itself. It balances modernity and classicism in almost exactly equal proportions, formal rigour with textural vitality and, as a result, has become an established favourite on the American concert scene.

Discographical Information

Other Zwilich: Sonata in Three Movements (1973–4; CRI 621); Chamber Symphony (1979; CRI 621); Symphony no. 2 (1979; First Edition Recordings LCD 002); Double String Quartet, and Concerto for trumpet and five players (both 1984; New World NW 372); Concerto for flute and orchestra (1989; Koch International Classics 3–7142).

Map references: Ernst von Dohnányi, *Variations on a Nursery Song* (1913; Koch Schwann CD 311136); Roy Harris, Symphony no. 3 (1939; Deutsche Grammophon 419780); Roger Sessions, Symphony no. 3 (1957; CRI CD 573); Thea Musgrave, Chamber Concerto no. 2 (1966).

Further reading: T. Page, 'The music of Ellen Taaffe Zwilich', in *New York Times Magazine*, 14 July 1985.

GYÖRGY LIGETI (born 28 May 1923)

Trio for violin, horn and piano: *Hommage à Brahms* (1982)

FIRST PERFORMED: Hamburg, 7 August 1982
SELECTED RECORDINGS: Disques Montaigne 782006
    Andre Cazalet (horn), Guy Comentale (violin), Cyril Huve (piano)
    [with: Johannes Brahms, Trio for violin, horn and piano in E♭ major, op. 40 (1864–5)]
RECORDED: May 1989
DURATION: 24' 14"

A contemporary composer who sets about writing a string quartet presumably must sense – unless he is radical or confident enough to shrug them off – the ghosts of Haydn, Mozart, Beethoven, possibly also Bartók, maybe the more substantial and immediate presence of Elliot Carter or of Brian Ferneyhough standing at his shoulder. The modern symphonist is expected to wonder whether anything has been left to say in that genre in the twentieth century, after Nielsen, Sibelius and Shostakovich. The fact is, though, that both forms have long, clearly enunciated histories and a huge literature of scores. Precisely because of that, the composer has a choice: he might write a work that is palpably 'in the tradition', that consciously draws on or alludes to the works of the masters; or else he might prefer to work more ironically in the interstices, the little, unexamined places left unexplored like patches of virgin woodland amid a snarl and rumble of converging motorways.

But what of a form that has virtually no history, that was created, for the nonce, as late as 1864–5, and that reached an immediate and apparently unsurpassable apotheosis. All forms generate a kind of inertia. Just as a novel about whales or a picture of flayed meat will inevitably set off expectations based on *Moby Dick* or Crucifixion imagery, so too do certain combinations of instruments sustain in their conjoint voices the echo of a masterwork; there is, for instance, a whole modern genre based on the instrumentation of Arnold Schoenberg's *Pierrot lunaire*. However, virtually nothing has been written for horn trio, more properly, for a trio consisting of violin, horn and piano. There is Johannes Brahms's op. 40, written in 1864–5, the Hungarian (and adoptively Austrian) György Ligeti's 'Homage to Brahms', and very little else.

Two masterpieces in an underexploited form, separated by rather more than a century, they make an obvious and attractive concert and record pairing, though the connection between them is not quite as clear-cut as Ligeti's dedication suggests. Even so, it is worth considering them as a pair. The horn occupied an important place in Brahms's sound-world, as witnessed by its dramatic prominence at the climax of the First Symphony, over which he was still agonizing in the mid-1860s. The sound of the horn had a powerful bucolic symbolism for Brahms, and seemed to represent the return of some half-remembered song from long ago. Brahms was, however, conscious that the instrument's most common device – the famous 'horn fifths', so called – had gone past being the brass player's stock-in-trade and was now a rather banal cliché. The tonic–dominant–tonic figure (or minor sixth, perfect fifth, and major third) was easily played on pre-modern horns. Ironically, its most famous appearance was not played on a horn at all, but in Beethoven's op. 81a Piano Sonata, where the three-note figure was marked 'Le-be-wohl' in an echo of the composer's *adieu* to his pupil Archduke Rudolph. Brahms conscientiously avoids using the figure until towards the end of his slow third movement, where he sounds a melancholy farewell in descending 'fifths' to his mother Johanna Brahms, who had recently died.

Though the modern valved horn was available to Brahms, he specified the use of the 'natural' or *Waldhorn* for his op. 40, thus restricting the horn player to the notes of the harmonic scale and such others as could be 'stopped' by the hand inside the bell. This restricted Brahms's harmonic language somewhat, but enhanced the slightly melancholy feel that Brahms sought in the first and third movements and the dour minor-key middle part of the scherzo.

Perhaps the most substantial point of contact between Brahms's work and Ligeti's is one of mood. The Horn Trio was one of the few works Ligeti wrote in a rather fallow period after the completion of his phantasmagorical opera *Le Grand Macabre*, and it has a sombre, almost elegiac quality that is untypical of his earlier output. His health was poor, and the opera had been very largely concerned with the failure of the imagination in the face of death. However, the end of the 1970s also marked a new direction in Ligeti's work, a move away from the huge, static 'sound-clusters' he had deployed in such works as the orchestra piece *Atmosphères* (and even more dramatically in the organ piece *Volumina*, also written in 1961), and away from the deliberately grotesque, parodic approach that culminated in *Le Grand Macabre*. Ligeti's earlier music was rarely concerned with movement; the scandalous *Poème symphonique* for 100 metronomes (1962) was the most extreme case, but even the more conventional *Lontano* (1967) saw Ligeti swamping the harmonic developments that can be traced in the score in a massive (literally massive) criss-crossing of contrapuntal devices. His music always sounds, as the last title hints, as if it is coming from very far away, and in a language that is neither quite familiar nor entirely alien.

That is very much the impact of the Horn Trio. It is a modernist piece by a modernist composer who clearly feels that he has come to the end of the phenomenon we know as modernism. Setting it against Ligeti's earlier output gives the sense that he has stopped in his journey and looked back at his own work, and beyond it, to the music of the recent and more distant past. In so far as it has antecedents, they are the two harpsichord works, *Passacaglia ungherese* and *Hungarian Rock*, written in the immediate aftermath of *Le Grand Macabre*. Typically both pieces represent a trade-off between harmonic and rhythmic movement on the one hand, and stasis on the other, and they are a useful corrective to any suggestion that Ligeti has turned into a neo-conservative *pasticheur*; his use of passacaglia in the final movement is completely individual, and his recent experiments in concertante writing for piano and orchestra (1985–8) and violin and orchestra (1990) demonstrate the complexity of his understanding of genre.

It begins, rather unexpectedly, with a clear echo of the 'Lebewohl' horn figure in an unfamiliar and rather distorted form. The opening movement, marked *Andantino con tenerezza*, has each of the three instruments moving independently, with the horn playing a mysterious, non-tonal melody. Though Ligeti specifies a modern, valved horn, perversely he asks the performer to pass 'uncorrected' those false upper harmonics that would normally be corrected by adjusting hand position within the bell. Though the trio only coincides briefly in the central passage of the opening movement, there is already a much stronger sense of 'development' than in any of Ligeti's earlier work (even if here the most obvious echo is American minimalism, which Legeti examined in the middle movement of the 1976 *Monument–Selbstportrait–Bewegung* for two pianos, with its references to Steve Reich, Terry Riley … and Chopin). The Horn Trio is ferociously fractured, but at the same time reaches toward a moment of almost glacial calm; Ligeti describes the conclusion as 'deep frozen', and it is probably not too fanciful to see in it the fantasy of a sick man to put himself and his music in cryogenic suspension and escape the painful hurly-burly of the late twentieth century.

That confused energy is expressed rather more positively in the vivid scherzo that follows, a wild polymetric dance written 'as if Hungary, Romania, and the entire Balkan peninsula were situated somewhere between Africa and the Caribbean'. Ligeti relocates the interest in folk music he had derived from Bartók squarely into mid-Atlantic, and there is an open, jazzy feel to the horn writing in this movement. The horn disappears at the start of the *Alla marcia* third movement, a relatively conventional ABA structure with considerable dislocation and variation in the closing recapitulation, where the horn-calls reassert themselves; it is typical of the piece, and of Ligeti's work as a whole, that just at the point where it seems most extravagant and *sui generis* he will introduce an explicit echo of conventional practice. Here, perhaps, it is Beethoven rather than Brahms who is invoked. It may be worth reinforcing the point that this 'homage' contains not a single identifiable allusion to Brahms's music, but works by a kind of shuttling of time-scales.

The final movement is by far the most profound, a bleakly philosophical lament that stretches the passacaglia form of the music almost surreally. Again, the descending 'farewell' motif is prominent, leading to an astonishing climax where the piano thunders remorselessly in the lowest register, leaving the horn and violin to communicate hopelessly at their extremes of pitch. It is one of the most powerful moments in all of contemporary music, no less so for being disturbingly ambiguous. It is unmistakably concerned with death. Looking back and forward, it addresses both the music of the past and its listeners in the present, *quasi lontano*, from a point of great philosophical distance.

Discographical Information

Other recordings: Shulte, Purvis, Feinberg (Bridge BCD 9012); Gawriloff, Baumann, Besch (Wergo WER 60100).

Other Ligeti: String Quartet no. 1: *Métamorphoses nocturnes* (1953–4; Deutsche Grammophon 431686); *Atmosphères* (1961; Deutsche Grammophon 429260); *Aventures/Nouvelles aventures* (1963/1965; Wergo WER 60045); *Passacaglia ungherese* and *Hungarian Rock* (1978; Wergo WER 60100).

Map references: Béla Bartók, Sonata for two pianos and percussion (1937; Music & Arts CD 648), String Quartet no. 6 (1939; Collins Classics 11882); Steve Reich, *Piano Phase* (1967; Elektra Nonesuch 79169).

Further reading: P. Griffiths, *György Ligeti*, London, 1983.

SOFIYA GUBAYDULINA (born 24 October 1931)

The Seven Last Words (1982)

FIRST PERFORMED: Moscow, 20 October 1982
SELECTED RECORDING: Melodiya SUCD 10 00109
　　Vladimir Tonkha (cello), Friedrich Lips (*bayan*), Collegium Musicum Chamber Orchestra, conducted by Timur Mynbaev
　　[with: *Rubayat* (1969, baritone, chamber ensemble; texts after Omar Khayyam, Khakani and Hafiz); *Vivente – non vivente* (1969–70, synthesizer)]
RECORDED: 1989 [1979, 1988]
DURATION: 40' 39"

After a brief period of active suppression following the Bolshevik Revolution, the Communist authorities in Russia recognized that they would not be able to stamp out religious worship. Fearing the creation of a radical underground like the early Christian cells, they increasingly turned a blind eye. The situation was very different when it came to the expression of religious ideas in works of art, literature and music. The Estonian composer Arvo Pärt (born 1935), already deemed suspect for his use of serialist techniques and aleatory devices in the early symphonies, was heavily censured by the authorities for the overt statements of religious faith in his choral work *Credo* (1968). As late as 1982, Sofiya Gubaydulina's *The Seven Last Words* received its first performance stripped of all religious references; given the work's internal references to Old Orthodox Church music and to earlier works on the Passion, it seems unlikely that the audience, doubtless well used to coded messages in art, was fooled.

　　Born in the Tartar Soviet Socialist Republic, Gubaydulina has a diverse ethnic and cultural background. Her claim to unite the traditions of East and West (common enough in modern music) has a rather special significance, since she comes of mixed Roman Catholic, Jewish and Orthodox parentage, and her paternal grandfather was a Muslim *iman*. She shares something of the spiritual intensity of her reclusive countrywoman Galina Ustvolskaya (born 1919), whose work is not explicitly liturgical but is, in Ustvolskaya's own words, 'infused with a religious spirit' to such an extent that the very concept of 'chamber music' dissolves in its visionary and universalizing presence. Gubaydulina has the same ability to instil even small-scale instrumental works with enormous passion and intensity. Few, though, have quite the dramatic impact of *The Seven Last Words*.

At the Moscow Conservatory, Gubaydulina was quickly identified as a potential trouble-maker and warned off her 'mistaken route'. She took great comfort when Dmitry Shostakovich, one of her final examiners and a man who knew the price of unorthodoxy, encouraged her to follow just such a path; Shostakovich had also claimed that *he* was influenced by Galina Ustvolskaya, not *vice versa*. After graduating, Gubaydulina worked as an accompanist at the Moscow Theatre Institute and as a house composer at the official Studios for Documentary Films and Animated Cartoons, an apprenticeship very similar to that of Alfred Schnittke in feature movies. She later went on to work at the Electronic Music Studio in Moscow, a period of research which yielded *Vivente – non vivente* (1969–70), written and performed on the ANS synthesizer and still perhaps the most impressive electronic piece by a Russian composer. Gubaydulina's interest in performance was encouraged by her association with the percussionist and instrument collector Mark Pekarski, for whom she wrote the 1972 Music for Harpsichord and Percussion Instruments, subsequently adapted into a vocal piece with orchestra and a text by Marina Tsvetayeva *Hour of the Soul* (1974, 1976–88).

In 1975, she co-founded the improvisation group Astraea with fellow-composers Vyacheslav Artyomov (born 1940) and Viktor Suslin (born 1942), using rare and ethnic instruments from the Caucasus and Central Siberia, and occasionally involving Pekarsky and the gypsy singer Valentina Ponomareva. Astraea's delicately woven textures (which can be heard on a concert recording from Davos in 1990, released on Leo Records) give a fair representation of Gubaydulina's distinctive sound. She has stated that her two guiding stars are Bach and Webern. They come together most explicitly in the opening pages of *Offertorium* (1980), the violin concerto she wrote for Gidon Kremer. Here elements of Bach's 'royal theme' from *The Musical Offering* are subjected first to Webern's distinctive orchestral approach (a version of the technique known as *Klangfarbenmelodie*, in which tone-colour is more significant than pitch) and then sacrificed to a network of delicate improvisational lines that seem to suspend like wisps of incense over the eternal qualities of Slavic chant and church music.

That is the essential opposition in Gubaydulina's music, and it comes as much from her own psychological pull between the aery and the earth-bound, as it does from a stylistic debt to Bach's firm harmonic grasp and Webern's surreally shifting chromaticism. It is a tension that achieves its symbolic apotheosis in the image of the suffering Christ, suspended between earth and heaven, and between agony and triumph. Though the musical language of *The Seven Last Words* is frequently quite 'Western', the emotional tenor is not and is certainly markedly different from that of Gubaydulina's two main models, identically named works by Heinrich Schütz and Joseph Haydn.

There has always been a slight degree of confusion about the title, which refers not literally to Christ's seven last *words*, but to his final utterances, as recorded in the Synoptic Gospels. These are familiar enough: 'Father, forgive them, for they know not what they do', 'Verily, I say unto you, this day thou shalt be with me in paradise', 'Mother, behold thy Son', the anguished 'Eloi, eloi, lamma sabbachtani' ("My God, My God, why hast Thou forsaken me?'), 'I thirst', the death-rattle 'Consummatum est', and the final, almost peaceful 'Father, into Thy hands I commend my spirit'. For a composer of Gubaydulina's temperament and background, the philosophical background to the drama is very different than for Schütz and Haydn. The Eastern (Orthodox) Church has always placed less emphasis on Christ the victim than on Christ the Victor, and Orthodoxy takes a much more dialectical view of the Incarnation, the Crucifixion and the whole question of Christ's divinity. The drama of the Cross is therefore both intensely physical and intensely spiritual, rather than a transcendence of the one by the other, as in the West.

Something of this is apparent in the slightly earlier chamber piece *In croce* (1979), in which organ lines representing incarnated humanity intersect with the spiritual domain, represented by a cello, in a symbolic version of the Crucifixion. Essentially the same device recurs in *The Seven Last Words*, though this time the 'breathing' sounds are conveyed by a solo *bayan*, a button accordion. Gubaydulina had explored its potential in the 1978 solo piece *De profundis*, and had begun to develop non-standard performance techniques for the instrument. These are also evident in the other solo part, where woody textures and harsh, spikey sounds suggest a strong internal contrast to the cello's more typical sound.

Where *The Seven Last Words* most obviously differs from *In croce* is in the addition of a large string section. This is both a musical and a programmatic addition, for the orchestra represents the eternal verities of the Church, communicated in overlapping hymnic phrases which seem to echo down long corridors of time, relatively undisturbed by the troubling drama of the foreground. Gubaydulina quotes directly from Schütz, and more implicitly from Haydn, in the first and last of the seven distinct movements of the partita or suite. The emotional pitch rises steadily to a savage climax before disintegrating into those thin filaments of untempered sound which are characteristic of Gubaydulina's work with Astraea, but which here convey a whole range of associations from the rent veil in the temple to the cyclical nature of time. Gubaydulina was profoundly moved by her first reading of T. S. Eliot's *Four Quartets* (as was Viktor Suslin, see below) and in 1987 wrote an impressive *Hommage* for soprano and octet which incorporated those parts which evoke the mystical dichotomy of the Crucifixion and the eternal, self-renewing nature of its symbolism.

It is as well to remember that *The Seven Last Words* was first presented to Russian audiences as simply *Seven Words* (that is the designation on the Cyrillic half of the Melodiya cover), an act of censorship rendered toothless and irrelevant by its powerfully coded drama. Only the young Ukrainian Alexander Shchetinsky (born 1960) has shown similar strong interest in the *bayan*, and concert performance in the West is likely to be limited by a shortage of expert *bayan* players; Lips is the acknowledged leader in the field and he re-creates the part for the more recent RCA Victor recording, below, which may be preferable purely on the clarity of the sound. Despite some irregularities in recording quality, most seriously a distracting loss of resolution at the highest pitches, where the dramatic intensity is likely to be greatest, the Melodiya version is authentic and very powerful; it is also desirable for the pairing with the synthesizer piece *Vivente – non vivente*, which explores similar philosophical ideas in a more abstract way, and the *Rubayat* after Persian texts which exposes a lighter and more lyrical strand to Gubaydulina's output.

Discographical Information

Other recordings: Milman, Lips, Moscow Virtuosi, Spivakov (RCA Victor Red Seal 09026 604662); Berger, Hussong, Diagonal CO, Rosensteiner (Wergo WER 6263).

Other Gubaydulina: *Rubayat* (1969; Melodiya SUCD 10–00109); *Misterioso* (1977; Melodiya SUCD 10–00491); *De profundis* (1978), *In croce* (1979; Koch Schwann CD 310091); *Offertorium* (1980 [with: *Hommage à T. S. Eliot* (1987)]; Deutsche Grammophon 427336); *The Garden of Joys and Sorrows* (1980; Koch International Classics 3–7055).

Map references: Vyacheslav Artyomov, *A Symphony of Elegies* (1977; Melodiya SUCD 10–00078); Galina Ustvolskaya, Symphony No. 4 *(Prayer)* (1985–7; Etcetera KTC 1170); Viktor Suslin, Sonata for cello and percussion (1983; Koch Schwann CD 310091).

Further reading: J. Lang Zaimont, in *The Musical Woman*, Westport, Connecticut, 1984.

ANNEA LOCKWOOD (born 29 July 1939)

The River Archive: A Sound Map of the Hudson River (1982)

REALIZED: as part of an installation, Hudson River Museum, Yonkers, New York, 1982
SELECTED RECORDING: Lovely Music LCD 2081
    Natural sounds recorded *in situ*, April–December 1982
DURATION: 71' 29"

Describing Annea Lockwood as 'avant-garde' is rather like describing John Paul II as 'a Catholic'; both a truism and a considerable under-statement of the facts. For thirty years, Lockwood has been exploring the boundaries of musical imagination with an impressive resistance to fashion or convention. While in recent years she has begun again to work with regular instruments and with voices, the bulk of her output has been conceptual or electroacoustic. A Violin Concerto (1962), written when she was twenty-three, was a sole concession to classical genre. It suggested a good technical grounding rather than originality, though the chamber settings of texts by Kafka, St John Perse, and Heloïse, Abbess of Paraclete, from the same period, are considerably more impressive.

Born in New Zealand, she transplanted to Europe, studying composi-tion with Peter Racine Fricker in London, electronics under Gottfried Michael Koenig at Cologne and Bilthoven in the early 1960s (this was also the period of Stockhausen's directorship of the hugely influential Cologne Courses for New Music) and the still more *recherché* field of psychoacoustics with Peter Grogono at the University of Southampton. She was strongly drawn to the work of the American avant garde, in particular Cage, but also the accordionist–composer Pauline Oliveros (born 1932), and the members of the Sonic Arts Union (who included Robert Ashley, David Behrman, Alvin Lucier and Robert Mumma); and in 1973, after a brief period as 'non-lecturer' at the Anti-University of London, she emigrated there. At least some of her work from this period now seems unrescuably time-bound – *Bus Trip* (1971) is probably the only musical work to specify 'free love' – and too closely bound up with the knocked-down Situationism of the 'happenings' movement. *Love Field*, a tape piece from 1964, may suggest something similar but it is in fact a threnody to John F. Kennedy, named after the Dallas airfield from which the president began his fatal motorcade to Dealey Plaza.

Lockwood's experiments with ambient sound developed more fully later. In the mid-1960s she created several works for glass objects, light bulbs and fluorescent tubes, bottles and jars, specially made mobiles, which could be tapped, bowed, sometimes even snapped or shattered.

Consciously or not, and certainly some time before she moved to the USA, these experiments tied her into a well-attested American tradition. It may be worth noting that Benjamin Franklin (who represents the pragmatic, technics-obsessed strand of early Americanism) invented the glass harmonium; later experimenters include the maverick instrument-builder Harry Partch (who made his 'Cloud Chamber Bowls' out of Pyrex dishes) and the composer–choreographer–performer Meredith Monk (born 1942), who accompanies vocal performances with rubbed wine glasses. It is characteristic of Lockwood, though, that she should take an existing line of inquiry and stretch it to its limits, or *ad absurdum*. It has been the acceptance of absurdity that has sustained her career.

In that, she is closely allied to John Cage. Taking his cue, Lockwood set about 'permanently preparing' the most canonical of modern instruments, though also the most populist, since she used warped and out of tune upright bar-room models. Her *Piano Transplants* (1968–72) exposed a series of pianos to air, earth, fire and water. Abandonment in the open air created 'natural' effects like those of an Aeolian harp. In other placements, an instrument was buried to form a 'piano garden'; one was semi-submerged in a lake at Amarillo, Texas; while a fourth was burned in London, following a séance to summon up the ghost of Ludwig van Beethoven. The event was scrupulously taped (though there was a certain coyness afterward about what the great man may have dictated from beyond the tomb).

Since the early 1970s, Lockwood has been largely concerned with sound sculpture and with environmental sound. Though she remains an independent, almost isolated, figure, there are some connections between her work and that of Lucia Dlugozewski (authorities disagree on the birthdate) and the 'city portraits' of composer–vocalist Joan LaBarbara (born 1947; married to the electronic composer Morton Subotnick). What distinguishes Lockwood, even to some extent from her original inspiration John Cage, is her insistence on natural sound as an absolute, with its own supra-human logic. *World Rhythms*, a 1975 piece whose title anticipates the 'World Music' movement of the 1980s, requires a large gong to be beaten ritualistically at very slow intervals, the decay of each tone being transformed by the resonance of a multi-tracked ambient tape. This is also related to projects like *Spirit Songs Unfolding* (1977, tapes, slides) and *Conversations with the Ancestors* (1979, mixed media). However, Lockwood's most important single project has been *The River Archive* (1970–), an ambitious attempt to compress actual ambiences into a highly metaphoric aural structure. Lockwood has insisted this is not a 'documentary' project, but an attempt to capture highly specific states of mind and body associated with the 'sonic texture' of particular locations. The first major piece to be derived in this way was *Play the Ganges Backwards One More Time, Sam* (1973–4), but the most important is unquestionably the Hudson River 'sound-map'.

Over a period of several months, Lockwood made *in situ* recordings at various points on the watercourse, from the headwaters at Lake Tear of the Clouds on Mount Marcy, right down to the Hudson Channel at Staten Island, New York City, where it joins the Atlantic. There are fifteen sections, of between three and five minutes in length, deployed in geographical but not chronological sequence. These are edited into a single continuous suite, lasting something over an hour, initially intended for use in a multi-media exposition at the Hudson River Museum in Yonkers. Textures vary according to time of day, season, weather, presence or absence of human activity, and the musicality of the piece derives from a 'complex mesh of rhythms and pitches' beyond the capacity of even the most ambitiously notated piece, and certainly far beyond human performative means.

How does all this differ from so-called New Age tapes and discs of natural sound – waterfalls, rain, the sea – marketed as aids to meditation or relaxation? So careful and specific are Lockwood's selections and editing that it is impossible to leave the piece playing as mere 'background' or ambient sound. Water-drop and wind effects have long been among the most laboured clichés of electronic and ambient music, and it is testimony to Lockwood's highly refined aural sense that she has been able to invest these sounds with textural interest and surface detail without tampering with the recordings in any way. The piece has an almost structural quality, with carefully modulated 'movements', which nonetheless flow into one another almost subliminally and are often only obvious by reference to the timing chart; individual sections are not indexed on the CD. More detailed sounds like birdsong or barge hooters emerge out of a less strongly differentiated background with often startling dramatic impact, while effects like the creaking ropes and spars at the Norris Park marina, Staatsburg, set up rhythmic patterns of considerable subtlety and complexity, certainly far beyond anything likely to be encountered in a notated score. There is, of course, an additional, metaphoric component, as the river 'moves' unchangingly towards the sea, but here too Lockwood avoids cliché or mystical vagueness; there are no contrived climaxes or lyrical diminuendos, nor does the ending merely sound like an arbitrary edit. The only proof of the work is to hear it.

Discographical Information

Other Lockwood: *End* (1970; Sveriges Radio RELP 1102); *World Rhythms* (1975; New Wilderness Audiographics 7704); *Malolo* (1982; Finnadar 90226); *Night and Fog* (1989; Lovely Music LCD 3021).

Map references: John Cage, *In a Landscape* (1948; Chant du Monde LDC 278.1067). François-Bernard Mâche, *Terre de feu* (1963; Candid-Vox CE 31025); Douglas Lilburn, *Soundscape with Lake and River* (1979; Kiwi Pacific SLD 59).

Further reading: A. Lockwood, 'The River Archive', in *Source*, x (1973).

KEVIN VOLANS (born 26 July 1949)

White Man Sleeps (1982, revised 1986)

FIRST PERFORMED: London, 1982; London, 1986
SELECTED RECORDING: Landor CTLCD 111 *Cover Him With Grass*
  1982 version: Robert Hill, Kevin Volans (harpsichords), Margriet Tindemans (viola da gamba), Robyn Schulkowsky (percussion); 1986 version: Smith Quartet: Steven Smith, Clive Hughes (violins), Nic Pendlebury (viola), Sophie Harris (cello)
  [with: *Mbira* (1980), Deborah James, Kevin Volans (harpsichords); Robyn Schulkowsky (rattle); *She who Sleeps with a Small Blanket* (1985) Robyn Schulkowsky (percussion)]
RECORDED: April 1984 [April and July 1989]
DURATION: 22' 18"

Kevin Volans is the first South African composer of the post-Sharpeville generation to make a major impact outside his homeland. Like his compatriot John Joubert (born 1927), who moved to Britain as a student immediately after the war, Volans found it impossible to pursue his compositional interests in South Africa and emigrated to Europe. There, however, the resemblance pretty much ends, though both men have been concerned to some extent with finding a new role for tonality, which from different perspectives each considers too fundamental a phenomenon to subordinate to an organizational ideology like serialism. Though Joubert has frequently suggested that his (mainly vocal) output is deeply marked by his African upbringing and by his reaction to political events in the Republic, his upbringing was almost entirely English and Anglican, and he now seems stylistically as well as personally naturalized; his pieces about the Boer War, based on Hardy's poems (1985), and about the Sharpeville Massacre might just as easily have been written by an historically aware and liberally minded Englishman. Volans has not severed his ties with South Africa, and his main creative motive has been, as he points out in the notes to this recording, 'a reconciliation of African and European aesthetics'. Though it does not include the 1982 tape piece of that name, the compilation *Cover Him with Grass* is dedicated to the philosophical travel writer Bruce Chatwin, who died in 1991. Volans's own artistic odyssey has been no less wide-ranging.

He became aware of the European avant garde during his under-graduate studies. After a year at the University of Aberdeen (whose geographical and intellectual position might be said to mirror in the Northern Hemisphere that of the Witwatersrand in the south), he moved to Cologne and studied music theatre under Mauricio Kagel, piano under Aloys Kontarsky, and composition under Karlheinz Stock-hausen (precociously understudying the master's composition seminars). Volans was instinctively suspicious of the more doctrinaire attitudes of the avant garde, which seemed to reflect a kind of urban rootlessness that elevated attitudinizing above style, abstract ideas above music, and aligned himself with the 'New Simplicity', a tendency named and headed by the Nuremberg composer Walter Zimmermann. Though principally hostile to conceptualism, among its more positive aims were a return to rigorous harmonic organization and a fresh reap-praisal of diatonic music. Zimmermann had begun to record and tran-scribe *lokale Musik* in Bavaria, and Volans, with money from West German Radio, returned to the area round his native Pietermaritzburg to document native forms and make 'soundscape' pieces for broadcast. Similar to David Lumsdaine's (born 1931) later Outback recordings in Australia, these electronic pieces – *Kwazulu Summer Landscape* and the synthesized *Studies in Zulu History* (both 1980) – were, however, unmis-takably research pieces. Two years in the early 1980s as a lecturer at the University of Natal in Durban put him close to the source of South African music. Subsequently Volans has lived in Paris and in Donegal.

He divides his output so far into three main cycles, though the most recent, significantly described as a 'Slow Homecoming', has to be seen as a longer-term synthesis of the first two. These alternately reflect that attempt to 'reconcile' African and European philosophies. The first group, to which the original version of *White Man Sleeps* belongs, was known as 'African Paraphrases' and made direct use of field transcrip-tions from Natal. By the later 1980s, Volans was ready to switch per-spectives. Instead of assimilating African modes to the style and instrumentation of European chamber music (as he had with the first version of *White Man Sleeps*), he began to attempt 'Translations from the European', casting Western art-music forms in an African context. The many separate movements of the Second String Quartet, *Hunting: Gath-ering* (1987), were described as 'expeditions', an interesting choice of ter-minology, suggesting cultural penetration at a different, not necessarily 'higher', level of organization.

The transitional piece is the later, string quartet version of *White Man Sleeps*, originally written for the Kronos Quartet (and sampled on an Elektra Nonesuch recording [9 79163 2]) but played here by the young

British Smith Quartet. This piece, too, involves an interesting shift of terminology. What were 'dances' in the original become, more neutrally, 'movements'. At the time he wrote the first version Volans was, in his own words, 'still very much a Cologne composer', and he grew to consider his treatment 'unacceptably Germanic'. However, there is a lot to be learned about Volans and his music by looking at the earlier piece, precisely because the source material is less 'masked' than in the string quartet version which he clearly now considers a more accurate representation of his intentions.

The title of the piece derives from an episode in traditional *nyanga* panpipe music, where the players set aside their pipes for several cycles and dance to the quiet chirrup of their ankle rattles while the *baas* rests. It is, then, concerned with a moment of suspension. The music's static harmony has been likened to American minimalism, a connection Volans explicitly rejects. 'A Cologne composer', he is still very much under the influence of Stockhausen's pointillistic 'moment-form' (to compress two separate stylistic developments). However, he is also drawn by what he calls the 'existential' qualities of African music, which he then rather paradoxically characterizes as 'a music of *being* not *becoming*', hardly the normal order of priority in existentialist thinking. Volans has rejected the notion of 'style' as a pre-compositional stance, and if he shares anything with the Existentialists it is his belief that the specific decisions that make up a moral or aesthetic act precede its stylistic essence.

His French models are earlier and more explicitly musical. In *White Man Sleeps*, he uses transcriptions of Shona *mbira* music, Tswana and *nyanga* panpipe dances, San bow music and related forms such as Basotho *lesiba* music, but he has scored his original sources for an instrumentation associated with the French baroque. *White Man Sleeps* was intended to complement two earlier pieces, *Matepe* and *Mbira* (both 1980, the latter included on this recording), in which he had attempted to synthesize the plucked sounds of ancient *mbira* by retuning harpsichords to the seven equal steps of the traditional Shona octave. The players improvise on a forty-eight-note pattern which goes through a rather freely construed 'cycle of fifths', which can be repeated as required. The players are so synchronized that each has a rhythmic pattern starting one note later than the other, allowing the music to be experienced either as one accumulative pattern or a combination of three separate patterns in which each is independent and in no way subordinate to the others. He achieves the same effect in the solo percussion piece *She who Sleeps with a Small Blanket*, performed here by its dedicatee Robyn Schulkowsky in a wonderfully tempered live version.

In *White Man Sleeps*, this 'interlocking' was not a feature of the source material, and Volans also added his own 'invented folklore' to explore further the non-Western tuning (he had already decided to add viola da gamba, an instrument fitted with movable frets and so capable of accommodating the new tuning); it was this aspect that he regarded as excessively Europeanized, but *White Man Sleeps* and the subsequent string quartet are pieces which depend very greatly on a rather fugitive shift of cultural perspective. What ultimately separates the two versions is Volans's sense of time and change within time. Though the source materials and the sonority of *White Man Sleeps* are in their different ways unfamiliar, its strict synchronization renders it a far more 'European' work than the string quartet version, but the restoration of equal temperament, instrumental hierarchies and a much more conventional timbral profile gives the later piece a sound and structure which are both part of and a million miles from the classical quartet repertoire; it is an effect often noted in John Cage's String Quartet in Four Parts (1949–50), and it is odd how often Volans's titles, with their pictorial compression, resemble Cage's less neutral ones.

The other main change between the two versions of *White Man Sleeps* is that Volans changed the order of dances or movements for the string quartet, placing the weakest (his view) first, allowing the music to quieten steadily as it advances. There is considerable logic for this (*She Who Sleeps* has the same dynamic, and it is so characteristic of Volans's work that it stands some risk of becoming a manner), but I keep returning to the original version, not just because its sound is so endlessly fascinating, but also because structurally it has a tense, bent-bow feel which is lost in the string quartet. Perhaps because the Smith Quartet, gifted as they are, tend to plod a little in the uneven time-signatures and frozen harmonies of the first and last movements (they sound very much as though they might have somewhere else to go after the piece is finished), the actual performance is less than compelling. The Kronos Quartet, for whom the revision was made, fare better over the same two movements, sounding wholly at ease with the rhythms, and they also give a marvellous account of Volans's Second Quartet *Hunting: Gathering* (1987) on a CD 'single' [Nonesuch 79253].

If revision is a relatively accurate gauge of an artist's intention, then *White Man Sleeps* provides a rarely detailed instance (though he works similar changes with the 1984 *Kneeling Dance*). It catches Volans at the point of switching and reversing cultural polarities. It demonstrates that estrangement is often better achieved by subtle manipulations of normality than by out-and-out oddity. It is, however, fascinating to hear a modern – and modernist – composer exploiting seventeenth- and eighteenth-century instruments without subjecting them to 'postmodern' irony. At the time of writing, Volans's first opera, *The Man who Strode the Wind* (1988–91) had not yet been premiered. Whether it represents a new stage in his 'Slow Homecoming', or another open-ended journeying like one of Bruce Chatwin's, with their endless dance between the strange and familiar, the timeless 'songlines', remains to be seen.

Discographical Information

Other recording: (movements I and V only) Kronos Quartet (Elektra Nonesuch 79163.

Other Volans: *Hunting: Gathering*: String Quartet no. 2 (1987; Nonesuch 79253).

Map references: John Joubert, *The Holy Mountain* (1963; Argo ZRG 5426 LP); Peter Sculthorpe, *Koto Music I* and *II* (1973, 1976; Move MD 3031); Peter Klatzow, Concerto for marimba and string orchestra (1985; Etcetera KTC 1085).

Further reading: K. Volans, *Summer Gardeners: Conversations with Composers*, Durban, 1984; P. Klatzow (ed.), *Composers in South Africa Today*, Cape Town, 1987.

BRIAN FERNEYHOUGH (born 16 January 1943)

Etudes transcendentales (1982–1985)

FIRST PERFORMED: Venice, September 1985
SELECTED RECORDING: Etcetera KTC 1070
   Nieuw Ensemble: Harrie Starreveld (flute), Ernest Rombout (oboe, cor anglais), Martin Derungs (harpsichord), Taco Kooistra (cello), Brenda Mitchell (soprano), conducted by Ed Spanjaard
   [with: *Superscriptio* (1981), Harrie Starreveld (piccolo); *Intermedio alla ciaccona* (1986), Irvine Arditti (violin); *Mnemosyne* (1986), Harrie Starreveld (bass flute), with pre-recorded tape; *La chûte d'Icare* (1988), Armand Angster (obbligato clarinet), with small ensemble]
RECORDED: 1989
DURATION: 27' 37"

Brian Ferneyhough is the guiding spirit of the 'New Complexity', a daunting and somewhat thankless designation at a period in which critics, audiences and a good proportion of his fellow-composers have trampled on the very idea of the avant-garde and elevated a species of populism above the old radical notion of musical progress. Ferneyhough's name has become a byword for 'difficulty', and that has been enough to banish his work to a well-mapped but inaccessible corner of contemporary music. Ferneyhough is an almost perfect example of a prophet with only token honour in his native country, acknowledged only ritually and with a kind of late-Jacobitical indifference (Paul Griffiths catches that exactly when he calls him 'our king over the water'). Though he is still rarely performed in Britain, the Second String Quartet

(1980) has acquired a perverse fame as an act of bracing self-discipline, an intellectual bungee jump rather than a piece of music to be savoured and enjoyed; by 1990 the Arditti String Quartet had given it in concert more than fifty times and recorded it twice [RCA Red Seal RL 70883, Disques Montaigne WDR 789002], astonishing figures for a 'difficult' modern work.

Ferneyhough first moved 'over the water' in 1968, to study under Ton de Leeuw at the Sweelinck Conservatory in Amsterdam. Since then, his professional life has played out on a long arc whose only logic seems to have been equidistance from his native Midlands; the first man, perhaps, to send himself *from* Coventry. Ferneyhough's *curriculum vitae* is an astonishing network of concurrent or overlapping professor-ships – Freiburg, The Hague, more recently San Diego – and of peripa-tetic masterclasses and guest appointments – the inevitable Darmstadt, the Civica Scuola di Musica in Milan, the Musikhogskolan in Stockholm – a feat of geographical co-ordination and organization of time that strongly suggests one of his own scores.

Ferneyhough, of course, speaks the *lingua franca* of advanced modern-ism. In an enlightening interview with Paul Griffiths (which was con-ducted by mail and so virtually amounts to a short autobiographical essay), he sensibly refuses to provide a stylistic definition of 'English-ness' in music. Instead, he argues for a series of mediations which locate musical 'influence' within specific logical boundaries: on the one hand, the realignment of national characteristics through the adoption or imposition ("by *force majeure*') of a powerful individual style, whose 'fin-gerprints and idiosyncrasies' are abstracted and then assimilated to the general culture; on the other, the almost mystical truism that 'any stimulus, however accidental, received in and through the English environment leads to the formation of an English composer'. In the middle, there is a perception which goes to the heart of Ferneyhough's thinking: that it is the musical infrastructure of a country, 'the totality of social institutions that engender, support and live from compositional activity', that conditions a composer's stylistic development. Though he concedes that he was partly formed by just such an infrastructure – the choice of scores to be found in the Coventry City Library, the brass band tradition in which he learned so much about instrumental sonority, the curriculum at the Birmingham School of Music and the Royal Academy of Music in London – it is equally true that he migrated from Britain without having made much professional contact with the main 'regulatory mechanisms'.

This sociological grasp is by no means incidental to Ferneyhough's musical thinking. It goes to the heart of his enormous gifts as a teacher, and his response to Griffith's question about what he learns from class-room activity also applies (with only minor editing) to his music: 'The infinite variety of nuance comprising human personality; flexibility in appreciating and thinking through the insights of others; how to avoid imposing my world-view and musical aesthetic on others; and – not least? – patience?' In thirty words, Ferneyhough provides the clearest possible framework for the defence. At least half of those words, or the associated concepts, directly contradict the blanket indictment that he is guilty of attempting to impose an inflexible intellectual system that obliterates expressive 'personality' and nuance. Knotty as much of the music is, the notion of Ferneyhough as a soulless commissar is palpable nonsense.

Much of it is very directly concerned with boundaries, but with the possibility of expressive freedom within those boundaries. Ferneyhough is, in the strictest sense, a heretic; all of his music is concerned with choice, *haeresis*. To write music is to make repeated, reasoned interventions into the 'unformed mass of creative volition'. His compositional roots are in the 'total serialism' that comes out of Webern, via Edgard Varèse, Karlheinz Stockhausen and Pierre Boulez (the Frenchman's early Sonatina for flute was one of the scores Ferneyhough found in despite of the Coventry Library), but turned in a direction which has been described as 'parametric polyphony' in which not just pitch and melody are counterpointed but all other aspects of the sound as well. Multilayered and immensely detailed, it is premised on the belief that *every* parameter of every separate sound in a piece can be the subject of multiple choices which do not necessarily condition one another; in other words, changing one parameter of a sound, its attack or timbre or intensity, need not mean that other parameters or other sounds in the same relative plane need to be changed in the same way.

These concerns (and, presumably, echos of the Boulez piece) help explain Ferneyhough's long-term attraction to the flute, an instrument with a range of three octaves over middle C and a particularly wide range of possible articulations, involving overblowing, microtonal slides, breath sounds, vocalizing, pad clicks, and so on. Almost all of these are utilized in *Unity Capsule* (1975–6), an extraordinary piece for unaccompanied flute often cited as an instance of Ferneyhough's near-unplayable 'difficulty' but also clear evidence of the enormous pains he takes to bring out the infinite variety of nuance in *instrumental* personality. Flute also plays a central role in the cycle of works that occupied him for much of the early 1980s and to which *Etudes transcendentales* belongs.

Ferneyhough calls the sequence *Carceri d'invenzione* after the eighteenth-century Italian artist Giambattista Piranesi's hallucinatory etchings of 'imaginary prisons'. Their weird, ectopic architecture becomes a metaphor for all the 'regulatory mechanisms' by which music is created and codified, rule-bound and contained, but with a startling expansiveness of inner space. The essential idea has much in common with the French philosopher Michel Foucault's conviction that prisons are the ultimate symbols and agents of social organization; again, it is hard to avoid the conclusion that Ferneyhough is making a more general socio-logical point, however abstractly and obliquely. The main substance of Ferneyhough's cycle lies in a chamber concerto for flute, *Carceri d'inven-zione IIa* (1984), with an associated solo flute piece (*IIb*, 1985), and two other works for similar forces: *I* (1982) for chamber orchestra, and *III* (1986) for eighteen winds and percussion. Around these Ferneyhough has placed a group of smaller-scale works which serve as prologue, epilogue and *intermedii*, and it is into the last category that the *Etudes transcendentales* falls. It is the only vocal piece in the sequence and one of only four vocal scores Ferneyhough had released up to that point.

In his liner-note for the Etcetera recording, Richard Toop describes the piece as a 'composer's diary'. It will be seen at once that it was composed over a longer period of time than the other pieces and that it acts as a kind of notebook (Ferneyhough admits to being an obsessive transcriber of fleeting ideas) in which the main compositional concerns of the sequence are set out. One of the most important of these is the opposition of extremes of sound, moving from the highly codified bat-squeaks of the piccolo in *Superscription* to the submarine sounds of the bass flute and tape sequence in *Mnemosyne*. The concluding piece, named after the Greek goddess of memory, finally makes explicit the group of chords on which the whole sequence has been constructed, but which are 'remembered' by the listener only subliminally.

The group of songs which Ferneyhough sets is closely concerned with the ultimate boundary of death, the point at which existential becoming ceases and lifeless being takes over. Prisons dramatize a paradoxical situation in which human beings are condemned to non-life, inactivity and also silence by stone walls, but may also find within the kind of freedom and transcendence which Jean-Paul Sartre detected in 'Saint' Jean Genet. Ferneyhough indicates this (in no way programmatically) by the opposition of the human voice with the hard, mineral sound of the ensemble. The nine moonstruck and mythological lyrics, written by Ernst Meister and by Ferneyhough's friend Alrun Moll, are marked by similar references and oppositions: 'Diamant berg' in the first song, 'Gold', 'Kratermund' and 'Skarabaën' in the fourth, 'Stalaktiten' in the last; the contrast of 'Rabe und Nachtigall', raven and nightingale in the opening 'Etüden'. In the final song of the sequence, Ferneyhough takes his examination of the relationship between text and music a step further; the singer doubles briefly as a percussionist, more 'hard' sounds, before breaking the last poem down into phonemes, vowels and consonants separately, until finally lapsing into speech. The obvious points of comparison are with Schoenberg's *Pierrot lunaire*, and Boulez's

Le marteau sans maître (1952–4, 1957) which also use permutations of a small ensemble, to convey the same fragmented, multidirectional approach which Ferneyhough had taken to even greater lengths (though with a more consistent instrumental sonority) in the 1967 *Sonatas* for string quartet. The soprano's downward octave swoops, which of course reflect the descending tonality of the sequence as a whole, also more or less explicitly recall the vocal part in Schoenberg's String Quartet no. 2 (1907–8), a work Ferneyhough greatly admires. There are several other musical references. Prominent among them is the Monteverdian *recitativo* of the sixth song, 'Der Grund kann nicht reden', the ground (or earth) cannot speak, with its harpsichord and cello accompaniment, and the fifth, in which Ferneyhough seems to refer to the rhythmic diversity and free polyphony of the Dutch composer Jan Sweelinck (1562–1621), who lent his name to the Englishman's first continental *alma mater*. This carries on in other parts of the sequence as well; for instance, the underwater music of *Mnemosyne* is intended to recall Debussy's prelude *La cathédrale engloutie* (1910).

The title of the present piece, though, invokes an odder parallel. It is also a variant on Franz Liszt's *Douze études d'exécution transcendantes*. Ferneyhough had earlier used the Lisztian title *Funérailles* (1969, revised 1977) for a piece for harp and string septet, and his comments about that work may illuminate what is going on in the *Etudes transcendentales*. It is clear that he intends no direct reference to Liszt's music in either case, though it may be that is setting his scores in opposition to the bravura virtuosity and 'expressiveness' of romantic music, for which he has no appetite whatsoever. There is a more general negative parallel in the sense that Liszt's works are essentially public and expansive, whereas Ferneyhough is concerned to create (as he wrote about *Funérailles*) 'microscopically fastidious textures … [which] prevent the material from breaking out of its essentially claustrophobic conceptual frame'. There is a sense in which all of Ferneyhough's work is a conscious alternative to the opera he shows no disposition to write, 'a rite taking place behind a curtain, or in the far distance'.

Ferneyhough's interest in the 'theatrical superstructure … [and] elaborately circumscribed symbolism of public events' is a central component of his approach to concert music. It is a drama on which he has no intention of raising the curtain. Like his famously impenetrable programme notes, this is not an act of mandarin contempt for his audience. It is an attitude rooted in a very practical and commonsensical understanding of how music is mediated. There is such thing as *the* new music audience; it is 'rather a chaotic mesh of special interests … [in which] one's imagined listener dissolves into a shimmering and impalpable mass of currents', into something, that is, that greatly resembles Ferneyhough's own music. He recognizes that the old intimacies of small concert or participatory chamber audiences no longer exist, that they have been overtaken by the giantism and number fetishism of the Symphony Hall approach and by the 'new reality' of recorded music. Ferneyhough's art is not the product of a detached control freak, but of a new kind of democrat. By seeming to keep us at a distance, Ferneyhough prevents that bland, rather literary identification with music which requires absolutely no understanding of it as music. Locked in our own cultural prisons (and longing for a key, or at least a tonal centre), we fail to hear the tremendous inner spaces, like Piranesi's incongruous rooms, that become available when a composer respects boundaries and makes his choices within them. By seeming to keep the mechanics of the music secret and hermetic, Ferneyhough enforces a new kind of attentive listening which transcends the narrow confines of the self and becomes a new sort of social act.

Discographical Information

Other Ferneyhough: *Funérailles* (1969, rev. 1977; Erato STU 71556); *Transit* (1972–5; Decca Headline HEAD 18); *Unity Capsule* (1975–6; Editions Stil 31085 83); String Quartet no. 2 (1980; Disques Montaigne WDR 789002).

Map references: Arnold Schoenberg, *Pierrot lunaire* (1912; Elektra Nonesuch 79237); Pierre Boulez, *Improvisations sur Mallarmé* (1957; Hungaroton HCD 11385).

Further reading: P. Griffiths, interview in *New Sounds, New Personalities: British Composers of the 1980s*, London, 1985; R. Toop, interview in *Contact*, xxix (1985).

MICHAËL LEVINAS (born 18 April 1949)

La conférence des oiseaux (1985)

FIRST PERFORMED: Paris, 11 and 12 May 1985
SELECTED RECORDING: Ades 14.104 2
  Martine Viard (the Hoopoe and other birds), Michaël Lonsdale (narrator), Daniel Berlioux (the birds), Ensemble l'Itinéraire: Patrice Bocquillon (flutes), Patrice Petitdidier (horn), Philippe Di Betta (saxophones), Didier Agostino (double bass), Fréderique Garnier (harp), Anne Berteletti (piano), Ichiro Nodaíra (synthesizers), Nicolas Piguiet (percussion), Gaston Sylvestre (percussion, sound effects), conducted by Michel Swierczewski
RECORDED: October 1986
DURATION: 53'

Even in his instrumental works, Michaël Levinas turns the concert platform into a 'magic space'. His work is dominated by the sad, interior theatre of *commedia dell'arte*, with its mysterious transformations and masks, its sublimated passions and strange dislocations of personality and language. Before he ever turned to opera, Levinas treated the orchestra itself, or individual instruments like the piano (on which he is also a professional performer) as a dramatic stage where simple representation, or what he calls allegory, can be made to leap the gap into poetry.

The *commedia* enters modern music in Schoenberg's *Pierrot lunaire*, but to a Frenchman of Levinas's generation, its curiously admixed sentiment and violence are just as likely to have come from Marcel Carné's film *Les enfants du Paradis* (1945), whose epic reach is deliberately contained within *trompe l'œil* spaces, or from Samuel Beckett's claustrophobic early plays. Significantly, one of Levinas's first major works was inspired by Beckett's latter-day version of the *commedia* in *Fin de partie* (*Endgame*). *Clov et Hamm* (1973) was premiered at the inaugural concert of the Ensemble l'Itinéraire, which Levinas co-founded with Gérard Grisey (born 1946) and Tristan Murail (born 1947). Trombone and amplified tuba take the roles of Beckett's two old men, shouting, arguing and weeping drunkenly into the instruments in an extended version of Mauricio Kagel's instrumental theatre in *Atem* (1970). The instrumental parts are placed against a background of clattering dustbin sounds inspired by Japanese Noh percussion and a tape of building – 'nail' and 'hammer' – sounds, which together evoke Beckett's dismantled world.

In a later piece, *Les rires du Gilles* (1981), a tiny ensemble mimics the 'laughter' of a cymbal, dropped down a staircase. Amplification and electronics have allowed Levinas to create 'virtual' spaces which dramatically alter the normal relationship of instrument and performer, and of both with the audience. The sheer oddity of spatial relationships and juxtapositions is most obviously derived from the Surrealists. Levinas's first really important work was an accompanied piece for amplified bass flute, *Arsis et Thésis, ou La chanson du souffle* (1971), in which the performer's breath sounds are as important as those produced by the flute. In the two pieces called *Concerto pour un piano-espace* (1976, 1980) Levinas explores the acoustic 'volume' of his own instrument by turning it into a 'grotto' from which the amplified sound of a small ensemble reverberates, associating it with the Villa d'Este caves explored by Liszt and with the great religious buildings of the Renaissance. There is a related study for piano alone (1977), and a duo for piano and harpsichord (also 1977) which examines tiny themes derived from a music-box. In *Reminiscence d'un jardin feerique* (1987) for orchestra, he constructs an imaginary and thoroughly magical acoustic environment, somewhat like Kaija Saariaho's in her *Jardin secret I* and *II* (1984–6), and certainly less disturbingly surreal than that of his own *Ouverture pour une petite fête étrange* (1979) for two orchestras and tape.

Here Levinas mimics the weird irruptions of Piranesi's 'Interior of a Palace' (Piranesi's drawings have also profoundly influenced Brian Ferneyhough), in which a crowd falls down before the lights, smoke and wheeling birds that break in through the palace's ripped-away roof. As in his use of music-box and, in the bass flute piece, of extreme close-up (a filmic device important to Carné), the music works by manipulations of relative scale.

All of the above pieces, except *Arsis et Thésis, Piano-espace* no. 1, *Reminiscence*, and the two piano pieces, can be heard on another Musique Française d'Aujourd'hui CD [Ades 14072–2] which is the ideal introduction to Levinas's work. His most remarkable work to date, though, is the brief opera *Le conférence des oiseaux*. The eldritch bird-calls of *Ouverture* are still there, but the spaces have become immense, metaphysical. The opera is based on the great twelfth-century mystical epic of the Persian Sufi poet Farid Ud-Din Attar. It belongs to the same narrative tradition as Chaucer's later *The Parlement of Foules*, but in Attar's poem the linked narratives are used to unfold the principles and central tenets of Sufism, in which the hermetic strand of Islam – the Way – is expounded in allegorical tales and riddles.

The essential outline of Jean-Claude Carrière's libretto is easily told. The birds of the world are summoned to a meeting by a fanatical priestess in the form of a Hoopoe, a magnificent crested bird that glories in the Latin name *Upupa epops*, and which in Persian mythology bears the holy sign *Bismillah* – 'In the name of the Father' – graven on its beak. In the original poem, it is the other birds who recognize the need for a king. In Carrière's version, their leader initiates the search by expressing misgivings about lives spent in divisive squabbling over a few grains of corn or a tiny patch of territory. Over many years, the Hoopoe has traversed 'un espace immense', and has discovered that the birds already have a king. The Simorg has already made himself known to creation by letting a feather fall in China on which is written 'Seek me out'.

The birds are immediately hesitant, unwilling to abandon their comfortable ways. The Hoopoe tries to talk them round with a parable, but every intended flight is abandoned. Eventually, some few are prepared to undertake the perilous journey. They make their way across parched deserts to the gate of the Simorg, somewhat like the biblical Gehenna. The Simorg's Chamberlain at first refuses them entrance and the Hoopoe apologizes for having misled them. But then the curtains are pulled back and the birds recognize that the Simorg – a hermetic pun on *si* (thirty) *morg* (birds) – is nothing more than a reflection of themselves. The journey is not over, but has just begun. The Way is open, but there is no guide or moral compass.

Previous to *La conférence*, Levinas had only given out one vocal score, the 'chant en escalier' *Voix dans un vaisseau d'Airain* (1977), though he had also adapted songs by Debussy and Berlioz. He was drawn to Attar and to operate out of a conviction that marvellous opera of the sort the poem suggested could represent an idealized extension of his earlier 'allegorical' style. In terms that recall Michael Tippett's insistence that musical setting destroys the verbal music of a poem, Levinas addressed himself to the problematic intersection of speech and pure sound: 'When words are made into song, are they not already the mask or the sublimation of speech; are they not already poetry instead of allegory?' The first striking technical and dramatic detail about *La conférence des oiseaux* is that it consists largely of speech rather than singing. All the parts are taken by just two vocalists with a narrator passing comment from time to time, and taking incidental parts like the Owl and the Chamberlain. Levinas insists that this is not contemporary 'théâtre pauvre', but a version of the *commedia*'s multi-plication and 'disincarnation' of character. Even the central part of the Hoopoe, conceived for the remarkable voice of Martine Viard, is intro-duced by her (in this production, male) partner. During the convoca-tion debate it is she who takes both sides in the argument, where it might have been more obvious dramatically to divide the lines between vocalists.

As in Levinas's earlier scores, a great deal of use is made of electronic reverberation to suggest the immensity of the quest and the vast spaces over which the birds range. In this recording, the narration is by the fine actor Michaël Lonsdale, whose precise, rather priestly intonation is very closely miked and placed in an artificial acoustic that makes him sound as if he is inside the listener's mind; it is he alone who unfolds the final revelation, underlining the inward and mystical nature of the birds' discovery, and following Attar in applying it wholesale to mankind. In contrast to the narrator, Martine Viard's first appearance as the Hoopoe uses a grating, almost hysterical articulation in which words are enunciated while breathing in as well as out. As elsewhere in the score, the vocal delivery deliberately violates the normal patterns and cadences of speech, stretching vowel sounds out till words are vir-tually unintelligible, exaggerating plosives, and swooping wildly from one sound to another. There is, though, little evidence that Levinas has attempted the kind of literal transcription of birdsong for which his teacher Olivier Messiaen is noted; the hoopoe is one of many birds that appears in Messiaen's *Réveil des oiseaux* (1953), the partridge's call figures in *La Transfiguration de Notre-Seigneur Jésus-Christ* (1963–9), and the once-familiar nightingale is ubiquitous, but there is no sign that Messiaen ever took much notice of such notoriously garrulous birds as the Parrot and the Peacock. Levinas's non-specific 'exotic birds' do on occasion seem to make reference in their questioning cries and accompaniments to his teacher's *Oiseaux exotiques* (1955–6), but this may be no more than an incidental homage.

The background music, except during the perilous desert crossing, intrudes only seldom but always with great effect. The opening sequence is a twittering agglomeration of cries as the birds gather. It is never entirely clear, nor does it matter, which sounds are produced instrumentally by the small ensemble, which are miked sound-effects and which are on the accompanying tape. The instrumentalists are frequently asked to play with maximum timbral distortion, as in Levinas's earlier works, though there are also sequences of almost naive simplicity (most audibly from the saxophone), which recall the crude musicianship of comedy troupes and circus bands. Some of the tape effects are deliberately obvious, as when the birds frantically plead with the Chamberlain at the Simorg, or when during the Hoopoe's parable about the king shooting an apple off the head of his favourite slave a speeded-up recording of the 'William Tell' Overture gallops into earshot.

The element of humour is by no means incidental. Like his models, Levinas espouses a sort of dark comedy in which the most violent oppositions are presented with a perverse light-heartedness. It is a combination to which the original stage director Peter Brook was particularly suited, and Brook's production was by all accounts marvellous. However (my constant refrain) *La conférence* also works as a recorded piece, a 'disincarnated' philosophical fantasy which, though unquestionably a one-off, is deeply rooted in Levinas's complex cultural inheritance.

Discographical Information

Other Levinas: *Clov et Hamm* (1973 [with: *Concerto pour un piano espace 2* (1976), *Les rires du Gilles* (1981)]; Adda 14.072).

Map references: Olivier Messiaen, *Oiseaux exotiques* (1955–6; CBS M2K 44762); Pascal Dusapin, *Anacoluthes* (1988; Harmonic Records HAR 8721); Tristan Murail, *Allegories* (1990; Norway Music ALBCD 005).

Further reading: 'Qu'est-ce que l'instrumental?', in *Darmstadter Beitrage*, xviii (1982); A. Darbandi and D. Davis, trans. and intro. to F. Ud-Din Attar, *The Conference of the Birds*, Penguin Classics, 1984.

ISANG YUN (born 17 September 1917)

Symphony no. 3 in One Movement (1985)

FIRST PERFORMED: Berlin, 26 September 1985
SELECTED RECORDING: CPO 999 125 2
  Filharmonia Pomorska, conducted by Takao Ukigaya
  [with: Symphony no. 1 (1983)]
RECORDED: January 1991
DURATION: 23′ 52″

So extraordinary is Isang Yun's life story that anecdote has tended to take the place of serious appreciation and understanding of his music. There is, however, a strong autobiographical thread running through his compositions, particularly the symphonies, and the story of this first Korean composer to make a substantial international impact is worth retelling.

Yun's earliest acknowledged works only began to appear after his fortieth birthday. His youthful production had been seriously constrained by the Japanese occupation and colonization of Korea, and between 1941 and 1943 he was imprisoned for his opposition activities. This set an unfortunate precedent, though the next time Yun was denied his liberty, it was by his fellow-countrymen. In the later 1950s, after a period as a teacher of music, he emigrated to Europe. After periods of composition study in Paris and under Boris Blacher (1903–75) and the musicologist Joseph Rufer (1893–1985), he settled in Berlin. On 17 June 1967, he and his wife were abducted by agents of the South Korean secret police, illegally transported to Seoul, and there arraigned on charges of sedition and treason; the only evidence offered was an artistic visit to North Korea in 1963. Predictably enough, he was found guilty and sentenced to life imprisonment, his wife to three years. Yun's sentence was subsequently commuted to ten years. There were angry representations by the West German government, who properly regarded the original abduction as an act of terrorism. Major musical figures, including Boulez, Stockhausen, and Stravinsky, signed a petition requesting that he be set free, but Yun's release after two years in confinement was prompted less by international pressure than by Korean fears that his health was breaking down irretrievably, thereby handing the West a cultural martyr. The Yuns returned to West Germany and took out citizenship in 1971.

It is clear that the experience of gaol affected Yun profoundly. Early dramatic works like the opera *Der Traum des Liu-Tung* (1965) had been richly coloured and mildly dissonant. He finished a sequel *Die Witwe des Schmetterlings* while in confinement (1968); the two were performed as a diptych in Nuremberg early in 1969 under the portmanteau title *Träume*. His subsequent work was, by contrast, stressed, personal and philosophical, expressing a highly individual world-view which places personal suffering and tragedy within a cosmic framework. This was first made evident in the instrumental piece *Piri* (1971) for oboe or clarinet, whose colour (black) and 'breathing' sounds represent the human condition, precariously poised between earth and heaven. It is also the theme of the profoundly moving Cello Concerto (1976) which was inspired by the sound of a temple gong in the Korean prison, announcing the death of another inmate, and is closely related to the symphonic cycle that Yun began seven years later.

Yun is not a composer of 'Korean music' in any consistent sense. His training in Seoul and in wartime Japan was almost entirely in Western (which effectively meant German) forms, but he quickly became disenchanted with the systematic rigidity of orthodox serialism (the English translation of his teacher Rufer's textbook was *Composition with Twelve Notes Relating Only to One Another*, 1954) and remained suspicious of Cage's 'oriental' indeterminacy. Yun destroyed most of his early works – there are, for instance, no String Quartets nos. 1 and 2 – but the first survivors are still in a bleak, central European idiom that contrasts sharply with his later scores. Though his prison experience was undoubtedly a turning-point in his life, it is clear that he had begun to change direction before 1967.

The Third Quartet and the *Musik für sieben Instrumente* (1959) are both on record (Yun is nothing if not generously recorded) and usefully document his earlier style. In the works that followed he sketched out elements of what he later called 'tone composition', which combines serialist principles with a long-lined melodic approach derived from Korean music, in which individual notes have their own specific character, independent of their harmonic or melodic function. This is evident in the next chamber work after *Musik. Loyang* (1962) is scored for nearly identical forces – flute, oboe, clarinet, bassoon, violin and cello, with harp and four percussion in place of the horn – and it sounds far more individual and expressively coherent. Over the next five years, Yun extended the approach to both instrumental and orchestral scores; *Fluktuationen* (1964) and *Reak* (1966) are in the latter class. *Reak* is a first example of the typologically divided orchestra of the symphonies, with strings, brass and woodwinds all suggesting different states of being and consciousness. Yun uses devices taken from Korean court music: ornamentation, admonitory clapper sounds, and big percussive climaxes. The music also uses pivotal notes which are deployed quasi-melodically, as centres of musical energy, but which give the overall movement of the score a sense of vertical or harmonic coherence. This device reappears in the symphonies.

Conscious of his own fragile health, Yun set himself the task of writing one symphony per year during the middle 1980s. The intention was that the completed cycle would represent a single, multi-faceted work reflecting the composer's experience and philosophical stances. The four-movement First (1983, included on the above record) is an essentially public piece, directly confronting Yun's apocalyptic views on weaponry and environmental attrition. It has a rather editorializing tone, very different from the impacted inwardness of the Cello Concerto, and is marked by logical restatement and illustration, with a peroration which again reflects the climactic moments of a Korean court performance. The Second (1983) is more abstract; largely concerned with timbres, it also introduces some of the symbolic tonal devices that contribute to the central drama of its successor.

The one-movement Third Symphony is the pivotal work of the sequence and the most immediately accessible. Its three-part structure – fast–slow–fast – is constructed so as to enact the central philosophical opposition of heaven and earth, and the human attributes of *yin* and *yang*. As in *Reak*, different orchestral groups convey different aspects of the drama. The strings, which play in a gentle compound time, represent the heavenly realm. The brasses and percussion, assigned a pounding $\frac{4}{4}$, convey the material and subterranean demonic realms, while the woodwinds, given a moderate but complex $\frac{5}{4}$, represent the 'ethical' and intermediate world of the human. (For a very similar symbology, see the entry on Sofiya Gubaydulina's *Seven Last Words*.)

The opening measures interrupt the pure sweep of the strings with an aggressive burst of brass and a questioning response from the woodwinds, establishing in miniature most of the dramatic and harmonic material of the work as a whole. It would be dull to the point of banality merely to juxtapose contrasting philosophical realms, so to give his treatment the dramatic impetus required of symphonic argument, Yun has the opposing realms collide and interpenetrate, with instrumental groups drawing sustenance from other forces; this becomes increasingly antagonistic and urgent in the climactic third section. The central part has a calmer identity as successive winds – bassoon, oboe, horn, flute, clarinet, with violin and trumpet speaking for opposing realms – engage in a debate that sounds like a conclave of the gods in Greek literature, with the same ambiguity of divinity and incarnation.

The final section is by far the most intense and clearly calls upon some of the language devices that appeared in Yun's *Exemplum in memoriam Kwangju* (1981), his response to an earlier Korean parallel to the democratic rising of Tiananmen Square and its suppression. The closing passages conclude a troubled opposition of *yin* and *yang* melodic outlines. The symphony ends with gestures of chastened acceptance from the lowest woodwinds, the bass clarinet and the contrabassoon, set over nudging reminders of the limits of human capability and the immensity of the struggle to come.

Yun's two subsequent symphonies are essentially continuations of the melodic and philosophic implications of the Third. Its immediate successor (1986) is subtitled *Im Dunkeln singen*, and is again transparently autobiographical, suggesting the violent disruption of the composer's life and career by imprisonment and his discovery, while 'singing in the dark', of a new means of expression. The Fifth (1987) is almost as philosophical as the Third, but with a calmness and poetical mysticism reflected in the baritone part, a setting of verses by the German-born Jewish poet Nelly Sachs, who fled to Sweden at the start of the war and there began to study the literature and iconography of the diaspora.

Yun has continued to write. Two fine *Kammerkonzerte* in 1990 demonstrated there was still much music to be written out of his intense personal experience and the philosophical energy (or *ch'i*) that came of suffering. His symphonic cycle, though, is perhaps the most important of the late twentieth century, combining the intense emotion and national identity of Sibelius, the psychological and philosophical complexity of Nielsen, and the ironic balance of public persona and inward, suffering self one associates with Shostakovich.

Discographical Information

Other Yun: String Quartet no. 3 (1959–61; CPO 999 075); *Garak* (1963; Adda 581166); Octet for winds and strings (1978; Adda 581166); *Exemplum in memoriam Kwangju* (1981; CPO 999 047).

Map references: Hwang Byung-ki, *Sup/The Forest* (1963; Arcadia ARC 1996); Paik Byung-dong, *Memorandum auf eine Linie* (1981; Seongeum Sel–RO 197); Kang Sukhi, *Inventio* (1984; RZ LC 8864).

Further reading: H. W. Heister and W.-W. Sparrer, *Der Komponist Isang Yun* [in German], Munich, 1987.

HENRI DUTILLEUX (born 22 January 1916)

L'arbre des songes: Concerto for violin and orchestra (1985)

FIRST PERFORMED: Paris, 5 November 1985
SELECTED RECORDING: CBS MK 42 449
    Isaac Stern (violin); Orchestre National de France, conducted by Lorin Maazel
    [with: Peter Maxwell Davies, Violin Concerto, 1985]
RECORDED: 1987
DURATION: 24' 24"

In the words of his friend Jean Roy, Henri Dutilleux has long been 'resigned to the masterpiece'. In half a century – his first acknowledged work dates from 1941 – he has signed less than fifty pieces, working slowly and patiently, and with great attention to detail. He has written very little vocal or dramatic music, next to none since the early 1950s, and his instrumental music is limited to piano works, a couple of early duos, and the remarkable string quartet *Ainsi la nuit* (1975–6). Dutilleux's particular genius is for orchestral scoring. His earliest acknowledged work was the symphonic suite *Les Hauts de Hurle-Vent* (1941), a programmatic piece inspired by *Wuthering Heights*. Since then, there have been two remarkable symphonies (1951, 1959), the dream-like *Métaboles* (1965), a meditation on Van Gogh's painting *La nuit étoilée* called *Timbres, espace, mouvement* (1978), an equally visionary meditation for strings, cimbalom and percussion called *Mystère de l'instant* (1989) and two concertos. The first, for cello and orchestra, was subtitled *Tout un monde lointain...* (1970); the present work underlines Dutilleux's almost oriental conviction that music partakes of the sacred, of ritual and magic, and that it should be removed from the mechanical and quotidian (or from any notion that music is mere entertainment).

The interlinked themes that determine his aesthetic philosophy are themselves governed by these convictions. Dutilleux sees music in terms of time-and-memory, always considered as a Proustian unity, and the cyclical nature of the natural world. To some extent, his compositions can be considered to work in pairs, each one mirroring and transforming the other. The Piano Sonata and the First Symphony have many structural characteristics in common. The String Quartet, with its appended notes about 'frozen' time (Proust again) somehow anticipates the 'snapshots' of *Mystère de l'instant*. However, a slightly wider angle of vision suggests that all of the work is insistently self-glossing. Though the five-part *Métaboles* is the 'purest' and most abstract of Dutilleux's pieces, exploring instrumental colour and expressivity in a quite schematic, albeit virtuosic, way ('Incantatoire', 'Linéaire', 'Obsessionel', 'Torpide', and 'Flamboyant'), it both anticipates the organic metaphor of *L'arbre des songes* (unity-in-change, the constancy of dream), and acts as a kind of formal bridge between the two symphonies which immediately precede it, and the later concertos.

Though he is a consummate orchestrator, Dutilleux is not naturally a symphonist, lacking the linearity of imagination that discipline requires. With benefit of hindsight, both symphonies have elements of the Bartókian 'concerto for orchestra', while *Métaboles* suggests a debt to the baroque concerto grosso with its multiple soloists and 'replenishing' orchestral parts. Even before attempting a concerto Dutilleux had occasionally used smaller groups within or against the main orchestral line, as in the Second Symphony, significantly nicknamed 'Le double', where a smaller chamber group clusters round the conductor, translating and sometimes contradicting his instructions to the full orchestra behind; he did something similar in the first half of *Timbres, espace, mouvement*, where the higher-pitched strings are rested and the cellos are gathered at the front.

If Dutilleux is not a symphonist in the strict classical or romantic sense, he is certainly not an orthodox concertante writer either, and he recognizes that certain conventions about concerto writing place the contemporary composer in a rather ambiguous position. With that in mind, he has shown no interest in writing bravura showpieces (either for Rostropovich in *Tout un monde lointain*, or for Isaac Stern, who plays here with formidable discipline and understanding) but rather, works in which the soloist and the orchestra interact in a much closer, perhaps more 'organic' way. Dutilleux regards the arbitrary separation of distinct movements as fatal to music's powers of 'enchantment', so he links the four main sections of the piece by three orchestral interludes, each one distinguished (as in *Métaboles*) by a different characteristic. The work's complex unity comes much less from the usual interaction of soloist and orchestra – *concertare* has a subtle etymology, poised between contention, agreement and confluence – but from a group of ringing instruments (vibraphone, celesta, bells, and Dutilleux's favourite cimbalom, a mallet-struck zither originating in Hungary) which adumbrate the soloist's material. Their function is to chime out a sort of non-chronological time, much as in the closing part of *Ainsi la nuit*, which was labelled 'Temps suspendu'. The device of 'doubling' is evident in the use of the cimbalom to underscore the soloist's ideas, but also towards the end of the second interlude, when the violin shadows the single orchestral line, and again during the subsequent slow movement when it is joined by a plaintively anachronistic oboe d'amore.

Dutilleux's music can often sound old-fashioned, even antique, but this is true only episodically. In his early years, he was very drawn to the ideas of Jeune France, a group founded by Olivier Messiaen with André Jolivet (1905–74), Daniel-Lesur (born 1908) and Yves Baudrier (born 1906). Jeune France was dedicated to an authentically French idiom, sensual and poetic, and was opposed to the dry Germanic neo-classicism of the period. Dutilleux is clearly not a conservative in any derogatory sense. He admits to drawing on the Belgian Eugène Ysaÿe (1858–1931), a composer who was also known as 'the world's greatest violinist', as well as on Niccolò Paganini (1782–1840), who also held that title (and probably holds it still), but Dutilleux's use of 'the past' is very much in keeping with French philosophical thought (Proust, Bergson, even Sartre), with a powerful infusion of oriental ideas. The present grows out of the past much as a tree grows, by a cyclical process of growth and decay, with a powerful simplicity of basic structure (historical time) overlaid by a more rapid progression of seasonal time; the insistent multiplication and replacement of lyrical ideas in the Violin Concerto are linked metaphorically to the budding, growth and decay of leaves. The oneiric element is also important. Dutilleux suggests that dream is itself cyclical, curving in and out of chronological time the way that the *cantus firmus* of chiming instruments moves in and out of 'real time' (a concept that has, interestingly enough, become very important in electronic music).

It is important not to confuse Dutilleux's interest in temporality with nostalgia. His approach to time has much in common with that of the great semiologist Roland Barthes in his essay *Camera lucida* (a useful background source for understanding the 'photographic' *Mystère de l'instant*) where he draws a distinction between the idea of the past as 'what is no longer' and that of the past as, more simply and positively, 'what has been'. A further, equally useful, distinction helps explain Dutilleux's shift from literary to visual analogies in his work. Barthes talks about literature's 'Dearth-of-Image' as against photograph's 'Totality-of-Image', and about the way in which many old photographs yield up a single detail, or 'punctum', which is not significant in any associative sense (as was Proust's famous morsel of cake) but simply in itself. Dutilleux's music does not seem to conform to any overall associative structure, as a straightforward tonal composition would, nor does it reduce to mechanical manipulations of a 'note-row', as in a serialist work. Its materials are as self-explanatory or as gnomic as a dream, and they are equally free from the inertia of chronological time. Where Messiaen sought to bring time to an end, Dutilleux attempts to work outside it altogether; consequently, he sounds much 'cooler', much less ripely sensual, much less apocalyptic. A last distinction of Barthes's, that between 'art' and 'magic', probably makes better sense of this music than any other formulation. *L'arbre des songes* is a musical spell, a prophecy in reverse, authenticating the musical past and guaranteeing its future.

Discographical Information

Other Dutilleux: Sonata (1947; Olympia OCD 354); Symphony no. 1 (1951) [with: *Timbres, espace, mouvement, ou La nuit étoilée* (1978)]; Harmonia Mundi 905159); *Tout un monde lointain...* (1970; HMV ASD 3145); *Ainsi la nuit* (1975–6; IMP Masters MCD 17).

Map references: Eugene Ysaÿe, Sonatas for solo violin, op. 27 (1895; Mobile Fidelity MFCD 921); Olivier Messiaen, *Chronochromie* (1959–60; Koch Schwann 311015); Gérard Grisey, *Modulations* 1976–7; Erato STU 71544).

Further reading: H. Dutilleux, 'Musique et creation', in *Revue Contrechamps*, Paris, 1989; C. Glayman, interview in *Entretiens*, Paris, 1991; also R. Barthes, *La chambre clair*, Paris, 1980, trans. by R. Howard as *Camera lucida*, London, 1982.

WITOLD LUTOSŁAWSKI (born 25 January 1913)

Chain 2 (1985)

FIRST PERFORMED: Zurich, 31 January 1986
SELECTED RECORDING: Deutsche Grammophon 423 696 2
  Anne-Sophie Mutter (violin), BBC Symphony Orchestra, conducted by
  Witold Lutosławski
  [with: Lutosławski, Partita (1988), Mutter, with Philip Moll (piano);
  Igor Stravinsky, Concerto in D (1931), Mutter, Philharmonia Orches-
  tra, conducted by Paul Sacher]
RECORDED August 1988
DURATION: 16' 27"

Chain 2 was written for and first performed by the German virtuoso
Anne-Sophie Mutter and one must assume that the composer-conducted
world premiere recording on Deutsche Grammophon authentically
reflects Lutosławski's intentions. But however valuable the pairing with
Stravinsky and Lutosławski's own later Partita may be, it is also worth
looking at at least one of the other available versions. Though the three
pieces entitled *Chain* do share certain compositional devices, there is no
intrinsic connection between them, and nothing substantial is gained
from hearing them as a continuous suite, as they are presented on the
rather shaky Polskie Nagrania version (see below), recorded live at the
1984 and 1986 Warsaw Autumn Festival (an event Lutosławski helped
establish), and in Katowice. Much more interesting, and certainly more
valuable as an introduction to Lutosławski, is the Thorofon Capella set,
also featuring the Polish violinist Krzysztof Jacowicz, which provides
some very useful context in the form of three earlier pieces which illuminate the development of Lutosławski's approach.
  A generation older than his contemporary Krzysztof Penderecki,
Lutosławski's first compositions were neo-classical in style, with a
strong nationalist infusion; and were directly influenced by Karol Szymanowski (1882–1937), the presiding genius of Polish music in the preceding generation. Lutosławski's first major work was the *Symphonic
Variations* (1938), which received its concert premiere on the eve of the
war. He was inducted into the Polish army, but was captured and
briefly held by the Germans; he spent the bulk of the war years giving
clandestine piano recitals in private houses in Warsaw and playing
cabaret songs in a café with his fellow composer Andrzej Panufnik. The
First Symphony was written during this period, very slowly (adverse
circumstances aside, Lutosławski has never been a quick or prolific
writer), and premiered in Katowice in 1948, a dense, atonal work that
promptly fell foul of a fresh outbreak of post-war 'socialist realism'.

The Concerto for Orchestra (1950–4) made use of folk materials, somewhat in the manner of Szymanowski's adaptation of Tatra songs in his influential ballet *Harnasie* (1923–31), but cast (as the Bartókian title suggests) in irregular rhythms, and dramatically modulated tone-colours. Like the bright *Preludia taneczne* (1955), 'dance preludes' orchestrated from a chamber piece, the Concerto was ideologically unimpeachable, but as political restrictions were lifted again in the mid-1950s, Lutosławski returned again to a highly personal vision of atonality, and once again Bartók was the immediate inspiration. *Muzyka zalobna / Funeral Music* (1954–8, included on the Thorofon Capella set) has the simplicity of structure associated with Anton Webern, rather than the more prodigal disposition of material one finds with Arnold Schoenberg or Alban Berg. Its two main movements are built canonically around just two intervals, a rising tritone, and a descending semitone, but what is most fascinating about a piece intended as 'funeral music' for Bartók is the tremendous sophistication of Lutosławski's sense of time. *Funeral Music* saw his first experiments with internal divisions of the orchestra, contrasting strands of music that wove together in a slow, stately polyphony that was to become much more vibrant and adventurous in future.

In 1958, Lutosławski was clearly primed for some new understanding that would take him a step beyond orthodox serialism. The use of extreme *divisi* in the strings (where each plays different pitches rather than playing together in groups) had been used to dramatic effect by Iannis Xenakis in *Metastaseis* (1953–4), which Lutosławski seems to have heard premiered at Donaueschingen in 1955. The real revelation, though, came from further afield. It is difficult to overestimate the impact radio had on the dissemination of new music in post-war Europe, and for special local reasons, particularly in Poland. Also in 1958, Lutosławski caught a broadcast of John Cage's Concerto for piano and orchestra (1957–8), one of his most extensive works and one in which chance – or 'aleatory' – procedures played a significant part.

Lutosławski was, by his own account, profoundly affected by a piece which seemed to conform with his own deeply held convictions about the performance of music. Much has been made – too much, perhaps – of Lutosławski's incorporation of 'limited aleatorics' in his work after the 1960s. The very essence of the term is its first element: *limited*. Though Lutosławski was, one suspects, constitutionally resistant to the idea that every aspect of music could be determined in accordance with system, as in serialism, he was certainly not advocating an abject surrender to chance; one thinks of Cage's own hostility to 'free jazz'. The composer was to retain control of the essential harmonic language, but the point of 'limited aleatorics' was that the internal textures of a piece would be ceded, quite naturally, to the performers. What Lutosławski sought was a middle ground between free improvisation, where the performers generated the total musical environment, and the 'closed' score, where the composer commanded every single musical parameter.

Lutosławski sent the original manuscript of *Gry weneckie/Venetian Games* (1961, see Thorofon Capella recording) to John Cage, with a grateful dedication. It was his first major essay in 'open' writing, and was scored for a chamber orchestra of twenty-nine instruments. Though there is only a rather limited part for solo flute in the third of four short movements, the piece as a whole anticipates the 'aleatory counterpoint' of the Third Symphony (1981–3), a work that reflects the delicate playfulness of *Venetian Games*, and the more venturesome concertante approach of *Chain 2*.

With the three *Chain* pieces, Lutosławski intended, as he explained to Richard Dufallo, to 'create something new in the field of sequences of musical thought'. What the three pieces have in common is that they are constructed in a series of overlapping links. These segments of musical activity would operate independently of one another, and would fall across conventional divisions between movements. This had been anticipated in *Venetian Games* where three independent and undeveloped sections were compressed and 'carnivalized' in a final section that raised the totality of musical information to a new level of understanding. In the third of the *Chain* pieces (1986) the orchestra suggests a sequence of unrelated 'moods' which are combined and transformed into what the composer calls 'multi-moods'.

Chain 2 is somewhat simpler in outline, but the interplay of soloist and orchestra is quite different from that in a classical concerto. Lutosławski describes it as a 'dialogue', but it is not simply a dialogue between the violin and the ensemble. It is also a dialogue between two independent but complementary harmonic 'chains', and it is a dialogue between the two competing (but here again complementary) modern philosophies of composition, the 'open' and the 'closed'. Only the second and fourth movements, marked 'A battuta', are precisely synchronized by the conductor's baton. In the first and third (and a small but significant passage in the fourth movement) an element of strictly controlled chance takes over, allowing the performers to play *ad libitum*; the conductor merely indicates a starting point, leaving the performers to determine their own phrasing of the material.

Since the Third Symphony, Lutosławski's main concern has been not so much the organization of time as such, as it was in *Venetian Games*. Rather, he has been trying to 'release' those harmonic possibilities still inherent in the chromatic scale of twelve notes, even after two generations of serialist dominance, and to 'release' (again!) the latent energy of performers who have been constrained by the requirement to follow first the composer's and then the conductor's every gesture to the letter. The rhetoric of liberation is obviously important to an artist of Lutosławski's nationality and background, but the broader enterprise of reconciling the highly thematic language of serialism with tonality marks him down as the main successor to Igor Stravinsky (which makes the Deutsche Grammophon pairing an effective one), and heir to a line that runs back to Claude Debussy (1862–1918) and Maurice Ravel (1875–1937).

There is a certain irony in the disposition of freedom and constraint in the two main language systems of modern music; where serialism seems to be rule-bound, it is also 'freer' in terms of melody and polyphony than the looser constructions of tonality. This is one of the things that Lutosławski is concerned with in *Chain 2*, and (though Krzysztof Jacowicz performs impressively on his two versions) Anne-Sophie Mutter is an ideal interpreter of the piece. Though she has been associated for much of her career with contemporary music, her background is actually in the romantic repertoire, and her virtuosic approach is well suited to the continuous solo part in *Chain 2*, particularly the rhapsodic opening movement. Where the first three movements of *Venetian Games* were quite independent, in *Chain 2* musical material actually overlaps the division of movements, creating a sort of fractured unity. There is something of the same effect in Elliott Carter's First String Quartet (1951, q.v.) and also in Henri Dutilleux's violin concerto *L'arbre des songes* (1985, q.v.) except that Dutilleux dispenses with movement breaks altogether in favour of a dreamlike continuum, while Lutosławski allows his musical material to 'jump' across apparently arbitrary breaks with the abrupt logic/illogic of dreams.

Lutosławski's orchestra is frequently divided into smaller instrumental groupings, which are used to highlight the emotional coloration of the solo voice, but he also uses the whole orchestra in an ironic echo of the call-and-response of the classical concerto. Its interventions are sometimes quite brutal, as in the hectic second movement, effectively the scherzo, where the 'joke' is sprung with devastating effect; yet these interruptions can also confirm the soloist's resolve, as in the slow third movement where she seems to respond to the slow, almost tragic disintegration of metre with a renewed purpose. That happens again in the forceful final movement, where a huge onslaught of sound reduces her to silence for the first time, only to return with a powerful declaration of independence that transcends all the foregoing material but restores the straightforward emotional assertiveness of the opening movement. Her conclusion anticipates the 'multi-moods' of *Chain 3*, just as the piano cadenza to some extent parallels some aspects of the piano part in Partita (1984, orchestrated 1988 and included in the same recording), one of several works Lutosławski has developed from chamber pieces.

Chain 2 is a dramatic, vibrant piece. It succeeds triumphantly in both its main purpose, setting free the performers (chiefly, but not exclusively, the soloist) from their enslavement to the ringmaster–conductor and demonstrating that the language of tonality still represents, in contemporary parlance, a 'renewable resource', one which has not been exhausted even by the long history of classical writing.

Discographical Information

Other recordings: (see text): Jackowicz, Filharmonia Pomorska, Ukigaya (Thorofon Capella CTH 2041); Jacowicz, National PO, Kord (Polskie Nagrania PNCD 04).

Other Lutosławski: *Variations on a Theme of Paganini* (1941; Koch Schwann CD 310 088); Concerto for Orchestra (1950–4; London 425694); *Musique funèbre: in memoriam Béla Bartók* (1955; London 430844); *Les Espaces du sommeil* (1975; Philips 416387); *Mi-parti* (1976); *Chain 3* (1986; Deutsche Grammophon 431664).

Map references: Witold Szymanowski, Violin Concerto no. 2 (1932–3; Marco Polo 8.223291); Maurice Ravel, *Tzigane* (1924; Sony Classical M3K 45952); Andrzej Panufnik, *Sinfonia sacra* (1963; Elektra Nonesuch 79228); John Cage, Concerto for piano and orchestra (1957–8; Etcetera KTC 3002); Henri Dutilleux, *L'arbre des songes*: Concerto for violin and orchestra (1985).

Further reading: B. A. Varga, *Witold Lutosławski Profile*, London, 1976; S. Stucky, *Lutosławski and His Music*, Cambridge, 1981; R. Dufallo, interview in *Trackings*, Oxford, 1989.

KAIJA SAARIAHO (born 14 October 1952)

Lichtbogen (1985–1986)

FIRST PERFORMED: Paris, 13 May 1986
SELECTED RECORDING: Finlandia FACD 361
    Endymion Ensemble, conducted by John Whitfield
    [with: Magnus Lindberg, *...de Tartuffe, je crois* (1981, piano, string quartet); Jouni Kaipainen, Trio I, op. 21 (1983, clarinet, cello, piano); Eero Hämeenniemi, *Efisaes* (1983, piano, twelve solo strings)]
RECORDED: 1987–8
DURATION: 19' 27"

I spent 1979 as a visiting lecturer at the University of Tromsø in the north of Norway. One Friday evening in mid-October, near the start of the *mørketid*, the day-long darks that everybody forgets to mention when they rave about the Midnight Sun, I left the teaching block in the centre of town and walked home. I had been giving a class on the English Metaphysical poets. Donne had been sticky ("Merk bot dis flay'), Herbert an uphill struggle, Crashaw obviously impenetrable. The only one of the 'set' poems that had coaxed a glimmer of enthusiasm was Henry Vaughan: 'I saw Eternity the other Night'. Tromsø stands on an island; my flat was in Hungeren, on the mainland. The streetlights thinned out past the Ice Cathedral and the road darkened. Primed with Henry Vaughan, a couple of half-litres of øl and the Hans Christian Andersen quality of the first snow (it is, I have to say, the kind of place that can support an Ice Cathedral without a blush of incongruity), I turned round at my front door to see the Northern Lights billowing silently back and forth across nearly 180° of night sky.

It is routine, of course, to comment on the silence. 'Everybody says that', everybody said. But it seemed essential that one day I would hear music that conveyed something of that weird spectral harmony, with its sudden transitions and leaping shifts of intensity. In January 1989, on a torrentially wet night in London, I heard Lontano give a concert of Kaija Saariaho's music at St John's, Smith Square. Not long afterward, I found the Endymion Ensemble's recording of *Lichtbogen*, Saariaho's hymn to the northern 'arches of light'.

Though her work frequently resembles some upper-atmospheric phenomenon of late modernism, it manages to communicate very directly and with great humanity, for all its cosmological references and adventurous use of computers and live electronics. Writing about Saariaho's exquisite *Jardin secret I* (1984–5), a computer-generated work for tape, her compatriot Risto Nieminen defined its essential quality as 'orchestration in miniature'. In places it recalls the extreme refinement of Webern, in whose work the pitch-intervals of the note-row have almost become less important than the timbres and rhythmic codes of much smaller sound-groups. In place of harmonic sequences, there are tiny scintillas of melody, almost prismatic in their variety and speed of variation. In the orchestral *Verblendungen* (1982–4), acknowledged as her first major score, Saariaho herself introduces the metaphor and develops a range of references to light and dark which is not just metaphoric (joy, birth, dazzlement, death, shadow, blindness) but also functional. Remarkably, *Jardin secret I* has virtually all the richness of the earlier orchestral piece; the distribution of loudspeakers and musical events places the listener in the midst of a mysterious but never entirely anomalous space, an aural experience somewhat akin to recent experiments with 'virtual reality'. Saariaho has written two further works with the same title or subtitle – *Jardin secret II* (1984–6) is for harpsichord and tape, *Nymphea (Jardin secret III)* (1987) is for string quartet and live electronics – and it is in this direction that her work seems to be developing, extending the performance resources and sonority of existing instruments rather than leaving them entirely behind.

This is evident in *Petals* (1988), in which the cello may play untreated or with live electronics, but her experimentation in this field had begun as early as 1982 (the year of her first visit to IRCAM) with *Laconisme de l'aile* in which a solo flute is softly ring-modulated through a circle of microphones. Even very early work like the student piece *Bruden / The Bride* (1977) for soprano, two flutes and percussion, and later essays like the related ... *sah den Vogeln* (1981) for soprano, flute, oboe, cello and prepared piano, or *Im Traume* (1980) for cello and piano are already concerned with the plasticity of sound, the desire to make it move with the almost instantaneous transitions and transformations. *Lichtbogen's* immediate successor *Io* (1986–7) is built on the sonorities of bass and bass flute, but here the transformations are more conventionally developmental and linear. The title's associations of divine rape (Jupiter visiting Io in the form of a cloud) and, by extension, of a small astronomical satellite attending a huge, gaseous planet (like Jupiter's moon Io) are never allowed to become programmatic, but they cast some light on Saariaho's intentions.

Like other young Finnish composers growing up within the powerful magnetic field of Jean Sibelius, she has been forced to define herself relative to his increasingly nebulous influence before breaking free of it. In *Verblendungen*, she almost seems to echo Sibelius's slow transformations of tempo and distinctive use of repetition and scalar themes. These had more in common than might appear with the serialist technique she studied first under Paavo Heininen (born 1938) and then at the Hochschule in Freiburg under Klaus Huber and Brian Ferneyhough, but their more radical significance has been lost or overlooked by the late 1960s. Together with Eero Hämeenniemi (born 1951) and the rather younger Jouni Kaipainen (born 1956) and Magnus Lindberg (born 1958), she formed Korvat auki, the Open Ears Group, in a bid to shake Finnish music free of its increasingly narrow provincialism. Though they began their studies under senior Finnish composers like Heininen, Aulis Sallinen and Einojuhani Rautavaara, the other members of the group followed Saariaho abroad to make contact with the central European avant garde.

Of all the group, she has nonetheless probably remained closest to her native roots. She is an heir to Sibelius, developing his language rather than merely reacting against it. Her sound palette is much smaller and purer, her orchestration increasingly miniaturized to the point where it enters the inner space of sub-harmonic and microtonal information. In overall impact, she is closer to Henri Dutilleux, whose exact balance of rapture and rigour she seems to share; she certainly never writes as sloppily as Sibelius sometimes did. If her works have a dreamlike quality, they are dreams which have a 'grammar'; the terminology is her own, a 1989 vocal piece, but it has been pounced on enthusiastically by the critics.

I have selected the Endymion Ensemble recording of *Lichtbogen* because it sets Saariaho in the context of the Korvat auki composers rather than because it seems to me a better performance of the work. It is on the face of it rather remarkable that a composer under forty should have the same piece recorded twice within a year for the same label. The Avanti Chamber Orchestra give a strong reading on Finlandia FACD 374, but it seems to me slightly time-bound in the sense of being more mechanically pulsed – it is also briefer by some three and a half minutes – and thus less responsive to a score which is at least in part about the suspension of time.

Lichtbogen was Saariaho's first successful attempt to compose instrumental music using a computer. Sustained string tones with gradually increasing bow weight had been a signature device since *Verblendungen*. Here she subjects cello harmonics to electronic analysis producing a graphic representation of the 'vertical' aspects of the music. The rhythmic patterns were generated in accordance with a computer program devised by the composer. Rhythmic states metamorphose without abrupt breaks but according to no immediately discernible logic, and the impression of the music is of tremendous inward movement at the micro level, but absolute stillness overall. One might almost be listening to the internal vibrations of a crystal, indiscernible from the hard exterior; or, of course, one might be hearing the silent music of the aurora borealis, with its leaping, rolling waves of colour and timeless calm. Clock time only reasserts itself towards the end, with a steady pulse on the glockenspiel.

The instrumental score is for percussion, piano, harp, string quintet with double bass, with the flute taking the principle role, as so often in Saariaho's work. Towards the end of the piece the flautist, whose sounds are progressively distorted, intones mysterious phonemes which are actually drawn from a French version of Henry Vaughan's poem 'The World': 'J'ai vu l'éternité l'autre nuit'. My other reason for preferring John Whitfield's reading of *Lichtbogen* is his handling of these passages (I say his because I cannot gauge the extent of Saariaho's involvement), which are given a dry, aspirated sound, as far as can be from verbal language, and in sharp contrast to the robot-voiced sci-fi effects on the Avanti Chamber Orchestra version. These seem to me to introduce a false note.

Saariaho might be described as a metaphysical composer. Her aesthetic is mysterious, cosmic, beyond the reach of everyday logic, but she also has an ability to yoke very heterogeneous ideas together without violence and to make aural poetry out of prosaically simple materials.

Discographical Information

Other recording: Avanti Chamber Orchestra, Saraste (Finlandia FACD 374).

Other Saariaho: *No and not* (1979; Ondine ODE 796); *Petals* (1988; Neuma 450–73); ... *à la fumée* (1990; Ondine ODE 804).

Map references: Brian Ferneyhough, *Cassandra's Dream* (1970; Neuma 450–72); Magnus Lindberg, *Kinetics* (1988–9; Ondine ODE 784); Cecile Øre, *Calliope* (1989; Norway Music BD 7021).

Further reading: K. Saariaho, 'Shaping a Compositional Network with Computers', in *Proceedings of the 1984, International Computer Music Conference, Paris*, Berkeley, Computer Music Association, 1985; R. Nieminen, 'A Portrait of Kaija Saariaho', in *Nordic Sounds*, 1986; L. Otonski, 'The Grammar of Dreams', in *Finnish Music Quarterly*, iii (autumn 1989).

GE GAN-RU (born 8 July 1954)

Gu Yue (Ancient Music) (1986)

FIRST PERFORMED: New York City, 1986
SELECTED RECORDING: Mode 15 – *Sonic Encounters: The New Piano*
   Margaret Leng Tan (piano)
   [with: John Cage, *Primitive*, and *In the Name of the Holocaust* (both 1942); Alan Hovhaness, *Orbit no. 2* op. 102 no. 2, and *Jhala* op. 103 (both 1952); George Crumb, Five Pieces for piano (1962); Somei Satoh, *Cosmic Womb* (1975)]
RECORDED: 1988
DURATION: 18' 25"

Up until the mid-1970s, Communist China was more or less isolated from the major developments of twentieth-century European music. During Mao's Great Proletarian Cultural Revolution, it had been virtually impossible to hear or study Western music, a situation roughly analogous to that in Japan in the period of extreme nationalism before the Second World War. For most Chinese music students, the first significant instance of cultural thaw was a lecture series given at the Beijing Conservatory in 1979 by the British composer Alexander Goehr, which represented their first exposure to contemporary compositional techniques. Meanwhile in Shanghai, the most individual and enterprising member of the nascent Chinese avant garde had already made considerable strides forward, and was to some extent spared the tiresome reinvention of the wheel that was the undeserved fate of his contemporaries.

Ge Gan-ru had managed to study Western music secretly during the Cultural Revolution, and when his home town conservatory reopened in 1974, he enrolled as a violin student, writing a relatively orthodox Violin Concerto (1976) before transferring to the composition department, where he was given an assistant professorship. Disappointed by his rate of progress, he resolved to leave China, and in 1983 emigrated to the United States to study with Chou Wen-chung (born 1923) at Columbia University; two years later his compatriot Julian Jing-Jun Yu (born 1957) also left to make his home in Australia, a fact that further underlines a persistent thinness of support for new music even in the 'new' China. Ge arrived in New York without possessions or resources; but with the same characteristic application that had seen him through the confused and often brutal aftermath of the Cultural Revolution, he began to make a living writing music for film and television productions on Eastern themes, and gaining a reputation for his concert scores, which were taken up by such fashionable opinion-leaders as the Kronos Quartet.

Though John Cage is often credited with the first successful musical synthesis of East and West, Chou Wen-chung was the first Chinese composer to make the journey in the opposite direction, arriving in the United States immediately after the war, exasperated by the 'quiescence' of Eastern music, but also convinced that it represented the passive, *yin* half of a new global synthesis. This is very much the context for Ge's experiments, though he has gone even further than his teacher in assimilating the essential qualities of Chinese music to Western technique and (in most cases) instrumentation. His much-raised 1990 score for the PBS documentary *Tang Dynasty* used ancient instruments, and he has written two large scale pieces for *koto* and orchestra, the first of which, *Questioning the Sky* (1987), used Chinese instruments, the later, *Gu Zheng Concerto* (1988), conventional Western forces.

Largely, though, Ge has concentrated on devising new means of articulation and sound production for European instruments. Though his only major repertoire piece to date has been *Wu* (1986) for piano and chamber orchestra, premiered by the Pittsburgh New Music Ensemble and later rescored for full orchestra, he has been more innovative when working with a much narrower instrumental palette. His first genuinely important work was the solo cello piece *Yi Feng* (1982) which dispenses with melody and considerably downplays pitch relationships in order to concentrate on microtonal and timbral gestures, glissandos, variable tempos and other devices not normally integral to Western music. These sound still more alien when played on a retuned and amplified instrument and combined with folkish simplicity of expression.

Gu Yue was commissioned and written for Margaret Leng Tan, and takes its place very logically at the apex of a four-decade survey of 'extended' piano technique, following premiere recordings of two Cage pieces for prepared piano, 'Eastern' works by Hovhaness (born 1911) and Crumb, and an electroacoustic piece by the Japanese Somei Satoh (born 1947). It is, perhaps, Ge's most obviously traditional work to date, ironically so since it achieves this effect by mimicking ancient Chinese instruments – one per movement – by radical manipulation of the most orthodox of Western instruments. Much of the music is produced inside the piano, by direct contact with the strings. The opening movement imitates the sonorities of the gong and has a mysterious, ceremonial quality that is immediately reminiscent of some of Cage's earliest pages, but also the rapt attentiveness of Takemitsu's *Uninterrupted Rest* (1952, 1959) and *For Away* (1973). The two middle movements have a more restless quality and a highly variable timbre, characteristics of the instrument they are imitating: the *qin* or seven-stringed zither, and the *pipa*, a lute-like instrument that somewhat resembles the Japanese *biwa* made familiar by Takemitsu's music.

Heard – as they are intended to be on this recording – in the context of Cage's and Crumb's pianistic experiments, they are both very similar (to the extent that 'prepared piano' is no longer so alien a sound) and utterly new, thus reflecting the irony of Ge's title: *Ancient Music*. The final and longest movement uses the piano as a drum; it marks time for a dark processional that seems to spiral slowly inwards until the deceptively simple rhythmic contour collapses on to itself. Though almost naive, the effect is much subtler than all the criss-crossing variation of American minimalist music; and it brings the piece to a suitably unresolved conclusion that contains unmistakable echoes of the opening gong-music, thus implying a constantly renewable cycle of sonorities. From a composer of Ge's relative youth, it is an astonishingly restrained and mature performance; and Tan brings typical concentration and commitment to her interpretation, as she does elsewhere to a much admired album of Satoh's music [*Litania*, New Albion NA 008].

Critics searching for the Next Big Thing have been quick to spot the Pacific rim as a likely location, and there is only a certain small irony in the fact that Ge, unquestionably the most gifted of the younger generation of Asian composers, should have made his home in the United States. He is, however, still under forty and may yet find the occasion to return to his birthplace.

Discographical Information

Other Ge: no others listed at press time.

Map references: John Cage, *Bacchanale* (1938; Doron DRC 3002); Tōru Takemitsu, *Uninterrupted Rest* (1952–9) [with: *For Away* (1973)]; Decca HEAD 4); Somei Satoh, *A Gate into the Stars* (1962; New Albion NA 008); George Crumb, *Makrokosmos I, II* (1972–3; Centaur CRC 2050/2080).

GEORGE BENJAMIN (born 31 January 1960)

Antara (1987, revised 1988–1989)

FIRST PERFORMED: Paris 1987; revised version first performed London,
 May 1989
SELECTED RECORDING: Nimbus NI 5167
 London Sinfonietta, conducted by George Benjamin
 [with: Pierre Boulez, *Dérive* (1984); *Mémoriale* (1985), Sebastian Bell
 (flute); Jonathan Harvey, *Song Offerings* (1985), Penelope Walmsley-
 Clark]
RECORDED: 9 May 1989
DURATION: 19' 44"

During the summer of 1984, George Benjamin was studying at IRCAM,
Pierre Boulez's Institut de Recherche et Coordination Acoustique-
Musique, in Paris. IRCAM is located in the basement of the controversial Centre Pompidou, a post-modern 'inside-out' building in the
place Saint-Merri where buskers like to gather. At the end of each day,
Benjamin emerged from the hyper-modern atmosphere of Boulez's 'sub-
marine' studios below street level and encountered a group of Peruvian
exiles playing folk music on ancient panpipes known as *antara*. The
juxtaposition of prehistoric and futuristic musics struck Benjamin
forcibly, and when he was commissioned to compose a piece to mark
IRCAM's first decade of research three years later, he returned to the
idea.

Benjamin's reputation took some time to recover from two critical
knee-jerks: his 'precocity' as a composer; and his association with
Olivier Messiaen, who had given him lessons in his teens. In fact,
Benjamin has not been at all prolific, the characteristic usually associated with precocity, and Messiaen's 'influence' on him has been
limited to some highly technical harmonic devices in his first completed
works; at least some of these could be traced back further to Claude
Debussy, or attributed to Benjamin's own dogged examination of tonal
colour. Messiaen was probably more important to Benjamin for the
encouragement and sponsorship he offered a young musician from a
country where new compositional talent was not always adequately
fostered.

Like Messiaen, Benjamin has shown little sustained interest in
chamber or instrumental music; since the early Piano Sonata (1977–8),
which draws on Messiaen's keyboard writing, he has completed only
one significant piece for small ensemble – Octet (1978) – one piece for
solo flute – *Flight* (1979) – a duo for cello and piano (1980), and a
handful of piano works. His gift is for orchestral writing of a highly

evolved sort and these smaller-scale works inevitably sound like preparatory exercises. Benjamin first came to wider public attention in 1980
when *Ringed by the Flat Horizon* made him the youngest composer ever
to have a piece performed at the London Proms; he was twenty. The
work was inspired by some lines in T. S. Eliot's *The Waste Land* and by
a photograph of lightning striking in the desert. It shares the same
dramatic quality and thematic thrust as its successor *A Mind of Winter*
(1981). This, too, was inspired by a literary text – Wallace Stevens's
poem 'The Snow Man' – and it remains Benjamin's only vocal setting to
date. Though less climactic than its predecessor, with its vertical chordal
flashes, it concerns the transformative power of the imagination, the
'mind of winter', over material with which it is identical in substance,
as a snowman is to the surrounding snow. The vocal line is not distinct
from the instrumental accompaniment, but emerges out of it. This is an
important indication of the way in which his work was to develop, and
it represents a first symptom of impatience with a music substantially
rooted in chords.

His next important work, however, marked the pinnacle of his
chordal approach. *At First Light* for chamber orchestra (1982) has been
Benjamin's most popular work, both in concert and on record. For the
last time, he draws on an external 'text', in this case J. M. W. Turner's
painting 'Norham Castle: sunrise' whose radiant colour and post-
modern lack of 'finish' or resolution are both reflected in Benjamin's
tonally bright but carefully ambiguous orchestration of chords; just as
the voice gave shape to the music in *A Mind of Winter* so in *At First
Light* an oboe registers a solid musical shape and the Turnerian
glimmer.

At this point, Benjamin's work changes quite markedly and his rate
of production (never hasty) slows up a good deal. The logic of his
musical language inevitably led him to explore microtones – non-
Western subdivisions of the chromatic scale – and there followed a relatively fallow period during which he studied microtonal language (and
the technology available to give it substance) at IRCAM. Benjamin had
never been drawn to electronic music, simply disliking the sound.
However, the working atmosphere and prevailing ethos at IRCAM was
resolutely plugged-in and he began to experiment with a pair of electronic keyboards tuned to quarter-tones. The tape piece *Panorama* (1985) is
unremarkable, even conventional; but *Antara*, completed two years
later, represents a new departure.

Dedicated to the French composer and ondes martenot player Tristan
Murail and his wife, *Antara* reflects Murail's efforts to give electroacoustic the same melodic, rhythmic and rapid contours as virtuosic
instrumental music. Whereas in much contemporary music microtones
add no more than a few post-modernist spangles to a relatively conven-

tional structure, they are part of the substance of *Antara*. The piece is scored for two flutes (doubling piccolos), trombone, bass trombone, two percussion, three violins, two violas, two cellos, double bass and two keyboards hooked up to the massively powerful 4X computer at IRCAM. The 4X allowed Benjamin to compose both microtonally and virtuosically. Intrigued by the sound of the native panpipes – as Louis Andriessen had been in *Hoketus* (1977) – and by the ironic juxtapositions of the place Saint-Merri, Benjamin used the 4X to devise a kind of 'meta-ensemble', synthesized, but increasingly inseparable in the score from the 'acoustic' piccolos and flutes, just as the two percussionists' bells and anvils blend seamlessly with electronically manipulated resonances from the metal pipes which entwine the Centre Pompidou.

For all its technological sophistication, *Antara* is a resolutely 'classical' work, though it draws more on medieval polyphonic procedures than on nineteenth-century orchestral language. An opening 'panpipe' solo generates the first of the work's microtonal but still clearly articulated themes, one which is recapitulated just before the brilliant, dramatic climax and shimmering coda. A second melody 'hockets' between the two flutes (a 'hiccuping' effect which was much used in medieval music, where a line of melody was fragmented, sometimes into single notes, and assigned alternately to two or more performers: Andriessen exploits the same device and it re-emerges in Benjamin's own later *Cascade* of 1990, subsequently absorbed into a larger work) before brass and percussion abruptly silence it. It is tempting to read some programmatic intention into this interruption for it gives way to a long central section in which ancient and modern musics seem to dance together in distinct but complex lines, again dominated by the flutes, before disintegrating in a tremendous thunder of sound from the anvils and from the keyboard-processed sound of the Centre Pompidou's external pipes. There are climaxes reminiscent of *Ringed by the Flat Horizon* and a similar coda in the strings, but *Antara* is absolutely distinctive and original, and redirects Benjamin's attention away from nineteenth-century chordal writing towards a more polyphonic style that combines medieval and non-Western procedures.

His subsequent work has taken him even further beyond the chordal and allusive style established in *Ringed by the Flat Horizon*. Benjamin insists that *Cascade* refers not to any actual physical waterfall, but to the way in which the work is constructed and perceived. It is interesting nonetheless that it should be a title with some resonance in English romanticism, rather than something from the natural sciences. As in a waterfall, the basic material of the piece is absolutely simple, and the component elements are virtually inseparable and indistinguishable in isolation. So free is the material from the usual harmonic functions that it can be deployed from the highest to the lowest registers, right across the rhythmic spectrum, varied in speed and duration, overlapping barlines, and even being shared by instruments in the 'hocketing' manner of the earlier piece.

It is perhaps easier to distinguish the constituent components of *Antara* than the simpler but more closely integrated cells of *Cascade* (which has not yet been recorded). Partly because of this, there is greater emphasis on the individual capabilities of the instrumentalists in *Antara*. The London Sinfonietta soloists perform with characteristic precision and expressiveness under the conductor's baton, and it is unfortunate that the piece is so 'obscenely expensive' (his own reckoning) to give in concert, because of the computer programming required. Benjamin has since decided to prepare a tape version of the electronic part; with some reluctance, for the whole rationale of the piece was to humanize and invigorate electronic resources and this the recorded version does with considerable panache.

Discographical Information

Other Benjamin: Piano Sonata (1977–8; Nimbus 45009); *Ringed by the Flat Horizon* (1979–80) [with: *A Mind of Winter* (1981), *At First Light* (1982)]; Nimbus NI 5075.

Map references: Olivier Messiaen, *Chronochromie* (1960; Koch Schwann CD 311015); Alexander Goehr, *Metamorphosis/Dance* op. 36 (1973–4; Unicorn-Kanchana UKCD 2039); Robin Holloway, *Romanza* op. 31 (1976; Chandos ABR 1056).

Further reading: P. Griffiths, interview in *New Sounds, New Personalities; British Composers of the 1980s*, London, 1985.

TIM BRADY (born 11 July 1956)

Symphony in Two Parts (1989)

FIRST PERFORMED: Montreal, 28 April 1990
SELECTED RECORDING: Justin Time: *Imaginary Guitars* JTR 8440 2
  Brady (electric guitar, with multi-track tape)
  [with: *Dead of Winter* (1991); *Imaginary Guitars* (1991); *Time Lapse Exposure* (1992); Paul Dolden, *Physics of Seduction: Invocation* no. 1 (1991); Alain Thibault, *Incertitude pourpre* (1991); René Lussier, *Roche noire (chronique irlandaise)* (1991–2)]
RECORDED: January–April 1992
DURATION: 15' 33"

Tim Brady has declared that he plays not one instrument but two: the electric guitar and the twenty-four-track recording studio. In that he is a descendant of the guitarist and engineer Les Paul, who developed the first solid-bodied electric guitar in 1941 and also pioneered such important aspects of sound recording as multitracking and overdubbing. Paul went on to devise many of the technical innovations – transducers, electrodynamic and floating bridge pickups – that made electric guitar the definitive sound of popular music from the late 1950s onwards. Brady belongs to a generation of composers whose first musical experience was not nineteenth- or even twentieth-century 'classical' repertoire but rock and pop. He was strongly influenced by producer George Martin's multi-layered arrangements for the Beatles, in which Martin transformed the basic guitar format of a conventional beat group with an unprecedented range of *trompe l'oreille* effects and synthesized sounds. Interestingly, Brady seems to be less influenced by Jimi Hendrix than most electric guitarists (or less *directly* influenced, since Hendrix's innovations are ubiquitous), preferring a cleaner, drier sound, which is much less reliant on electronic artefacts like distortion and feedback.

Perhaps because of its 'popular' music associations, 'serious' composers have shown surprisingly little interest in the electric guitar. It has on occasion been used for tonal or dramatic variation, as in Michael Tippett's opera *The Knot Garden* (1966–9), in John Buller's troubadour song cycle *Proença* (1977), but there are still relatively few scores which exploit its enormous harmonic and colouristic potential. The Norwegian jazz guitarist and composer Terje Rypdal (born 1947) has written a good deal of ensemble and concerted music for electric guitar and was probably the only composer before Brady to give the instrument such a central emphasis. Perhaps the best known concert piece for electric guitar is Steve Reich's 1987 *Electric Counterpart* which also calls for a tape part, or for ten additional guitarists. I have already mentioned Betsy Jolas's *Episode huitième* (1984), but it is exceptional. The composer and ondes martenot virtuoso Tristan Murail (also born 1947), has included electric guitar in his *Random Access Memory* sequence (1984–7). However, the majority of electroacoustic composers, who might be expected to appreciate the instrument's pioneering importance in the area of live signal processing – familiar rock music staples like wah-wah pedals, 'fuzz-boxes', Octividers, and so on – have been somewhat resistant, perhaps again put off by popular music associations. So far, no one has taken the electric guitar's compositional potential further than Brady, who has also greatly increased its profile by commissioning work from like-minded composers such as non-English Britons Sinan Savaskan and Michael Cobas Tomain and by those fellow Canadians included on the disc above.

The title piece – *Imaginary Guitars* – is a fantasy piece in which Brady uses studio processing of no less than twenty-two overdubbed guitar parts in non-standard tunings to create the illusion of a single meta-instrument capable of almost infinite tonal and rhythmic complexity. In a curious way, this runs counter to what increasingly seems the main thrust of his work. On previous records, Brady had been working in what was identifiably a jazz context, and he has always *sounded*, despite his enthusiasm for rock, like a jazz guitarist. His *Inventions* album teams his own dedicated ensemble Bradyworks with guest soloists John Surman, an influential British saxophonist/composer, and bassist Barre Phillips, and is inspired by ideas in the French theorist Jacques Attali's book *Bruit* in which the very concept of 'composition' is called into question. Two earlier records on the same Justin Time label suggest that Brady's career has come full circle. *Visions* is an impressive five-movement work for conventional orchestra with a substantial unscored part for the Canadian-born trumpeter Kenny Wheeler; the record also includes more straightforwardly improvisational duos and guitar solos, an interest that resurfaces on *Double Variations*, where Brady stacks up 'orchestral' backgrounds for fellow-guitarist John Abercrombie (who responds with some uncharacteristic sequences for guitar synthesizer).

What is interesting about *Imaginary Guitars*, as David Olds points out in his liner-note, is that none of the pieces included are in any sense 'about' the guitar in any self-consciously technical sense. Like the L'Itinéraire composers in France – Murail, Gérard Grisey, and Michaël Levinas – Brady sounds on occasion as though he might have been influenced by the radical sonority pioneered by the maverick Italian Giacinto Scelsi, who virtually dispensed with the traditional compositional concerns – linear progression, counterpoint, hierarchical or vertical harmony – in favour of sound-for-its-own-sake. Brady does share an interest in simple octaves, non-functional pitches and timbres, and suspended musical time, but he is too dramatically linear a player and composer to be cast in the same mould as the L'Itinéraire group. He traces back many of his own compositional devices to the guitar itself, and to the basic opposition of single notes and great masses of sound, like a rock guitarist's lead lines and power chords. Brady considers guitar playing to be a 'daily lesson in economy of means' and suggests that his own compositional output, 'regardless of the medium, has been increasingly informed by this guitaristic tendency to use the most concise musical gesture possible in creating a piece'.

In Brady's case this derives more from rock music than from Scelsi. It is evident at once that his 'symphony' bears only a rather oblique, if not ironic, relationship to the cumulative development, counter-argument and musical density associated with classical symphonic language. In a curious way the guitar symphonies of Glenn Branca (born 1948) are far less in need of inverted commas. However dehumanized and minimal Branca's low-tech guitar parts might be, however ambiguous the effect (John Cage declared the Second Symphony, *The Peak of the Sacred* (1982),

to be hypothetically Fascist), they are far more conventionally symphonic than Brady's, and almost Brucknerian in impact. The Canadian
uses the term in a way that restores the word's original meaning of
'simultaneous sound'. Rich polyphonic passages are set against scrabbly
patterns which recall the highly abstract approach of British free player
Derek Bailey. Sections in which detailed pick-and-single-string lines
appear to function quite conventionally over rich electronic washes are
suddenly subverted by unexpected microtonal slurs and wildly ambiguous quasi-tonal passages. In musical terms, the effect is a little like
stepping into an empty lift-shaft. A familiar enough analogy in improvised music, but Brady creates an aura of weightlessness, very similar
to that evoked by the Beatles' complex unresolved chords and by
George Martin's to superimpose harmonically unrelated sounds to give
non-functional texture to the music.

The opening is dense and chordal, with a number of implicit tonal
centres playing off against each other. From these, almost as if from a
single serial chord, there emerges a long winding line for guitar that
contains the basic substance of the piece. Its relationship to the 'orchestral' sound is not at all the same as that between a solo instrument and
the ensemble in a concerto; a better parallel might be a work like
Witold Lutosławski's *Chain 2* in which the relationship between soloist
and orchestra is. In Brady's Symphony there is little impression of
dialogue or of exchange and variation, but rather a constant development of ideas in which the 'soloist' responds to but remains uncon-
strained by the backgrounds; they are, of course, not separate entities at
all, but aspects of a single logical progression. In that respect, it is very
similar to Reich's *Electric Counterpoint*. The 'orchestral tape overdubs
twenty individual guitar parts using real-time effects but with no
further electronic processing. Brady's commitment to economy of
gesture contrasts very sharply with the rather heavy-handed approach
of Paul Dolden, Alain Thibault and René Lussier on this record. The
recent *Time Lapse Exposure* is a live performance piece for solo guitar,
with a minimum of extended technique; towards the end, Brady briefly
uses a 'hammering-on' method and a small element of digital delay to
create a polyphonic environment. The effect is sparse and disciplined.
By contrast, Dolden's aural chronicle of Irish–Canadian immigration
features a dense, overcooked tape of guitar, bass and drum parts,
collaged with interview material from Brady's parents and a bizarre
recording of ex-Prime Minister Brian Mulroney singing 'When Irish eyes
are smiling'! Dolden's *Physics of Seduction* no. 1 (parts 2 and 3 are for
harpsichord and cello respectively) wears a rock influence very much
less lightly; interest here tends to focus almost entirely on the technological sophistication of a patiently layered instrumental backing. Using
MIDI technology to sample natural and synthesized sounds, Thibault's

Incertitude pourpre is a powerful impressionistic piece, but again the problem would seem to be the composer's inability to subordinate technology to music.

This is Brady's great achievement. Without attempting to mimic conventional instrumentation, his Symphony steadfastly refuses to draw attention to its own technological novelty, accepting the capabilities of the guitar and the studio as a given rather than an aesthetic end. Where it leads is, of course, temptingly uncertain.

Discographical Information

Other Brady: *Visions* (1985–8; Justin Time Records JTR 8413 2); *Double Variations* (1987–9; Justin Time Records JTR 8415 2); *Bradyworks* (1988–91; Justin Time Records, JTR 8443 2).

Map references: Terje Rypdal, *Whenever I Seem to Be Far Away* (1974; ECM 1045); Tristan Murail, *Vampyr!* (1984, electric guitar; from *Random Access Memory*); Glenn Branca, Symphony no. 6: *Devil Choirs at the Gates of Heaven* (1986; Blast First! BFFP 39); Steve Reich, *Electric Counterpoint* (1987; Nonesuch Digital 79176).

1990s

The disintegration of the Soviet Union accelerates the Balkanizing tendency of the later 1980s, opening up the cultures of the constituent republics to international recognition. There is also a renewed emphasis on religious music (now freely rather than covertly expressed), which chimes with the so-called 'New Age' sensibility to bring composers like Arvo Pärt, John Tavener and Henryk Gorecki unprecedented attention. The compact disc quickly consolidates its claims to be the ultimate in musical reproduction and most companies launch huge reissue programmes, transferring recent and 'historical' recording to the new format, but also sponsoring entirely new cycles of classical repertoire. By the mid-1990s, it is possible to sustain the illusion that almost every significant work in the Western tradition is available on CD. For the first time since the war, and not just because the perspective is foreshortened, it is not possible to identify one or two dominant styles . . .

1990 Leonard Bernstein and Aaron Copland die, a year after Virgil Thomson. Olivier Messiaen, Jean Langlais, Andrzej Panufnik and Luigi Nono all die during 1991. An old guard is slowly disappearing . . .

1992 Henryk Górecki's *Symphony of Sorrowful Songs* tops the album charts, outselling even rock recordings . . .

JOHN CORIGLIANO (born 16 February 1938)

Symphony no. 1 (1989–1990)

FIRST PERFORMED: Boston 15 March 1990
SELECTED RECORDING: Erato 2292 45601
   Chicago Symphony Orchestra, Stephen Hough (piano), John Sharp (cello), conducted by Daniel Barenboim

RECORDED: (live), 15–17 March 1990
DURATION: 40′ 37″

This stands at the end of our period as a further confirmation that not only are classical forms still viable in purely technical terms, they are still capable of great emotional and even political urgency. Corigliano's First Symphony was inspired by the 'feelings of loss, anger and frustration' the composer felt as he witnessed many friends and colleagues succumb to the AIDS epidemic. The work is a memorial to absent friends, three in particular, and quite specific musical memories are woven in the fabric of the work, in a thinly veiled reference to the Names Project AIDS Memorial Quilt, a vast participatory work in which relatives and friends paid their own tribute to AIDS victims.

The long opening movement is subtitled 'Apologue: Of Rage and Remembrance', and takes its emotional dynamic from those two contrasting moods. As in other works, Corigliano begins with the A which his father would have called for to tune the New York Philharmonic, where he was concertmaster for many years. The opening section is marked 'Ferocious' and gives a powerful sense of bottled-up anger finally breaking out, as the percussion section explodes over the initial string figures. Once the full orchestra is engaged, the pulse is determined by a heartbeat effect on the tympani which accelerates and slows with the mood of the music, rising to a hysterical climax towards the end of the movement, before dying away entirely.

Sandwiched in the middle of this roughly symmetrical ABA movement is a plaintive elegiac passage which introduces Corigliano's memories of a pianist friend, represented by an offstage piano playing a version of an Albéniz tango which the composer's friend had loved. Like all such devices, it has an eerie effect, which is partly lost on this live concert recording from the premieres. As the brasses that had begun to build up the tension of the opening section begin to make their presence felt again, the mood gradually changes and the heartbeat accelerates, leading into the wild final passages. Passion exhausts itself, and the piano is briefly heard again.

Twenty years earlier, Corigliano had arranged his *Gazebo Dances* for piano, four hands, dedicating the final 'Tarantella' to a record executive friend who was also an accomplished player. The terrible irony of this is that the tarantella, with its fiercely accelerating rhythm, was originally associated with the cure of tarantula bites and the hectic madness these were supposed to induce. In a heartbreaking 'rhyme', this connects with the dementia which is one of the most distressing symptoms of advanced AIDS. It is a painful, unrelieved movement, interspersed with tragic glimpses of a more orderly consciousness.

By contrast the long third movement has a much gentler sound.

Entitled 'Chaconne: Giulio's Song', it draws inspiration from a tape Corigliano found of himself improvising with a cellist friend, now also dead. He derived a brief theme from materials on the tape and played it against a twelve-note ground which runs throughout the movement. Dominated by strings, it begins with nothing but cellos and basses, and at a crucial moment in the solo cello's song, it is joined by a second cello, representing another dead friend. This somehow opens the door for a whole procession of memories. Corigliano asked his librettist William Hoffman to write brief textual threnodies to other friends. These he then set, finally removing the texts, so that these short melodic cells sound enigmatically and in turn against the repetitive background.

When Giulio's theme is heard again, a trumpet repeats the angry-sounding A that began the symphony, building up the emotional temperature again, though now the pace is that of a funereal march. Chimes sound out the twelve notes of the chaconne, leading to a last outbreak which might be likened to the second half of a New Orleans funeral, except that the mood is still sombre and angry. When it dies, there is only the sound of the cello, playing a sustained A that ends the third movement and signals the beginning of the fourth. Here the music has pushed through into another dimension, evoking timelessness in shifting waves of brass sounds, beneath which the central motifs of the previous three movements are repeated, as in an echo. The end is peaceful and untroubled, drifting off on a long-held A.

It is impossible not to be moved by the work as a whole, or to be impressed by its integration of strong personal feeling and formal control. If Corigliano is still 'unfashionably romantic', the critics' standard response, he always communicates, which is his own first priority. In its themes, as in its musical language, the First Symphony looks forward as well as back, a compass bearing for the remainder of the decade and for the millennium beyond.

Discographical Information

Other Corigliano: Sonata for violin and piano (1963; Bay Cities BCD 1018); *Elegy* (1965; CBC Enterprises SMCD 5050); *Poem in October* (1970) [with: Concerto for oboe and orchestra (1975)]; RCA Gold Seal 60395 2 RG).

Glossary

I have tried to avoid undue technicality in my discussion of individual composers, works and genres. However, some terms which are new or centrally important to the period in question do recur and what follows is an attempt to explain my understanding of them. In many cases, there is a tension between common usage and a strict construction of terms, and I have tried to indicate wherever possible how and when this happens. Some words are likely to be encountered in the text in different grammatical forms, I have tried to cover the probable cognates – atonal, atonally, atonality – in the body of each entry rather than listing them at the head. In most cases the head-word is the form most frequently used. Since many terms occur in related contexts, there is a certain amount of repetition, even of hair-splitting. Though the list of concepts is not long, I have cross-referenced other entries with an asterisk (*).

Search in vain for definitions of 'symphony' or markings such as *allegro*. There are already a number of basic reference books available – *Grove's* pre-eminently, but also the *Harvard Dictionary of Music* (1944, *et seq.*) – and I have no desire to reinvent the wheel; where contemporary innovations seem to demand some rebalancing of earlier usage, I have tried to indicate in the main text how and why meanings may have changed.

There is also the problem of what overall term with which to characterize the music of the post-war period. 'Contemporary classical' sounds odd and expressions like the much-favoured 'new music' needs to be approached with some caution since it tends to imply innovative or avant-garde practice, not just much of recent origin. I have generally preferred the neutral 'contemporary composition', which contains no such implication.

One of the trendier novels of the late 1960s was Luke Rinehart's *The

Dice Man, in which the protagonist made moral – but mostly immoral – decisions on the throw of a die. That is essentially what **aleatory** means, derived from the Greek word *alea*. Aleatory music is written according to chance procedures, whether it be the toss of a coin, the shuffling of cards, the throwing of I Ching medals or yarrow stalks. The notes are then written down and fixed (sometimes also in the additional sense of being manipulated in order to make sense); there should in theory be no element of chance in a performance. As with so many revolutionary innovations, there is nothing inherently new in the basic idea – Mozart is said to have devised a musical game like *cadavres exquis* or Consequences in which fragments of melody were put together according to the roll of dice – but it was John Cage who made chance a philosophical and compositional principle. And it is Cage, too, who illustrates the limits of the definition and the differences between his kind of gaming and Mozart's. Aleatoricism is not the same as indeterminacy* or 'open scoring', where responsibility for the actual notes produced is devolved on to the performer(s), as in some of his works, and it only partially applies to works such as *Atlas eclipticalis* or the *Etudes australes* where the notation is determined by positions on a star-map.

Though he is still credited with inventing it, Arnold Schoenberg thought that **atonal** music was an oxymoron, implying music without tones, which is clearly not feasible. One of his preferred alternatives was 'atonical', more accurately suggesting a musical system without a tonic, or root note, on which a harmonic scale could be built. No one has ever seriously taken up the suggestion, which has meant that atonal and atonality have been systematically used and misused ever since, much like the related but very different serialism*. Like all technical terms, they belong to a particular historical juncture and become slightly treacherous when universalized. Atonal episodes, in which the twelve notes of the chromatic scale are sounded in a non-repeating sequence, had occurred (not frequently, but on occasion) in classical music, but it only was with the turn of the twentieth century, and the experiments of composers such as Skryabin and Schoenberg (and occasional mavericks like Charles Ives) that atonality *as a compositional principle* was attempted. The usual giveaway for untrained ears is a characteristic lack of closure in the harmony, similar to that sense of infinitude one hears in Wagner. Indeed, much of Schoenberg's thinking was inspired by the celebrated 'Tristan chord'. Perhaps with Wagner in the back of his mind, he preferred to think of his music as 'pantonal'. The notion that each piece had its own, equally valid tonal centre was one that perfectly suited the new century's obsession with relativism and non-hierarchical self-determination. Whether such concerns – or the term – survive the collapse of optimisms that came with the First World War, is open to question. However, ubiquitous atonal might have been as an adjective in preceding pages, readers will find that the substantive form has been treated with considerable suspicion.

Once music began to be conceived in terms of masses rather than of lines dominated by hierarchical harmonic relationships, it was possible to replace signifying chords with undifferentiated **clusters**. These are essentially groups of adjacent notes, played either by depressing an area of the piano or organ keyboard (as Henry Cowell was to do with his forearm), or else having groups of instruments play those notes simultaneously, and in the cases of strings and winds with the option of microtonal* intervals as well; this was essentially what Xenakis and Ligeti were to do. The term has a parallel use in a discipline which interested both of the latter. Astronomical clusters are loose agglomerations of stars without definite structure.

One of the difficulties facing modern composers has been how to express new sonorities and playing techniques in classical notation. Reginald Smith Brindle's excellent *The New Music: The Avant-Garde since 1945* has a very useful appendix on new notational symbols (for microtonal* intervals and clusters*, and for various non-classical performance devices). He also includes examples of **graphic notation**, in which black dots are replaced by diagrams or pictures, on the basis of which the performer is required to make musical decisions. In the early 1950s, radical composers began to use simple black squares (a little like ancient *neumes*) to indicate indefinite pitches, or bar-graph lines to suggest proportional relationships of pitch, duration and rhythm. Stockhausen devised a similar system, using a binary system of plus and minus signs. Later composers (Ligeti most prominently) introduced colours. Some simply drew pictures. Christopher Headington's useful *Illustrated Dictionary of Musical Terms* includes a page from David Bedford's *100 Kazoos* which contains passages in which players are asked to interpret images – a sylvan landscape, pterodactyls circling a tree – rather than read notes. The American Anthony Braxton now titles all his pieces with a wordless freehand graphic, the significance of which is entirely his own.

It is sensible to make a distinction between aleatory* *composition* and **indeterminacy**, which tends to refer to *performance*. Though all music is to a degree susceptible to interpretation and all performances, even of strictly notated pieces, will differ in some particulars, indeterminate works devolve almost all precise decisions to the performers, which means that every performance will be different. This leads us into such alphabetically close at hand terms and concepts as **improvisation** or what Stockhausen usefully called **intuitive music**. This is arguably the final mystery. Do improvisers really pluck sounds 'out of the air', or do they rely on a semi-conscious stockpile of formulaic responses, as many ethnomusicologists would argue? By what standard does one judge a performance in which a musician has been asked to stay awake for days, eat and think as little as possible and then produce sounds without forethought? Stockhausen thought that 'improvisation', tainted by jazz, inevitably involved some element of pre-determination and did his utmost to eliminate it in favour of pure intuition. Cage appeared to believe that reality was itself the most effective 'composer'; his views are expressed in a recorded lecture called *Indeterminacy*, which is available on Smithsonian Folkways 40804/40805.

Some years ago, a committee sat in London trying, among other tasks, to devise a sensible title for a concert tour of **microtonal** music. Suggestions included 'Between the Notes' and 'Stepping on the Cracks', which give some sense of what the word means and also of the superstitions attached to it. Essentially, a microtone is any interval smaller than a semitone (or half-step). Their limitation, in Western musical terms, is that they are not performable on a piano, though pianos have been constructed and adjusted to play quarter-tones, the most common microtonal interval, and Charles Ives and others experimented with them. Wind and string instruments are, of course, capable of playing any pitch 'between the notes', and less than wholly competent performers often do. The desire to break free of the fetters of Western harmony has led composers to explore musics – African, Asian, native American – which do naturally exploit microtones, and such effects are now common, if not acoustically commonplace. However, few have made such a dedicated and determined exploration of this territory as the Mexican pioneer Julian Carrillo, though the Dutchman Henk Badings and the American Harry Partch and Ezra Sims have been writing extensively using microtones and, in Partch's case, specially designed instruments.

Minimalism is often satirized as a highbrow version of punk rock, sweeping away the pretentious elaboration of its predecessors in favour of something refreshingly stripped-down and bare-boned. In his *Lectionary of Music*, Nicolas Slonimsky suggests that music is constantly in transit between Liliput and Brobdinag, returning to the former with the twentieth century's embrace of limited forms and one-dimensional harmonies. As with atonality, the term itself involves an apparent contradiction: surely Cage's *4′33″*, containing no deliberately produced sounds, is the ultimate act of minimalism? In fact the term is used for music which is often very dense and, in some cases, detailed. It was applied by the British critic Michael Nyman to a loosely neo-classical* generation of American composers, of whom John Adams, Philip Glass, Steve Reich, Terry Riley and LaMonte Young are the most prominent. These composers *tended* to abandon use of harmonic tension and rhythmic variation in favour of what Slonimsky, characteristically, calls a 'consonant quietus'. Perhaps the single most 'typical' exemplars is Terry Riley's once-fashionable *In C*, in which there are no changes of key until the very end, or Steve Reich's *Drumming*, in which rhythms are sustained and overlaid for very long periods, as in certain ethnic musics. However, the term stretches to cover large scale works such as *Harmonielehre* by John Adams (who alone of his contemporaries still finds it a useful category) and Philip Glass's massive trilogy of 'portrait' operas; and it is necessary to emphasize that minimalism is a multi-faceted tendency, not a rigid movement. (Its progeny have sometimes been grouped together as 'the New Simplicity', but this is not a term that has caught on, and ironically use of 'the New Complexity' to characterize music of a very different complexion is much more prevalent.) In his book on American minimalism, the Dutch composer Wim Mertens suggests alternatives including 'repetitive music', 'phased music' (in contrast to complex modulations), 'modular music', 'pulse music', and even 'trance music' (which might certainly apply to parts of Riley and Young). So uncertain and controversial is the term in application that one might even suggest it comes neither from Brobdinag or Liliput, but from Laputa.

They stayed somewhat aloof, even when both of them were living in California, but even though their respective followers seem to have achieved polite *détente*, Schoenberg and Stravinsky are still considered to be the two opposing pillars of twentieth-century music. Like most absolute oppositions, this is largely a critical confection. There was a good deal of mutual respect. Schoenberg famously believed that plenty of (doubtless fine) music would be written in C major, while late in his career Stravinsky produced masterful works in a serialist idiom. Nevertheless the stand-off remains a useful historical shorthand, Schoenberg's revolutionary on the one hand, Stravinsky's **neo-classicism** on the other. It is probably sensible to make a distinction between *neo*-classical music as such, in which there was always an element of self-consciousness and irony, pointing up the profound differences between twentieth century values and circumstances and those of the baroque, and *deutero*-classicism, which was a much more literal and slavish form pastiche, spurred by the desire 'to don papa Bach's wig', as Paul Griffiths sharply puts it. 'Back to Bach' was a rallying cry for many composers, including some for whom Webern's rigours were the descendants of Bach's. Stravinsky used eighteenth-century music as a kind of benchmark, offering a linear clarity that was missing in romanticism and its aftermath.

Nevertheless, there was never any doubt that Stravinsky was a twentieth-century composer. His compatriot Alfred Schnittke uses neo-classical references in an even more ironic, even satirical, way; but there are composers for whom the backward glance is absolute and self-sufficient, marking a rejection of most of what has happened since Mozart, and it is as well to be aware of the difference.

Just as 'modernism' is a different phenomenon from the merely modern, so **post-modernism** must not be confused with the contemporary. Both imply distinct – or in the latter case, increasingly indistinct and Procrustean – configurations of ideas. There has already been a move to outlaw 'post-modern' and its cognates as being so vaguely all-embracing that they are empty of real meaning. The problem, of course, as with 'neo-classicism'*, lies with the opening particle. In what sense is it 'after' modernism? Merely chronologically? dependently? ironically? There is good reason to think it may be all three, in different combinations, at different times, and relative to very different works. If modernism was largely concerned with time, with states of inner consciousness, with language systems and iconographies as integral, sometimes nationalized, entities, then post-modernism is cheerfully dismissive of time as a meaningful concept, equally cheerfully accepting of surfaces and of languages as uniformly meaningless. A composer like Schnittke is post-modern in his appropriation of earlier music and anachronistic juxtaposition of it with highly personalized language. Karlheinz Stockhausen's and Luciano Berio's respective idioms are modernist in their universalising strain, but again post-modern in their choice of materials and expressive contexts. John Cage is definitely post-modern in his relentless questioning of the very premises of artistic activity and consumption. It is, all the same, an uncomfortable category, and when critics begin to talk about 'post-postmodernism' or 'post-contemporary' art and music, it is perhaps best to follow Cage's famous instruction to the letter: *tacet*.

One certain characteristic of post-modernism* is its polymorphousness, and even, to complete the Freudian cant, its perversity. One way of demonstrating one's post-modern credentials is to prefix an array of music concepts with **poly-**. By this means, metres proliferate into polymetres, rhythms into polyrhythms, and of course, tonality, instead of being negated, as Schoenberg feared if 'atonality' became accepted usage, was converted into an open-ended and multi-faceted system with no single or restrictive hierarchy. Polyrhythms are far from new, and they are commonplace in modern jazz; what *is* unprecedented is the extent to which they become structural principles in contemporary music, dominating some compositions to the point where no single metre or even pulse can be isolated from a shifting grid of possibilities.

Strictly speaking, **serialism**, another greatly over-used term, only accurately refers to the music of Anton Webern and his more slavish imitators. That is because only Webern treated the 'series' quite so literally, brooking no repetition of it or within it until all twelve notes of the chromatic scale had been sounded in the music, and only then subjecting it to any transformation or variation. It is perhaps easier to define the term from the point of view of its *mis*use. Serialism, for instance, is not the same as atonality*. Nor does it adequately describe Schoenberg's music, as is often thought; though Schoenberg often composed using twelve notes, he rarely did so in the strict manner that his younger colleague pioneered and his note-rows often imply, even if they do not explicitly acknowledge, some sort of harmonic hierarchy. The desire to subject each and every parameter of composition (not just harmony) to serial organization, led to such evolutionary sports as 'total serialism' or 'integral serialism'. There has been a tendency, one to which I have occasionally succumbed, to characterize the music of the 'Darmstadt School' as serialist; this is also potentially misleading, on two counts, but justified insofar as the *lingua franca* of the Darmstadt composers (who never really represented a coherent movement) was Webernian. In the case of Schoenberg, and in the majority of others, to speak of 'twelve-note' – or '-tone' – composition is a great deal safer. No well-bred person ever talks of 'dodecaphony', once a favoured option, and its use nowadays is mostly ironic. Predictably, there is now also talk of 'post-serialism', though this is more useful than most such coinages in acknowledging that such music follows an idiom that belongs to the historical past.

Further reading

These are books that I have found particularly illuminating or helpful in understanding the music of the post-war period. In each case, I have given some indication of their relevant contents. I have avoided monographs on individual composers, most of which will be covered at the end of essays in part one. I have not included the latest edition of *Grove's* (1980), which is inevitably somewhat limited in its coverage of contemporary music, or the *New Grove Dictionary of American Music* (1986), which contains good essays on the major United States composers. Nor have I included our own *Contemporary Composers* (Brian Morton and Pamela Collins, 1991), which contains biographies, worklists and brief assessments of some 500 living and recently deceased composers; it was not intended as a discographical guide, but it may be a useful source of basic facts and repertoire.

There are several good histories and reference guides to twentieth century music as a whole, by Paul Griffiths, Norman Lebrecht, Wilfrid Mellers and others. In what follows, I have given precedence to the testimony of composers themselves, so collections of interviews are highlighted.

Pierre Boulez, ed. Jean-Jacques Nattiez, *Orientations* (English trans. Martin Cooper, London, 1986)
    Trenchant commentary on his own work and that of contemporaries and figures of the past by one of the most significant composer/conductors of the period.

Reginald Smith Brindle, *The New Music: The Avant Garde since 1945* (Oxford, 1975; 2nd edn 1987)
    A cogent but often demanding survey of post-war music which never shies away from tackling difficult ideas and concepts head-on. Brindle deals with 'The Historical Background' in two crisp pages, which gives a fair impression of the pace at which he moves. A composer himself, Brindle studied under Pizzetti and Dallapiccola, and was an active member of the Scuola Dodecafo-

nica in the 1950s and 1960s alongside Bruno Bartolozzi and Sylvano Bussotti; the slight Italian bias in his account is more welcome than not. Particularly valuable are the diagrams of tonal and rhythmic matrices, electronic systems, and the illustrations of graphic and other unconventional scores. There is also a very useful eleven-page glossary of new notation symbols.

Richard Dufallo, *Trackings* (New York and Oxford, 1989)
Dufallo is an immensely experienced conductor, with an impressive track record in contemporary music which is not, ironically, well represented on record. Each of the chapters in *Trackings* is headed with a photograph of him with the composer interviewed. These include Boulez, Cage, Stockhausen, Xenakis, Lutosławski, Penderecki, Tippett, Davies, Carter and Copland, as well as Peter Schat, Earle Brown, Jacob Druckman, Friedrich Cerha and some others. Offers valuable insights into the performance and institutional politics of contemporary music.

Cole Gagne and Tracy Caras, *Soundpieces: Interviews with American Composers* (Metuchen, New Jersey, 1982)
Relaxed but often perceptive interviews with a mostly radical or experimental cohort of American composers. Usefully complements Walter Zimmermann's *Desert Plants* (see below).

Paul Griffiths, *New Sounds, New Personalities: British Composers of the 80s* (London, 1985)
Contains interviews with Benjamin, Birtwistle, Bryars, Davies, Ferneyhough and sixteen others. Relative to my concerns here, it largely supersedes Murray Schafer's earlier *British Composers in Interview* (Toronto, 1963), which nonetheless includes useful interviews with Elisabeth Lutyens and other older British composers.

Michael Nyman, *Experimental Music: Cage and Beyond* (London, 1974)
Nyman's rather muted critical reputation as a composer has to be put down in part to the fact that as a music *critic* (mostly for the otherwise conservative *Spectator*) he had a rare gift for raising hackles. *Experimental Music* was significant in recentring contemporary music in the shadow of Cage rather than *sub specie* Anton Webern, as had been the norm.

John Rockwell, *All-American Music: Composition in the Late Twentieth Century* (London, 1985)
Rockwell is the immensely experienced chief music critic of the *New York Times*, a loyal but sensibly sceptical propagandist for the avant garde. *All-American Music* contains valuable essays on Milton Babbitt, Elliott Carter, John Cage, and Philip Glass, as well as lesser-known figures such as Ernst Krenek, David Behrman, Max Neuhaus and Walter Murch, and jazz and rock performers Ornette Coleman, Keith Jarrett, The Art Ensemble of Chicago, Neil Young and Talking Heads. Chapter notes also include valuable discographical information.

Karlheinz Stockhausen, ed. Robin Maconie, *Stockhausen on Music: Lectures and Interviews* (London, 1989)
Books on/by Stockhausen are far from scarce, but this is one of the best. Oddly, perhaps, the composer is clearer when speaking as if to himself than when he is attempting to communicate with a sympathetic interviewer. As a study in revolutionary aesthetics, it is second to none.

Walter Zimmermann, *Desert Plants: Conversations with 23 American Musicians* (Vancouver, 1976)

Now rather dated, but still containing valuable background information on innovative composer such as Robert Ashley and Conlon Nancarrow, suggesting that Zimmermann was pretty much ahead of the game when he was writing.

Index

Composers with own entry: name and main citation in **bold type**. Composers discussed in text; citation given in plain type. Discographical citations in italic.